83 Hours Till Dawn

83 Hours Till Dawn

By Gene Miller
in collaboration with
Barbara Jane Mackle

1971
DOUBLEDAY & COMPANY, INC.
GARDEN CITY, NEW YORK

There are certain themes of which the interest is all absorbing, but which are too entirely horrible for the purpose of legitimate fiction. These the mere romanticist must eschew, if he does not wish to offend or to disgust. They are with propriety handled only when the severity and majesty of truth sanctify and sustain them.

Edgar Allen Poe
"The Premature Burial"

Contents

83 Hours Till Dawn

Jake and the Boys

I didn't hear the knock. Mother's bed was closer to the door and she was up already when I awoke. Someone was outside our motel room door. Mother was talking to him. I didn't know what time it was. I knew it was still night. I remember the first thing Mother said, "Oh, no, no, no."

"What's the matter?" I asked.

She turned toward me and said, "Stewart has been in an accident." Then she turned back and said, "Is his name Stewart Woodward?" She was at the window peering out. The curtains were drawn.

She started to unbolt the night latch. I said, "Mother, don't open the door." I don't know why I said it. I just didn't want her to open the door. I had one foot out of bed on the floor.

"Barbara," she said, "there is a policeman outside and Stewart has been in an accident."

I saw the gun before I saw the man. I don't know who turned on the light. As Mother unbolted the latch, the barrel poked through and at the same time the man flung open the door. Mother didn't open it. He pushed it open. It slammed her back against the wall. He had the gun in his hand. I don't know much about guns but it looked like a rifle to me.

Then I saw him. He was a big man. He wore a leather jacket of some kind, a yellow sweater, I think, and dark pants. He wasn't mean-looking, I remember. He wasn't a hoodlum. He didn't have a mask. He held open the door with his arm and suddenly this other person rushed in under his arm. I thought it was a little boy. The boy had on a ski mask.

I wasn't scared exactly. You know how sometimes you are so astonished that you are completely calm? That's how I felt. Mother was angry, not hysterical, angry. She gets excited. We both thought we were being robbed. Mother was the one making all the noise. "Oh, for heaven's sakes," she said. "Take our money and take our jewelry and get out of here!"

The man said, "We won't hurt you. Get over there and sit on the bed." I sat on the edge of Mother's bed, closest to the door. Mother sat on my bed, back farther in the room. He said, "Put your hands behind your back. We're going to tie you up but we won't hurt you."

The small boy started tying Mother's hands. She was really angry. Distinctly, pronouncing each word very deliberately, Mother kept saying, "Get out of here! Take it! Take it! And get out!" I didn't even know where our purses were. Mother said, "You are not going to get anything anyway."

The man put the gun to my head. I tried to look at Mother over my shoulder. "Turn away," he said. I looked straight ahead. I was facing the wall and the television set and I could feel the barrel at my left temple. He kept bumping, nudging my head. It felt cold. I don't think Mother even knew what he was doing.

The small figure, the boy I thought, had Mother on the other bed, first tying her hands behind her, then her ankles with white rope. He was very quick. Mother was talking the whole time.

"Take our money and jewelry and get out!"

"Be quiet!" the man said.

I put my hands behind my back. I thought he would tie me up too. But he said, "No. We are not going to tie you up."

For the first time I began to get scared. It wasn't rape or anything like that. That never entered my mind. I didn't think they would harm us. I thought somebody was trying to get back at the family in some way.

I tried to look again, to see what was happening, and the man nudged me again with the gun barrel. "Don't look," he said.

"Mother," I said. "Do what he says."

I couldn't see what was going on exactly. Mother was struggling. The boy had a rag and he had her on the bed, pushing her down, and he had the rag to her face. It was chloroform. He didn't say a word.

"It's a harmless anesthetic," the man said. He said it at least three times. "It is harmless. This is a harmless anesthetic. It won't hurt you. We're not going to harm you. It is a harmless anesthetic."

I guess I believed him. I knew Mother was being chloroformed. I said, "Mother. Don't fight them! Don't fight them!"

She didn't say anything. I didn't think she was under. It seemed as if she was still struggling. Then the man grabbed my arm. His grip was strong, but not overly strong, and he pulled me to my feet and we started for the door. The boy left suddenly and he raced out with us. The whole thing couldn't have taken more than two or three minutes.

I didn't know what to think. The man had the rifle in one hand and he held me with the other. A car was right there, parked head-in at the motel. The engine was running, I think. The headlights were off. I didn't recognize the make of the car. I know it had four doors. The man put me in the back seat. The boy, the small figure, jumped into the back seat with me.

"Don't do anything wrong and you won't get hurt," the man said. "I've got the gun and I'm not afraid to use it."

My thoughts were all a blur, jumbled, indefinite. These people could be someone trying to get even with Daddy or something like that. I didn't think any further. I wasn't thinking about what might happen to me. I felt I could talk them out of it. I really did.

The man is reasonable, I thought. He is intelligent enough. He is very calm and very cool. He must be a horseman. He must. I didn't know too much about that situation. I knew that the horsemen once had a strike at the Hialeah Race Track and that some people were very unfriendly toward Daddy. I didn't know the facts. Gangsters or the Mafia never entered my mind.

Right away, before we even pulled out of the driveway, the man said, "Chloroform her!" I didn't want to be chloroformed.

Very quickly I said, "That's okay. I'll put my head down. I won't look at anybody. I don't want to see what you look like." I volunteered this immediately. So without waiting for an answer, I put my head down. I put my head down in this boy's lap. At least I thought then he was a boy, about fifteen years old, something like that. I didn't want to be chloroformed. That was all I could think of. I was cold and shivering. I was shaking so. I put my arms around his waist and held tightly. He seemed so small.

The driver didn't say anything. He just pulled out. This was at the Rodeway Inn on Clairmont Road just northeast of Emory University in Atlanta, Georgia, where I was a junior, and I remember seeing from the right rear seat the slanted roof of the Pancake House there. I was sprawled out, my feet stretching toward the driver's side, my head on the boy's lap. I felt a hand on my face.

"Oh, she is sick. She has a fever."

It wasn't a boy's voice at all. It was a girl's voice.

Those were her first words, "Oh, she is sick." I knew I was sick. I had the flu. Everybody had the flu. That's why my mother was taking care of me at the Rodeway Inn. I couldn't get into the infirmary at Emory.

The girl had a very distinct Spanish accent. My first thought was: She is Cuban. I'm from Miami. She is from Miami. I'm right. This has something to do with Daddy. Yes, that is what it is. But they don't want me, I told myself. I'm no good for anything like this.

I tried to get up. She pushed me down and started to chloroform me. By now she had on a big heavy black glove. It wasn't her bare hand. I could smell the chloroform. I pushed her glove away and said, "No, no, no," and I put my head down again in her lap. I lay perfectly still.

My mind was racing. How do I get out of the car? I knew the gun was in the front seat. I was thinking, I'll try to open the door and jump. She is a girl, not a boy. But we were traveling fast, very fast. I was trying to think of something, anything.

That's when the man spoke up again. "This is going well," he said, pleased with himself, cackling almost. "This is going extremely well."

He sounded so cocky and conceited, as if it was some sort of a game with him. He was having a good time really. These were thoughts that went through my mind before I knew what was going to happen.

He kept glancing back. "Don't let her look," he said. The girl put her hand over my eyes. It was the glove again. I kept turning my head and she didn't try too hard.

A minute later I struggled to get up again. I knew I couldn't get away lying down. He got mad then. "Chloroform her!" he said, shouting. "Put it on her mouth. Keep her head down!"

The girl pushed me down hard.

"Don't! Don't! Don't!" I said, trying to grab her hand and push it away. "I'll be good."

I was shaking. It was very cold. My teeth were chattering. They were making a noise. I was very conscious of this. Maybe it was from fear, too. I know I could see my breath frosted and I thought the temperature must be in the teens. I was very cold.

"Oh, she is cold and she is sick," the girl said, and she started rubbing my arm. "We won't hurt you," she said. "We won't hurt you. Just do as he says. We won't hurt you."

I felt some attachment for the girl at this point. I don't know if it was because she was a girl or because she appeared so nice. If I'm going to get away, she'll help me somehow, I thought. As long as she is here, I don't think anything will happen to me. She seemed so sympathetic.

We were going fast. I could see the driver's profile by the street lights or whatever. I closed my eyes when he turned around so he wouldn't catch me staring.

"I hope we don't get stopped by one of those red-neck Georgia cops," he said. Or something like that. I think that's what he said. "I've had enough trouble with them." I remember I thought he sounded immature, and conceited and cocky.

About this time I got another dose of chloroform. I don't know if it was intentional or not. I don't know what she was trying to do. She put her gloved hand over my mouth. It was faint but I could smell it. And it burned. My senses were not affected at all, but it was uncomfortable. I kept pushing her hand away. She had it all over my face. They didn't say anything else.

I was trying to think of something I could do. By this time I had started thinking kidnap. Kidnap for ransom. It just jumped into my mind. Then I thought, no, that can't happen to a twenty-year-old girl. Kidnaping is for children. I still believed they wanted me for revenge or something. They wanted something from Dad or Uncle Frank.

From the motion of the car, I knew he had turned hard to the left. An abrupt turn. And I felt him run over railroad tracks. He turned again and it was real bumpy and he didn't go far at all. Then he stopped. The entire ride to wherever I was hadn't taken fifteen minutes. I'm sure it was faster.

He leaned back from the front seat and said, "I thought I told you to chloroform her."

"She has been good," the girl said.

He looked at me and said, "Well, you'd better be good." Or something like that. I can't remember exactly. It wasn't quite that crude. "Remember, I got the gun," he said, and he got out of the car.

The girl began to talk. "You are missing an exam, aren't you?" she asked. I told her I was, "Yes, ma'am."

"What is the exam?"

"Economics," I said. When she asked me that, it was a real shock. Well, I thought, they know all about me. They've researched me and I knew this was all planned. I asked her a question. "Are you from Miami?"

She didn't answer. There was a long pause. "I can't talk to you," she said. "I can't talk to you."

We were alone briefly, perhaps a minute.

"How's she doing? She behaving herself?" It was the man. He was standing right outside the right rear window. "I can't find the flashlight," he said.

"I don't know where it is," the girl said.

"Well, find it!" he said. He was impatient. "I've got to have it."

"Maybe it is in the back," she suggested.

"No, it's not in the back," he said, and I sat up because they were looking around on the floor. I realized I was in a station wagon of some kind. The back end was full of stuff. I couldn't tell what. There was no light. It was dark. I know the engine was off but I think he had left the headlights on. He found the flashlight quickly. It was on her side. He saw me sitting up. "Turn away," he said.

By this time I knew exactly what he looked like. I knew even then I would never forget his face. My first impression was that he was fat and big, real big, you know, husky. I wasn't tremendously afraid of him although I knew he could hurt me if he wanted to. I remember his teeth and his eyes. I remember his eyes most, kind of small, eager. In a devilish sort of way, he was kind of an attractive man. I wasn't thinking about it then. I still didn't know what she looked like. She was all in black, a black sweat shirt, black stretch pants, and that knit ski mask. I could see her eyes in the slit. I remember seeing her eyes very clearly. They were green and they were close-set. That was all I could see. They were very pretty eyes.

Before he got out again, he said, "Keep her head down so she doesn't see the house. And this time chloroform her! Here is the gun," he said.

I don't know whether he gave her the gun or not. She started the chloroform again and I said, "No. I've been good so far. I'm not going to try to get away."

And I thought, a house! They are going to put me in a house. I knew I hadn't seen a house. I saw nothing but black.

Now, I thought. Here is my chance to get away.

She must have known what I was thinking. "Please don't try to get away," she said. "Don't do anything because we are not going to hurt you, I promise. I'll take care of you." She started asking me about school again. I knew she was trying to keep me talking so I wouldn't think about getting away. "What was that test you were talking about?"

I told her again, "Economics," I said. "Are you in school? Are you studying?"

She said, "No, but George . . ." Then she stopped. She knew she had said something wrong. I wasn't really listening. I could hear him walking. He was around the back of the car.

He came up and said, "Jake and the boys dug the hole too deep." He wasn't yelling it but it was loud. He wanted me to hear him.

That's when I thought they are going to kill me and bury me in the ground. I said to myself, I'm going to get away from here. There has to be something I can do instead of lie here and let it happen. I'm not going to die. So I was thinking, I can get to that door. Maybe if I can get away they won't come after me. He won't start shooting. There is a house there, I thought. My head was still down and I decided, okay, I'll run.

I jumped up and there he was, right at the window. He had the flashlight in my face.

"I thought I told you to chloroform her," he said.

"I tried. I tried," the girl said.

"I thought you were going to behave yourself," he said to me. He was mad again, gruff.

"I can't breathe, sir," I said. "I've got to get up. My nose is stopped up. I can't breathe."

I'm not sure about the exact sequence of things. He was away once, I know, when the girl said, "Oh. You're so cold. Here, take my sweat shirt." And she took off her sweat shirt. She had on a white Peter Pan shirt, I think. That's what comes to mind. I'm not sure. When she was taking it off, he was right there, and she gave it to me and I put it on.

I said, "Thank you. It is so much better." And I said, "You are so nice to me." I was trying to play up to her.

And she said, "But, oh, you are so nice and sweet," she said, really. She said it twice. She said, "You are so well-mannered." I was saying, "Yes, sir," "No, sir." I always do.

"You are so well-mannered," she said again. "You are such a nice girl." It was all so insane.

I kept thinking I could talk them out of it. He was standing outside the car when I put the sweat shirt on. He didn't say anything, nothing.

Then he tied me up. That was right after I had jumped up. He climbed into the back seat and tied my ankles together. I had my legs crossed. It seemed as if he used a cord. Rope of some kind, I couldn't tell. It didn't hurt really but it was pretty tight. He did my hands too, but they weren't tight at all. They were really loose. I knew I could get my hands free. I was sitting up in the back seat, and the next thing he was in the front seat, flashing the flashlight in my eyes. I lowered my head.

"I want to explain this," he said to me. "I suppose you know that you are being kidnaped."

I knew it was kidnaping. I sort of said, "Uhh uhh." I didn't say anything really.

"We are asking quite a bit of money," he said, and he emphasized the "quite," and he sort of chuckled. "It may take some time to get it," he said. "I'm sure your father can get it," and he sort of laughed again.

"Now," he said, "listen carefully to what I am going to tell you. I'm going to give it to you once and only once. You'd better get it. This is important.

"We are going to put you into an underground room," he said. "It is big enough to walk around in. But you can only get your air through a battery. And this battery will run seven days. You have a light down there and if you use the light the battery will run out in five days . . ."

He kept right on talking. An underground room? A battery? I couldn't believe it. It didn't make sense. I didn't know exactly what he was saying. I know he said an underground room.

He said, "There is a house nearby and we'll come and check you every two hours to make sure you are not trying to get out."

Then he said, and this doesn't make sense either, "You will be under water."

I might have misunderstood. Maybe he said under the water table.

He said, "There is a pump in there. And if the water starts to come in, turn the pump on. A light will go on in the house. A buzzer will go on in the house."

I thought this man is crazy. It was all coming at me so fast. I couldn't conceive of any room under ground where I could walk around which was under water. In Atlanta, Georgia? This was absurd. The man is crazy. And yet I was listening intently. I had to make sure I got it right.

"Now, if you put the pump on, you'll use up the battery a lot faster." And he started reciting some exact figures, amperage, and things like that. "If you put the pump on, we will know this, and we'll come get you out. But if you put a little crack in the wall, the water definitely will come in—and you are going to drown."

I remember him saying that. Exactly. I remember him distinctly telling me I would drown.

He went into all kinds of detail. He said something about a ventilation fan and a life-support system and hours and amps. I can't even change a fuse. I simply didn't know what he was talking about. I realized what he was saying, but I couldn't understand. He was going to bury me under the ground. I thought, no. It can't be. And he kept talking. I couldn't listen. I wasn't listening.

I said, "No! No! I don't understand! What are you talking about?"

I kept thinking, no, I'm not going to let him do it. I'm going to get away. Somehow I'm going to get away. He'll have to kill me or something, but he is not going to do it. I'm not going to let him.

When he finished, I said, "You don't know what it is like to be buried." I don't know why I said it.

He said, "Yes. I do." And he said something about being in prison.

I kept thinking something is wrong with this man. He probably was reading my mind because he said, "You probably think I am crazy." I didn't say anything. "They think I am crazy, but I am not," he said.

I said aloud, "Well, that's good." It was just spontaneous. I was sorry I said it. I said, "Please, sir, I've been good. Just put me in the house. Put me anywhere. You can tie me up. Please, sir, put me in the house."

He said, "No. I can't do that." Then he sort of reconsidered, I thought. "I'll have to ask the boss." He said that two or three times. "I'll have to ask the boss."

I was begging and pleading. "Please, I'll be good. You can't do this." I was beginning to panic.

He asked me, "Do you understand the instructions?"

I said, "No! No! I don't."

"All right," he said, and he was threatening. "One more time. This is it."

And he began to tell me again, only much quicker, not so much detail. He used the word "capsule." But I thought he was going to put me in a room. A room big enough to walk around in. Big enough to stand up in. He told me if I tried to break out, insects would crawl in. I risked being eaten by ants. That is what he said.

"Don't use the light," he said. "Only when you have to. Don't use the light and you will have air enough for a week."

I was trying to think of anything. "Daddy will pay the money," I said. "Listen, you don't have to do this. Daddy will pay the money. Put me anywhere you like, but please, don't bury me. Tie me up, anything. But don't bury me."

And he said, "Yeah. I know Mackle will pay the money."

That is when he used our name. He enunciated Mackle peculiarly, the accent on the first syllable. I didn't really think about it at the time.

"Please," I said. "Why can't you put me in the house?"

And he said it again, "I'll have to ask the boss."

"Can't you ask him now before you put me in there?"

He said, "No. I'll ask him later. I think he'll get mad."

"Don't worry, Barbara," the girl said. "We'll come check you every two hours. I'll be right there." She sounded so convincing, so sincere. I realized she knew my name.

"Do you have any nose drops?" I asked. I don't know why I said a strange thing like that. But I remember saying that, though.

The girl asked him, "Can't we leave her some nose drops?" He didn't answer. I'm sure they didn't have any. I thought maybe they could bring me some.

He was still shining the light. Sometimes he would let the

beam go down and I would look up, of course. Then he said, "I want your watch. I want everything you have that is metal."

I had on a long flannel nightgown, red-and-white checkered, with a white frilly collar, and underneath I had panties, that's all. I also had on an old pair of my brother's black socks. That was because I had the flu and my feet get cold at night.

He put the beam on the black bow of my nightgown. "How is that bow connected?" he said. I think it had come off in the laundry and it had a safety pin. He took it off.

"You can't do this," I was saying.

And he said, "Do you have any buttons? Any zippers?"

I had two buttons at the back of the neck. I don't know if he took them or not. I was thinking, I'm going to keep my watch. He had forgotten my watch. I slipped it up my arm. I have slim arms and the band was loose. I slid it up my arm a few inches.

Then he saw the ring on my finger. "This is what is going to identify you for your father," he said, and he took my hand and tried to get it off. It was an opal with two little diamond chips on the side. No initials inside. I've always liked it. It was my birthstone. I don't like jewelry generally. I hardly ever wear it. I don't like things that sparkle. Anything that jings or jangs, I can't stand. But I always wear my watch and ring to bed. It was on my right hand, fourth finger. He pulled and twisted and I said, "I'll get it off. Let me." He was getting very impatient.

I was so scared then I didn't feel how tight it was. And this is terrible, I was feeling very smug about the watch. I really did. He had forgotten and this was the one thing I had. Everything else they had. Everything else was going for them. I just wanted to know what time it was.

I was still trying to reason with the man. I just couldn't imagine someone wanting to bury someone alive. For what reason? There was a house nearby. I really believed this, absolutely.

He said, "You know, we are not in this alone. We have people down in Miami and up here, too. We have lots of contacts. It is not just us."

Then he turned to the girl and said, "Give her the shot now." To me he said, "We are going to give you a shot which is only half strength." He named the drug, but I can't remember the name. "It is going to numb your senses," he said. "It is going to make you feel that you don't care what happens to you."

I was still stretched out in the back seat with my hands and feet tied. I knew I couldn't get away with him there. She had a syringe and hypodermic needle, and she pulled my gown up and my pants down. "You don't mind shots do you?" she asked.

At first I had my hands in the way. "What is it going to do?" I asked. "Is there anything in it? There is not any air in it, is there?"

"It is not going to hurt you at all," he said. "It is only half strength," he repeated.

"Good God, girl," he said. "Is that all you've got on?"

And she said, "Oh, stop!" That's when he turned away. It was dark. I don't know how she saw. It didn't hurt at all. I was so scared maybe that's why I didn't feel it.

He turned around again and said, "Okay. Everything is ready. Pretty soon it is going to take effect. You won't care what is happening."

I said, "Yes, I will care." I kept thinking, this isn't going to happen. I felt I am going to talk these people out of this. He is not going to put me in there.

He said, "I want you to chloroform her again. And this time do it!" And she did.

I said, "No. The shot is going to work," and I pushed her off. This time the chloroform started to hurt. I could smell it. She had on the gloves. I could feel the smooth leather surface on front and cotton on the back and I fought to keep her off. I could feel the dryness on my face.

"Just be good," she said. "We won't hurt you."

. I didn't breathe. I turned my face to the side and I held my breath and I fell back and pretended to collapse.

He was outside again and he put the flashlight in my face and lifted my eyelids.

"She is faking!" he cried. "She is faking! Give it to me."

He grabbed me and he was very forceful. He pushed me down against the back seat and held me. The chloroform was on a cloth of some kind, and it was heavily saturated. I was struggling, squirming, trying to get away. But he was strong, too strong. He hurt. It started affecting me.

I felt dizzy and woozy. Things were going round. Everything was black. I heard loud noises in my head. It felt like hammering inside my skull. I remember trying to grab his hand and push it away and I couldn't. I don't know what happened. I don't know if I lost consciousness or not. I might have. I don't think so. I felt drained, terribly drained. Then he finally quit. I could still hear them talking.

He said, "Okay, let's get going." I felt him pick me up. He was having trouble getting me out of the car. He pulled me out on the driver's side. He couldn't get me right. And as he took me out, he found the watch on my arm and he stopped and took it off. I knew what he was doing.

"Poor little rich girl," he said. "She only has an Elgin."

I just couldn't believe he would say something like that. Here he was, so rough, then he was laughing, poor little rich girl. It all seemed terribly unreal. My parents had given the watch to me for my sixteenth birthday. It was automatic. I didn't have to wind it.

I was completely limp. He carried me no more than ten or twelve feet and put me down on the ground. It wasn't far at all. He left the car door open. The ground was grassy, I think, but I felt as if I was on a blanket. I was lying on my back. I could see some pine trees. Tall trees. I'm not sure.

"We're going to take your picture now," he said. "Smile."

I opened my eyes and now he had on a ski mask. I don't know why he put it on. He hadn't worn one before. They were standing together in front of the car. The headlights were on, I'm positive. They were very close and they were talking. He had a camera.

He put a cardboard sign under my chin. I couldn't read it. Then he said, "Now, smile. Smile." I didn't smile.

The flash went off and he took a picture and they waited. I guessed it was a Polaroid. In a little bit, he said, angrily, "This won't do! Your eyes are closed." I didn't know it. I didn't mean to close my eyes. It just happened.

"Now, open your eyes this time!" he said. He was impatient again. He wasn't directly over me, a few yards away. I just had to smile. I was thinking, if Daddy saw it, I didn't want him to think they hurt me. It was a sorry sort of smile. The camera flashed again.

"You are a good-looking girl when you smile," he said. That's what he said. Here he was, one minute so impatient, the next trying to make a joke out of it.

I could see them both in the headlights and now the girl didn't have her mask on. She had it off. I saw her short hair. I saw her distinctly. She looked like a nice person, I thought. Small, but not fragile. With her haircut and everything, she looked like a boy, too. I still felt some empathy toward her.

I was lying there, wondering how I was going to get away. There had to be someplace I could run. I remember moving my feet and they were still tied. How could I run? My hands were in front of me but they were tied loosely as if he didn't really want to bother.

He came over and he wrapped me up in the blanket. He just folded it over. It was underneath me. He picked me up and he had a hard time carrying me. He couldn't keep his balance. He kept lurching and wobbling and tilting me this way and that way. I felt some branches brush across my shoulders. We were in a forest or woods or somewhere. I didn't think there was an actual path. I remember the girl was walking behind.

"We have to make sure to cover her face so she doesn't see the house," he said. The blanket sort of hung there, flapping. She hurried around and put it over my face.

I hadn't said anything in four or five minutes. It had taken that long to develop the Polaroid prints and everything. I was still woozy.

"I'm pretty hard to carry, aren't I?"

He didn't say anything. He was having trouble. I remember he stumbled once.

"If you put me down, I can walk if you undo me," I said. I was trying to make a joke. I said, "You are not really going to do this. I told you I'd be good." Then I started through all that again.

"I've got to," he said. "The boss told me I had to."

"Well, let me talk to the boss, please. At least, put me in the car and give her the gun and keep it on me. Don't put me in there without talking to the boss."

"Well," he said, "I'll tell you what. I'll talk to the boss about it and see what he says."

And I honestly believed him. I was willing to believe anything. It was such a preposterous situation. I wanted to believe him. I wanted to believe there was someone else I could talk to.

He was still carrying me. "Will you give me my watch, please?"

"I'll give you the face of it," he said. I didn't know what he meant. I assumed he meant he would take the band and give me the works. He didn't.

Then, abruptly, he put me down. He sort of sat me up on the ground. My feet were dangling over the side into a hole or something.

"I want you to slide down in there," he said, and he was pressing down on my shoulders.

Up until then I thought it was a room; certainly a place big enough to stand up and walk around in. He put me down and he said, "Now straighten out."

My feet were in first. I was sitting somehow. The blanket fell off. I still couldn't see anything in the darkness. I remember thinking when my feet hit, this is too short for a room, an actual room. Well, I thought, this is something leading to the room. It is a passageway, a corridor or something. The room is down lower.

When I tried to straighten out, I couldn't. My feet wouldn't go all the way. And for the first time I could actually see. There was a light in there. I knew instantly this wasn't a passageway. It was a box. There were things in the way in the box. My mind was functioning, but it wasn't accepting.

I was petrified really. I was shaking. I was terrified. I was never so frightened in my life. I guess I became hysterical. I cried, "No! No! No! You can't do this!"

And very calmly, the man stood there and said, "Don't be such a baby."

Then he became real angry. He said something about water. I heard him say water. And then he screamed, "You didn't fix it? Get down in there, Ruthie! Fix it!"

I remember the Ruthie. That's the only time I ever heard her name.

She refused. "No!" she said. "No."

He was shouting at her, and slowly, very reluctantly, she climbed in right on top of me, actually on top of me, and started crawling headfirst in a big hurry. There wasn't enough room for two persons. My knees were up, bent up, and she was all over me, scrambling. I turned my face away. It was so unreal.

It was not just fear. It was disbelief. This is a dream, I thought. This is not happening, and somehow, she scrunched up backward and started out. I don't know how she got out. I don't know. I didn't see her turn around. She said, "Here is your water tube." I don't remember looking at it.

The drug, I guess, hadn't worn off completely. I was still woozy, but I knew I had to get out. Let them kill me. I had to get out. I was getting up and suddenly the top came down. It made a heavy thud. I pushed against it as hard as I could. It didn't do any good. He must have been standing or kneeling on it. In the car, I remembered, he said there was no possible way I could break out. No way. So don't even try. I'd only drown myself.

I guess I was screaming sort of. Not incoherently. I didn't do that. My mind was racing. I've got to say something. I've got to make them believe I'm hurt. Something. Or I have to tell something they have to know. I was talking constantly. I was desperate.

"You've got to let me out! Just a second! Wait! Wait! This is very important! I have to tell you something very important!"

And I could hear him screwing in the screws in the lid. I don't know how long it took. "Wait! Wait! I have to tell you something!"

Then he said, "Be quiet and listen now." I could hear him very distinctly. "Now turn on the fan. Your switch is in back of your head. You can turn it up and you can turn it down. This will bring fresh air in as long as the battery is running."

I reached up and found the switch on the left. I switched it on and it made a funny racket.

"It is not working!" I cried. "It is not working. Something is the matter with it."

He didn't say anything for a while, maybe for a few seconds. "No, it is all right," he said.

I said, "No! I can't work it. How do I do it? It isn't working right." Just anything. "Please let me talk to the boss," I said. I started that again.

"I'll talk to the boss," he said. "Don't worry. You are going to be all right."

I was talking into the air vent. I knew that if I could hear him, he could hear me. "I can't work it," I said. "I can't! I can't! I'll be good. Let me talk to the boss! I have to tell him something important."

Then I heard the dirt. I heard it falling. There are no words to describe it.

"No! Don't do this! Be reasonable! Listen to me!"

The first shovelfuls were very loud. After a while they became muffled. I don't remember any stomping or packing. I never saw a shovel. I was still talking. Then I tried to listen. I didn't hear anything. I thought, they've gone already. They've left me.

"Do you know how to work everything?" He was back. I could hear him very clearly. I could hear footsteps. "Do you know how to work the pump now?"

I said, "No! No! I don't. Tell me again. I don't know how."

"You know how to work it," he said. He said it sarcastically. "You understand."

"No. No. I don't," I said. "There is something I have to tell you. Let me up just for a second. This is very important."

Then the girl, Ruthie, spoke up. "Barbara," she said. She called me Barbara. "Don't worry, Barbara, we'll be back every two hours."

She sounded so compassionate. I trusted her. I thought, if she said she'll do it, she'll do it. Desperately, I wanted to believe.

"Please come back. Please come back and check me. Just talk to me." I was still asking about the boss.

And he said, "All you want is human contact." I heard him kind of laugh. I'm sure this doesn't make sense. When it happened and I was there it didn't make sense. "Human contact." That's the last thing he said.

"Yes," I said. "I do. I do."

After a while there was nothing. I couldn't hear anything. I started talking louder. "Don't go away. Don't! Don't! Please. Please come back!"

I pushed as hard as I could. Then I started pushing again against the top. And I was hysterical. "Oh, God! You can't leave me here!" I'd talk, then be silent waiting for an answer, then talk. There was nothing. Then I'd talk some more, begging, begging. And there was nothing. Only silence. That's when I knew they were gone.

Hey, Lady, Shut Up

At this imprecise moment of Tuesday, December 17, 1968, Jane Braznell Mackle, mother of Barbara Jane Mackle, wife of Robert Francis Mackle, sat on a rumpled bed in a franchised motel in Decatur, Georgia, suburb of Atlanta, room 137, Rodeway Inns of America, where an unlighted billboard advertisement outside, displaying the registered trademark "Solid Comfort" and "Old Fashioned Hospitality," depicted a gentleman in repose in a rocking chair, his shoes off, and a cat snoozing on the floor. Her legs, trim still at the age of fifty-one, bled from the abrasions of three falls to a parking lot pavement. The horizontal streaks of discoloration from rope burns were yet to turn an ugly black and blue.

Jane Mackle was blaming herself. "I was so stupid. I shouldn't have opened the door. It is my fault." Her feeling of guilt and self-castigation, if unjustified in the totality of an incredibly elaborate crime of abduction, appeared frightfully pertinent to her at that moment.

Jane Braznell Mackle, unpretentious, lively, unconcerned by money, a woman of charm, happily married for twenty-five years, somewhat high-strung perhaps, her excitability usually confined to a bridge foursome, kept "fussing," as she put it, at two uncomprehending DeKalb County police officers that morning.

"Do something," she demanded excitedly. "Isn't there any place you can look? Look in the bushes! Look in the side streets. Before they get away!" Except for the lone occasion that a forgiving policeman stopped her for running a stop sign once, she had never spoken to an officer of the law in the performance of his duties.

Jane Mackle had checked into the Rodeway Inn before noon four days earlier, a Friday the thirteenth, for the sole purpose of taking care of her daughter. Barbara had the flu, contracted in the midst of her final examinations for the autumn quarter of her junior year at Emory University, and it had been a miserable weekend.

On the day of the kidnaping, a federal agency in Atlanta, the National Communicable Disease Center, where office workers had already scheduled their annual Christmas party at the same Rodeway Inn, would formally add the state of South Dakota to a list of twenty-four flu epidemic states. In Washington, D.C., that day, the National Headquarters of the American Red Cross would deem the flu epidemic a "disaster situation," and in New York City, where a city commissioner estimated 500,000 cases, a spokesman for the Pharmaceutical Society of New York State would report that New Yorkers had to wait an average of two hours to get their prescriptions filled. Doctors at the Atlanta center described the malady as a new Hong Kong variant of an influenza virus.

In the week before the kidnaping, Barbara had telephoned

home twice from her small and shared one-closet corner room 208 in McTyeire Hall, a dingy, old and depressing college dormitory with a communal bath down the hall.

"She always phones. She never writes, except for notes on birthday cards, Mother's Day cards, you know," her mother said. Barbara's roommate, Ramsey Owens, a tall blonde from Tunicia, Mississippi, had the flu too, and Barbara had given Ramsey all her medicine.

"Robert had talked to Barbara that Thursday, and he was about ready to make her come home. She couldn't get into the infirmary at Emory because it was full," Jane Mackle recalled. "But Barbara wanted to stick it out. That Thursday night we telephoned again. She couldn't even talk. Her voice was gone. She was hoarse, her nose was stopped up, she had a headache and nausea, she ached all over, and she admitted she had a temperature of 101.

"Barbara just never cries," her mother said. "Never. But that night on the telephone she was crying. I asked her, 'Do you want me to come up?' And she said, 'Yes, please.'"

Barbara's roommate Ramsey had finished her last final examination before Barbara began hers and Ramsey had left that Thursday afternoon for Christmas vacation. Barbara, too ill to be alone, moved for the night into Smith Hall, another woman's residence dormitory, not that her whereabouts were of any great concern to Emory University, an institute founded by Georgia Methodists in 1836. In the fashion of the time, Emory had abolished its sign-out policy for unmarried coeds.

Jane Mackle caught the first non-stop Eastern Air Lines flight at 7:15 A.M. from Miami International Airport to Atlanta Municipal Airport the next morning, and took a taxi to the Rodeway Inn on the eastern border of Emory University's wooded and hilly campus. She registered and was shown into room 137. It had two double beds, one of which was a "Pleezer," where for the deposit of a quarter, a mechanical vibrating massage would make the guest "sleep relaxed" and "wake refreshed."

After her mother telephoned, Barbara drove to the Rodeway in her year-old Pontiac Firebird, an olive-green vehicle the family called "the Green Hornet," and she parked beside a rainspout which someone else's bumper had already squashed. The car had originally belonged to Jane Mackle, but Barbara had more or less appropriated it for college.

"I took her temperature right away and she still had 101," Jane Mackle said. She had brought to Atlanta a medicine kit which contained a thermometer. "Barbara could barely whisper. It wasn't Barbara at all. She had all her books with her and she was upset because she had loaned her econ notes to a boy in her class who hadn't returned them and she needed them for a test and couldn't find him.

"She was really furious about those notes," the mother said. "He was supposed to bring them to her dormitory; she told me the professor practically made up his test from his classroom lectures."

At 2:50 P.M. that Friday, ten minutes early, Barbara Mackle, pale and feverish, walked into the stone and red-tiled Rich Building at the School of Business Administration to take a three-hour final examination in the History of Economics.

Peter Murr, a classmate, saw her. "You look terrible," he said.

"Thanks a lot," replied Barbara.

"What's the matter?" he asked. "Are you sick?" He wanted to know why she was taking the test.

"I want to take it and get it over with," said Barbara, a girl seldom unnerved by examinations.

Marshall Louis Casse III, a plump and round assistant professor with mutton chop sideburns, also took quick note of his student's health.

"You don't want to take this test do you?" he asked Barbara.

"No, sir," she said. "I guess not." He told her she could make it up later. He dispatched Barbara to the dean's office and the infirmary once again, where after waiting an hour and twenty-five minutes, a doctor told her there was nothing she could do but rest.

A cold rain turned to sleet in Atlanta that dreary afternoon, and besides the flu, Barbara's strep throat, an ailment recurring with tiredness, flared up. She returned to room 137 at the Rodeway Inn and went to bed.

She felt somewhat better Saturday and insisted on taking a second final examination from 3 to 6 P.M., the American Civil War, taught by Bell I. Wylie, a professor with four doctorate degrees and a reputation for asking obscure questions. She took the examination, saying nothing of her temperature, and confident that she had scored well, she left the History Building alone in the darkness of dusk.

It was windy, and as she walked through the seemingly deserted campus to her parked car several blocks away, she had a peculiar feeling of uneasiness. Months later she would recall, "I was scared. I don't know why. I hate to say it. It wasn't a premonition, not really. I just had this peculiar funny feeling."

At the motel that Saturday evening the telephone rang about seven o'clock. By this time Jane Mackle had felt a cold coming on too, and an assortment of medication, aspirins, cough medicine, Contact capsules, an NTZ squeeze-plastic nasal spray, prescribed pills from Miami, and Kleenex so covered the single bedside table between the beds that there wasn't room for the telephone. It lay on the bed. At night it went on the floor.

Jane Mackle answered the ring.

"I have a registered letter for Barbara Mackle." It was a man's voice. She didn't recognize it.

"He told me he was taking somebody else's place and he had promised he would hand deliver the letter," Jane Mackle recalled.

"Barbara, your economics notes!" she exclaimed.

Quite mistakenly, Jane Mackle assumed that the boy who had borrowed the notes had mailed them to Barbara special delivery at McTyeire Hall.

"Never mind," she said. "It's too late tonight. I'll stop by the dorm tomorrow." She thanked him and hung up.

Later that evening she talked to her husband in Miami and asked him if he perchance had mailed Barbara a registered letter. Assured not, she felt sure she was right about the notes.

That evening and again Sunday and Monday, Barbara's friend, Stewart Hunt Woodward stopped at the Rodeway Inn. The relationship between Barbara and Stewart, as the DeKalb County police would later so aptly demonstrate, was a little difficult to understand. Put very simply, he was her best friend.

"I know that sounds funny," Barbara would tell her family. "But I enjoy his company more than any person I know, any girl. We enjoy being together. We're always together."

Although there had never been a wild, head over heels romance, they were quite close and genuinely fond of each other. Stewart Woodward, a senior majoring in business economics, was a year older than Barbara. An alert and quick student, Stewart had made the dean's list for scholastic excellence, studying hardly at all.

His hair was a blondish brown, he had green eyes, and a wiry, medium build.

They had met in a Health Education class during the winter quarter of Barbara's freshman year. They sat next to each other. Stewart asked her for a date, Barbara accepted, then changed her mind at the last minute. In the classroom he kept kidding her about it and asked her again. This time she went and they attended a fraternity dance and discovered what they already suspected: they truly enjoyed each other's company.

Sporadically Barbara dated two boys from Duke, one from Harvard, and a few others from Emory, but she was never serious. At age twenty she had yet to fall hopelessly in love. She and Stewart would go everywhere together, the movies for *Bonnie and Clyde*, canoeing, horseback riding, bicycling on a bicycle built for two at historic Stone Mountain, a great gray-granite monolith northeast of Atlanta, with a skylift, a river boat, a gristmill (circa 1865), and a 732-bell carillon left over from the 1964–65 New York World's Fair. Stone Mountain attracted them Sunday after Sunday. In winter it was ice skating. In the spring, kiteflying at Grant Park, where after an hour in futile attempt to fly a drugstore kite with a handerchief tail, two small boys showed them how. Stewart was always supplying Barbara with reading material, *Harper's*, the *Atlantic Monthly*, and the *Federal Reserve Bank of St. Louis Review*, with whose monetary policies he usually agreed. "Here, read this! Read this!" he would insist, thrusting upon Barbara the book *Stalingrad*. He convinced Barbara that the Vietnam war was wrong. Stewart had visited the Mackle home in Coral Gables, Florida, and the family knew him well.

Barbara had first begun her major in mathematics at Emory. After her first course in economics, though, she switched to economics. She found it fascinating. Stewart came by that Saturday night to help her with her third and last final examination, Macroeconomics 210, the study of the economy as a whole. Macro, as opposed to micro, encompassed the entire subject of economics, and Barbara found it her hardest course. Stewart knew it well. For the final, the students had the option of selecting either "poverty" or "inflation" for testing. Barbara selected "inflation."

She would write in the margins of her text, "Ask Stewart," "Ask Stewart," and Stewart, propped comfortably in the motel chair, would supply answers and interrogate her about the national income and output. Jane Mackle, deemed the whip by Barbara and Stewart, served as a straw boss and nurse. "Study," she commanded. She gave Stewart a bottle of NTZ. He, too, had developed the sniffles.

On his way home to his apartment Saturday night, Stewart stopped at Barbara's dormitory to see if her notes had been returned. They were there waiting for her in a red loose-leaf notebook. They had not been mailed. The boy who borrowed them had returned them himself. Stewart didn't think anything about it. Neither did Barbara or her mother when he brought the loose-leaf notebook with him when he returned to the Rodeway Inn on Sunday. No one thought to mention the telephone call the night before. Sunday night they felt well enough to dress and have dinner at a nearby Morrison's Cafeteria. Stewart drove them in his white 1965 Ford.

All day Monday Barbara remained in the motel room in her bathrobe. She didn't dress. She had prevailed upon Stewart, who had finished his own final examinations, to stay in Atlanta until Tuesday, and by the time he dropped by she had another long list of questions for him.

The battery cable on Barbara's Firebird had corroded slightly and Stewart brought along a tool kit that afternoon to fix it. He parked his Ford at the other end of the parking lot, and as he carried his tool kit to her car, a man in an overcoat, driving what Stewart believed to be a royal-blue Buick, went by slowly, looking at him over his shoulder. Stewart felt a little odd. He wondered if the man suspected him of stealing the tools. He certainly didn't look like a mechanic.

The weather, gray, damp and unpleasant, hung on unchanged for the fourth consecutive day, and the motel confinement had Jane Mackle climbing the walls. Her cold was worse.

"I'm tired of looking at that nightgown," she said. "I'll get you another one."

"I need socks, too," said Barbara.

Stewart and Jane Mackle drove to McTyeire Hall where Jane Mackle began packing for the holidays. She picked up a pair of dark blue woolen knee-high socks. Barbara had confiscated them months before from her brother Bob, a quiet and controlled young man three years older than she. He had graduated in 1967 from another school in Atlanta, the Georgia Institute of Technology. Their father, Robert, had been born in Atlanta.

At the Emory dormitory that afternoon, Jane Mackle also picked up the clean nightgown for Barbara. It was the red-and-white checkered one Grandma Del Braznell had given Barbara as a Christmas gift the year before, knee length, long sleeved.

On campus near the Rich Building later, Jane Mackle noticed a man staring at her in another car. Oh, she said to herself, "I know I'm parked wrong." She didn't give it a second thought.

As Stewart opened the door to leave about ten o'clock that night of Monday, December 16, he paused and said, "Well, don't talk to any strange men." He said it all the time. It was good for a laugh.

Neither mother nor daughter turned on the Motorola color television before the eleven o'clock news. Barbara put her books on the floor beside the bed and her glasses on the bedside table. She was nearsighted. Usually she wore contact lenses. But because of the flu, her eyes had been watering and she hadn't had on her contacts in four or five days. Barbara carefully puffed up the pillows so she could keep her head up while sleeping. She had to breathe through her mouth.

She didn't worry about an alarm clock. Jane Mackle, a light sleeper, instinctively awoke at 7 A.M. Once during the night, Jane Mackle awoke and listened in the dark to Barbara breathing.

"Barbara, are you awake?"

"Yes," she said. "I can't sleep. My head is stopped up."

It was one of those perfectly sensible nighttime responses she wouldn't remember.

Jane Mackle crawled out of bed and parted the curtains to let enough light come in so that she could see her Wittnauer watch on her wrist. It was three o'clock. She climbed back into bed. For the next hour she lay in bed unable to sleep.

"I kept listening to see if Barbara would get back to sleep," said Jane Mackle. "Her breathing wasn't even."

"The knock on the door startled me," Jane Mackle said.

"Who is there?" she asked.

"I thought he said a detective," she recalled later. "Maybe he said, 'A policeman,' I'm not sure. He said, 'There is a young boy in a white Ford and he has been in an accident. He is in the hospital and he is asking for you.'

"I immediately thought of Stewart, of course. I even wondered at the time, if Stewart had been in an accident, why hadn't we heard earlier."

"Is his name Stewart Woodward?" she asked then.

"Yes, that's his name," the man replied.

From the still-darkened room she could see by the light of an ornamental green lantern outside a clean-shaven man wearing a latticed and visored cap, lettered "Police." It had a badge on it. Not illogically, she responded to a request for help.

She never remembered turning on the room light. As she unhooked the chained latch, the man abruptly shoulder-bashed open the door, ripping the anodized aluminum stripping from the door.

Jane Mackle, surprised and angered rather than frightened, couldn't believe he had a real gun. To her, it looked like a "long wooden pretend gun." She guessed later it might have been a shotgun. She didn't know much about guns.

When the second small figure, quick and darting, started to tie her hands behind her back, Jane Mackle quickly spun inward on her finger, a 3½-carat-diamond ring, so that only the band showed—indignantly crying all the while, "For heaven's sakes, take our money and take our jewelry and get out of here! Get out!" It was a family keepsake. Her father had given the diamond to her mother when she, Jane, was born in 1917. She thought a boy had tied her up. He looked about twelve or thirteen years old, and he didn't seem to notice the ring.

The "policeman" never took off his cap. "He was chunky and he had a round face, a moonface. He spoke well and spoke softly. He didn't look like a hoodlum or anything like that."

Sprawled back on the bed, Jane Mackle struggled to keep from being chloroformed. "It was either chloroform or ether and I could hear him saying, 'Give her more! Give her more!'

"When I realized the boy was going to keep at it until I went out, I decided I would just pretend I did. I didn't inhale and I don't think I lost consciousness. Almost the second I quit fighting, he put this adhesive tape across my mouth and raced out. I looked up and I saw just a flickering of Barbara's nightgown going out the door between them."

Oh, my God, she thought, they are going to rape Barbara. Frantically, Jane Mackle rolled across the bed to get the phone.

It was on the floor. Somehow, she pitched herself to the floor, knocked the receiver off the hook and started screaming.

"The adhesive tape was so loose it was almost falling off. The boy had just slapped it on. He almost missed my mouth."

She lay on the floor, the single piece of tape askew, screaming into the telephone, and there was no response. She would have to dial for the night clerk and she couldn't. "I couldn't hear anything, not even a dial tone."

Barefooted, wearing only a shortie flannel nightgown, her hands and legs securely bound, Jane Mackle struggled to her feet, and hopped across the room and fumbled for a pair of scissors in the medicine kit. She dropped them. She doesn't remember whether or not the door was ajar.

She hopped outside, oblivious to the twenty-four-degree chill. "And I screamed and screamed and screamed."

"Please. Help! Help! Help!" she cried. "Somebody help! Please help!"

"I got absolutely no response," she said. "I couldn't believe that no one heard. I know they heard." No one responded.

The horn, she thought suddenly. Barbara's Firebird was parked one space to her right in front of room 139. She knew it was unlocked. Screaming still, she hopped from the sidewalk off the curb to the asphalt pavement, retaining her balance.

At the right front door she fell. She staggered to her feet and fell again.

"Help! For heaven's sakes help me somebody! Help!"

Except for her own room, Jane Mackle did not see a single lighted window in the motel. Of the 120 rooms in the motel, 71 were occupied that night.

She struggled to her feet, sliding up against the car. With her hands behind her, she realized she had to back toward the door handle, grab it and depress, and pull open the door.

Suddenly, unexpectedly, she tumbled over backward. This time she hurt herself. She hardly knew it at the time. Bruised, bleeding, her lips and mouth so dry and flaky from the chloroform that she would feel it for a week, she again struggled to rise from the asphalt pavement.

"I had a hard time getting up. I was afraid I couldn't do it."

Then she had the door handle in her hands. The door opened easily. She backed into the seat, plopped downward, and put her chin on the steel rim of the horn and pressed hard. "And I didn't let up."

A minute or so before the demanding blare of the Firebird, Beverly Jenkins had awakened. She was in room 139 next door. Mrs. Jenkins, a young woman in hope of becoming a Certified Public Accountant, worked for the Rodeway Inn as a bookkeeper, and slept over occasionally instead of going home. She thought she had heard a struggle. She said she didn't hear anyone screaming. At the sound of the horn, she arose and peeked out the drapes, her room still dark. From her window she could see in the distance, perhaps a hundred yards to the south, the imposing new Veterans Administration Hospital on the adjoining property. Once before, quite literally, a little man in a white coat had come to the Rodeway Inn to retrieve an escaped or wandering patient.

Beverly Jenkins telephoned the night-desk clerk. "Walter," she said, "another crackpot is on the loose."

Walter W. Perkins, a bald-headed Michigan native of fifty-four with a penchant for poetry, a singsong voice, and a $379 hearing aid built into his spectacles, had worked as a night clerk for hotels for sixteen years.

Perkins hurried across the lobby, methodically locked the front door, hurried back across the lobby and let himself out the back door, carefully locked that door too, then sought the source of the disturbance. "I trotted. I stepped lively," said Perkins, "and I found the lady in distress. She was blowing the horn for all it was worth."

"Hey, lady!" he shouted. "Shut up! You'll wake up all the guests!"

Jane Mackle lifted her chin.

"What's the matter with you?" Perkins cried. "We run a nice place here! We don't carry on like this!"

"For heaven's sakes, help me!" Jane Mackle said.

He saw the adhesive tape dangling from her face. Dumfounded, he pulled it off her chin.

"They robbed me and took my daughter."

"Calm down. Calm down," said Perkins in disbelief. "I thought it was some sort of mother-daughter disturbance," he would say later.

"Call the police!" Jane Mackle demanded. "He just stood there and fussed at me. He didn't do a thing."

Perkins, ever the discreet innkeeper, confessed later, "I was interested in keeping the peace and quiet. That's all. I didn't ask any questions."

Perkins started to leave. He felt he had to get back to the lobby. After all, the doors were locked.

"Would you please get the pair of scissors and cut me loose," Jane Mackle demanded frantically. The scissors were lying just outside the door. He cut the cord from her hands. She hopped back into the room. Perkins hesitated. Unaccustomed to escorting ladies into motel rooms, he stood there in the open doorway.

"I had to telephone the police myself," Jane Mackle said. "I asked him for the number."

"Call the DeKalb County police," said Perkins.

She handed him the book. He looked up the number for her. The police dispatcher in Decatur logged the call at 4:11 A.M.

"I had to cut the cord from my feet myself," Jane Mackle said. Perkins hurriedly excused himself and hastened to the lobby to unlock the doors.

Approximately two miles away, DeKalb County officers Walter Baer and S. L. Bawmgras routinely drove through a shopping center where they had been rattling store doors to make sure they were locked.

"A 1018 at the Rodeway Inn on Clairmont, room 137," droned a flat, unemotional voice from the dispatch room. Baer, twenty-two years old, only seven months on the force, automatically decoded the 1018 as an emergency.

"Signal seventy-seven," the dispatcher added.

"A seventy-seven?" Baer repeated aloud. "That's kidnap."

Accelerating, he flicked on the red, flash-swivel light atop car 29, deliberately left off the siren, and sped toward the Rodeway Inn.

"A lady was outside alone in front of the door," said officer Baer.

"It seems as if they were there right away," said Jane Mackle. "It couldn't have been more than a minute or two."

The crime of kidnaping had not entered her mind. "I didn't think of it, not once," she said. "I saw my black leather purse where I had left it on the table." Barbara's purse, of John Romain make, sat undisturbed on the floor. Neither had been touched. Jane Mackle's contained about $150. It was still there.

"When I realized they hadn't robbed us, I knew they were

after Barbara. They wanted Barbara. That was all I could think of and I just nearly died. All I could think of was rape."

Verging on hysteria, desperately grasping for explanation and logic, Jane Mackle telephoned Stewart Woodward. Had he really been injured in an automobile accident?

"Stewart," she said, "they've taken Barbara. Someone broke in and took Barbara. Can you come over right away?" It was about 4:15 A.M.

Young Woodward lived off-campus in a third-floor apartment at 2577 Shallowford Road, about five miles away. He was there in a few minutes. He didn't bother to take the time to put on socks.

"How often do things like this happen in Atlanta?" Jane Mackle asked the two uniformed policemen. "I used to like Atlanta. Do you have many rapes in Atlanta?"

"I was so sure that's what had happened," she would say later. "I wanted somebody to tell me everything was going to be all right. They kept saying, 'I don't know. I don't know.'"

"She was terribly upset and terribly disturbed," said officer Baer. "We tried to quiet her down. She kept pacing back and forth. It was hard to get information from her."

Jane Mackle wanted to telephone her husband. Officer Baer suggested she wait, please. He wanted the descriptions again, slowly, please.

Despite the initial radio designation of kidnap, officer Baer tended to discount it. "I thought it was some sort of sexual abduction." It didn't make much sense, a boy and a man disguised as a policeman breaking into a motel at 4 A.M., chloroforming a mother and taking her daughter. The acts of a sexual psychotic are not the acts of a rational man, Baer told himself.

He wondered, as would other investigating DeKalb County detectives, if Barbara Mackle had fled of her own free will in league with her captors. Could it all be an elaborate ruse?

"I tried to tell them Barbara was a coed at Emory and a nice girl," Jane Mackle recalled. "And one of the policemen said very sarcastically, 'A coed at Emory a nice girl?' It really annoyed me. I was so upset anyway.

"They asked me about Barbara's boyfriends. I told them she'd never gone overboard about any boy, she'd never lost her head."

The two officers looked suspiciously at Stewart Woodward. "He's just a friend," Jane Mackle tried to explain. Somehow, in the emotions of the moment, they incorrectly concluded that Stewart was Barbara's fiancé.

"Can you think of any reason why anyone would take her?" officer Baer asked Stewart.

He couldn't. Officer Baer knew nothing of the Mackles, their wealth, their status, their position—or who Barbara Mackle was. To him, she was a girl who had disappeared from a motel room. When he wrote his report several hours later that morning, he misspelled the name. Mackel, he wrote.

"Kidnaping—(at gunpoint)," he would type under case report 60-1321. He listed "Mrs. Mackel" as witness one; Stewart Hunt Woodward as witness two.

In the stilted jargon of the usual police document, he would chronicle the "above incident":

"Upon arrival talked to witness number one, who stated that while she and her daughter, above victim, were seated on the bed talking in room 137, Rodeway Inn, 1706 Clairmont Rd., Decatur, Georgia, they were interrupted by a knock on the door. When witness number one asked who it was, a male voice answered that he was a detective who had information concerning a young white male involved in an auto accident driving a white Ford. Victim's fiancé, witness number 2, drives such a vehicle.

"Mrs. Mackel opened the door at which time a white male, medium build, wearing a black leather jacket, a cap and carrying a shotgun, entered the room and put a rag or cloth saturated with chloroform on her face. Subject was accompanied by a young white male approximately 12 years old. Witness said young boy tied her hands and feet with white cord and put a strip of adhesive tape over her mouth. Subject then took victim, a white female, age 20, 5 feet 10 inches, 120 pounds, brunette, brown eyes, wearing a red and white checkered flannel nightgown, out the door.

"Mrs. Mackel stated incident occurred at approximately 4 A.M., and thought it took her approximately five minutes to work free from bonds and call the police. Her face was purple and wrists and ankles severely bruised from rope. Reporter and employee for the Rodeway Inn who lives in adjoining room to where incident occurred stated she was awakened at approximately 4 A.M. this date by what appeared to be sounds like a struggle going on in room 137, but that she did not see anyone until a few minutes later when Mrs. Mackel came out to call for help.

"Witness number two, an Emory University student who came to scene after being called by Mrs. Mackel, stated a few hours earlier that he noticed a white male driving a late model Buick or Olds, color blue, hanging around the area and staring at him when he looked back at him. Subject ran and got in vehicle and left. Victim is also a student at Emory University.

"A lookout was placed with radio. No further description available . . ."

The staring subject who ran, it seemed, was the man who had looked at Stewart as he carried the tool box about 3 P.M. the afternoon before. That was the only lead they had. It was a bad one.

"Do something! Do something!" the distraught mother had exhorted the two officers that morning. "Isn't there any place that you can look? I'm so scared. I'm so scared."

Soon a plainclothes DeKalb County detective, Mac E. Dover, arrived and started asking all the same questions again. Officers Baer and Bawmgras promptly departed to search dead-end streets, lovers' lanes, and all the local "cracks," as they called them, where a rapist might take a victim.

At first Detective Dover mistakenly thought Jane Mackle was intoxicated. "When I first saw her she appeared looped," said Dover. "I was wrong. She was hysterical and she obviously was in pain." He looked suspiciously at both Jane Mackle and Stewart.

Stewart noticed the detective's cuff links, miniature handcuffs. He disapproved. Impatient, yet outwardly calm, Stewart felt nothing was being done. Jane Mackle asked him to telephone her husband.

For two, three minutes or so Stewart tried to call out. The night clerk kept informing him that he couldn't reach the long-distance operator directly. The switchboard was closed.

"Hang up. I'll make the connection for you and call back," Perkins said. Perkins, too, had trouble. Four minutes. Five minutes. It seemed forever. Stewart kept interrupting him. It was already a few minutes after five o'clock.

When the night clerk finally made the connection, Stewart gave the long-distance operator the unlisted number of the Mackle residence in Coral Gables, Florida, 665-7242. He let it ring and ring and ring. No one answered.

I Need You, Billy

Long before the black edge of night yielded to the tinctured
pink of sunrise over the Riviera Country Club of Coral Gables
that Tuesday morning, the telephone rang unanswered in the
stately and vacant home of Robert and Jane Mackle just off the
fairway to the twelfth hole of the golf course.

Stewart Woodward, suddenly realizing Barbara's father would
not be at home, hung up and tried again to reach a long-distance
operator.

Jane Mackle, anxiously pacing, noticed Stewart's predicament.
"Stewart," she said, "Mr. Mackle is in Villa 73."

Unable again to arouse the unperturbed night clerk on the
switchboard, Stewart bolted out the door toward the lobby. He
found a pay booth.

Poet Perkins, the night clerk, had telephoned Mrs. Jenkins, the
motel bookkeeper. She had stayed in her room. She didn't want to
get involved.

"Here is the latest news—from your neighbor breaking up your
snooze," Perkins informed Mrs. Jenkins cheerfully. "The guest in
room 137 has been robbed and her daughter taken away." He
didn't quite believe it.

An exasperated Stewart Woodward finally got his call through
to Barbara's father.

Robert Francis Mackle, at fifty-seven a deeply tanned man,
perceptive, decisive, and candid with a southern friendliness and
softness of manner, a large man with direct blue eyes with a
smudge of gray in a full head of black hair, looked the very
personification of corporate prosperity, the successful American
executive—as if he belonged in a four-color bourbon advertisement
in *U. S. News & World Report*. He and his two brothers, Frank, Jr.,
and Elliott, the Mackle Brothers, Frank younger at fifty-two and
Elliott the oldest at sixty, qualified easily as Florida's best-known
home builders and land developers.

Reaching, not groping, Robert Mackle caught the telephone on the first ring that morning at the Key Biscayne Hotel and Villas, which he and his brothers had built and owned since 1953.

He recognized Stewart's voice instantly. The boy had visited the family in Florida on three previous occasions over two years.

"Something terrible has happened, Mr. Mackle," Stewart began. "I don't know of any way to tell you except come right out with it."

"What is it?" said Robert Mackle, abruptly awake.

"About an hour ago someone broke into the motel where Barbara and Mrs. Mackle are staying. A man said he was a policeman and that someone in a white Ford had been injured. I drive that kind of car. So when Mrs. Mackle opened the door they came in and tied her up and took Barbara."

"Wait a minute. What do you mean, they took Barbara?"

"They took Barbara. A man and a little boy. They tried to chloroform Mrs. Mackle and they took Barbara."

There was a pause. Robert Mackle did not respond immediately. "How sure are you of everything?" he asked in disbelief.

"The police are here but they don't know what's going on."

"Just the local police?"

"Yes, sir."

"When I hang up, you call the FBI immediately and tell them to come right out. Will you do that?"

"Yes, sir."

"I want to put a lid on this. I don't want any publicity until we find out what's going on. And leave the telephone open because I'll be calling back."

"Well, Mr. Mackle, the switchboard isn't open. I'm calling from a pay booth. You can't call in."

The man erupted. "I want that damn switchboard open! Tell them no damn fooling about it. I want it opened! I'm going to my home now and I'll be in touch with you. You call the FBI."

Robert Mackle, stunned and bewildered, had recognized instantly the nature of the problem. Almost instinctively, he reacted as he had to uncounted hundreds of the lesser crises of his business and profession: Keep quiet. Find out the circumstances. "I knew it was serious. I knew it was desperate." He also knew he needed help from a cool head, someone he could trust. He telephoned an employee of his company, Billy Dale Vessels.

At that moment Vessels' wife, Susanne, a pale attractive redhead, sat at the dining room table of her home in a full-length housecoat addressing Christmas cards. Often she was up at five o'clock. The odd hour for the telephone to ring didn't surprise her particularly. Billy's friends from Oklahoma were always calling in the middle of the night.

Only the previous week, a somewhat inebriated classmate from the long-ago of the Cleveland Tigers, Cleveland High School, Cleveland, Oklahoma, had interrupted the sleep of the Vessels household in wistful reminiscence. Never again had the Tigers had a football tailback like Billy Vessels. With a cast on his left wrist, fractured so recently the coach did not want him to play, Vessels one afternoon in 1947 ran 97 yards, 95 yards, 93 yards, 90 yards, and 63 yards for touchdowns against a rival from the Indian country of Fairfax. This happened before the collegiate glory of All-American designation twice at the University of Oklahoma and selection as the best collegiate football player in the United States in the year 1952. The Heisman Trophy, a gold-plated figure of a fullback in flight, frozen atop a large and heavy base, reposed on the Vessels cabinet of long-playing records. Vessels had worked for the Mackle Brothers in a public and corporate relations capacity for ten years.

"Is Billy there?" the caller wanted to know.

"Well, yes," said Susanne hesitantly. "But he is asleep."

"This is Robert."

"Robert who?"

His voice, distorted under emotion, had made Mrs. Vessels suspect she had another drunk on the line from Oklahoma. She called her husband to the phone.

"I need you, Billy," Robert Mackle said.

Billy Vessels, a compact bull of a man physically, with the power and swiftness of youth, if not intact at age thirty-eight, still formidable, listened intently.

"All right, I'll meet you at your home in a few minutes," Vessels said. He dressed hurriedly and grabbed his black all-purpose raincoat. Like so many other migrants from the Midwestern plains states to the warmth of South Florida, he no longer owned a topcoat. He sped toward the darkened Mackle home at 4111 San Amaro Drive, Coral Gables. It was a five-minute drive.

Robert Mackle made a second hurried call. He called his brother Frank at the Plaza Hotel in New York City. Frank Mackle was in New York for a business appointment that day with Peter Cats, of Francis I. duPont & Co., a member of the board of directors of a company owned by the Mackles. The thought crossed Robert's mind that he was scheduled to be in Washington that day for an appointment with Clarence S. Pautzke, assistant secretary of the Department of Interior.

"I knew that Frank would know what to do," said Robert. He didn't ask anything. It wasn't necessary. He told him what he knew.

"Robert called me at 5:20 A.M. He was broken up. His voice was trembling terribly," said Frank Mackle. "I kept thinking, well maybe it's just a college prank, perhaps it is not as serious as it appears.

"I telephoned Dr. Ed Lauth, a physician and personal friend in Miami Shores, and I told him Robert was driving to his home from the Villas and suggested that he go over immediately. I was worried that Robert wouldn't make it. Then I telephoned Elliott, our other brother."

From Villa 73, a modern two-story pale green structure trimmed in coral and set back only a few yards from the beach and the glass-smooth Atlantic Ocean, Robert Mackle half-ran a hundred-yard walkway westward toward his new black-topped Lincoln Continental, a vehicle he had purchased six weeks before. Nobody is in the Villa! The thought struck him as he ran. Someone might call. When he reached the car he drove up the half circle to the main entrance of the hotel, and letting it idle under the three-lane canopy, he hurried to the front door and yelled across the lobby to the night-desk clerk.

"Any calls coming to Villa 73, transfer them immediately to my house."

Robert Mackle drove the twelve miles from Villa 73 at the hotel on the island of Key Biscayne to his home in a state of incredulousness. "I kept thinking I'll wake up. This is a nightmare." He drove toward the mainland on Rickenbacker Causeway, a four-laned palm-lined strip of highway across Biscayne Bay named for an old friend, Captain Eddie Rickenbacker, a World War I flyer who shot down twenty-six Germans.

In the first astonishment of Stewart Woodward's telephone call, Robert Mackle had thought of the crime of kidnap for ransom. Had he pondered the matter, as he would in the terrible agony of unknowns in the days ahead, he would have realized that his station in life, his position in the community in which he resided, subjected him to the greed of the criminal far more than the average man.

For Robert Mackle, inseparable from his brothers in the corporate world in which they lived, was hardly average about anything. Nor was the family nor his daughter, Barbara.

The man who sped across Rickenbacker Causeway had a title: Vice-chairman of the board and chairman of the executive committee, the Deltona Corporation.

Deltona stock would open at $54 on the American Stock Exchange in a few hours that morning of December 17, its assets listed at $127,887,537. The firm held in excess of 90,800 acres for development in the vicinities and communities of Deltona, Spring Hill, Panama City, Orlando, Tampa, Sanford, Daytona Beach, Lake Maitland Terrace, Cocoa Beach, and its newest and most publicized acquisition, Marco Island.

If a thoughtful kidnaper had so desired, he could have requested and received the company prospectus and the Marco Island brochures: Billowing sails and sleek hulls of the annual regatta on the azure calm of the Gulf of Mexico, the spacious four-bath homes at $54,200 (homesites not included), the bikini-clad water skiers aswirl off the overpoweringly white sand of a four-mile crescent of beach, and the ad man's enticements: "The ultimate in Twentieth-Century resort and leisure living," "all the haunting allure of the South Seas,"—"Florida's Last Frontier."

The tires of the Lincoln whined loudly as they raced over the metal grating of the drawbridge of the Rickenbacker Causeway. As Robert Mackle put his foot to the brake and stopped and waited for the red light just beyond the toll booth, he could see to his left the Miami Seaquarium advertisement of another Florida species. In arched fiberglass imitation, a huge tiger shark circled around and around.

You Are Safe. Do Not Be Alarmed

I started screaming and pounding to try to get out. With my fists I hit the walls as hard as I could. With all my strength. I braced and pushed. I remember doing that.

I guess I lost control completely. Nothing was real yet. I don't think I'd recovered completely from the drug. I was screaming, "God, no, you can't leave me! God, you can't leave me here!" This was out loud. "You have to let me out." That's when I started talking to myself. I didn't stay hysterical very long. I really didn't. Maybe thirty seconds or something like that. I was breathing hard. From the pounding I guess. I was screaming and pounding—and the pounding helped. The physical exertion helped. I don't know exactly how, but it helped. I was panting hard and I could hear my heart beating. I guess if there was a peak of terror, it was right after they left. That was it.

Then everything sort of just hit me. It became real. I knew. Until then I couldn't believe what was happening. And then all of a sudden I accepted it. Even when they were putting on the dirt I thought, they are going to let me out. I hadn't accepted it. Suddenly, I was beyond that. I realized what was happening.

I started thinking, now, look Barbara. Just calm down. I do that often. I sort of talk to myself. Now just calm down. They are going to come for you in two hours. This screaming and hollering will get you nowhere. You're doing this to yourself. This is ridiculous. There is no way it'll be a week. It can't be a week. Daddy will get the money. And they'll be back in two hours.

In two hours, I thought, I know I'm going to think of something to make them let me out. It isn't going to take that long. I'm going to have the best story I ever thought of. Then it struck me. Daddy isn't home. He won't answer the telephone. If they try to call him, they won't be able to reach him. When they come back in two hours, I won't tell them where he is unless they let me out. This was pretty silly, but I was trying to think of anything, just anything. I knew Daddy was at our villa at the Key Biscayne Hotel. He always stays there when Mother is out of town. He doesn't like to stay at home by himself.

I calmed myself down. I was still terribly scared, of course, but I knew what was going on. I started looking around and I realized my hands were still tied. I got the cord off easily. First I switched the fan on. I wanted to see if I could work it. I knew I could. But it was hard to work. It was a small rounded metal switch which stuck out, protruded outward a half inch or so, from the wall above my left shoulder. It went up and it went down. In the middle position the fan would stop. That's how it was. Up or down, the fan would stay on. I had to fool around with the switch and get it just right to turn it off. I couldn't turn it off very easily. Something had to slip just right. I couldn't see the fan but I could hear it. It had to be in a compartment behind my head. I knew that. I didn't feel the air at first, and I wasn't thinking about the flu at all. I wasn't conscious of my health. The fan made a loud noise and, really, I was thankful for the noise. To hear nothing was horrible. I looked around and I could see the switch for the pump on the other side. I guessed that is what it was. I saw the water tube and the barrels or whatever you want to call them at my feet.

My feet were still tied and I couldn't stretch out. I tried to reach the cord to untie my feet and I couldn't. That was horrible. The lid was maybe twelve or fourteen inches over my head. If I rose up, I bumped it. Finally, I turned on my side and sort of folded up. My hands would barely reach my feet. If I could have gotten to the cord, I think I could have undone it in a few seconds. I kept trying and trying. The rope wasn't so tight. The position was so awkward. I remember I just wanted to get my feet undone. I just had to. It probably took me three or four minutes.

So I kept looking around. There was a red flowery sofa pillow with a single black button. I saw a box of Kotex and decided to use it as a pillow. I stuffed the Kotex box behind my neck, then put the pillow on top of the box and sort of propped myself up. That's how I'd slept at the Rodeway, propped up so I could breathe, halfway up. That's when I noticed my nose was still stopped up and I couldn't even breathe through my nose. Under the Kotex box there were some instructions. I remember seeing them before I untied my feet. I picked them up and read them very carefully. I counted three pages. Everything was typed in capital letters and double spaced. I could see that they were Xeroxed or something. I could see that they weren't originals.

DO NOT BE ALARMED   YOU ARE SAFE

YOU ARE PRESENTLY INSIDE A FIBERGLASS REINFORCED PLYWOOD CAPSULE BURIED BENEATH THE GROUND NEAR THE HOUSE IN WHICH YOUR KIDNAPPERS ARE STAYING. YOUR STATUS WILL BE CHECKED APPROXIMATELY EVERY TWO HOURS.

THE CAPSULE IS QUITE STRONG. YOU WILL NOT BE ABLE TO BREAK IT OPEN. BE ADVISED, HOWEVER, THAT YOU ARE BENEATH THE WATER TABLE. IF YOU SHOULD BREAK OPEN A SEAM YOU WOULD DROWN BEFORE WE COULD DIG YOU OUT. THE CAPSULE INSTRUMENTATION CONTAINS A WATER SENSITIVE SWITCH WHICH WILL WARN US IF THE WATER ENTERS THE CAPSULE TO A DANGEROUS DEGREE.

YOUR LIFE DEPENDS ON THE AIR DELIVERED TO YOUR CHAMBER VIA THE VENTILATION FAN. THIS FAN IS POWERED BY A LEAD-ACID STORAGE BATTERY CAPABLE OF SUPPLYING THE FAN MOTOR WITH POWER FOR 270 HOURS. HOWEVER, THE USE OF THE LIGHT AND OTHER SYSTEMS FOR ONLY A FEW HOURS COUPLED WITH THE HIGHER AMPERAGE DRAIN WILL REDUCE THIS FIGURE TO ONLY ONE WEEK OF SAFETY.

SHOULD THE AIR SUPPLIED PROVE TO BE TOO MUCH YOU CAN PARTLY BLOCK THE AIR OUTLET WITH A PIECE OF PAPER. A MUFFLER HAS BEEN PLACED IN THE AIR PASSAGE TO PREVENT ANY NOISE YOU MAKE FROM REACHING THE SURFACE: IF WE DETECT ANY COMMOTION WHICH WE FEEL IS DANGEROUS, WE WILL INTRODUCE ETHER TO THE AIR INTAKE AND PUT YOU TO SLEEP.

THE FAN OPERATES ON 6 VOLTS. IT HAS A SWITCH WITH TWO POSITIONS TO SWITCH BETWEEN THE TWO AVAILABLE CIRCUITS. SHOULD ONE CIRCUIT FAIL . . . TO THE OTHER.

THE BOX HAS A PUMP WHICH WILL EVACUATE ANY ACCIDENTAL LEAKAGE FROM THE BOX WHEN YOU TURN THE PUMP SWITCH ON TO THE "ON" POSITION. THIS PUMP USES 15 TIMES AS MUCH POWER AS YOUR VENTILATION FAN (7.5 AMPS); YOUR LIFE SUPPORT BATTERY WILL NOT

ALLOW THE USE OF THE PUMP EXCEPT FOR EMERGENCY WATER EVACUATION.

THE LIGHT USES 2.5 TIMES THE AMPERAGE OF THE AIR CIRCULATION SYSTEM. USE OF THE LIGHT WHEN NOT NECESSARY WILL CUT YOUR BATTERY SAFETY MARGIN SUBSTANTIALLY. IF YOU USE THE LIGHT CONTINUOUSLY YOUR LIFE EXPECTANCY WILL BE CUT TO ONE THIRD OF THE WEEK WE HAVE ALLOTTED YOU BEFORE YOU ARE RELEASED.

YOUR CAPSULE CONTAINS A WATER JUG WITH THREE GALLONS OF WATER AND A TUBE FROM WHICH TO DRINK IT. BE CAREFUL TO BLOW THE WATER FROM THE TUBE WHEN YOU ARE FINISHED DRINKING TO AVOID SIPHONING THE WATER ONTO THE FLOOR WHEN THE TUBE END DROPS BELOW THE WATER LEVEL.

YOUR CAPSULE CONTAINS A BUCKET FOR REFUSE AND THE PRODUCTS OF YOUR BOWEL MOVEMENTS. THE BUCKET HAS AN ANTIBACTERIAL SOLUTION IN IT: DON'T TIP IT OVER. THE LID SEALS TIGHTLY TO PREVENT THE ESCAPE OF ODORS. A ROLL OF WAX PAPER IS PROVIDED—USE IT TO PREVENT SOLID WASTE FROM CONTAMINATING YOUR BED. KOTEX IS PROVIDED SHOULD YOU NEED IT.

BLANKETS AND A MAT ARE PROVIDED. YOUR WARMTH DEPENDS ON BODY HEAT SO REGULATE THE AIR TO PREVENT LOSS OF HEAT FROM THE CAPSULE.

A CASE OF CANDY IS PROVIDED TO FURNISH ENERGY TO YOUR BODY.

TRANQUILIZERS ARE PROVIDED TO AID YOU IN SLEEPING—THE BEST WAY YOU HAVE TO PASS THE TIME.

THE VENTILATION SYSTEM IS DOUBLY SCREENED TO PREVENT INSECTS OR ANIMALS FROM ENTERING THE CAPSULE AREA. YOU RISK BEING EATEN BY ANTS SHOULD YOU BREAK THESE PROTECTION SCREENS.

THE ELECTRICAL COMPONENTS BEHIND THESE SCREENS ARE DELICATE AND THEY SUPPORT YOUR LIFE. DON'T ATTEMPT TO TOUCH THESE CIRCUITS.

WE'RE SURE YOUR FATHER WILL PAY THE RANSOM WE HAVE ASKED IN LESS THAN ONE WEEK. WHEN YOUR FATHER PAYS THE RANSOM WE WILL TELL HIM WHERE YOU ARE AND HE'LL COME FOR YOU. SHOULD HE FAIL TO PAY WE WILL RELEASE YOU, SO BE CALM AND REST—YOU'LL BE HOME FOR CHRISTMAS ONE WAY OR THE OTHER.

I read it and I was there and still I couldn't quite comprehend. It was awfully hard to believe.

And I wondered, God, am I going to die? I said I don't feel like I am. Do people feel like they are going to die before they do? I don't know. Or is it the same feeling I have now? And they don't know it? I was talking to God. I don't say formal prayers, you know, formal recitation. I just talk. And somehow I knew I was not going to die.

I started reading the instructions again. "Do not be alarmed. You are safe." I laughed. I couldn't help myself.

So, okay, I'll have to turn the light out because I'm using too much battery. In a minute, not now. Tranquilizers. I wonder where they are. I don't want them yet. I want to be very awake, very alert, when they come back in two hours.

Drowning. I'm not afraid of drowning. I don't believe that. All that dirt. That's not true.

And for the first time, really, I looked closely at the plywood lid. The light made it yellowish. I could see stamped there some writing; identifying the shipment number of the wood, I guess. I know I was getting wet. Everything was damp. I pulled up the blanket. It was a yellow frilly one and it was damp, too. I was cold.

After ten minutes or so I began to think about Mother. Had they hurt her? Had she gotten away? I didn't think they had hurt her. Had she called the police? I was hoping she hadn't called the police. That might make things worse. Mother is going to call Daddy at Key Biscayne. That's what she'll do, I thought.

I was thinking of how upset Daddy would be. Daddy! That's it! When the two hours are up, I'll ask to speak to Daddy. I am sure he is going to ask to speak to me to make sure I'm alive. And they'll have to let me out to talk to him. If I get out, just once, they'll never put me back here again. Never. They'll have to shoot me or something. Kill me. If I can only talk to the boss. I'm sure I can convince him there is no need for this. No need at all. There is the house.

In my mind I reconstructed the telephone call from Mother to Daddy. I saw Mother dialing, how Daddy would react when he first heard.

I thought he might have tears in his eyes. He wouldn't cry. One time before I saw tears in his eyes. It was about 1955 or

1957 and we were at the hospital, Daddy, Bobby and me. Mother had to have surgery. Precancer, they thought. And Daddy told Bobby and me. I think he started to cry. He had to leave the room. He said, if something happens to Mother, we'll make it. It was the only time I ever saw tears in his eyes.

When Daddy heard about me, I thought, he would calm down, and he would get everyone working on it. He would think about calling Bobby, I knew, but I didn't know if he would call Bobby right away. Yes, I knew he would tell him because our family is very close and when it really comes down to it, we talk about things. They'll tell him, yes. I was going through all this minute detail, trying to think of anything—so as not to think of where I was. How would Bobby react? He would be calm and calm down Mother and Daddy. I knew he could.

It is funny the things that come to your mind. I thought about school and I said well, I won't have to take that macro exam. Look where I am! I thought about Barbara Law, my little sister in Delta Delta Delta sorority. She is from Coral Gables, too, and when Mother came up I knew the company plane would fly to Atlanta and take us home for the holidays. I had offered her a ride home and she was excited. I knew she'd have a hard time getting another commercial reservation because of Christmas.

I said to myself everything is going to be fine. Everything is going to be all right. And I read the instructions again, a third time.

. . . USE OF THE LIGHT WHEN NOT NECESSARY WILL CUT YOUR BATTERY SAFETY MARGIN SUBSTANTIALLY. IF YOU USE THE LIGHT CONTINUOUSLY YOUR LIFE EXPECTANCY WILL BE CUT TO ONE THIRD OF THE WEEK WE HAVE ALLOTTED YOU BEFORE YOU ARE RELEASED. . . .

Yes, I said, I have to turn out the light. It was a small white light, about the size of a Christmas-tree bulb, and it was in the top left corner of the box, and I reached for it. I could feel the heat. I turned it off.

Then I got scared, real scared. As a little girl I'd always been afraid of the dark. It was one of those unreasoning fears that I knew was stupid. But I couldn't help myself. That's the way I'd always been.

I started to tense up. I tried to put it out of my mind. I couldn't

do it. I said, no, no. But I had to turn it back on. I just had to. I
was angry at myself, but I had to.

So I turned it on—and it didn't help. I could feel the panic
building up anyway, getting worse and worse. Something is
going to happen! I've got to get out of here! The pump! The
pump! That's it.

I had thought about the pump before but I didn't want to use
the battery. He told me it would turn on a red light and buzzer
in the house. The panic was getting unbearable. I turned on the
pump. It made a horribly loud noise. I actually jumped, it startled
me so. It sounded like a broken kitchen Mixmaster going off in my
ear. I didn't expect anything like it. It was almost overbearing. I
kept switching it on and off. I don't think I was too rational. In my
mind I could see the light and the buzzer going on and off in the
house.

They are going to come for me now, I thought. They'll think
it is an emergency. He'll be mad, very mad, but I'll be able
to talk to him. I'm going to tell him there is something I have
to tell them that is very important. I'll tell them Daddy is not
at home. I turned off the ventilation fan so I could listen and hear
better. I listened for the footsteps.

And nothing. There weren't any.

I just left the ventilating fan off. The panic subsided. I had a
hold of myself. I could hear myself breathing again. And I noticed it was getting a little stuffy after a few minutes. It began to
get warm. It felt good. I felt drowsy. I thought, this is great. I'm
going to sleep. It was just that fast. Then I began to wonder about
getting enough air. I turned the fan back on, and it started getting
cold again right away.

Well, they'll be here in a little bit to check, I thought. They didn't
come on the pump because they know I'm faking. They're in the
house.

In that first hour or so in the box I would just get control of myself when the fear and the dread and the panic would start building
up again. It came in waves. I could feel it coming. I started
pounding again. "Can you hear me? Help! Something is the
matter!" And when I lost control, I'd grit my teeth and beat as hard
as I could. I could get good leverage, too, and I would brace
myself and strain as hard as I could. My muscles didn't ache
or anything at the time. I wasn't thinking about them. I clenched

my fists and beat and beat very deliberately. Maybe some air would come in, some water, some daylight. After a while, I calmed down again.

I remember thinking, I wonder if I'm bugged. I wonder if they've got a microphone in here somewhere? There were all sorts of things, pails, some food, a sack, and stuff in the bottom of the box, and I hadn't even bothered with them. The idea of the bug crossed my mind but I dismissed it.

I had no conception of time. Right from the beginning I was waiting for those two hours. So I decided, okay, I'll count seconds. Sixty seconds per minute for sixty minutes. That's three thousand and six hundred seconds and doubled, that's seven thousand two hundred seconds. I started counting. Not aloud, but to myself. It was a long count. I left the light on.

I counted the long way. I thought of every number by itself like two thousand three hundred and forty-eight; two thousand three hundred and forty-nine; two thousand three hundred and fifty. I'm sure I counted two complete hours. I counted slowly.

When I reached seven thousand and two hundred, I turned the fan off and listened. Nothing. Absolute silence.

Well, I thought, maybe I counted wrong. I'll start again at six thousand. I knew I couldn't possibly have missed that much. Six thousand and one; six thousand and two . . .

When I reached seven thousand and two hundred again I knew it had been more than two hours. That's when I realized that everything they said wasn't true. The pump didn't turn on a red light and buzzer anywhere. There wasn't any house. And there was nobody there. They are not coming back, I said. They are not coming at all. They are not ever coming back. Ever. Ever.

Ergo, Barbara Will Suffocate

Wrenched from sleep at the Plaza Hotel in New York City, Frank Mackle that morning thought immediately of his own daughter, Nancy Radcliffe Mackle.

"Check on Nancy!" he called to his wife, Virginia.

If Barbara had been kidnaped, and he couldn't exactly accept it, had Nancy?

Nancy, the first Mackle daughter in three generations, was two years older than Barbara. Barbara would have been named Nancy Radcliffe, after their great grandmother, had she been born first. Both girls attended college.

Nancy, a senior studying psychology, had finished her exams at the University of Florida in Gainesville the previous Friday, and unlike Barbara, she lived in an apartment off campus. She had accompanied her parents to New York so she and her mother could go Christmas shopping. They had arrived the evening before and it was snowing. As a child of the Florida sun, Nancy, although twenty-two, had seen snow only once before. She had to buy boots and play in the snow in Central Park. That night Nancy stayed up and watched the Johnny Carson television show until one o'clock. Her parents were asleep in a second room of their suite. A moment or two after she turned out the lights, Nancy heard someone fumbling at the door with a key. From the light under the door, she could see a man's feet in the hotel corridor. He's got the wrong door, she thought. It struck her as amusing. Without knocking, he walked away. She dropped off to sleep.

"Wake up, Nancy. Wake up!" It was her mother. It took her several minutes to comprehend. She remembered the fumbling at the door. Yet she couldn't believe what her mother told her. Kidnaping? "There's got to be a catch somewhere," she told her mother.

Her father, in pajamas and robe, was on the telephone again. He called his son, Frank III. Frank III, twenty-four, and his wife, Loretta, and their two young children, Laura and Frank IV, lived seven blocks from "Uncle Bob" in Coral Gables.

To Loretta, kidnaping seemed preposterous. Everything was so sketchy. Groggy, not fully awake, inclined to disbelieve, she went back to sleep. It was still dark despite the switch back to standard time from daylight-saving time. Feeling a little ridiculous, Frank III looked at his sleeping children and made sure the doors were locked. He poured himself a cup of coffee. He expected a second telephone call telling him it was a false alarm. Maybe Barbara had stayed out all night. Uncle Bob, he told himself, might be upset about nothing. He decided to stop by his uncle's home on his way to work at Five Points, the location of the executive offices of the Deltona Corporation, 3250 Southwest Third Avenue. He could stop by in an hour or two. Whenever he went to work.

From the Plaza Hotel, Frank Mackle, Jr., booked airline reservations for Miami on two flights, at 8:30 A.M. and 9:30 A.M. He was afraid they couldn't make the first one. He was right. Caught in the snarl of Manhattan's morning traffic, slowed by a construction project, the taxi arrived at Kennedy International Airport five minutes too late. "It was a strange ride," said Nancy. "Nobody could say anything. There were so many questions." Hippies? College boys drinking? A misunderstanding? They caught the second flight. Frank Mackle knew his son would meet them at Miami International Airport. He knew he would tell from the expression of his son's face the seriousness of the situation. Computing mentally, he calculated 60 per cent; he convinced himself, 60 to 40, he would see his son smiling.

From the Rickenbacker Causeway some few moments before six o'clock, Robert Mackle had turned left and sped southwestward to his home. As he pulled into the half-circle driveway to the front door, he saw Billy Vessels waiting for him. Neither man spoke. Robert quickly inserted a key into an automatic-burglar-alarm lock, disconnected the alarm and unlocked the door. The Christmas wreath hung on the door. They stood for a second on the marble entrance, down two steps from a more formal foyer, under an unlighted antique glass chandelier hanging from the high ceiling of the stairwell.

"Tell me everything that has happened," Billy Vessels said, and Robert Mackle repeated what little he knew. From a red telephone in the game room, Billy Vessels put a call through to room 137 of the Rodeway Inn.

Jane Mackle, terribly distraught, her nightgown torn and bloodied, had yet to hear—or even think—of the word kidnap. Roger L. Kaas, the first FBI agent on the scene, mentioned it some moments later.

"Would there be any reason for kidnaping?" he asked.

"Oh, no," said Jane Mackle. It was the furthest thought from her mind.

"Well, it could be," Stewart Woodward spoke up.

"Is there any money in the family?" agent Kaas asked.

"Oh, I don't know," Jane Mackle replied evasively. For years she had abhorred conversations about wealth.

"Well, yes," said Stewart flatly. "They are connected with the Deltona Corporation."

Jane Mackle's emotional condition disturbed both Robert and Billy Vessels. She told them the police had asked her about photographs of Barbara.

"Your place is with Jane," Vessels said when Robert hung up.

"My place is where I can get Barbara back."

"I think you should be with Jane," Vessels repeated. "She needs you."

"There is a 7:15 Eastern flight to Atlanta," Robert conceded. "I can make it." He had driven his wife to the airport for the same flight the previous Friday.

Billy Vessels telephoned Eastern Airlines. He asked for two first-class reservations. He decided he was going too.

Elliott arrived about six-thirty. Robert Mackle kept glancing at the telephone. Someone had to be there to answer it. He thought of Jane's sister, Ann Braznell Briggle. She lived with her husband, Dr. William F. Briggle, a dentist, about four and a half blocks away in Coral Gables. They were family. He telephoned.

Bill Briggle, a grayed and rigidly scheduled man Robert's age, had just stepped out of the shower.

"Bill," Robert began, "don't say a damn word to anybody, not even Ann, but get some clothes on and get over right quick."

From the tone of his voice, Bill Briggle knew it was an emergency. "Ann's lying right here," he said.

Robert's voice broke. "Here, talk to Billy Vessels."

Vessels told him Barbara had been kidnaped, and asked him to come over immediately. Bill Briggle told his wife.

"Oh, my God, no!" cried Ann. She believed it instantly. She was five years younger than Jane. Because the Briggles had three sons, no daughters, they looked upon Barbara as a daughter almost. Her husband told her to tell no one. No one!

"Why are you up so early, Mom," her oldest son, Bill, wanted to know. He was home from the University of Tennessee for the holidays. As a cousin he had served as an escort at Barbara's debutante party two years before.

"I guess I didn't sleep well last night," Ann Briggle lied. For five hours that morning, after her sons had left the house, she would pace the floors like a caged animal.

Dr. Briggle, ignoring his undershorts, slipped on a pair of pants, a polo shirt, and slippers. He arrived at the Mackle home within five minutes. Dr. Lauth, called earlier from New York, arrived a few minutes before. In the game room Billy Vessels hurriedly flipped through family photo albums in search of recent pictures of Barbara. He figured the FBI might want them.

"Robert was terribly upset," said Dr. Briggle, "but he was tracking straight. There was no panic." Robert Mackle worried still about the telephone. If his daughter had been kidnaped, and as yet he truly did not know, someone had to be there to answer every call. A call could be vital. It was as simple as that. "Bill," he said, "will you stay here until we get someone in?"

Robert Mackle and Billy Vessels took off for the airport. Vessels drove his car, a new Oldsmobile 442. He knew he was in better condition to drive than Robert. He left the car in valet parking and they walked hurriedly toward the Eastern counter. "We're late," Vessels kept saying. They were running close.

"I don't want anyone telephoning Bobby," Robert Mackle said. It might not be necessary. Somehow, everything might have a logical explanation. It made no sense to call his son until he had to. His son was in Philadelphia in his first year at Wharton Graduate School of Business and Finance.

"You'd better call Ed Lauth and tell him not to call Bobby," Vessels said. "He might take it on himself. I'll get the tickets." He rushed off.

For the first of uncounted times that day, the ring of the telephone startled everyone in the Mackle household. Dr. Briggle picked it up. It was dead. There was no one there.

A moment later it rang again. Dr. Lauth raced up the stairs so he could listen on the bedroom extension.

Robert Mackle had made both calls. He thought he had dialed incorrectly and hung up too soon. He instructed Dr. Lauth not to telephone Bobby under any circumstances. "Let's find out first." He suggested they might telephone Jane at the Rodeway Inn.

"We'll do that," said Dr. Briggle. He already had. From the telephone in the game room, which was a direct WATS line for long distance, he had talked to Jane a few minutes before. "We couldn't tell very much. She was in pretty bad condition. The police were there."

At the airport, Robert Mackle and Billy Vessels boarded the plane. In the full-throttled thrust and roar of four wing-jet engines, Flight 122, Miami to Atlanta non-stop, lifted from a 10,500-foot strip of concrete for a scheduled one hour and forty minutes. The two men sat in silence. They drank a lot of water.

Once, his voice cracking, Robert Mackle said simply, "Barbara is not the kind of girl you violate." He didn't know. He didn't know.

At the Mackle home in Coral Gables, William H. O'Dowd, Jr., waited near a red telephone in the red-carpeted den. It wasn't a particularly large room. A cobbler's bench sat before an Early American divan across from a walled, upright, brick fireplace-barbecue grill where the Mackles often cooked with charcoal on the maid's two nights off, Thursday and Sunday. Full-length wooden shutters closed off a lift-up bar built into a corner. A shuttered cabinet also contained a black-and-white television set. For six years after the home was built in 1954, the Mackles practically lived in the den. Then in 1960 they put in a pool and built a game room, a huge all-purpose room 30 by 45 feet, and the den more or less became a passageway into the game room. Both rooms had telephones. The red one in the game room was the WATS line. A second red one in the den sat on a black combination bench-desk on an interior wall paneled in knotty pine. A red pencil stuck out from an inkstand holder. A pad of paper lay on the desk. Robert Mackle had written on it the number of the Rodeway Inn in Decatur, 404 634-6291. Elliott had written the number of the Miami office of the FBI, 379-2421. Pasted upon the telephone months before, so it would be seen when anyone picked the receiver off the cradle, was a bright red-orange label with two other numbers:

"Courtesy of Coral Gables Fireman's Benevolent Association. Fire or First Aid: Emergency call 446-7685. Police: 446-6464."

The phone rang. O'Dowd grabbed it.

"Is Jane there this morning?" It was a matronly voice, obviously a friend of the family. O'Dowd quickly disposed of the caller.

Elliott Mackle and the dentist, Dr. Briggle, had left earlier. "Don't use the telephone needlessly," Elliott said. "Keep it open. I'll be at the office." Frank III stopped by briefly about 8:50 A.M. Skeptical, uncertain, he went on to the office, too.

O'Dowd, a quiet-spoken, six-foot-four-inch man of forty-seven, subdued, restrained and generally unflappable, had worked for the Mackle organization since 1950. When hired, the company had no idea of how bright he was. He went to work as a timekeeper on a construction site. Genuinely shy, he had neglected to tell anyone he was a graduate of the Harvard School of Business Administration.

As O'Dowd waited in the den, the Negro maid arrived, walking to the home from a bus stop three houses away on the closest thoroughfare, Bird Road. She had to walk on the edge of the street pavement on San Amaro Drive. There were no sidewalks. Home-owners in Coral Gables preferred it that way. The back kitchen door was latched from the inside and the maid had taken from her purse her own key to the front door when O'Dowd opened it for her.

Mrs. Agnes Banks recognized O'Dowd as someone from the company. She didn't know his name.

"Mr. Mackle," O'Dowd said, "had to go to Atlanta. If the telephone rings, please let me answer it."

"Oh, did Barbara get worse or something?" Agnes knew she was ill. She thought O'Dowd looked at her peculiarly.

"No," he said. "She is fine."

Agnes, a Georgia-born grandmother of three at age forty-five, walked off, positive something was wrong. She slipped into her green, white-collared uniform and began her cleaning. The home was already immaculate except for a pile of photo albums strewn over a round table in the game room.

Agnes had worked for the Mackles since the week after Barbara's birth in 1948. She took care of her as a baby, refereed in futility joyful pillow fights between Barbara and Bobby when their parents were away, and generally prepared dinner, stayed until the evening dishes were put away at six-thirty or seven o'clock, and kept everything as Mrs. Mackle wanted it—"just right." "If Barbara was ever mad at me, I never knowed it," she would say.

From the kitchen about 8:40 A.M., the gardener and handy man, Walter Powell, hollered, "Aggie!" He had driven up in his old pickup truck, a 1956 green Chevy he had purchased cheaply from the Mackle Company years before. He noticed O'Dowd's car in the driveway.

"Aggie didn't know what was going on. Ah thought something had happened to Mister Robert. He got sick or something. Nobody tells us nothing," Walter recalled. Slender and graying at fifty-four, Walter, as he was always called, had worked for the Mackles since 1947. For years Barbara had bought him a pack of Juicy

Fruit chewing gum every time she went to the store. When he began to wear false teeth, Barbara switched brands. Dentine didn't stick as much as Juicy Fruit. Every Monday Walter did the outside lawn work and on Tuesday the inside, waxing floors, polishing silver. Tuesday was the pool day too, and this Tuesday he hooked up the long, flexible vacuum-cleaner-styled tube and let it sink slowly to the bottom. Occasionally, he would get a golf ball. The pool and patio were off the game room at the back of the home, close to the fairway.

O'Dowd watched and said nothing.

At 9:10 A.M. the telephone rang. O'Dowd grabbed it. He was nervous.

"Hello," he said.

"Robert Mackle?" It was a distinctive male voice.

"No," O'Dowd replied evenly. "He is on his way to Atlanta." There was a long pause.

"Well," said the voice, "tell him to look under a palm tree in the northeast corner of the house—under a rock about six inches down."

"Where did you say it was?" O'Dowd scrawled furiously on the pad.

"The northeast corner of the house," he repeated hurriedly.

"Don't go so quickly," said O'Dowd. "I can't take it down."

"That's all," the voice said. O'Dowd heard only the deadened nothingness of a broken connection.

He hadn't recognized the voice. It was no one he knew. It had sounded faintly foreign, not Spanish certainly, possibly Canadian, scornful. Immediately he dialed the Deltona Corporation and repeated the message.

"Wait a second, Bill," said Neil E. Bahr, the firm's executive vice-president and chief operating officer. "Let me record you." O'Dowd again repeated the message.

"Don't do anything," said Elliott Mackle, cutting in on another extension. "Don't go outside and look yourself. Wait for the FBI. They're on their way over here now." O'Dowd wondered if the kidnapers could conceivably have the Mackle home under surveillance. It all seemed so improbable. Look for a palm tree and dig under a rock.

In the decrescendo whine of jet engines on the concrete apron of Atlanta Municipal Airport, Robert Mackle and Billy Vessels were on their feet inside the slowly moving DC-8, waiting for the stewardesses, now putting on their white gloves, to open the door. It was 8:55 A.M. They had no luggage. They ran for a taxi. Panting, hardly able to catch his breath, Robert Mackle told the driver, "The new Rodeway Inn on Clairmont Road in Decatur." He knew there were two Rodeways. He didn't want the wrong one. They were easy to mix up. "Please hurry. It is urgent." Robert Mackle knew the way. He had stayed there a few months before.

"I kept looking at my watch," said Jane Mackle. "I didn't think they'd ever get there. It seemed forever. I remember seeing the taxi stop and Robert get out. I started crying."

Two men stood on the walkway outside room 137. They already had registered and moved into the adjacent room 135. The door was ajar. Robert Mackle saw them but didn't stop. Billy Vessels stopped.

Roger Kaas and William J. Watry, FBI agents, introduced themselves. Kaas showed Vessels his credentials. They remained outside.

Robert Mackle put his arms around his wife and she sobbed on his shoulder. "If I hadn't opened the door," she wept. "Barbara tried to stop me." Her condition shocked him, the rope burns, the abrasions, the blood stains, the discoloration. Her face was shell-white, puffy. She kept blaming herself.

"Jane," said Robert Mackle, "from what we know right now, you had nothing to do with it. We're going to get Barbara back." He had himself under control. He held his wife in his arms.

"We've been through a lot together and we'll get through this," he said. "We're going to get Barbara back."

Some moments later Robert Mackle stepped outside. Vessels introduced him to agent Kaas and another man, a dean from Emory University. Robert Mackle didn't catch the name.

"We don't have a thing to go on yet," agent Kaas admitted candidly. "We know nothing. Our men are talking to Barbara's friends on campus."

The dean took offense. "What right do you have to be on our campus without notifying us?"

This is the one thing Robert Mackle felt he didn't need, an argumentative dean. "This is the FBI. I want to hear his story," Robert Mackle said. Unimpressed, unaware, and glaring accusatorily, the dean persisted.

Agent Kaas said something about the hour that the university administrative offices opened. The dean, increasingly agitated, wasn't interested.

"Our agents are on your campus," agent Kaas said very coldly and firmly.

Billy Vessels, face flushed, muscles tightening, erupted in wrath. "Get your ass out of here!" he said to the dean. The dean departed.

Robert returned to room 137. Billy Vessels joined the two FBI agents. The phone rang. Agent Kaas listened momentarily, and then asked Vessels to summon Robert.

"I think we've had a real break," agent Kaas began. "Do you know a man named O'Dowd?"

When O'Dowd had telephoned the Deltona executive offices at Five Points, agent James Downing had relayed the information about the rock and the palm tree to the Miami office of the FBI. The Miami FBI, in turn, had notified both the Washington and Atlanta FBI offices.

"It appears to be a genuine kidnaping," agent Kaas told Robert Mackle. "We know what we're dealing with."

Immensely relieved, Robert Mackle felt as if someone had lifted an invisible boulder from his shoulders. Agent Kaas wanted to know about palm trees in the northeast corner of the yard.

There were four in the back yard, three royal palms on the east side of the property under Barbara's upstairs bedroom window. In the extreme northeast corner of the property, just inside the property line, croton shrubs grew next to a power pole. But also on the northeast side, five yards from the edge of the house, was a clump or cluster of Phoenix palms, a dense decorative outgrowth of subtropical shrubbery, about five feet in diameter. "Somebody might call that a palm," Robert Mackle said.

At the executive offices at Five Points, agent Joseph H. R. St. Pierre asked James E. Vensel, Deltona's senior architectural engineer, to drive him to the Mackle home. Vensel knew the way and the home. Agent St. Pierre wanted to approach the house cautiously. Conceivably, the house could be under surveillance. On Pinto Court, the far side of the golf course, agent St. Pierre and Vensel stopped and parked. They had an unobstructed view of the northeast corner of the home from about 360 yards across the fairway.

Inside the home, standing at the sliding glass doors, O'Dowd saw the car stop. My God, he thought, someone is watching the house. What's keeping the FBI, he wondered. Two morning golfers, nonchalant and dawdling, played through the twelfth hole, agent St. Pierre and architect Vensel watching suspiciously from one side, O'Dowd watching nervously from the other.

Agent St. Pierre and Vensel toured the neighborhood, detected nothing abnormal, and pulled into the Mackle driveway. At closer view, O'Dowd recognized the car and Vensel. He was glad to see them. They talked briefly in the game room. "You stay here," St. Pierre said. St. Pierre strolled outside. Conscious of footprints on the well-kept and mowed Bermuda grass, he neither left any impressions nor saw any footprints. He inspected every palm tree on the premises. At first he didn't see the right one. The clump of Phoenix palms on the northeast side didn't look like ordinary palms. But beside it, a few inches from a small fern, he saw a single coral rock, a chunk no larger than a man's fist. It was the only rock in the entire yard. The earth around it was firm.

Agent St. Pierre retreated momentarily. He found Walter, the gardener. O'Dowd had already asked Walter if he had a shovel.

Walter Powell had no idea of what was happening. He made one reasonably correct deduction, though. The man now asking for the shovel had to be a "detective man." From the bed of his pickup truck, Walter reached for the long white-ash handle of his shovel.

Very carefully, St. Pierre lifted the rock and instructed Walter where to dig. "Take it easy," he said.

"Ah was scared to death," said Walter. "Ah didn't know what I was digging for. Ah thought it must be a time bomb."

He gently drove the blade of the shovel down all the way. The earth appeared normal. It wasn't loose.

"Bring it up," said St. Pierre. "Okay, now again. Easy."

On the second shovelful, St. Pierre saw a rolled white paper protruding from a black rubber stopper of a broken bottle.

"Get out!" St. Pierre said.

Walter Powell, half expecting to be blown to kingdom come, scampered across the lawn to the safety of his hibiscus bushes.

The blade of the shovel, six to eight inches under the surface, had smashed a fragile tubelike no-neck bottle, four inches in depth. St. Pierre wondered if it had come from a scientist's laboratory of some kind. With a razor or knife or scissors, someone had trimmed about a quarter of an inch from the bottom edge of the rubber stopper so that a note, folded longways once, and tightly rolled, would fit inside. One end still stuck inside the stopper. Delicately, St. Pierre picked it up by the edges. It was clean except for a few fragments of glass and fresh flecks of dirt. He walked across the pool deck and patio to the game room. He needed tweezers. Agnes ran upstairs to the master bedroom and from a drawer of the vanity table in the bathroom, she took a pair of Jane Mackle's eyebrow tweezers.

Carefully, St. Pierre unrolled the paper. There were three sheets, 8½ by 11 inches. Someone had typed double space on the first page and single space typed the other two. St. Pierre could tell they were not the originals. This was a Xeroxed copy.

With O'Dowd and Vensel peering over his shoulders, he spread the sheets on the round table in the game room and began to read.

ROBERT MACKLE:

Sir, your daughter has been kidnapped by us and we now hold her for ransom. She is quite safe, if somewhat uncomfortable. We offer no proof of our possession of her at this time. It will arrive by mail in a few days. Barbara is presently alive inside a small capsule buried in a remote piece of soil. She has enough food and water and air to last seven days. At the end of the seven days the life supporting batteries will be discharged and her air supply will be cut off.

The box is waterproof and very strong—fiberglass reinforced plywood—she has little chance of escaping. The box is in an unusual and lonely place. She has no chance of being accidently stumbled upon.

Contemplate, if you will, the position into which this puts you. If you pay the ransom prior to the seven days, we will tell you of her whereabouts. Should you catch the messenger we send to pick up the ransom, we will simply not say anything to anyone and ergo Barbara will suffocate. The messenger knows only one of us and he will report to us via radio from the pickup site. We will immediately know his fate.

Should you catch all of us, we will never admit anything as to do so would be suicide *and* again—she will die. As you can see, you don't *want* to catch us for to do so would be condemning your lovely and intelligent daughter to death. The police may allow you to have a free hand prior to the return of your daughter should you be so callous as to contact them. If you ask the police to advise you in this matter please be aware that their very presence will scare us off. We can see no way for you to secure the safe return of your daughter other than to obey our instructions explicitly.

1) Although we will always anticipate the involvement of the police in this situation, be assured that if your communication with them or their actual presence is detected, we will break off negotiations with you immediately. We have tied into several of the possible means of communications that you have with the police and we feel that you will be unable to contact them without our knowledge.

2) The ransom will be $500,000 in recently issued $20 bills. Here are the requirements you must meet in this matter:

The notes must not be older than 1950 issue.

No more than ten notes may have consecutive serial numbers; ie., the notes must have a great variety of serial numbers and not be merely shuffled.

The notes must be Federal Reserve notes of standard configuration.

No more than one-half of the notes may be uncirculated.

No form of marking on the bills is acceptable. Please note that the bills will undergo a minimum of eight hours of intense examination before we allow you to have knowledge of the subject's whereabouts. We have planned a series of 44 tests on a large representative sample of the bills. These tests include every chemical and physical test of any remote applicability. No omission, shaving, spotting, cutting, counterfeiting, irradiating, ad nos will go undetected.

3) The bills should occupy no more than 4000 cubic inches and thusly fit into a standard large suitcase of inside dimensions 31.5″ long×18.75″ high×6.25″ deep. Purchase such a suitcase and lock the bills inside.

When you have the money in readiness, call all the Miami area major newspapers and place the following ad in the "personal" section of the classified advertisements:

"Loved one—please come home. We will pay all expenses and meet you anywhere at any time. Your Family."

Prepare your car for a trip and on the night of the ads' first appearance we will call you at your home after midnight to advise you of where you must go to deliver the money. You must be the one to deliver the money, Robert. You will dress yourself in an all-white outfit. You must use the Lincoln to deliver the money.

In order to prevent the instructional call being traced it will be very brief and no portion of it will be repeated. If the phone rings more than three times or the connection takes longer than 15 seconds we will not contact you. You will have a limited period of time to make the rendezvous so you should be ready to leave your house within one minute of receiving the phone call in order to be within the time limit. You will proceed to the area of the meeting within the legal speed limit as if you were in no hurry. We will not meet you if you fail to show within the time limit which is only a short time longer than you will require to drive to the pick up site. Any unusual police activity or other activity in the area of the pick up will cancel the appointment.

When you arrive at the pick up site you will know it by a signal of three short flashes repeated continuously from a flash-light directed at the windshield of your car. When you see the signal you will stop the car and immediately take the suitcase toward the light. The light will be mounted on top of a box. The suitcase should be placed within the box. You will then return to your car and proceed back up the street, in the direction from which you came and go home. Any deviation from this outline will result in your death. Our messenger will have you in his sights from the time you leave your car. Within twelve hours after you deliver the money you will receive another phone call advising you of your daughter's whereabouts. A letter will be sent also to insure the finding of your daughter.

It was 10:10 A.M. O'Dowd shuddered as he read the last paragraph. Brutal, he thought. Brutal. Whoever they are, they are trying to tear apart Robert and Jane. They are trying to force them to act quickly. He knew that he—as well as the entire Mackle organization—would act on the premises that everything was true. They had no choice.

Already, agent St. Pierre was on the telephone to the Miami

FBI office, rereading aloud, word by word, the entire note, "Sir, your daughter has been kidnapped . . ." his mind racing ahead. Buried alive. Half a million dollars. An ad in the classified. What kind of nut do we have here?

Deliberately, he pressed firmly two fingers to page one and four fingers to the reverse side of page three. He wanted his prints on the document for identification purposes. He realized he couldn't mark it in any visible manner. Conceivably, a kidnaper might want it back. A kidnaper might demand its return. He put it in a manila envelope.

If there was any doubt in the collective mind of the FBI that the abduction of Barbara Jane Mackle was a genuine kidnaping, it vanished abruptly. Agent St. Pierre remained at the home. Another agent, Edward J. Putz, rushed to the home. Vensel, the architect, took the ransom note to the Deltona executive offices at Five Points where agent Downing waited. The FBI wanted Downing to take the ransom note and fly immediately to Washington so that its crime laboratory scientists could analyze it. Before he left, though, Downing took the elevator to the third floor, carefully inserted the ransom note into a clear plastic sleeve, and made four copies on the firm's Xerox 2400, Xeroxing the Xerox.

The morning at Five Points had been pretty hectic. The front-desk receptionist, Carol Murray Lambert, a small fine-spun blonde with blue eyes and pale lipstick, had been surprised to see everyone already there when she arrived at 8:30 A.M. "Mr. Elliott," she said, "was wearing a red sports shirt." She had never seen him in a sports shirt before. "He was very upset. I thought something had happened to Mr. Robert. I didn't know what."

In the Deltona office, the secretaries, Mrs. Lambert, Mrs. Mary Fox and Mrs. June Owens, referred to the Mackles as Mr. Elliott, Mr. Robert and Mr. Frank. "Mr. Mackle" alone was too confusing.

The morning office routine fell to pieces. Neil Bahr opened his door and said, "There will be a Mr. Fred Fox here from the FBI. Please show him right in. There may be some telephone calls from the FBI in Atlanta. Please put them right through."

The telephone rang and Melvin R. Mathews, an employee of the firm at Marco Island, wanted to know if Elliott Mackle would fly over later in the day, and if not he, Neil Bahr? He needed to know, he said. Mrs. Lambert checked the Daily Reminder book —December 17, 1968, 352nd day, fourteen days follow—and she could see Mr. Elliott was scheduled out on one of the company Beachcrafts. No one had time to talk to Mr. Mathews. "Tell him that no one will be over today and that he will understand later," Neil Bahr instructed Mrs. Fox.

"I didn't know what to think. I wondered if Mr. Robert had been shot or something," said Mrs. Lambert.

Fairly early that morning—sometime after O'Dowd telephoned —suddenly convinced, young Frank III left the office hurriedly. Intent, worried, he went directly home. He had heard of the ransom note. His wife and children were alone. He wasn't at all certain that they were safe. The ransom note seemed utterly fantastic. He felt that his wife and children would be safer in a locked car moving at random on the public streets. He put them in the car and drove them. They had a few hours to kill before his father would fly into Miami International from New York.

Radio newscasters had not mentioned the crime. They knew nothing about it yet. The story would break shortly.

In the pressroom of the Atlanta Police Department that morning, Orville Gaines, a reporter for the Atlanta *Journal,* made his routine telephone calls to the fifteen police agencies he checked daily in the metropolitan area before the paper's first Metro edition at noon. The copy deadline was 10:45 A.M. Between 9 and 9:30 A.M. Gaines telephoned the DeKalb County police station. He knew the radio dispatcher. He had been calling there for fifteen years.

The dispatcher told Gaines that they had a kidnap working, some Emory coed. He wasn't sure. It might be a crank.

Gaines telephoned his city desk. From a nearby café, John Crown, the city editor, retrieved reporter David Nordan about 9:30 A.M. Neil Swan, an assistant city editor, assigned Nordan the story. "It looks like a girl ran away from home, but check it out anyway."

Reporter Nordan drove the fifteen minutes to the DeKalb County police station. For all practical purposes, the FBI had control of the investigation by this time. The only DeKalb County detective on the case, Mac E. Dover, was on the Emory campus. Dover had in his possession as evidence adhesive tape taken from the trash basket of room 137 and rope he found on the dresser. He planned to give it to the FBI with receipts to keep the chain of evidence intact for possible admission in a courtroom some day.

If antagonism had arisen between the FBI and the DeKalb

police, reporter Nordan didn't detect it. Much later, DeKalb County Captain J. C. Smith would say, "The FBI took it over. We got disgusted. They just ignored us." Captain Smith wasn't at all convinced it was a bona fide kidnaping. "Too much is too pat," he said. "We're pursuing the possibility of either personal revenge or some kind of emotional involvement."

Reporter Nordan soon had officer Baer's initial report. "It is public record once the report is put on our books," said Captain Smith. Nordan telephoned his office.

"He had the girl's name, 'Barbara Mackel,' from Miami, no specific address," said Swan, the assistant city editor. Swan recognized the name Mackle. A Mackle from Miami? He had worked for four years on the Miami *Herald*. "Get the address," he told Nordan. Swan asked another reporter, Bill Collins, to telephone the Miami *News*, also an afternoon newspaper, and find out where the Mackles lived in Miami. Within ten minutes the *Journal* knew it had a very hot story.

Reporter Nordan corrected the spelling of Mackle for the De-Kalb police department and informed a lieutenant he knew casually that Robert Mackle was a wealthy man. "He seemed surprised. I don't think anyone there had any idea who the Mackles were," said Nordan.

Now that the *Journal* had the story, should it go with it? Durwood McAlister, the managing editor, wasn't about to just break it willy-nilly. If it was a legitimate kidnaping, publication might jeopardize the life of the girl. Someone was always damning the newspapers for being irresponsible. It was approaching eleven o'clock.

Up four flights in the same building, Don McKee, a cool and grayed young reporter for the Associated Press, who had covered every major civil rights disturbance in the South since Martin Luther King in Birmingham five years before, had the tip from the *Journal*. McKee telephoned the Atlanta office of the FBI. For the AP, he volunteered to put a lid on the story. He acted on his own initiative.

The agent he talked to would say only the FBI was investigating. He couldn't go beyond that. He would have to say no comment. McKee informed the *Journal* that AP was holding. AP alerted its Miami office of the situation.

The *Journal*, with its 11:40 A.M. stereotype deadline approaching, called the FBI office three times. Nordan telephoned. "Some-one told me they had nothing to say." Reporter Collins telephoned. "I told them we had the story and that we were going with it unless they stopped us. He wouldn't even acknowledge that he knew what I was talking about." McAlister, the managing editor, also called. "I told whoever answered the phone that we had the story and that we had heard that the FBI was asking AP to hold it. I told him that if they wanted us to hold, we wanted to hear something. The man I talked to said he was not authorized to speak and that the man who could was out to lunch. I told him if we didn't hear in fifteen minutes, we were going with the story in the next edition."

The *Journal* long-distance operator put in a call to the Mackle residence. Although the number was not listed in the public di-rectory for Greater Miami, the Southern Bell Telephone Company 113 information operators had it designated NPT—for non-pub-lished tell, 665-7242. Anyone telephoning long distance could have the number. Swan, the assistant city editor, identified himself and asked for "Mr. Mackle."

"He is on his way to Atlanta," a man replied.

"Is there anyone there from the family?"

"No. Nobody is here."

"Who are you?"

There was a pause, "I'm the yardman," the man said. How in the hell did the newspaper find out?

Swan hung up. "I think I just talked to the FBI," he said. He had.

At the Mackle residence, agent St. Pierre told the maid and the gardener what had happened and questioned them.

"He said one of the children had been kidnaped," recalled Agnes.

"Is it Barbara? Is it Barbara?"

He told her it was. "I busted up and started crying. He told me I had to get a hold of myself, that we're going to go through the day just like nothing happened, and that to keep Barbara alive I shouldn't say anything, not even to my husband. He said I should answer the telephone just like I always did."

Walter Powell, his hands calloused by his yard labor, kept thinking about that rock. "It wasn't there when Ah done the lawn yesterday. Ah knowed it wasn't. Ah'd seen it if it was."

At a second Deltona office Tuesday morning, west of Five

Points on Coral Way, assorted newspapermen kept trying to reach
John F. Bonner, vice-president of corporate relations. Bonner
used to be one himself. The six-button telephone of Marguerite
Yessman, his secretary, at one time lit up simultaneously. She knew
that Deltona's convertible preferred series A stock had been listed
on the American Stock Exchange for the first time that morning.
My, she thought, that stock must be doing well. She was French-
Canadian and she had once typed some of Barbara's French papers
for her.

Bonner, a boy from Illinois who hurled a discus 156 feet 4
inches for Harvard before he worked on newspapers for twelve
years and for the Mackles for ten years, wasn't there. He had
gone to see his lawyer that day about his will.

Ben Funk, an Associated Press reporter in Miami, reached him
in his attorney's office at 11:10 A.M.

"Do you have a photograph of Robert Mackle and his family?"
Funk wanted to know. "In case we need it."

"Well, I guess so," said Bonner, and he thought, heavens to Betsy,
Nixon is appointing Robert to something. Because Robert Mackle
knew the President-elect fairly well, the Deltona executives had
been kidding him about being appointed the ambassador to Bia-
fra.

"My secretary can dig one up for you. What's up, Ben?"

"Don't you know?" the AP man asked.

"No," said Bonner, and Funk told him there was a report of a
kidnap of Barbara out of Atlanta. "There is a hold on the story.
It's not out yet."

"Oh, my God," said Bonner.

He telephoned Elliott Mackle at the Deltona offices.

Tight and clipped, Elliott Mackle said, "Forget it. Forget it.
There's nothing to it."

Bonner didn't believe him. "I'll see you in a few minutes," he said.

Elliott Mackle and the few Deltona executives who knew what
the note contained isolated themselves in the modern conference
room at Five Points, pouring coffee from a huge silver serving
pitcher on a marbled coffee table.

Once, before the Xeroxing of the note, Neil Bahr had bolted out.
Did anyone have eyebrow tweezers? The secretaries, still unaware,
sensing some unexplained crisis, started calling the girls on the
second and third floors of the office. They found a pair.

Bill O'Dowd left hurriedly. He had an appointment.

Carol Lambert fended off perhaps five telephone calls from newsmen.

Charles Bremicker, manager of the Key Biscayne Hotel, called too.

"Are the rumors true?"

"We just don't know anything," said Carol Lambert. Whatever it was, it had to be horrible. She just knew it.

It was twelve noon. "I think I'll skip lunch," she said. "I think I'd better stay here."

A few minutes after the hour, a teletype operator in the Atlanta office of the Associated Press wheeled a chair to a keyboard, began to perforate a strip of paper, and seconds later a bulletin clacked out over the AP's main A wire to its six hundred clients across the country.

ATLANTA, GA. (AP)—TWENTY YEAR OLD COED BAR-BARA JANE MACKLE, DAUGHTER OF A WEALTHY FLOR-IDA LAND DEVELOPER, WAS KIDNAPED IN HER NIGHT-GOWN FROM AN ATLANTA MOTEL EARLY TODAY BY A SHOTGUN-WIELDING DUO, HER MOTHER TOLD DEKALB COUNTY POLICE.

MRS. MACKLE REPORTED THAT HER DAUGHTER, A JUNIOR AT EMORY UNIVERSITY IN ATLANTA, WAS TAKEN AT GUNPOINT AFTER THE KIDNAPERS GAINED ENTRY BY CLAIMING TO BE FROM A POLICE AGENCY.

THE ACCOUNT OF THE INCIDENT WAS GIVEN BY MRS. MACKLE IN A COMPLAINT OF "KIDNAPING AT GUN-POINT" RELEASED BY POLICE TO THE NEWS MEDIA.

The story moved at 12:05 P.M., Eastern standard time.

We're Surrounded by Cobwebs

In their private penthouse executive dining room on the eighteenth floor, the senior officers of the First National Bank of Miami usually began their every-Tuesday luncheon at 12:15 P.M. They were a few minutes late this Tuesday. Robert W. Bruce started with a cup of soup.

"Mr. O'Dowd is here," said a receptionist, interrupting.

Robert Bruce, president of the bank, a large, flat-toned, precise and unemotional man of fifty-four, expected him. O'Dowd had telephoned ten to fifteen minutes before.

"Bob," O'Dowd had said, "I need to see you right away. It is urgent."

"We have the senior officers' lunch today, Bill," Robert Bruce had replied. It was a ritual. "What about afterward?"

"No," said O'Dowd curtly. "I need to see you now."

Bruce hung up, puzzled, his mind neutralized. The Mackles had dealt with First National since the 1940s. He knew O'Dowd as treasurer of Deltona. He had played golf with him. This wasn't like him at all.

Wordlessly, he arose from the dining table and ushered O'Dowd into another smaller unused private dining room.

O'Dowd wasted no conversation. He wanted $500,000 in $20 bills as soon as possible. He showed Robert Bruce a Xerox copy of the ransom note. Bruce hurried back into the executive dining room. He asked two men to please step outside, Carl H. Bruns, the vice-chairman of the board, and Ray F. Basten, an executive vice-president of the holding company which owned the bank, Southeast Bancorporation, Inc. Eight other senior officers looked up, mystified.

O'Dowd set forth the facts again. Suddenly, he noticed he was trembling. He grasped a chair to steady himself. He had to sit down.

There was no question that the First National Bank of Miami would loan the Mackles the money—if it had it. "There were no reservations. We didn't know their intimate financial worth, but we had important knowledge of their general over-all worth," Bruce said.

The crucial question was: Could the bank come up with twenty-five thousand $20 bills in an afternoon? Could anyone? Robert Bruce had no idea. The bank's amount of cash on hand fluctuated enormously with need, days of the week, payrolls, the tourist season, the Christmas season, the mutuel handle at the dog and horse tracks.

"I'll find out," said Basten, and he left in search of James Sumpasis, the head teller, a tight-lipped Yankee from Maine with an owlish look and a disposition toward secrecy. Basten found him in the first-floor lobby, a spacious modernistic room, shielded from the sidewalk entrances by goldlike "money tree" screens, where forty tellers conducted the public affairs of the bank from 9:30 A.M. to 2 P.M. First National qualified as Florida's largest bank. Its deposits that day totaled $669,046,137, and it was Sumpasis' job to know how much cash the bank had on hand, down to the last penny.

If the bank couldn't come up with the money from its own vaults immediately, it would just have to get it elsewhere, Bruce decided. He began to think of borrowing money from his competitors, other banks in Miami. He knew he could if he had to. Perhaps some of the department stores. Thinking aloud, Bruce said, "We can telephone the Federal Reserve in Jacksonville, and, if necessary, get them started south with a Brink's armored car." Jacksonville was 349 miles from Miami.

O'Dowd said some FBI agents would be over soon. He said he wanted to get back to the Deltona office at Five Points. Bruce told him he would telephone him just as soon as he had an accurate reading on the situation. "We'll have someone sign a note," O'Dowd said.

At Five Points, Carol Lambert, the front-desk receptionist, heard about the kidnaping from Kay Sargent, a secretary in the accounting department. Miss Sargent had turned on her car radio on her way to lunch.

"Which daughter?" she wanted to know. "Do you know which daughter has been kidnaped?" Carol Lambert and Mary Fox stared at each other in disbelief. There was a small transistor radio in the lower left drawer of Carol Lambert's desk. She didn't want to turn it on. She didn't want to touch it.

When Elliott Mackle realized that the news of the kidnaping was on the radio, he asked Mrs. Lambert to please put a call through to Bobby immediately. He didn't want Bobby to hear of the kidnaping of his sister by radio. Carol Lambert spun the Rolodex directory on her desk and had the switchboard operator upstairs give her a WATS line.

Robert Mackle, Jr., known as Bobby in the family to distinguish him from his father, lived in an 1870 downtown third-floor apartment in Philadelphia with another Wharton graduate student, Walter Becky, whose father was a General Electric executive in Cincinnati. "I was studying for my final exam in quantitative analysis. That's pretty much pure stat, statistics, and I hated it," said Bobby.

His uncle Elliott was on the telephone. "Bobby," he said, "Dr. Lauth wants to talk to you."

"Sit down and listen carefully," Dr. Lauth began. In that fraction of a second, Bobby could think of only one thing. His mother or father was dead. Someone was dead. He knew it. He felt oddly relieved when he heard it was the kidnaping. Barbara could have gotten lost and they thought she was kidnaped. But methodically, slowly and clearly, Dr. Lauth explained what they knew.

"He was straight and unemotional, and I just stood there and listened," said Carol Lambert, blatantly eavesdropping. "Will you make a flight reservation?" It was Bobby talking to her. "Philadelphia to Miami."

While Bobby held the line in Philadelphia, she dialed the Yellow Bird Desk, a special reservation service Northeast Airlines operated for executives. She had called often. "I need to know right away."

The reservationist for the airline, Barbara Conway, said no. Reservations had been full for days because of the holidays. "I can't confirm . . ." Then she stopped. "Oh, Carol?"

And Carol Lambert knew that the reservationist knew. "Wait a minute," she said. There was a pause. She confirmed the flight. "Anything we can do," she said, and there was a catch in her voice.

At the Rodeway Inn in Decatur, agent Roger Kaas told Billy Vessels, "The news is out." Soon it was obvious. Reporters began congregating outside the motel room. Vessels and agent Kaas went outside and politely requested on behalf of the family that they leave. The reporters meandered down to the street end of the parking lot and waited, watched. They wouldn't leave.

Robert Mackle had thought about calling Bobby all morning. With the news out, that settled it. "Get Bobby on the telephone," said Robert. Vessels, who was now screening all calls, reached him in Philadelphia. Bobby was packed, ready to leave. "There is no sense in you going home," his father told him. "I think you should come to Atlanta."

"Don't tell anyone about the ransom note," Vessels emphasized. "That isn't out. Nobody knows it."

Bobby's roommate drove him to the Philadelphia airport. Bobby's reservation to Miami had been changed. Flying to Atlanta was easier. He barged to the front of a line of waiting passengers. He had only a few minutes.

"There is a minor family emergency," he apologized. He made his flight. "I'm sure everyone thought I was lying."

At this juncture Robert Mackle knew very little of what was happening in Miami. After the initial contact, he kept asking, "Did they find the note?"

Around 11 A.M. agent Kaas had told him they had. "It is three pages long."

"What does it say?"

Agent Kaas said he didn't know. It was being flown to Atlanta from Washington.

"I couldn't find out anything about it," said Robert Mackle. Agent Kaas informed him that an inspector from the Washington office, Rex Shroder, was flying to Atlanta to take charge of the investigation and that he would have a copy of the ransom note. He would be in about 3:30 P.M.

The fact is that a gentle conspiracy, a protectiveness, had evolved within the Mackle family and Mackle organization, and Robert's brother, Elliott, simply did not want Robert to see the note yet. It was a cruel and terrifying document. At the moment, Robert could do nothing and Elliott knew it. This gentle conspiracy, a deep family concern for each other, would become much more pronounced in the desperate hours ahead.

"I was so relieved when Robert told me of the contact and the note," Jane Mackle said. "I knew they would have taken Barbara regardless of whether or not I opened the door. They would have taken her sooner or later anyway. I didn't really question the note. They told me they had it and it was being deciphered."

Frank Mackle, Jr., and his wife and their daughter, Nancy, arrived from Kennedy International at Miami International about 1:30 P.M. From the ramp Frank Mackle could see the face of his waiting son. He knew instantly. He knew whatever had happened was for real. The youngest of the brothers, and perhaps the most aggressive, Frank Mackle was a direct and forthright man, easily given to command. He decided that it might be best that his family and Elliott's family move to the somewhat isolated confines of the villas at the Key Biscayne Hotel.

This was also the thinking of the FBI. About this time Fred Frohbose, agent in charge of the Miami office, telephoned Rocky Pomerance, the 270-pound chief of police of Miami Beach, and asked him to check out and patrol the homes of Frank, Jr., and Elliott on Sunset Island Number Two, an exclusive residential area. No one drove across the single bridge of access to the island without a nod from the gatekeeper. Chief Pomerance, whose department prided itself on its ability to put an officer anywhere on its pink-sidewalked isle of paradise within three minutes after a call, responded himself. He took along his chief of detectives, Major Arthur "Red" Leonard. The gatekeeper recognized them. Elliott's wife, Milbrey, did not. Both the chief and detective wore civilian clothes. She wasn't about to let any strangers in her front door.

"Mrs. Mackle," said Detective Leonard, showing her his badge, "telephone Mr. Fred Frohbose at the FBI and ask him if he wanted us to stop by."

She telephoned her husband at Five Points instead. Soon agent Fox was on the line to straighten things out.

Detective Leonard suggested that Mrs. Mackle telephone her sister-in-law, Mrs. Frank Mackle, before they arrived there.

The nearby Frank Mackle home was wide open. Workmen were installing a carpet. Everything was a wreck. Mrs. Frank Mackle, who had just arrived from the airport, said they were all moving to Key Biscayne, but personally, she felt safer in her home on Miami Beach. The chief, feeling appreciated, grinned and said he understood. For the next three days cruisers patrolled the long one-block islands constantly and the gatekeepers looked suspiciously at everyone.

Frank Mackle read the ransom note at Five Points. He thought it gruesome and shocking and yet it struck him also as obviously well thought out, extremely well prepared. "We knew we had a real battle on our hands."

Around two o'clock Robert Bruce telephoned from the bank and asked for Bill O'Dowd. This was just before Frank and his son arrived. Everyone was highly conscious of using the telephone.

"Bill," said Robert Bruce, "that package you asked for is available." Sumpasis, the head teller, had told him they would be able to provide the $500,000 in $20 bills without recourse to the

Federal Reserve in Jacksonville or other banks. It was a good day for cash on hand.

Bruce also said he would send a messenger over. "So, if you don't mind, we'll get this note signed this afternoon."

No bank, as Bruce well knew, could lend money without a corresponding entry on the books, regardless of circumstances. The ransom money would be considered a commercial loan at the prime rate at that time of 6½ per cent, subject to cancellation on date of return.

If returned? If it could be delivered to a kidnaper? If the kidnaper contacted them again? If. If. And if everything went wrong—if they made payment, lost the money and discovered Barbara had already been murdered—the loan was still a legitimate financial transaction that some day must be repaid. The thinking went unsaid. It wasn't necessary to say it.

Before he hung up, Bruce said guardedly, "No one has come over yet," referring to the FBI.

At Five Points, O'Dowd repeated, "Bob Bruce says the package is available."

Agent Fred Fox didn't comprehend instantly. No one had anticipated that either the Mackles or the bank would be able to come up with $500,000 in $20 bills that quickly. Agent Fox said he would get his men over to the bank right away.

Said banker Bruce later, "We knew what had to be done. The money had to be recorded somehow. We wanted some guidance. This is where we had a little fumbling. The FBI didn't want to just take charge and tell us what to do. They didn't want to say, 'Do this. Do that.' There was no well-defined way of going about it. And nobody was going to tell us exactly how to do it."

The bank's three top working executives, Bruce, Bruns and Basten, closed the door and mulled over the possibilities. The bank used seven different Burroughs computers, and it was feasible to key-punch serial numbers of the bills. That way they could come up quickly with an electronic unscrambling on a sequence of numbers. But the computers were already programmed for the night's work. Key-punching would take a good deal of time. There weren't too many key-punch operators. They had thirty in all. The money could be microfilmed. A high-speed Recordak machine, used for photographing checks, would be faster. Technically, the photographing of U.S. currency could be a felony, punishable by law by fifteen years in prison and a fine of $5000. Under the circumstances, this didn't worry anyone too much. An FBI agent telephoned the Miami office of the Secret Service to explain the situation.

No one in Miami, the Federal Bureau of Investigation included, knew precisely how to proceed under the pressure of kidnaping. Miami FBI agents wanted to confer with the Washington office. The critical factor, of course, was to perform the task in such a way that someday, hopefully, the groundwork would be there for prosecution in a courtroom.

Sumpasis, the head teller, had other things to worry about. Physically, he had to collect the money. Without telling him why, Basten, quoting the ransom note, told him $500,000 in $20 bills. "No more than ten notes may have consecutive serial numbers . . . no more than one half the notes may be uncirculated . . ." That took time.

"Try not to use new money," Basten said. He emphasized secrecy. This Sumpasis was good at. Alexander McIntire, the comptroller, was apprised of the problem. FBI agents began arriving at the bank. They tried to remain inconspicuous. It wasn't easy.

Teller Sumpasis had another task. He was told that none of the twenty-five thousand $20 bills could be older than 1950. That made it necessary for someone to pull out all bills of the 1934 series. "You can go through a thousand $20 bills and not find a single '34 series," said Sumpasis. They were almost but not quite out of circulation as were 1928-series bills. Someone had to start screening, and one person, obviously, wasn't going to be enough.

Sumpasis, Carl Prom, an assistant vice-president, Gene Rothman, supervisor of tellers, and Mrs. Kay Treadway, an experienced money handler, began thumbing packet after packet. They kept to themselves in the bank's money room, off the lobby out of view, a glass-caged room opposite the walk-in vault. The other 1012 bank employees in the building and elsewhere knew nothing of their task.

They extracted about $2000 in bills of the 1934 and 1928 issues. In the process, they found two counterfeit $20 bills. A good teller can usually tell a counterfeit bill by the touch. Mrs. Treadway stamped the two bills counterfeit and set them aside. No banker was passing on a counterfeit bill, kidnaper or not. The fact is, though, that Mrs. Treadway didn't realize why she was sorting the money until she heard the eleven o'clock news telecast that night at home. The screening took approximately three hours.

Later in the afternoon Basten had the money taken to the so-called book vault on the second floor where the bank kept its journals and a Recordak microfilm machine. William W. Hillhouse, a bookkeeping clerk who expected to retire shortly, began photographing bills—something he had never done before in his life. An FBI agent watched him. Hillhouse would drop a stack of bills in a carriage and the machine, not much larger than a cash register, would spit them back neatly, clackety-clackety, in seconds.

The machine wasn't exactly color-blind, but on that day it wasn't reproducing the green too clearly. Green ink is used on the front side of every $20 bill for serial numbers. They could be read but not easily. An FBI man started talking to the Washington office again.

Frank Mackle, meanwhile, talked to Robert Bruce by telephone. Could the bank get a suitcase?

That was no problem, Bruce thought. He knew exactly whom to call. On the bank's twenty-member board of directors were two men who ran the two biggest department stores in town, Robert Macht, chairman of the board of Jordan Marsh, and Thomas C. Wasmuth, chairman of the board of Burdine's.

Bruce reread to himself the Xeroxed instructions. "The bills should occupy no more than 4000 cubic inches and thusly fit into a standard large suitcase of inside dimensions 31.5″ long×18.75″ high×6.25″ deep . . ." He telephoned Robert Macht.

"Macht thought I was kidding. He thought I was pulling his leg or that I was out of my mind," said Bruce. By the tone of his voice, as cold and as stern as only a banker's voice can be, Bruce conveyed to Macht that he was deadly earnest. "I'll send a man over right away to pick it up," said Bruce.

"We kept rereading that note and thinking this was really far out. We wondered if this character had taken his plot from a cheap dime novel," said Bruce.

Macht soon called back. The luggage was not standard. Jordan Marsh had suitcases that long and other suitcases that high and deep but the cubic content wasn't right. Bruce told him to please keep trying. The messenger from the bank and a Jordan Marsh executive went across Biscayne Boulevard to search the luggage at Jefferson's, another department store. No luck.

Bankers Basten, Bruns and McIntire sat in Bruce's third-floor office and sketched out the dimension on a marble coffee table. They rounded off the kidnaper's figures and checked his arithmetic on cubic content. "His math was accurate," said Bruce.

Bruce called Burdine's and put Wasmuth on the problem. He, too, ran into trouble. The catalog didn't have it. A luggage wholesaler couldn't find a piece of those dimensions.

"I had no idea what he wanted it for," said Wasmuth. "He said it was for a confidential matter. I believed him. He is not the kind of man to jest." Wasmuth had his luggage people start calling "the manufacturing reps" for the Florida area, Hartmann, Ventura, American Tourister, Samsonite.

"We came up with one good suggestion. I thought he might be able to find what he needed at a music store." Perhaps a case for an alto saxophone or another musical instrument might do.

By this time FBI agents at the bank had been apprised of the difficulty and soon agents from the downtown main office were quietly reciting dimensions to luggage clerks who had been asked the same thing an hour before. It was getting late. The stores, though, would be open late for Christmas shopping.

"It was about four-thirty or five o'clock when it dawned on us that we were going to have to take down the serial numbers manually," said Bruce. "It seemed as if this was the only way to do it and co-operate with the FBI."

Looking ahead to possible prosecution, it appeared to be the most logical approach: One man copy a serial number and another man verify the number. Both could testify in a courtroom. But how many people did they need? How long would it take? No one had the answer. Obviously, it had to be done now. Immediately.

There were five floors of assorted bank officers in the employ of First National, 118 in all, and some few had already left for the day. Bruce had all departments notified, the commercial loan department, installment loan, mortgage loan, investment, bond, comptroller, trust, Latin American, foreign, and others. "All officers were asked to remain at their desks. They were told only that we had an urgent assignment that would run into the night, nothing more," Bruce said. Their secretaries, tellers, nearly all other employees of the bank, left at their usual times.

About 5:30 P.M. eighty-five officers, all those found in the building, began congregating in the third-floor board of directors room around the long teakwood sectioned table and the twenty-four orange easy chairs. They lined the walls, standing alongside the full-length white curtain with its indirect lighting to make it look like a window. "We wanted to keep everything off the first floor, and the third floor was fairly easy to seal off."

Robert Bruce spoke briefly. "This is a serious occasion," he began. "It is a matter of life and death." He presented the problem: Copying and verifying serial numbers. "I ask that you do not ask questions," he said. "I ask that you stay until the job is done."

A group of strangers heard his remarks. "These gentlemen are FBI agents," Bruce explained, "and we are co-operating with them." They stood by as observers.

Only a few of the bank officers had ever counted money professionally. The officers were not tellers. Counting money was considered a clerical job, a teller's job. A good teller could count a thousand bills in fifteen minutes. But the bank had elected to go with its officers, not tellers.

Some of the officers telephoned their wives and told them they would be late. Others did not. At least one wife waited outside in her car for an hour, fuming impatiently, before her husband hurried outside and told her to please go home and don't ask questions.

An FBI agent brought over a stack of forms for recording serial numbers. It was a standard form with a carbon paper duplicate. Each page had two columns, numbered 1 to 50 and 51 to 100. For each bill to be copied there was a space for the series year, then separate blanks for each letter and number. Most bills had ten digits.

On each page there was a space for names. "Prepared by _____." "Checked by _____."

But it was soon apparent that the FBI had nowhere near enough forms. Miss Juanita Athey, secretary for Basten, solved that problem. She took out the carbon duplicates and made each sheet an original. Lieutenant Vincent Simon, a white-haired chief of the bank's Wackenhut guard service, escorted Sumpasis and Mariano Fernandez, the auditor, to the third floor with the $500,000. They carried it in two large canvas money sacks, decorated with the bank's four-ring sunburst emblem, supposedly a reproduction of an Aztec calendar stone. Sumpasis wasn't at all pleased with the procedure. The bank had just received part of the $500,000. He had always double-checked incoming money, either by counting or by highly sensitive scales. Today he had not had time. Sumpasis wasn't positive he had exactly $500,000. It disturbed him that the bank would utilize money that had not been verified.

Lieutenant Simon held his ten-man guard staff beyond quitting time. Four night guards just arriving joined the force. He posted them at the doors and stairways. No one was allowed on the third floor except bank officers. One guard quickly detected Miss Athey. She wasn't an officer. "I'm sorry, I'll have to ask you to leave." She needed her boss to bail her out.

Basten, a banker with a computerized mind, organized a team system for recording the serial numbers and had the packets of one hundred $20 bills issued two at a time so that no copier and verifier would have out more than $2000 at a time. Teams scattered out from the board of directors room throughout the third floor, confiscating desks and counter space among the potted palms in the corporate trust department and the personal trust department.

Bankers, loosening ties and rolling up sleeves, began their long and tedious labor. The copier would take off the purple currency strap, flip each bill separately, and write down the numbers. His verifier would recheck at his side. Both men signed each page. The verifier would restrap the packet. Much of the money had come from department stores and supermarkets and on each band was stamped the name of the store. An overprinted stamp, similar to a postmark, bore the date the money had been received at the bank and the teller who counted it.

Although hardly anyone within the bank had heard a newscast, most of the officers realized what they were doing. Some had been on the streets during the afternoon. An eight-column headline across page one of the Miami *News*, which hit the streets at 1:10 P.M., said; "Mackle's Coed Daughter Is Kidnaped From Motel." Still, quite obviously, everything had to be done in strict secrecy.

Someone realized they would soon have hungry men on their hands. To send them out wasn't feasible. Basten had his property-management man telephone Miss Mary Ruth Jones, the bank dietician for the employee food service. She was home. "I got the call about five forty-five and I called my cook, Joe Bellamy, and told him to meet me at the bank because we had to feed somebody.

"I just figured they had clients or a group working who couldn't get out. I stopped by the supermarket on the way and picked up eight loaves of bread." She needed help. One of the bank's four lady officers, Mrs. Marie S. Doland, suddenly found herself assigned to K.P. duty. "We started with ham sandwiches and when we ran out of that, we switched to tuna fish with lettuce and mayonnaise," said Miss Jones. "A few lucky ones got a slice of tomato. I'd say we made 250 sandwiches." There was plenty of coffee.

In Bruce's private office, Carl Bruns, the vice-chairman, suddenly had an idea. "I bet my wife has a suitcase about that size." He telephoned her. His wife, Bea, whom he married thirty-nine years ago, obediently dragged out from the floor of a linen closet her blue suitcase and measured it with a tape measure. It was almost perfect. She had purchased the suitcase from Jordan Marsh two years previously for a trip to Hawaii, Tokyo and Hong Kong. Once she took it to New York City and she waited and waited in the terminal during a snowstorm for the airline to deliver it. When the luggage finally arrived, she considered herself fortunate. There had been an accident. Other suitcases were split open, battered and unhinged. Hers had a dime-sized dent in the metal frame and a slight hole. A repairman later was able to hide the hole with her initials, BMB, for Beatrice Marjorie Bruns. One of the four white rubber stoppers had been lost. "I need to borrow it," said her husband without explanation. "I'll send someone out to get it. I'll be late tonight."

When he hung up, he realized his conversation might have been a little disconcerting. He had never needed a suitcase that fast before. What would his wife think? An FBI agent was available for the pickup. Bruns decided he would rather send someone his wife knew. John M. Sessions, executive vice-president, drove to the Bruns home in Coral Gables, and made polite small talk for a moment. Then he asked for the suitcase. Mrs. Bruns, sensing something was wrong, asked no questions. Sessions returned about 7:30 P.M. He brought with him one other item from the Bruns household, a bottle of Johnny Walker Black Label. It might be a long night.

At the Mackle home that afternoon and evening, FBI agents St. Pierre and Putz tried to have the maid act as normally as possible. At the suggestion of the FBI, Billy Vessels had already called the telephone company from Decatur and formally requested that the line be tapped. Recording equipment would be installed for the telephones in both the home and the Rodeway Inn. It wasn't in yet. At the home the telephone kept ringing and people kept coming to the door.

Most of Agnes' close friends knew the unlisted Mackle telephone number, especially other maids in the neighborhood. After the newscasts, they started calling.

"You mean to say you ain't heard? And you is there!" cried Mrs. Susie Rome. Years before, Mrs. Rome had met Agnes at two o'clock every afternoon at the playground with their "babies," Barbara in her baby carriage after her nap.

The two FBI agents stood right beside Agnes at every call.

"Ain't that bad about Barbara," said Mrs. Ora Liberty, the maid from across the street.

"I don't know anything about it," said Agnes, following instructions.

"The news is on the radio. Everybody knows it. Why don't you know it?" Mrs. Liberty persisted.

"I just don't know what's going on," said Agnes.

"You know damn well what's going on, it's on the news," said her friend indignantly.

Agnes' husband, who had fallen off a roof and injured his leg and couldn't work, called, too, and he started asking questions.

"Mrs. Mackle is out of town," Agnes replied. "Now you hang up and get off the line!"

James Buchanan, a reporter for the Miami *Herald,* rang the doorbell. Buchanan noticed the two agents in the foyer. Agnes told him no one was home. Milt Sosin, a reporter for the Miami *News,* wanted to borrow the telephone for a minute. Agnes told him she was sorry. Agent St. Pierre saw a brightly colored WTVJ television newscar parked across the street, and Lord Almighty, for all he knew the home might be under surveillance. The FBI asked the Coral Gables police for heaven's sake to keep the news media away.

Several well-meaning friends of the Mackles, Mrs. Robert Ford, Mrs. Stewart Patton, Peggy Golden Johnson and Lou Lyons, stopped by, and Agnes, verging on tears, told them Mrs. Mackle was in Atlanta.

Walter, the yardman, couldn't get anything done. "Ah was just moving about," he said.

The first of the silent calls began that evening.

Agnes had explicit instructions: Don't hang up. Keep saying, "Hello." Identify the residence.

The first one frightened her. She answered and no one said anything.

"Hello? Hello? Mackle residence . . . Hello?" Then, finally, the caller hung up.

Edgy, nervous, distraught, Agnes answered another unexplained call.

"Is Patty there?" a female voice asked.

In the background, Agnes heard someone plead, "Please, please hang up." Then the line went dead.

"That's Barbara," Agnes told the FBI man. "That sounded like Barbara. I know her voice. That was Barbara." She was trembling. The telephone man installed the equipment so that all conversations were taped.

In room 137 at the Rodeway Inn in Decatur, Billy Vessels would wait for the telephone to ring twice, then pick it up before the third ring. By the third ring, agent Kaas would have on earphones in the next room. Dr. Richard King, Jane's brother-in-law, telephoned from Hendersonville, North Carolina. Jane's brother and sister, Scott Braznell and Ann Briggle, telephoned from Miami. They were on a telephone together.

Scott, a year younger than Jane, ran a building-supply company with offices in Miami and Naples, Florida, on the Gulf coast. He was in Naples when he heard of the kidnaping, and he couldn't believe it. *Bob and Jane,* he thought, *are so protective of their children. Maybe they're worked up about something that has a simple solution.*

On the straightaway stretches across the nothingness of the Everglades, Scott Braznell accelerated his new Lincoln to the floor and the speedometer registered 120 miles an hour, the fastest he had driven since he was a kid.

"Someone at the yard thought I might overdo it and telephoned a friend in the State Police." A trooper escorted him part of the way. He kept asking himself why he hadn't taken the trouble to see Barbara when she was home last summer. "What kind of an uncle am I?" Now he was on the telephone trying to reach Jane from Miami.

Billy Vessels wasn't letting anyone talk to her. "This was my decision," said Vessels. "Jane had these terrible headaches and she was terribly upset."

"Ann and I thought we should fly to Atlanta," said Scott. "Billy said there was no need, there was no point. We decided we would fly anyway."

Vessels manned the telephone. To nearly all callers, he would say politely and firmly, "We will be in touch, please keep this line open. Don't call again."

He put in one call himself. He telephoned a close personal friend, Florida's Senator George Smathers. He reached him in Washington, D.C.

"Billy was apprehensive," Smathers recalled. "He wanted to make sure all the government agencies were in on the kidnaping. I told him the FBI would be up to its neck on this one, not to worry."

One incoming call to the Rodeway Inn startled Vessels. It was from the Associated Press in New York City. "No comment," he said curtly.

As Vessels sat on the bed in the motel room, a slow burning anger and bitterness welled up inside him. He wasn't thinking about Barbara. He could think only of Robert and Jane, the anguish, their suffering, their helplessness, his helplessness. Jane's headache grew worse. "We kept trying to get her to lie down. She wouldn't do it. She couldn't close her eyes."

"My head was in my lap practically," said Jane Mackle. "My head was splitting. The cigarette smoke was getting to me. It doesn't bother me normally, I'm used to it. But I had a cold and that room was terribly stuffy. They didn't want to let me out. I couldn't turn on TV. I just sat there. Every time I'd go near the window, I'd get pushed back. I remember they opened the door once and I started to breathe and they pushed me back," she said.

Every time the door opened, newsmen flocked toward it from the parking lot. Jane Mackle didn't see them. She was not told that the press—and much of the nation—already knew of the kidnaping of her daughter.

From the window Vessels and agent Kaas could see the Veterans Administration Hospital. Where do you get chloroform? Vessels asked, and answered his own question: a hospital. A hospital full of psychiatric cases. "That was my initial thought." Barbara and her mother had been there in the motel next to the hospital for four days.

Although Vessels had not yet read the ransom note, he knew too much to doubt the authenticity of the kidnaping. Others, less knowledgeable, suspected otherwise. At the DeKalb County Police Department, Captain Smith couldn't understand why anyone would take a twelve-year-old boy on a kidnaping. "It may or may not be a bona fide kidnaping," he announced to the press. By this time he also had a good idea of where the "alleged kidnaper" obtained the policeman's hat. Three nights before, DeKalb County officer Gerry G. Smith had stopped for a cup of coffee at the Pan Cake House adjacent the Rodeway Inn and put his size 6⅞th hat on a rack. Someone stole it. "I accused the waitresses of a practical joke," he said. He had filed a report: "petty larceny."

Ingrained skepticism glistened elsewhere. Fred Andersen, a bald, crusty and quick-witted rewrite man on the Miami *Herald*, telephoned every marriage mill in Georgia he could think of—Folkston, Valdosta, Augusta, Dalton, Columbus. Wouldn't that be a twist?

How did the boyfriend, Stewart Woodward, fit in? Could it all be a love triangle of some sort? Could Barbara have been taken away by a jealous suitor? Or was Woodward somehow involved? "He looked like a good suspect to me," said Dover, the detective from DeKalb County.

Vessels too wondered if "Stewart could be a participant." Vessels questioned Jane Mackle very closely. To Stewart he suggested things were in hand and that he might as well leave.

Stewart had telephoned his parents. His mother flew from Charlotte to Atlanta and Stewart met her at the airport and drove her to the Rodeway Inn. They had met the Mackles before in Hendersonville, North Carolina, where the Mackles owned a summer home. Stewart's mother, Mrs. Herbert Woodward, stopped briefly at room 137. Billy Vessels wouldn't let her in at first. He thought she was a reporter.

The FBI tended to discount Stewart as a suspect. Yet, it couldn't completely. There were too many unknowns. When Stewart Woodward and his mother got up about 4 A.M. the next day and drove home to Charlotte, North Carolina, the FBI had to make certain they were going home to Charlotte. Agents kept them under surveillance. Stewart, badly shaken by the crime, accepted the facts realistically. Under the circumstances, he understood.

The uncertainties of the crime, compounded by the absolute need for secrecy of the ransom note, led to other friction. When one agent learned that the DeKalb police had released officer Baer's initial report, he exploded angrily in front of newsmen at the motel, "These people talk too God damn much." He stalked off.

"I was annoyed, too," said Dover, the DeKalb detective. "Our department made a leak that never should have been made." Dover, for the life of him, couldn't understand the intense concern of the FBI. "The ball just never gets rolling so fast through normal channels." He had never worked a major kidnaping before.

On the Emory University campus that afternoon, an FBI agent scrutinized Barbara's administrative records. They reflected very little that seemed pertinent to the crime of kidnaping. She was a junior majoring in economics. Her grades were good. She had graduated in 1966 from Everglades School for Girls in Miami, an exclusive girls' school, where she won a Smith College award and a National Education Development Test award, made the National Honor Society, and served as president of a small class of seventeen during her senior year. She had been the class valedictorian.

In search of leads at Emory, FBI agents tried to find her friends, classmates, and Delta Delta Delta sorority sisters. Many had left for the holidays. An Associated Press reporter, Laura Foreman, walked in on five girls across the hall from Barbara's room at McTyeire Hall, once a man's dormitory, and found them taciturn and abrupt. "I'm not going to tell you a thing," said one young lady who declined to give her name.

Melaine Kofoed, a casual friend of Barbara's from Miami, couldn't think of anything she thought remotely helpful. "Barbara was not at all impressed by her background, her social status. That's what impressed me about her. She just went out of her way to make everyone feel the same." Melaine Kofoed recalled her last conversation with Barbara some weeks before when they met at the airport. "She liked Emory but was sort of tired of it. She was thinking about transferring to the University of North Carolina in Chapel Hill."

From a telephone booth outside the library at the University of North Carolina in Chapel Hill, Professor Marshall Louis Casse III telephoned the dean's office at Emory a few minutes after two o'clock. Casse was Barbara's macro econ instructor. He had excused her from one final exam the Friday before and he had driven the six-and-a-half-hour trip from Emory to the University of North Carolina that day for research on his Ph.D. thesis on Soviet monetary policies. He had heard of the kidnaping on the two o'clock news. Professor Casse dropped four quarters and a nickel into the slot for three minutes. He felt a little ridiculous, but, just possibly, he might be of some help. He had overheard a conversation the previous Saturday afternoon, someone asking about Barbara Mackle. It probably had no correlation at all with the kidnaping, he thought, but just in case the FBI or anyone wanted to talk to him, he would leave his telephone number. He told where he could be reached that evening.

Rex I. Shroder, an FBI inspector from Washington, arrived at the Rodeway Inn shortly after four o'clock to take over, and if ever a man possessed command presence, Shroder was he. Said Vessels, a boy from Oklahoma, "He came on strong—like an acre of onions. I was very impressed."

Shroder, a stern, straight Kansas-born man of forty-seven with a quick, hardened intelligence and a slight drawl, strong physically, with rimless glasses perched on a freckled face, his brown wavy hair graying slightly, looked directly at Robert Mackle and said immediately, "I want you to know that the director, Mr. Hoover, sent me down personally. He personally sends his sympathy and he wants you to know that the entire weight of his organization is in back of this investigation. I assure you that it is going to have a happy ending."

"He was the first person to say what I wanted to hear," said Jane Mackle. "He was so convincing, so sure. He really eased my mind. He said, 'I'll stake my job that you'll get your daughter back.' He told me that so many times."

Inspector Shroder turned to Robert Mackle. "I know how to handle these things," he said. Forceful, confident, intelligent, he took charge. There was no doubt in Robert Mackle's mind that this was the first team.

"I can't find out anything about this note," Robert Mackle said.

"I have it with me," Shroder replied. They went into the next room. Shroder had it in pieces and paragraphs. It had been dictated from Miami to stenographers in Washington. "I'll put them together for you," he said. "Please sit down."

Robert Mackle began to read. "Sir, your daughter has been kidnapped by us . . . We offer no proof of our possession of her at this time. It will arrive by mail in a few days. Barbara is presently alive inside a small capsule buried in a remote piece of soil. She has enough food and water and air to last seven days. At the end of the seven days the life supporting batteries will be discharged and her air supply will be cut off . . ."

He read the note in silence. No one spoke when he finished.

"I guess you are waiting for some kind of reaction?"

Shroder nodded affirmatively.

"Well, my reaction in reading it is terror, but on the other hand, I feel a lot better. I think we are dealing with some highly intelligent person and not some maniac who will chop somebody up."

Shroder broke into a grin. "We feel exactly the same way."

"If you can get any consolation reading something like that, I am consoled by the fact that they are highly intelligent people. I can think and I can hope and I can pray that no harm will come to her."

"Did you notice there is $500,000 ransom?" Shroder asked.

Robert Mackle couldn't have cared less. "My brothers have had this note for some time, I take it?"

"Yes, since this morning."

"Let's don't worry about that. That'll be taken care of."

Robert Mackle went back to his wife in the next room. There was no connecting door. He had to walk outside briefly in the cold darkening afternoon.

"Jane," he said, "the note is here. It is not in any kind of form that you can read. They want half a million dollars and they will return Barbara to us safely. It is a highly intelligent note and I feel much better about it."

"What are we going to do?"

"I don't think harm will come to Barbara. I want to go back and do some evaluating with the FBI." Robert Mackle did not tell his wife their daughter was buried alive. He just couldn't believe it. He couldn't NOT believe it either.

Billy Vessels had read the note a few minutes earlier, out of Robert's presence. The first name he saw at the top was "McNamara."

Hell, he thought, these people must be Cuban. They don't even know McNamara is no longer Secretary of Defense. McNamara was a name of the agent who transcribed the message. Vessels grinned.

Vessels knew basically what the note said even before he read it. He had talked to both Elliott and Frank at Five Points during the afternoon. They had briefed him. They didn't want Robert to read it. Vessels had disagreed. He told agent Kaas he thought the inspector should let him read it. One paragraph struck Vessels forcefully as he read. ". . . You must be the one to deliver the money, Robert. You will dress yourself in an all-white outfit. You must use the Lincoln to deliver the money." Use the Lincoln? Robert had owned the Lincoln only six weeks. Before, he had driven a Chrysler for two years. How much did the kidnaper know about the family? Where could he have learned that?

Bobby Mackle had arrived a few minutes after Inspector Shroder. Robert had seen him step out of the taxi. Bobby walked directly to the motel room and grabbed his father by both shoulders.

"Dad," he said, "we're going to get Barbara back."

"I knew he had been schooling himself to say that all the way down from Philadelphia," said his father much later.

Not once in the ordeal that lay ahead would Bobby break emotionally where anyone could see him. Outwardly, he would remain confident.

Bobby had stayed with his mother when his father read the ransom note in the adjacent room. "I tried to tell Mother that the kidnapers had let her see them and they had left her alive. They would leave Barbara alive, too. I tried to reason with Mother. I didn't quite believe it, but I kept reiterating it. I guess I made myself believe it."

"You've already seen them, Mother," he said. "They know it. Whether that was intentional or not, you have seen them. You saw the man. If they had intended to kill or harm Barbara, they would have taken you, too. They would have held you both for ransom."

One crucial decision had to be made fairly soon. Where should Robert Mackle be? In Atlanta or Miami?

Not once during the entire kidnaping did Inspector Shroder or the FBI flatly order Robert Mackle to do anything. Again and again, the options were his.

Robert explained afterward. "They would say here are the pros and here are the cons. Here is what we recommend. You can do one thing this way or another thing another way."

Inspector Shroder spoke up. "You've had your first contact in Miami. If everything we know about this type of case holds true, the next contact will be in Miami. I think you will be needed there."

"I think you are right," said Robert. It was six o'clock. He told his wife.

"No. I'm not going to go," said Jane Mackle. "Barbara is probably in an apartment or somewhere in Atlanta. I want to stay here. You go ahead and Bobby and I'll stay here."

Gently and firmly, Robert Mackle convinced his wife that she too should go home; not that he truly knew where his daughter was, but because he felt home was the place for her. FBI agents, he knew, would answer every telephone call to room 137.

"Let's let Rex handle this. He knows what is best."

"I figured there were things in the note I didn't know about," said Jane Mackle, consenting. "I didn't question them any more."

Robert Mackle packed for his wife. She was hardly in condition to do it herself. Robert knew there was an 8:15 P.M. Delta flight to Miami. Vessels called the airline. Delta offered him four seats in a DC-8 directly in front of the first-class sections, seats they often did not sell.

"You'll have to get the money and place the ad in the newspapers," said Shroder.

Robert Mackle wanted to know if the ad couldn't be put in right away for the bulldog or first edition of the Miami *Herald*.

"Well, not until we actually have the money," said Shroder. The kidnaper had written, "Prepare your car for a trip and on the night of the ad's first appearance we will call you at your home to advise you of where you must go to deliver the money."

The night of the ad's first appearance, he reasoned, would be the following night, Wednesday night, after the publication in

Wednesday morning's newspaper. Shroder knew the Miami office would work out the details.

In Miami, agent Wayne Swinney, a direct and forceful man usually concerned exclusively with organized crime and South Florida Mafia characters in residence and their guests, was trying to calculate all the possibilities on the want ad. A normal customer would have to place an ad in the personal column by 3 P.M. to make all editions of the Miami *Herald* for the next morning. It was already approaching four o'clock. Could the FBI get an ad in the *Herald* after the 3 P.M. deadline? Should they skip the first edition? What time did the first edition hit the streets that evening? Would the kidnapers see the ad and call Robert Mackle's home too soon? Would they call before he was home from Atlanta and before the money was ready? Would the kidnapers become suspicious if the ad wasn't in the first editions but made the later editions? What if they waited until the Wednesday afternoon edition of the Miami *News* and the Thursday morning edition of the *Herald?* Might that not delay the drop twenty-four hours?

What editions went to Atlanta?

Agent Swinney telephoned Jim Savage, a reporter for the *Herald*. He knew Savage well and he trusted him. Savage had been over to his office twice previously that day, trying to eke out information on the crime.

"Jim," he said, "we need some help real fast. It has to be absolutely off the record."

Reading from the ransom note, Swinney dictated the want ad. Savage took it on his typewriter and read it back slowly for accuracy. He knew instantly what it was.

Off the record, Savage wanted to know how much money was involved.

"An awful lot," said Swinney.

Reporter Savage took the want ad to John McMullan, executive editor of the *Herald*. There would be no problems. The ad could go whenever the FBI wanted it to go, regardless of deadlines. The *Herald* could stop its presses for a replate any time.

At first the FBI wanted the ad in all editions, including the first street edition, 42,000 papers from a press roll beginning at 6:10 P.M. Tuesday, dated Wednesday, December 17. United Air Lines flew fifty of those papers to Atlanta. Agent Swinney called back. "Skip the first edition," he said. He knew the money wasn't ready. He knew too that Robert Mackle hadn't left Atlanta yet. "Run the ad in the regular city morning edition," he said.

Editor McMullan took the ad and walked down a flight of stairs to the composing room and gave it to Phil Eaton, assistant to the paper's production director. "This is an important want ad," said McMullan, and Eaton, reading, realized it had to be connected to the kidnaping. "There should be as little discussion about it as possible. I think you will want to avoid the usual channels," McMullan suggested. No advertisement ever received closer attention.

Jane Mackle's brother and sister, Scott Braznell and Ann Briggle, had left Miami for Atlanta about five o'clock. In flight, a stewardess paged Braznell and gave him a message which had been radioed to the pilot. "There will be a Delta representative waiting for you with an important message in Atlanta." When they landed, there was another note, "Please telephone Mr. Robbe at the FBI. 521-3900."

Angelo Robbe, a bureau supervisor, told Scott Braznell the FBI had booked reservations for him and his sister to Miami. They would have to catch a return flight immediately. He didn't explain why.

"Look," said Braznell. "Where is my sister? I came up here to see her."

"I am sorry I can't help you in that respect," said Robbe. "The situation has changed. Please be on Delta flight 847. It leaves at eight-seventeen," he said.

At the Delta counter Braznell asked a clerk if anyone had made reservations for Braznell and Briggle. No one had. "Are there any reservations for Mackle?" It was a shot in the dark.

The clerk checked the manifest. "Yes," he said brightly. "We have a Miss Barbara Jane Mackle." He looked up expectantly.

Weeks before, Robert Mackle had told his secretary to make a reservation for his daughter to fly home for the Christmas holidays. By chance, the flight was Delta Air Lines 847, December 17.

As they stood there, someone handed the clerk their reservations for the same flight. Scrawled on a note was, "In connection with the Mackle kidnaping."

"I think you can cancel that reservation for Miss Mackle," Braznell said lamely. "She won't be using that tonight."

As Scott Braznell and Ann Briggle boarded the jet, they saw

Robert, Jane, Bobby and Billy Vessels sitting in a compartment up front of the first-class section. Someone had wrapped a blanket around Jane's bruised legs. She had Barbara's coat and Barbara's purse in her lap.

"Sonny, what are you doing here?" Jane said to her brother. "Ann, oh, Ann," and the pent-up emotion burst in a tide of wracking sobs. The sisters embraced.

Almost incoherently, Jane Mackle cried, "I don't know why I'm leaving Atlanta. Barbara is here. I know she is here."

Scott Braznell had never in his life seen Jane in such a terrible emotional state. "She was almost in a stupor."

Billy Vessels felt he should physically separate the sisters.

Robert stepped in. He separated them. "Go back and sit down, Ann," he said. "You are breaking yourself up. You are breaking Jane up."

The Mackles had left the Rodeway Inn shortly after seven o'clock. Agent Jack Keith had diverted newsmen momentarily by the simple act of standing outside the door for questioning.

"We are getting them away from the motel," he said. "They just need a little peace and quiet."

Only two newsmen from WSBT-TV had pursued the Mackle car, and they gave up when the Mackle car, driven by agent Kaas, went through a "no admittance" gate at the airport and an airport police car shined a spotlight on the news car.

As the Delta jet waited on the apron, the captain announced over the public address system a delay of twenty to thirty minutes. He had been ordered to wait for delivery of a mechanical part needed in Miami. An FBI agent walked forward from his seat in the rear of the jet, and a moment later the captain announced on the speaker without explanation, "We are now ready to leave." Someone else could deliver the freight.

Frank Mackle and Dr. Lauth met the airliner at Miami International Airport at 9:45 P.M.

Frank walked straight to his brother and put his arms around him. It was Robert who spoke. "Frank," he said firmly, "we are going to get Barbara back."

The ride home was hurried. Jane Mackle was surprised to see the lights on and the curtains pulled. She hadn't pulled the front room draperies in years. A stranger, agent St. Pierre, opened the front door for them. Elliott was there too, waiting in the den near the red telephone. So were several other strangers and Agnes.

"Mrs. Mackle, she was all apart," said Agnes. "I tried not to cry, but I cried anyway."

"Do we have the money?" Robert asked his brother.

"Yes. The bank has already called," said Frank. "They're getting it together now."

At the First National Bank of Miami, the eighty-five officers still worked in almost absolute silence, broken by the snap of rubber bands going around "bails," $20,000 bundles of $20 bills. Occasionally someone would whisper, correcting a number, reciting it softly a third or fourth time for accuracy. The hours stretched from eight to nine, to ten. Bruce stepped from his office. "It looked like nothing so much as a deadly serious poker game."

Not everyone realized precisely why they were listing serial numbers. Miss Athey still had not heard of the kidnaping. At the top of each page she read the single word "Mackle," and, of course, she knew who the Mackles were. But why did they need the money? No one told her. Why couldn't they take a check?

Lieutenant Simon took a telephone call from a worried wife. "Ma'am, I'm a guard," he said. "Your husband is busy and he can't come to the telephone."

Always before, the wife said, his secretary would telephone her and tell her that he was going to be late. Was his secretary there?

Near eleven o'clock it became apparent the listing was about finished. Basten had run out of fresh packets. The bank officers were beginning to leave. In less than six hours, they had copied in pen and pencil and verified in excess of six million digits on 296 pages.

FBI agents from the crime laboratory in Washington had arrived in Miami and they were waiting to take Mrs. Bruns' suitcase and photograph it for identification purposes—if the money would fit. Someone from the FBI had found another suitcase of the same approximate dimensions, slightly larger, inferior, and obviously a very cheap piece of luggage. "It looked like something you would use to send home laundry from college," said Jack Sessions.

An agent had paid thirty-seven dollars for it. "Extortion," someone deadpanned.

It was then the bankers realized they didn't have $500,000.

They were $100 shy. Just as Teller Sumpasis had feared, the shortage occurred when the incoming money wasn't verified.

Someone suggested that maybe the missing five $20 bills might be caught inside the Recordak microfilming machine. A banker dismantled the apparatus. They weren't there.

Basten said they could get the extra $100 in the morning out of the bank's "over and short" fund. It wouldn't be delivered tonight anyway. Would the money fit? That was the important question.

Basten, graying at fifty-seven, distinguished, dignified, a banker through and through, was down on his hands and knees on the beige wool carpet of Bruns' private office, personally packing the suitcase.

"Is it going to fit?" asked Sessions.

"Yes, Jack. It'll fit," Basten said, and he marveled at exactly how well. He closed it to make sure it would close.

Then the money was removed and put again into two sacks and returned to the first floor. An FBI agent took the suitcase. He would have it back the first thing in the morning.

The bank's two huge walk-in vaults, controlled by time locks, had been closed since six o'clock. It was approaching midnight. Sessions had already made arrangements by code with the ADT Protection Service to get inside a special coin-wrapping room, protected by electronic apparatus sensitive enough to detect the smoke of a cigarette. Gerald Fitzgibbons, a Wackenhut guard, would stay there all night. That settled that.

At the Miami office of the FBI, where the lights burn all night every night, agent Swinney tried to piece together the fragments of the crime, known and unknown.

"We're surrounded by cobwebs," he said.

So He Lied

I'm being left here to die. This is it, I thought. The thought entered my mind, why wait? Instead of waiting a week, why not just turn off the fan. I would get warm and drowsy and sleepy and it would be so easy.

Then I said to myself, Come on, Barbara, you know better than that. You'll make it. And I turned on the light and I started talking to myself again. That helped. I tried to make myself cry then. I said, well, I'll cry. I'll feel better. But I don't know why, I just couldn't.

I rarely actually cry. You know how some girls cry. Just about everything. I don't. I never show my feelings in front of other people. Except when I broke down on the telephone to my parents, I can hardly remember when I cried last. It might have been while watching the funeral of President Kennedy but nobody else was in the room. I am usually very quiet. I don't talk about emotions. Crying for someone else is different than crying for yourself. I don't like to cry for myself. I don't know why. I'm funny about that. I guess the last time I cried was when Sandy, our collie, died. He was my dog and he was about thirteen years old and followed me everywhere I went. He was part of the family and when he died I went up in my room and cried.

As I lay there, trying to cry, I began to think about the kidnapers. I kept thinking of him, not her. Look, I said, if he was going to let me die, he wouldn't have gone to all this trouble. This box and this fan and everything. If he wanted me to die, he would have just killed me, right? That's how I felt. Okay, maybe he won't come back. But he'll tell somebody. And somebody will come and get me out. It went back and forth in my mind.

But what happens to me if something happens to him? How will anyone know I'm here? There are just the two of them. Or was he telling the truth about other people? Do other people know exactly where I am? I knew I was somewhere in rural Georgia not too far from Atlanta. But I wasn't relating to the university or any specific place. I knew it was pretty hard to find your way around rural Georgia unless you know exactly where you are going.

What if they are killed? The way he was driving that certainly was possible. What if a policeman stopped him and he got scared and clammed up and just forgot the whole kidnap—the ransom and everything—and just left me here? So many things could happen. It really frightened me that they might get killed on the road.

Then I thought, that's ridiculous. There are other people. So there isn't a house. So he lied about that. But there are other people. He is not in it by himself. He talked about the boss, Jake and the boys. Jake? Jake knows where I am. Good old Jake. I tried to laugh but I couldn't. There must be a Jake. I didn't want to think about it.

I tried again to make myself laugh. Whenever I sing I always laugh. My voice is so terrible. I can't sing at all. So I started to sing, Jingle Bells, Jingle Bells, Jingle all the way. Oh, what fun it is to ride in a one-horse open sleigh. I made myself be happy. I love Christmas and I sang "Deck the Halls." Deck the halls with boughs of holly, fa la la la la la, la la la la . . .

Actually, I can't remember the exact sequence of things. I can't remember what I was thinking at exact times. I know I started singing after counting. I knew I had turned off the light. I didn't want to waste the battery. I would get scared again and then I would think, why should I be afraid of the dark? Nobody is going to get me in here. I wished someone would. For rush at the sorority house, we had revised all the songs from Camelot. I knew Camelot by heart. I had the album with the original cast, Robert Goulet and Julie Andrews. We took the Seven Deadly Sins and made them the Seven Deadly Deltas—they play basketball, volley ball and swim. It kind of made me laugh because we are the worst sorority in sports. I started to sing all of those songs. I sang, "Follow Me." That is my favorite. I think it is the most beautiful song on the album. Merlin going into the cave. Follow me, far from day, far from night, and I began to wonder how other people would react if they were down here instead of me. I remember thinking about Nancy; my cousin, Nancy Mackle. I'm extremely fond of her. She is Uncle Frank's daughter. She is a year younger than Bobby; two years older than me, and we're just exactly opposite, physically and every other way. She is a kind of extrovert. She is lively and vivacious and bubbles in a crowd. Nancy's the kind of person everyone just enjoys being around. I wondered what Nancy would do down here. I was thinking of girls at Emory, the girls who have good control of themselves. They wouldn't panic like I do. I was thinking of Bette Brunell. She was going to be my roommate but she got married. She is five feet ten inches tall, slim like I am. I move around a lot and she does, too. She would be like me in here. Then, I said, now listen, Barbara. This is unique. That's the one thing about this thing. It is unique.

And then it happened. You know how a light bulb flickers just before it burns out? That's what it did. I had the light out and I reached up to turn it on. It flickered and it went out.

I said, No!

I had my hand on the switch. My hand was shaking. This was the worst possible thing that could have happened. I couldn't see my hand. I couldn't see anything. My hand was trembling and I took it off the switch and I didn't touch it. Oh, no. It hasn't gone out! Then I tried again. It didn't work.

That's when I sort of cried aloud, "Oh, God. You can't do this to me." I wasn't hysterical. I didn't pound at that point. I knew that was futile. But this was almost as bad as when they first left me. This must have happened about an hour or so after I counted—maybe four or five hours after I had been buried.

It was black. I didn't realize how much the light meant. Even though I had managed to keep it off, I knew it was there, and every time I really had become afraid, I had turned it on. I would say, okay, okay, everything is all right. It was so reassuring.

Then in the darkness I remembered the tranquilizers. And I was so mad at myself. Where were they? Why didn't I find them before? Why was I so stupid?

And then I really became hysterical, not shouting, not crying, this time, but desperate and hopeless. I felt complete desperation. I was perfectly still for a long time. I don't know what I was thinking about. I guess I wasn't thinking. I just lay there.

I started thinking about the tranquilizers again. I had never had a tranquilizer in my life before. I guessed they must be little capsules in a bottle or tablets in a container like Bayer Aspirin. I remembered there was a paper bag and I felt for it and found it. Inside were apples. I was going through it for the first time. There was some bread there. I'm sure it was bread, and some chewing gum. I didn't open the gum. I was still feeling for the tranquilizers. I felt a piece of candy and unwrapped it and I tasted it. It was a caramel. I wasn't hungry at all. I kept feeling around for the tranquilizers and I couldn't find them.

Well, this is just something else that he lied about. He could have put them down at the bottom of the box. I remember straining and trying to get down to the bottom, feeling around with my feet. I was really wearing myself out, reaching and stretching and straining. I finally decided that if they were at the bottom, I could never get to them. I was still mad at myself for not looking before the light went out and I was mad at myself for being so gullible and believing all those things. The tranquilizers were just another thing he said that was not true. I remember thinking the ether—just like the tranquilizers—wasn't true either. And I made some racket intentionally to cause a commotion and make them come and put ether in the fan. I knew this was ridiculous. I tried the pump twice. I knew they wouldn't come. This was about four or five hours after they'd gone. The second time I turned on the pump the noise helped. It was so much louder than the air fan. All that sound was directly behind my head. It was different. It relieved me. I let it run, oh, maybe thirty seconds. I didn't want to use up the battery. With my feet I could feel a blanket down there. It was real wet. I could tell that right through Bobby's socks. I remember I couldn't stretch my feet out all the way at the bottom of the box. Things were in the way. The pails, the food, the blanket I guess. If I lifted my legs as if I was doing a calisthenic exercise, I could stretch out at the top of the box but not at the bottom. I knew I was getting very uncomfortable. I'm five feet eight and three-quarter inches tall and I knew there just wasn't enough room. There was a thin plastic mat underneath me and I kept switching from one side to the other trying to get comfortable. I guess I was on one side or the other practically the whole time. I could feel my hips getting sore. I'm not very hippy to begin with. I didn't know it then but they were turning black and blue.

I didn't pay much attention to the dampness at first. I remember the blanket at the bottom was wet and the blanket around me was getting wet, too. I had it half under me and half over me and after a while there was this dripping from overhead. At first I wondered if something was wrong with the box. I put my hand up and I felt the droplets, or condensation. I can't remember seeing them before the light burned out, just feeling them after it was dark. Maybe my breathing caused them. I don't know. I pulled the blanket up and used it as a hood to keep off the dripping.

I hadn't had anything to drink yet. I was very thirsty and I kept thinking about a conversation Bobby and I had Thanksgiving at home. I don't know how the subject came up but Bobby said anyone can live without food for a long time. Water is more important. You have to conserve your water. I remember him saying that and I was thinking I don't know how much water I have. I had better conserve it. I was worried about drinking too much. When the girl, Ruthie, had climbed in and crawled all over me, she had pulled up this thin long black tube. It was rubber and it was real small. My lips were all burned and terribly swollen from the chloroform and when I tried to drink my lips hurt. I had to suck real hard. It took forever for the water to come up the tube and when it finally came it tasted terrible. It tasted so bad I didn't drink very much. I knew I had to blow it back. I knew the water had to go all the way back into the container or whatever it was. When I blew I must not have blown hard enough because after a minute or so I realized I was getting wet. I had put the tube next to me. For a second I wondered if the box was leaking. Then I realized. I tried again and I did it real hard.

Sometime later I pulled the hose out of the container. I don't know how it happened. I think I was sucking on it. I had to drink a little even though it tasted so bad. The tube wasn't hooked in anywhere. All of a sudden I wasn't getting any water. It was loose. This scared me again. I knew I had to get the tube back in and the water container was down by my feet, toward the left.

I sort of scrunched up and leaned over sidewise, half sitting, reaching as far as I could. I kept trying to flip the tube back in the top of the container.

And then, suddenly, I was stuck. I really panicked. I was over on my left side and my legs were up in back of me, and I was reaching with my right hand as far as I could. I was caught all over, up and down and sideways.

And while I was stuck, I realized I was going to be able to get the tube back in. I wasn't close enough to touch it but I was close. So I went right ahead, casting blindly sort of. And I actually hit it. A lucky shot in the dark. And I fed the tube into the jug. I did all this before trying to get unstuck. I guess I was that way, jammed up that way, for forty-five seconds or maybe a minute. I discovered I could go on down a few more inches, and even though that was the wrong way I did it, and somehow I squirmed around and I managed to get back up.

I became conscious of the flu. I don't know when my fever broke. I didn't think about it. I just remember that my head was completely stopped up. I couldn't breathe through my nose. It wasn't runny. I didn't sneeze or cough. I didn't have to blow my nose. It was just stopped up and I had to breathe through my mouth. It makes me extremely nervous. You know how when you lie on one side during the night and one side of your nose will drain to the other and one nostril will be clear? Well, that never happened. They didn't leave me the NTZ. I thought about that.

I began to think about mental torture and I remembered a teacher I had in the seventh grade. The teacher was Mr. John McGuire and I had a crush on him. Seventh-grade girls always have a crush on a teacher. He was single and twenty-eight. My brother had him before me and he knew the family. He told this story about this man who was in a prison camp of some kind who could undergo mental torture. This is how I remembered it. I might not be correct. But, anyway, whenever they were trying to interrogate this man and break him down in any way, he would slowly build a house in his mind, you know, brick by brick. He took himself completely away from the people who were torturing him. Everytime they would start to get to him—and I know this sounds funny—a brick would fall. But he would just methodically pick it up. Slowly, he would build this house to keep his mind on something else, diverting himself. I remembered Mr. McGuire sitting in the classroom telling us this. And he talked about himself. I remember he said we should all be able to talk to ourselves. Talk to yourself, he said, and be able to control your emotions.

I didn't think about building a house with bricks. I thought about decorating our Christmas tree. I know this sounds funny, but I decorated our Christmas tree in my mind three or four times. The bulbs and ornaments have been around for years and I thought of each one specifically. I made some of them. Three of them I sprinkled sparkle in names, Daddy, Mommy, and Bobby. This was when I was ten or eleven years old.

I love to decorate. All the Christmas decorations are in boxes on a shelf out in the garage and in my mind I would have Dad go out and get them. He would have to get the ladder and I could see him going up each step. He would take the boxes down, one by one, and I would open them, and look at each ornament. They are breakable, and very carefully, I would decorate the tree. I would lay out all the pieces of the manger, too. Daddy always put the lights on himself. He wouldn't let anyone touch the lights. That was his job. I put the top on, a pointed ornament with a little bulb in it. I would put on the angel hair and the tinsel. The tree was always in the game room. In the living room I would put the lights on the mirror and fix the little china reindeer and the little china Santa Claus on a sleigh. There were gold threads for reins. That's

mine. I always do that. I would have to put the Christmas grass
underneath it. I thought of every little minute detail I could. I
remember I also wrapped presents in my mind. I like to have
different bows and I thought of some fancy ones. I wrapped
Mother's presents, two wool nightgowns and a wool robe. They
were very pretty. And if she didn't like them, I might take them
myself. I thought that too. I had already bought Daddy's gift in
Atlanta and sent it home. It was a light for the bar in the den. It
was a man in a tuxedo and a top hat clinging to a light pole and his
nose was a red light. I hadn't bought Bobby's gift yet. I was supposed to wait until I got home to buy him some cuff links at
the Diamond Center in Miami. That's where Daddy bought me my
ring.

In my mind, I went into great detail on the ransom payoff. I
invented all sorts of versions. Some of them, I guess, were pretty
corny. I really believed other persons were involved. I really did.
I thought I am so glad Stewart is still in Atlanta until Dad or
Bobby gets here. I knew Mother would call Stewart. I knew she
would. He doesn't get excited about things. I knew that Mother
would be very excited. I was glad that he was in town. I thought
Mother would call Dad first and I thought Dad would say, Don't
call the police. We'll handle it. On television the kidnapers
always say, Don't call the police. I don't know why I thought
that. At the Rodeway the kidnapers didn't say anything about the
police—except that the man, George, pretended he was one.

In the first version I didn't think much about the money at all.
I had Dad calling the bank; no particular bank, just a bank, and
they put the money in a cardboard box. That was it. They put the
money in a cardboard box and wrapped it up. I thought of it as a
small box. I didn't think much about the amount of money.
Maybe $5000. Honestly. Honestly. I don't think of ourselves as
having money in the family. Nobody really does. I don't think my
friends think of us as having money. I hope not. Daddy is always
kidding me about being an expensive daughter. It is a family joke.
Mother is very reasonable about money. I just don't think about
money. We don't talk about having money. When I ask Daddy, can
we have a boat? he says, nope. When I stop and think about it
though, I guess my allowance is quite a bit. Daddy puts in my
account at the bank $150 a month. Anyway, Daddy had the
cardboard box and in my mind I put him on the plane, a com-

merical plane, Delta. We like Delta. You don't have to wait very
long for your baggage. We've timed other airlines. Delta is very
fast. Bobby was coming to Atlanta, too. I remember thinking that.
Daddy called him. I thought of Daddy driving out to the Rodeway,
stopping at the red lights. I've driven it so many times. You go
down Moreland and on Moreland you catch the turnpike and it
puts you straight into the airport, I-20, then I-85. I went minute by
minute, second by second, giving them plenty of time, so that when
it was time for them to come and dig me up I would know it and
I could be ready.

I remember I still had them in the room at the Rodeway Inn.
In the same room. They were waiting for some sort of contact. I
thought of different versions of how Daddy would be contacted.
One, I remember, was my mailbox at Emory. We have a regular university post office and there are two persons to every little
mailbox. My number is 23521 and I share it with a boy named
Don Mackler. We are assigned alphabetically. I've never met him.
I keep forgetting to check my mailbox and Stewart checks it for
me. It has a combination to it. In my freshman year Stewart would
write little messages because I would neglect my mail. Stewart
would get the message from the kidnapers, I thought, and give it
to Daddy.

I thought of Daddy dropping off the money. This was occurring
at night. It was dark. And Daddy was scared. I thought he might
drop it at the Atlanta airport where the private planes land. I just
saw him dropping it off in the dark and driving back and everyone
was asking him how did it go? How did it go? And he said all
right. We're going to get her back. He drove back and Bobby and
Mother were excited. He said we should hear from them real soon.
So I imagined a dark shadowy figure picking up the money and
getting into an old-type car and driving away. I remember Mother
and Daddy and Bobby all sitting around the Rodeway waiting
for the phone call. And in my mind Daddy jumped when the
call came in. He would say, Jane! Jane! Get a paper and pencil.
He is always yelling at Mother, Jane! Jane! I remember they had
to go buy a shovel. They got a little Army shovel. And I was
thinking it is about time now. The car is pulling up just about now.
I didn't know where I was but the car was pulling up. I didn't
think they would have any trouble finding me. The kidnapers
might have left a flag or something. I remember listening for their

footsteps. It is about time now. And I turned off the fan so I could hear.

And I couldn't hear a thing.

So I went back and started inventing delays. The airplane was late. That was one delay. The weather was real bad. It took much longer for Daddy to get up.

Maybe the kidnapers had had trouble giving the details about where the ransom would be. Maybe they wanted to make sure it wasn't marked money. They were going through it very slowly, making sure nothing was wrong. The kidnapers delayed in calling afterward. That was another delay. They wanted to get away before they called. They are not as far along as I thought. Daddy is just now arriving at the Rodeway. This is stupid, I know, but I thought someone would tell them about me by slipping a note under the door. That would be the instructions on where to deliver the money. Maybe the kidnapers didn't want the money delivered at the Atlanta airport. The airport is kind of open. They could get caught. There is a dead end there and maybe they thought that if Daddy brought the police they would get caught.

So I changed the dropoff to Stone Mountain. Again, Daddy had the money in the cardboard box. It had brown paper and string around it. The things I thought about were so ridiculous. The delivery was going to take place at the gristmill at Stone Mountain. Daddy had to make the delivery inside where it has spider webs. I just had the picture of a kidnaping in my mind. I don't know where I got it from; not from any particular movie or television show. I thought about the different entrances and exits to Stone Mountain so that the kidnapers could get away. So Daddy drove up again. He was alone. He was in the Firebird. He made the dropoff. The same thing. And a dark shadowy figure picks it up. I didn't picture any one in particular. I even had Dad's car having a flat tire. They would have to stop and have it fixed. That's another delay. I would always give them plenty of time and take them right up to the time they would arrive to dig me out. Not quite to the point where they would get me out, but almost.

But I knew something had happened. I gave them so much time. Then it struck me. Everything could have happened in Miami. Not in Atlanta at all.

It must have been a day and I had to go to the bathroom. I've got very good kidneys for a girl but I had to go very badly. No bowel movement. That didn't happen. I didn't have much to eat in the days before because of the flu and I wasn't hungry at all when I was buried. You can imagine how awkward everything was. I was searching around to find something, a cup or anything, and he hadn't left anything. At my feet there was this plastic pail and I figured that was what it was for. It was bell-shaped and it had a top to it, a lid sort of, curved slightly, and I had to put that down underneath me. I could only go a little bit at a time because it was so flat and I knew I had to be careful or it would spill. Everything was so difficult in that compressed space. It was very difficult to move and I was as careful as I could be. I couldn't sit up. I had to try to move it back level and find the pail and tilt and pour. I didn't know where I was pouring because everything was so black and at least 50 per cent of the time I got it all over me. Some of it poured on the outside of the pail. I didn't want it to get into the other drinking water containers. The second or third time I got it right and I could hear it hit. There must have been some water in there. Even though I had to go some more, I didn't. If he had just left a cup or something, really.

I kept thinking about the kidnapers. And things kept coming back to me.

After I was drugged, before he buried me alive, I looked up, I remember. He was standing on the ground and I was in the box and I was groggy still and my mind wasn't accepting this thing.

I know I said, "Please don't tell Daddy where I am. Daddy will get the money for you, but please don't tell him where I am."

I know I said that and I'm sure it didn't make any sense to them.

He said "Mackle will know all about it." The way he said, MACK-le. It was so distinctive. I've never heard anyone enunciate it that way. This was before the girl came down.

There was a reason why I didn't want him to tell Daddy I was buried alive.

You see, Daddy has claustrophobia.

It is not extreme. I've never had a fear of being closed in but Daddy does. He doesn't even like to ride elevators, especially small ones. He merely says, "I'll walk," and Daddy doesn't like to walk that much. Even at Bobby's apartment in Philadelphia, Daddy would walk. It was a real small elevator. He doesn't like tunnels and he doesn't like to be in a small closed room with a lot of people. He just likes to feel he has plenty of room. This thought definitely crossed my mind when they were burying me.

I hoped they wouldn't try to frighten Dad by telling him how small the box was. I knew he would get the money just as soon as he could and something like this wasn't going to help.

Loved One—Please Come Home

Late the Tuesday evening of December 17, Assistant Professor Marshall Casse received a telephone call. He had driven that day from Emory University to Durham, North Carolina. He planned to drive to the University of North Carolina at Chapel Hill the next morning where he could work on his thesis among the books on Soviet economics in the library stacks.

His caller apologized for the late hour. He identified himself as an FBI agent. What could Professor Casse tell him about someone asking for Barbara Mackle at the Emory campus? It could be important.

On Saturday morning, December 14, three days before the kidnaping, Professor Casse had begun grading final exams in his office in the Rich Building on the Emory campus. This was the exam that Barbara missed because she was ill. He had taken a break about two-fifteen in the afternoon and while walking on the first floor near the main office he overheard a man say, "There is someone in the office," emphasizing the word is. A girl was with him.

Professor Casse saw approaching a man approximately six feet tall, fairly heavy, he thought, perhaps 240 pounds, with a full dark and striking beard. To Casse, the man reminded him of jazz trumpeter Al Hirt. Casse was from New Orleans.

"He was dressed for the street, better than she, dark pants and I think a gold cardigan sweater, buttoned down the front, regular shoes. He was six or six one, and I remember they were of considerably different heights. She was five feet one or so, quite petite actually. She was dressed rough. Rough is the word I thought. Sweat shirt, dungarees or blue jeans, tennis shoes, and her hair was

very short, a pixie haircut, and she looked quite young at this time."
Swimmer's haircut, he thought.

"Do you have a list of students in this school?" the man asked.

"Yes, there is such a list, but I don't have one," said Professor
Casse. "I suggest you come back on Monday morning when the
office is open."

"Does school continue until Wednesday?" the man asked.

"No, classes were over as of last Wednesday, exams continue
until next Wednesday," the professor replied.

"Then we can't find her in class," the man said to the girl.

"Is there someone particularly you are looking for? Could I help?
Who are you looking for specifically?"

At this point the bearded man mentioned the name of a person.
Professor Casse thought he said, "Ruth Scherer."

"Ruth Scherer is my secretary," Professor Casse said. "She is the
secretary for the department."

"Well, then that ought to make her easy to find," the man
responded quickly and easily, almost nonchalantly, the professor
would think later.

As the couple left, the professor followed them to the door of the
Rich Building and watched. The entire encounter puzzled him
slightly. Why should they ask for a list of students, then say
they were looking for Ruth Scherer? She couldn't be mistaken for
a student. She had a son in college. He watched them get into a
blue foreign-made station wagon. He thought it was a Volkswagen.
He looked at the license plate. They were from Massachusetts. He
read the number, intending to jot it down. The professor seldom
wore a watch but he looked at the clock, thinking of Mrs. Scherer.
Maybe it was nothing at all. But perhaps Mrs. Scherer knew them
and was expecting them. Before he went back to grading exams,
he telephoned her at home.

"Do you know anybody from Massachusetts with an Al Hirt
beard?" She said she had no idea who he was talking about.

About four o'clock that same afternoon Professor Casse was
walking down the stairs toward the drinking fountain. On the
ground floor, in an alcove underneath the stairway, there was a
Coke machine, a cracker machine, a copy machine and three
public telephones attached to the wall.

Professor Casse, almost directly above, stopped and listened.
The same man was on the telephone. He seemed annoyed.

"Operator, I have had a good deal of difficulty with this telephone. I can't get the Emory number, Emory University number." There was a pause of a minute or so.

Professor Casse just stood there, a half flight above, and out of sight, listening.

"I am looking for Barbara Mackle. It is an emergency," and he lowered his voice. Professor Casse knew Barbara, of course, but he did not know who her father was.

The professor thought he heard him say "McTyeire Hall."

"Can you get this number for me?" and again the man lowered his voice. Professor Casse heard him hang up.

Deliberately, Professor Casse again descended the stairs. He looked closely at the couple again. They didn't seem to notice him.

He heard the man say simply, "She is at the Rodeway Inn."

And the girl, seemingly surprised, replied, "What is she doing there?" They left hurriedly.

On Monday Professor Casse was back in his office grading papers about 10:30 A.M. From his third-floor window he again saw the man with the Al Hirt beard and the girl with the swimmer's haircut. Mrs. Scherer was in the office. He called to her and he pushed up the window. Together they looked out over the parking lot and saw them get into the blue foreign station wagon. Mrs. Scherer said she did not recognize them. Obviously they weren't trying very hard to find her in her office. That's the last he had seen of them.

The FBI man on the telephone wanted to know if Professor Casse had written down the license number.

No, he hadn't. But he was positive about the Massachusetts plate and he was certain it had one letter and five numbers. He thought the letter was a Y. He was sure two of the numbers were a 0 and a 2. Or a 2 and 0. He was positive it was blue and he was positive it was a station wagon. He thought it was a Volkswagen.

The FBI man thanked him and wanted to know where he could find him Wednesday if necessary. Professor Casse said he would be in the stacks at the library.

The lead looked good. Certainly it had to be pursued. Could computers isolate by IBM card all the station wagon Volkswagens painted blue, registered in the Commonwealth of Massachusetts? How many would there be? Would the Y and the 2 and 0 help?

The beard and the girl opened other possibilities. Were they looking for a man who had just shaved a beard? Could Mrs. Mackle have mistaken a ski-masked girl for a twelve-year-old boy? Who were they and why were they asking for Barbara Mackle? Could they be from Miami?

Behind the closed draperies of the Mackle home in Coral Gables, the three brothers that night tried to think of anyone who might dislike them enough—hate or detest—to kidnap Barbara. In the twenty-three years since the end of World War II the Mackles had built in excess of 30,000 homes. Was it conceivable that a homeowner, demented or mad, was so deranged he would kidnap Robert's daughter? It seemed absurd. Had their company ever fired an employee who vowed revenge? Had anyone ever before so much as mentioned the word kidnap? Had anyone ever threatened Barbara in any manner? The answers were negative. The only public dispute involving the Mackles in recent years concerned the Horseman's Benevolent and Protective Association. Frank had served as the national president of the association in 1966. Robert had been president of the Florida association during the 1967–68 season when the HBPA, as it was called, negotiated separately with the three Miami tracks, Tropical Park Race Track, Hialeah Race Course, and the Gulfstream Park Racing Association, Inc. Mackle's group had won concessions from the track owners, a slight percentage increase in the track's mutuel handle for purses. The jockeys, dependent on the horsemen for their rides and in agreement with their views, had called in sick and boycotted Hialeah on opening day the previous February, and feelings ran high. But the boycott had been resolved quickly. To the Mackles, any connection to the kidnaping seemed utterly impossible. Yet they forced themselves to try and think of everything.

Dr. Lauth put a salve on Jane Mackle's throbbing finger, bandaged it, doctored the abrasions on her legs, and gave her a sedative by hypodermic.

"I accused him of giving me a shot to knock me out, and he said no, he was just giving me a vitamin shot. He also gave me antibiotic pills and cough medicine. My cold was terrible." Jane Mackle collapsed on her bed upstairs fully dressed. Dr. Lauth suggested she be left alone until morning. Agnes went home in a taxicab. Elliott and Dr. Lauth later left for their homes.

In the game room no one slept, not the FBI agents, Vessels, Bobby, nor Frank and Robert. "You never know the thoughts that

go through your mind," said Robert. "Where is she? Is she all
right? Is she out of her mind? The FBI kept saying there was
nothing to this buried box. Mechanically, it couldn't work. They
were trying to give me every comfort in the world.

"I never told anyone—not my wife, not even Bobby, although he
probably realized it, but I knew Barbara was in a box of some kind.
The ransom note was so intelligent in my estimation. I felt she was
in a box for security reasons. In a cell perhaps. There would be
people around her. Or even, I thought, the box might be in one of
those caves up in Georgia. I thought they might have her in a
trailer. Or even a box inside a trailer. Maybe they were driving the
trailer to Miami.

"The one thing I couldn't visualize was anyone so inhuman as to
bury anyone alive. I just couldn't accept that. I know the FBI
didn't believe it. Everything else in the note, okay. But you just
couldn't bury someone alive and have her remain mentally sane.
I couldn't have."

Robert Mackle did not mention his abhorrence of elevators,
close confinement, small rooms, tunnels. No one else mentioned it
aloud.

Bobby thought of his dad's claustrophobia.

"I remember one occasion when I was very young, I might
have been four or five, maybe it was much later, I don't know, but
anyway we used to live by a cemetery and Dad said to me one
day, 'When I die, put me in a mausoleum. No matter what, don't
bury me in the ground.' That stuck in my mind." Bobby doubted
that the kidnapers of his sister had buried her alive. "Obviously,
they knew Dad real well. They knew about the Lincoln. We figured
they probably knew his voice, too, and he would have to take the
call—whenever it came," said Bobby. "The buried box, we thought,
was just a scheme to make him come up with the money quick. The
FBI thought it was a ruse. It wasn't feasible."

The night lingered, and the windup eight-day Guild Crest clock
on the paneled wall over the red telephone in the den ticked so
loudly it could be heard across the room. No one said anything.
Finally, about 5:30 A.M. the faint flop sound of a 120-page newspaper striking the concrete porch outside broke the stillness.

The Miami *Herald* of December 18, 1968 lay wrapped in a
polyethylene sleeve, and deep in its fourth section, after the paid
death notices and the cemetery lots for sale, long columns of

unbroken agate type chronicled the wants and needs and every-day dreams of every man, $1.35 a line a day or $.75 a line for a week.

"Need Super Bowl tickets, Call Steve at 666-0424," proclaimed one advertiser, and Steve Klisanian, an exercise equipment sales-man, would eventually listen to the game on radio because of a local television blackout and the scalper's price of $100 a ticket.

"Lost: Ladies' gold watch. Initials V.B.D. on 'L' Bus 864-8621," said another, and Virginia Dare, Miss Virginia Bell Dare, who took home the Hialeah bus from the U. S. State Department pass-port office where she worked, would have to buy a new Wittnauer.

The classified advertisers of that morning, presumably seeking "fast results through low-cost," promised twelve dollars in "instant cash" to blood donors, all types needed, and Maria, spiritual reader and adviser, and Ho-Ho the TV Magic Clown, announced their availability, along with a gentleman, 38, wishing to meet lady under 36 for companionship. Several of the more institutionalized business enterprises typically beseeched: "No Date Tonight? Don't stay home and watch TV. Call the Meeting Place, PL 7-9389," or, if one preferred, "Join the new large Nudist Club. Rt. 1, Box 568, Fort Lauderdale, Dial 1 584-7584," where often the telephone was temporarily disconnected at the customer's request.

Three of the forty-one ads published under the 01-03 Personals on that morning appeared quite personal, intelligible and fully meaningful only to those directly concerned. "Da-Da, please call or come home. Urgent. Love S and A." And, "Modesto, please come home or call. I'm sick. I love and need you. I will go any place with you."

Billy Vessels heard the flop outside and sprang to his feet, flung open the front door and slipped off the polyethylene wrapper. Ignoring the black type in six columns on page one, "Miami Girl Abducted From Atlanta Motel," Vessels turned hurriedly from the back pages forward, past Peanuts, Blondie, Li'l Abner, and at the very top of the second column from the right on page 20-D, he found what he was looking for:

> LOVED ONE—please come home.
> We will pay all expenses and meet you
> anywhere at any time.
> Your family.

The classified ad, inserted when the presses stopped after the first edition, appeared in 352,620 papers that morning.

"It jumped out at me. It was so obvious. Too prominent. Anyone in the world would know," Vessels thought.

Soon Ann Briggle came over and saw her sister, awakening fully dressed, the bedspread unturned, the bed still made from the day before. "Jane looked better, but she was awfully sore. The cuts and wounds were scabby on both her legs. Her lips and cheeks and mouth were sore, chapped, really, as if she had been in a winter storm. She was so sick physically. She kept coughing. She would hold herself as she coughed. When she fell, she had hurt her back. I could see the black-and-blue marks and I rubbed her with Ben-Gay and put hot towels on her to relieve the pain. She wasn't comfortable lying and she wasn't comfortable sitting. She couldn't sit and she couldn't stand, and she kept walking."

Downstairs, Billy Vessels kept busy. "I was taking all the calls and getting rid of people," he said. Impatiently, he would say the same thing repeatedly.

"If you have something to contribute, please help. Otherwise, please get off the line and don't call again."

Vessels was startled to see newspaper and television reporters congregating across the street in the shade of the Ficus trees heavy with Spanish moss.

Probably every major daily newspaper in the nation published something about the crime that morning in varying degrees of prominence. The New York *Times* had conservatively played a United Press International account.

"ATLANTA, DEC 17 (UPI)—A fake detective and a tiny accomplice barged into a motel room before dawn today and kidnaped the daughter of Robert F. Mackle, millionaire Florida land developer and friend of President-elect Richard M. Nixon . . ."

The Mackle relationship to the President-elect, naturally, made the story more newsworthy. That particular morning the editor of the *Times* had a two-column picture of the President-elect on page one, paying a call to U Thant, the Secretary General of the United Nations, and the kidnaping story on page 25. The Mackle relationship to the Nixons was never truly close but the Mackles genuinely liked both of them. Before Nixon's nomination the previous April the Mackles had Mrs. Nixon, daughter Julie and David Eisenhower over for cocktails. As a senator from California and as

Vice-President in the 1950s, Nixon had often stayed at the Key Biscayne Hotel where he discovered the psychotherapy of sun and sand and surf. In the informality of vacationing at the Villas, where the Mackles met the Nixons, the senator had taught Jane how to make a lime gimlet. Barbara had met Nixon as a child. She and her daddy were walking along the beach one day when Nixon, the swimmer, emerged from the ocean. Once Barbara had barged into the Nixon villa to see her parents, tracking in splotches of oil from the beach on her feet. Her daddy shooed her away. The Mackles' and Nixons' children were exactly the same ages, Bobby and Tricia, Barbara and Julie, and Nixon had studied law at Duke University at the same time Jane attended the university. They didn't know each other then. Nixon said he never went out socially as a student. He said he was poor and studied all the time.

Not too long ago, before the 1968 campaign began in earnest, Nixon had been playing the Riviera Country Club golf course bordering the Mackle home, and he stopped unexpectedly one day during Jane's Tuesday bridge club gatherings, wanting to know if he could get out of the hot sun for a moment. He was told he could if he played bridge. In the air-conditioned coolness of the Mackle game room, the thirsty golfer drank a can of Budweiser beer instead. Briefly they commiserated about their daughters. Why wasn't Julie going to Duke? Why wasn't Barbara going to Duke? Barbara had visited the Duke campus before she selected Emory. Julie's father had lobbied unsuccessfully for the principles of coeducation and lost to the female exclusiveness of one of the "seven sisters," Smith College.

In that summer of 1968, Barbara worked at a telephone information booth at the Republican National Convention at Miami Beach. For the occasion she had her hair cut. Nearly always before, her mother merely trimmed her long black shoulder-length hair. This time a beautician cut it quite short and brother Bobby teased her. "Hello there, Prince Valiant," he said cheerfully, and for the convention, Robert Mackle just had to buy his daughter a fall. Nixon never made it over to the Key Biscayne Villas during the convention, and consequently he never saw the three-volume set of books Robert Mackle had left for him in Villa 15, *The American Heritage of the Presidency*. They were a gift ungiven. The books stood upright on an end table near two oversized divans L-shaped into a corner in the Mackle game room that second morning of the kidnaping as Jane Mackle came down the stairs determined to see that her guests were properly fed.

Hardly anyone felt hungry. Dr. Lauth insisted that Robert Mackle have breakfast whether he wanted it or not. He extracted from his coat pocket an aluminum packet of chocolate-flavored Instant Breakfast. It was a powdered substance, dissolved in milk for drinking, and he had long prescribed—or forced—his own four daughters and son to drink it when they were in too big a hurry for breakfast. He had taken the supply from the kitchen cupboard over the stove in his own home before returning to the Mackle residence early that morning. Robert Mackle would have just as soon swallowed castor oil. "You've got to maintain your strength on this thing, Bob," said Dr. Lauth. "You've got to keep your equilibrium." He also gave Robert a vitamin shot. Bobby had a touch of strep throat and Dr. Lauth gave him penicillin. Some of the FBI men also accepted Dr. Lauth's medication.

Inspector Rex Shroder arrived somewhat later and introduced Robert to a well-built white-haired agent about Robert's age, Leroy L. Kusch.

"This is your double," said Shroder to Robert.

"What do you mean, my double?"

"Your walks are similar. Your heights are identical. You both have the same round face, and if we put a little black in Lee's hair, he can pass for you in a dim light. He is your double. It might be that Lee can make the delivery of the money," suggested Shroder, watching Robert Mackle closely for his reaction. "We want to have someone out here who can do this."

Robert Mackle said nothing. He had no intention of letting anyone else deliver the money. But he approved of the FBI thinking. Inspector Shroder also said that he would like to borrow Robert's Lincoln for a while. He had two thoughts in mind. He wanted installed secretly an infrared camera for night photography and a hidden microphone for transmitting. Billy Vessels could drive the Lincoln to a Texaco station at Five Points directly across the street from the Deltona executive offices and leave it there to be gassed and prepared as if for a long trip in compliance with the ransom instructions. There would be a black FBI agent, Leo McClarin, waiting for him at the gas station dressed in a Texaco uniform. It was all arranged. Vessels could then walk over to the Deltona offices.

Vessels delivered the car. At the Deltona office he picked up some correspondence involving a business dispute which the Mackles had thought of while wracking their brains for possible leads the night before. It was meaningless.

Vessels and agent Frank Smith then drove in Smith's car to the First National Bank in downtown Miami after Smith made sure they were not being followed. At the bank a guard had saved a parking space for them in an adjacent parking garage accessible to the third floor where Robert Bruce, the bank president, waited for them in his office. Sumpasis, the head teller, and Mariano Fernandez, an auditor, accompanied by Wackenhut guards, carried the money in sacks from the first-floor coin-wrapping room to Bruce's private office. A guard carried the empty suitcase.

"Here I was on the third floor to collect $500,000 and I was overdue on a personal loan on the first floor," said Vessels. The thought occurred much later. At the time he felt the weight of the responsibility of representing the family.

"We all felt a little foolish about the missing $100," said Bruce, the bank president. "We sent down and had a voucher put in for the five other $20 bills." Somewhat later it became an in-house joke at the bank: What department was to be charged with the loan? The commercial loan department eventually handled the paper work. No one that morning was joking about anything. "We were all keyed up like race horses," said Bruce.

When Vessels saw the suitcase he became upset. "I became very suspicious. Everyone had made such a production out of the ransom note and I thought the note had said a new suitcase." This one wasn't new. He didn't like it. Vessels wasn't aware of all the problems encountered in finding it. "There were some very distinctive marks on it." He searched it thoroughly, looking for a microphone or any sort of concealed electronic homing device. "This rubber stopper is off," he said accusingly. Convinced finally that this was the best they could do and that the suitcase was in no way tampered with deliberately, Vessels watched sullenly as the bankers repacked the empty suitcase.

"To me it was fantastic the way the money fit," said Vessels. "I don't think they could have put in another bill." Vessels lifted the unlocked suitcase. "It was so damn heavy I couldn't believe it," he said. It weighed seventy-five pounds. From Bruce he took the key to the suitcase and a piece of paper dated December 18, 1968.

It said: "RECEIVED OF THE FIRST NATIONAL BANK OF MIAMI—$500,000. Five Hundred Thousand And 00/100—" Vessels signed first Elliott Mackle's name, then "by" and his own name. Bruce signed too.

As two FBI agents walked in front of him and two Wackenhuts behind, Vessels carried the suitcase toward the car. A young lawyer in a hurry, totally unaware of what was happening, arrived at the third-floor door to the parking garage just as Vessels did, and started to push his way out at the same time.

A guard physically shunted the gentleman aside. He didn't like it at all. "Let me out!" he bellowed, and when he was ordered to remain where he was against a wall, he demanded to know everyone's identity. He could see the bank guards were Wackenhuts.

"I'm going to sue Wackenhut and I'm going to sue the bank!" he cried, and indeed, as keyed-up as a race horse himself, he would return to the bank the next day and demand to see someone in authority. Bruce would attempt to pacify the young attorney without explaining the circumstances. It wasn't easy. "The poor fellow, he was treated rather shabbily," said Bruce.

A second FBI car, more or less riding shotgun, followed Vessels and agent Smith to the Mackle home. Unobtrusively Vessels took the suitcase inside and set it down in the den beside the fireplace.

"It was just sitting there," said Vessels. "No one paid any attention to it."

The ad was in the paper. The money was ready. Soon the Lincoln would be ready. They would simply have to wait for the telephone call.

"We will call you at your home after midnight to advise you where you must go to deliver the money," the instructions had stated. It was a few minutes before twelve noon. How long would they wait?

What Do You Want, Father?

At the Catholic Rectory of the Church of the Little Flower on a broad and palm-lined avenue named Anastasia deep in the residential grandeur of Coral Gables, the Reverend John Christopher Mulcahy had a few minutes to kill before lunch. He was in his room reading when the buzzer buzzed on his number-six extension telephone on a desk beside his bed. Someone had asked for a priest and Mrs. Irene Kappes, the secretary in the lobby downstairs, had referred the call to him.

"Hello, Father Mulcahy speaking."

"Father who?"

"Father Mulcahy."

"What is your name?"

"Father Mulcahy."

"Is this a priest? Are you a Catholic priest?"

"Well, I suppose I am. Yes, I am," said Father Mulcahy, amused, wondering to himself just how good a priest he was. He was a young man, younger in appearance than his thirty-one years, black-haired, small of stature, and he spoke softly in a tenor voice with the lyrical brogue of Ireland. He was from Killaloe, County Clare, Ireland, and he had lived in America a little more than six years.

"Father, promise me that you will not tell anyone what I am going to tell you except the person I designate. Father, this is a matter of life and death."

It was a hard and precise male voice. "Very fierce, just like a young lawyer," Father Mulcahy would remember. "He was very well-spoken and very well articulated. His voice almost had a kind of ring to it." In the vernacular of his adopted homeland, Father Mulcahy wondered just what sort of kook he had on the other end of the line.

"You promise me this now, Father? It is a matter of life and death," he repeated.

"Well, I suppose so. Yes."

"I am the kidnaper of Barbara Mackle."

Father Mulcahy didn't believe him. Skepticism overwhelmed him. Someone was always putting a priest in a position where the priest had to do something. What did this nut want? A few bucks? The Mackles were parishioners of the Church of the Little Flower and the Monsignor and everyone had spoken of them the day before when they had heard of the kidnaping. Father Mulcahy did not know the Mackle family personally. He had been appointed to the church as an assistant pastor only seven weeks before and there were two thousand families who belonged. He knew the Mackles lived somewhere nearby in the Gables. That was about all. He said nothing. He listened. He let the man talk.

Later Father Mulcahy would recall the conversation. "He told me that Barbara Mackle was okay. He said that the last time his men, his people, checked on her that she was all right. He said she was up in Georgia, outside Atlanta, and that she was buried in a coffin and the lids had nails in it. That is what he said. He said she was okay. He said she was buried underneath the ground, fifteen or twenty inches under the ground, and that she was being well taken care of. He said she was a bit sick and she didn't have much clothes."

To Father Mulcahy, the caller appeared mentally unbalanced. What he was saying seemed preposterous.

"It is very cold up there, Father."

"Yes, I know it is," the priest replied, containing his disbelief.

Father Mulcahy would later try to remember the man's exact words. "He told me there was a little food and some water in the coffin and there was a battery to provide her air for five or seven days. I'm not sure. He said two days were gone already. He said, 'When the battery runs out, she runs out, too.' I'll never forget that. Exactly, these were his words, 'When the battery runs out, she runs out, too.' That kind of hit me. And he said if Mackle didn't come through, that was it."

Who was he? Why had he called the church? What did he want?

"What am I supposed to do?" Father Mulcahy asked at the time. It was probably a hoax, he thought. His inquiry was purely intellectual, not emotional.

"He told me he wanted me to go to the Mackle home and tell

Mr. Mackle that he had called and that their daughter was alive. To speak to the father and no one else. He said the whole place was full of cops, detectives and FBI men; that he had checked there. Speak to no one, only the father, no one else, and tell him that his lovely daughter will die unless he followed the instructions. He said lovely daughter."

"Look," interrupted the priest during the call. "Follow what instructions?"

"I am sure they have already found them," the man replied. "The instructions were left beneath a rock near a tree. You can tell Mackle to follow the instructions exactly—or his lovely daughter will die."

"What is the address?" the priest asked perplexed.

"Come on, Father. They are your parishioners."

The man gave him the address, 4111 San Amaro Drive, Coral Gables. "You will probably hear from me again."

"Good-by," said Father Mulcahy, his mind diverted totally. What if it wasn't a hoax? The magnitude of the possibilities frightened him. His intellectual involvement dissolved in his own emotions.

It could be real, Father Mulcahy thought. "These people could be watching me right now." He didn't know what to think.

Without a word to anyone, he walked down the stairs and out the front door and climbed into his green Ford Mustang.

The other priests had started lunch without him. The telephone call had taken perhaps three minutes.

Bill O'Dowd, the treasurer for Deltona, also had an errand that Wednesday. The kidnaper's ransom note had instructed, "You must be the one to deliver the money, Robert. You will dress yourself in an all-white outfit." Although Robert Mackle owned a dozen white shirts, he didn't own a single pair of white pants. As O'Dowd discovered, December in Miami was not the season for white pants.

"Billy Vessels called me about the white clothes and he told me Robert wore a size forty-one. I went to Burdine's downtown and they didn't have any white slacks. So I drove to South Miami to a men's store that advertised it could always fit any size. And they didn't have anything. I stopped by Sears, Roebuck in Coral Gables and they didn't either."

His fourth stop was a Tall Man's shop in Dadeland, a fashionable

shopping center in the southwest section of the county, and again
he could find nothing. In a large Jordan Marsh store in Dadeland,
O'Dowd finally found what he wanted: piles and stacks of slacks,
white ones included. They were on sale. Clearance—50 per cent
off.

"But they didn't have any 41s," said O'Dowd, a lanky tall man
who wore a size 34 himself. "So I bought a 40 and a 42."

"I'll take them with me," he said, and he was sure that young
lady who waited on him wouldn't have known if he wore a 26 or
46. He paid her $18, plus tax. He heard again from Vessels.
This time the FBI wanted two of everything, two white golfing
caps, size 7¼ and 7⅛. Since he already had two white slacks, it
wasn't necessary to go back. Without realizing it, O'Dowd had
purchased the exact size for agent Kusch, Robert's double. O'Dowd
didn't want to stop for the caps at the Riviera Clubhouse on the
course adjacent to the Mackle home. "I knew there would be a
lot of questions." Instead, he purchased the caps at the nearby
municipal-owned Coral Gables Biltmore Golf Course. There were
no questions. He delivered the merchandise to the home, not
wanting to intrude, and departed quickly for the Deltona offices.
O'Dowd and James Vensel, another Deltona executive, would
accept all incoming telephone calls for any of the Mackle brothers
there for the next few days. They were recording nearly every call.

In the master bedroom of the Mackle home, Jane Mackle insisted
she see the news on television that noon. Her sister-in-law, Anne
Braznell, who stopped by briefly, couldn't prevent her.

"And then they showed Barbara's picture," said Anne Braznell.
"Jane put her head in her hands and cried, 'Oh, God. Where is she?'
It was pathetic." Soon someone would unplug the cord.

Downstairs, Agnes Banks, the maid, noticed that both television
sets were off. Usually, faithfully almost, she watched "Love of
Life" and "As the World Turns" every day, but this Wednesday
she did not want to see any television or read any newspapers.
She had found the morning paper stuck under a couch in the den,
unaware that Bobby had hidden it there from his mother.

On one occasion Jane noticed the FBI agents opened all their
mail. She was a little surprised. "Even our Christmas cards." Most
of the cards had been sent prior to the kidnaping. Elaborate and
artistic cards from friends, oblivious to the horror or uncertainty
of the moment, had little notes wishing the family a merry Christ-

mas and a happy New Year. "Even our Christmas cards," she repeated. She felt useless, ineffectual, unable to do anything.

Some few aspects of the Mackle household continued normally. Ann Briggle, Jane's sister, had to empty the garbage. As she stepped on a step-on lid to a sunken container outside, photographers lolling on a lawn across the street leaped to their feet.

Jane Mackle happened to be watching from the bedroom window. "Oh, Ann," she said, "you just had your picture taken emptying the garbage." It was one of the few times they laughed.

The four-tone chimes of the doorbell, a common musical imitation of Big Ben in London, rang in electronic harmony through the Mackle household, and the FBI agent who had watched the priest park his car, walk up the walkway, and press the doorbell, opened the front door.

"I would like to speak to Mr. Mackle," Father Mulcahy said through a second and closed outside screen door. Nodding wordlessly, the agent departed.

Robert Mackle came to the foyer and he could see the priest outside. "Please," he said to the FBI agent, "I don't want to see anyone. Let's not have a crowd around the house. I just want as few people as possible. Tell the Father some other time."

The FBI agent again opened the door. "What do you want, Father? Unless you can make a contribution . . ."

"I don't know if I can or not," Father Mulcahy interposed, and he mumbled something about it not being a question of seeing a priest. "I would like to speak to Mr. Mackle. It is about Barbara."

The door swung open and Father Mulcahy walked into the darkened foyer, the chandelier above unlit. The walls were parqueted and grass-clothed. The priest felt surrounded by large men, crowding in closely. "Take it easy," he grinned. He introduced himself and Robert Mackle stepped forward.

"I have a message for you Mr. Mackle," he said quickly. "I don't know if it is for real or not. I was asked not to speak to anyone but you. No one else."

"These are FBI agents, Father," said Robert Mackle, "and I would like for them to be present."

"All right," said Father Mulcahy, and Robert Mackle led him into the formal living room, an elongated green-carpeted room in the front of the home faintly reminiscent of an old-fashioned unused front parlor. It was much quieter than the game room.

Bookcases flanked an immaculate marble fireplace, and the *Reader's Digest* and a World Atlas lay on the underneath shelf of a coffee table. The furniture was traditional. At one end of the room sat an antique desk, which had once belonged to either President John Adams or President John Quincy Adams. Jane Mackle could never remember which. Near it was a Steinway baby grand piano. She had practiced on it as a child and so had Barbara, who had taken lessons since she was eleven and had become quite proficient. There was so much of Barbara's sheet music stuffed into the piano bench that the lid wouldn't quite close. Father Mulcahy walked toward a divan under two large oil portraits on the wall. He noticed them as he sat down. They were paintings of Barbara and Bobby each at age two.

Never in his life had he such a rapt audience. The attention was riveted. "They were very intense, tremendously alert. I could hardly breathe," recalled Father Mulcahy.

"Now just start at the beginning, Father," said Inspector Shroder evenly.

"He was the headman," said the priest later. "He told the others not to ask questions. I got the impression he was directing traffic."

Father Mulcahy repeated everything he could remember. Two agents began to take notes as he spoke. Then, afterward, Inspector Shroder questioned him closely to make him amplify and clarify.

Father Mulcahy couldn't tell what they were thinking. "Do you think he was the uh . . . This is for real?" he asked finally.

"Yes," said the inspector. "You talked to the kidnaper."

"The FBI was tremendously elated," said Robert Mackle. "We all were. We knew this was it."

Jane Mackle walked down the circular stairs about this time. "I saw the priest and I said, 'Oh, do you know anything?' and he had a somber face too. He came up and shook my hand."

The FBI had wanted permission to install immediately a telephone tap at the church. That would be no problem.

As the priest reached his car, newsmen surrounded him. Generally, they assumed he was there to comfort the family. "Have they heard from the kidnapers?" someone asked.

"They have reason to believe their daughter is alive and unharmed," Father Mulcahy said. He did not elaborate. He knew he might receive other calls and he knew he needed God's help. He wanted to be alone to pray.

The afternoon dragged. There was very little to do but wait. Dr. Lauth realized that the tensions would intensify during the evening and somehow he had to persuade and convince Robert Mackle to rest while he could. Edward J. Lauth, Jr., a muscular, tall and angular man of forty-six from Cedar Rapids, Iowa, was a family doctor of the old school. He made house calls. He accepted so many night calls that his wife learned to sleep right through his departure and return during the night. As director of the Centro Hispano Catolico for Miami's refugee Cubans, he had so many poor patients that in his private records he would jot down "can pay" for patients like the Mackles. He was an informal man, quick to call practically everyone he met by their first name, yet a man of deep personal convictions. Quite probably he was the most articulate physician in Florida on the subject of abortion. He opposed liberalization of the laws. Three times he had pressed his views successfully before the Florida Legislature. He kept himself in superb physical condition, jogging a mile and three-quarters around the La Gorce Country Club golf course in Miami Beach before his office hours.

He had virtually abandoned his practice after the telephone call from Frank Mackle at the Plaza Hotel in New York the morning before. He had become the physician-in-residence at the Mackle home, and when he began his soft sell to get Robert Mackle to bed, Robert knew it and respected his judgment.

"Now, Bob," he said, "we need you. We think we'll need you tonight. You are terribly tense and I understand that, and medically, there is not much I can do. But I can give you a pill to let you get a little sleep. I'll make a deal with you. If you have one more of these Instant Breakfasts, I'll fix you a bourbon myself and then I'll give you a pill. You drink the bourbon and go upstairs. I think you'll sleep for just about three hours." As with many nondrinkers thrust into the role of barkeep, Dr. Lauth employed a heavy hand.

Robert Mackle followed the doctor's orders. "I looked at my watch and it was a quarter to one. I was so tired I hardly made it up the stairs. I plopped into bed." He slept. When he awoke, he looked at his watch. It was exactly a quarter to four.

"While Robert was sleeping, we considered the possibilities of

Lee Kusch taking his place," said Frank Mackle. Robert was up-set earlier in the day. Rex Shroder wanted Lee ready as a back-up man. If, but some chance, Robert's condition worsened, we would have someone to throw into the gap. We didn't discuss this in front of Robert.

"When he came down, he looked good, much better, aggressive. I knew he would go. There was no question about it," said Frank. He knew his brother.

Inspector Shroder, to the contrary, was not at all convinced. For the time being, he said nothing. He would be able to discuss it later.

Before sunset at 5:43 P.M., Billy Vessels and an agent left to pick up the Lincoln. It was dark when he drove into the garage. An agent pulled down the overhead doors, closing off the view from the street.

"They wanted me to go out and look at it," said Robert Mackle. "And I went out and they opened the trunk."

There, sprawled out inside, was a brawny agent, Larry Coutre, an ex-halfback from Notre Dame. He was cradling a shotgun. He had an oxygen tank and the trunk latch had been modified so he could open it from the inside.

"What is this for?" Robert asked.

"We think you should have some protection," someone said.

"No," said Robert, containing himself. "Just get him out of there."

They were introduced. They shook hands. "We recommend that Larry go with you," the inspector said.

"I'm not going to do it," said Robert.

"Well, we'll talk about it."

The FBI had installed a hidden radio-transmitting unit in the car. A microphone was concealed in the driver's air-conditioning vent. The regular antenna served as the aerial. Any conversation in the car could be monitored at FBI headquarters and at the Mackle residence.

The bureau technicians had not been able to install the infrared stroboscopic lighting equipment and camera necessary to take photographs in darkness without detection. The equipment, al-though not too bulky, would have had to have gone under the hood for concealment, and because of the way the engine was situated in relation to the grille, the engineering and modification just wasn't feasible in the time available.

In the game room, the conversation turned again to an agent hiding in the trunk. Under no conditions would he intervene, the FBI declared. He would be there solely in case of extreme emergency. It was one of the few times that Robert Mackle adamantly decided to go his own way.

"Look, the note said prepare for a trip," he argued. "Maybe it'll be a long trip. I'm likely to go one place and get instructions somewhere else. Then maybe I'll have to go to a third place. I might wind up in Palm Beach," said Robert Mackle. The FBI had calculated much the same and had told him so. He could expect any number of diversions before a final destination.

"Maybe somewhere along the line they will stop me," said Robert Mackle. "Suppose they say, 'Open the trunk. We want to make sure no one is with you.' On that one chance alone, I am not going to take a chance on having anyone else in the car."

"We respect your wishes," said Inspector Shroder. "Either you or Lee can do it that way." He was still leaving himself—and Robert—a way out.

"If you are worried about my life, forget it," said Robert Mackle. "The point is to try to get Barbara back, not protect me."

"If someone shoots Dad, it wouldn't do too much good to have someone jump out of the trunk afterward," Bobby told his uncles. "If Dad is going to get shot, we'll know it. We'll hear it. It would be pointless for an agent with a shotgun to jump out and then try to save his life." Bobby worried more about his father's ability to deliver the money than the risk of assassination, murder, or gunfire from a sniper despite the threats in the ransom note . . . "Any deviation from this outline will result in your death," the note said. "Our messenger will have you in his sights from the time you leave your car." Robert Mackle felt much the same. What if he couldn't follow the instructions? What if they weren't clear? What if he couldn't deliver the ransom? He feared this more than his own life.

And what if the call never came?

The only sensible course was to try to think of every contingency, every angle, everything that the kidnapers might demand.

"Suppose this man calls and asks me to bring the ransom note?" said Robert.

"We're ready for you," said Inspector Shroder, and he produced three Xeroxed pages.

Robert Mackle had noticed the tire was missing from the trunk of the Lincoln. What about that?

"That's perfectly obvious," suggested an FBI agent. "Tell him it is a brand new car and you never opened the trunk before. You hadn't, had you?" Robert Mackle agreed that was reasonable.

No one wanted the kidnapers to panic over the used condition of the slightly battered blue suitcase even though the ransom note had not specified that it be new. A detail of FBI agents, scouring and rummaging through luggage stores and wholesalers all over the county, finally came up with another one. It was a flawless light green, a "Socialite," made by U. S. Trunk, $32.75, and the dimensions were within half an inch of what the ransom note had ordered.

An agent found it at the Miami Diamond Center, one of the city's largest jewelers. The salesman, Arthur Koff, knew personally the FBI agent who purchased the suitcase. He attached no significance to the sale. He assumed it was a gift for someone at the office who was either retiring or being tranferred.

"Don't bother to wrap it," the agent said. "I'll take it with me."

Soon it had been delivered to the Mackle residence. The keys were still in an envelope. Billy Vessels scrutinized it closely, flipping it over, opening it up, examining it thoroughly, and he could find absolutely no identifying marks on it. The new green one was obviously superior to the old blue one. On his hands and knees on the red carpet of the den, Vessels switched the money from the blue to the green. Agent Edwin J. Sharp helped him. Lee Kusch, a white-haired veteran agent of twenty-two years, stood by as an overseer. If they turned up $10,000 short, no one could say he touched that money, he noted, grinning, not wanting to handle it. He applied his manual talents to a prime rib of roast beef, proclaiming great dexterity as a carver. It helped the tension. No one ate very much. Again, the twenty-five thousand $20 bills fit perfectly. From its weight, though, the suitcase snapped open. Vessels locked it briefly, then decided against that. "Let's not give him any problems at all," he said. They worked with it until it presented no problems.

Dr. Lauth again gave medication to the ailing. It seemed as if everyone had a cold. "Doc, it's okay if you use Army reject needles, but do you have to use them from World War II?" agent Kusch joshed.

"How do you know it isn't reject serum?" Dr. Lauth shot back.

FBI agents set up telephone-monitoring earphone equipment on a card table in the den near the regular red telephone. The second the phone would ring, an agent would put on the earphones. "My instructions were to let it ring twice, then pick it up on the third ring," said Robert Mackle. "The agent would be listening before I answered.

"We kept going over my instructions. One of the things I was told to do, no matter who called, no matter what, was to keep the party on the line as long as I could," said Robert.

"Tell them that you are brokenhearted," said an agent. "Tell them that you are desperate. Keep talking. Tell them anything to keep them on the line. You are going to get some crank calls, but then the kidnaper is going to call. So the longer you hold him the better chance we have tracing him."

In an age of electronic communication to the moon, the tracing of a hurried telephone call within a major metropolis in December of 1968 was not the simple matter generally assumed by a public that took its telephones for granted and viewed all manner of fictional missions impossible on television.

The Miami office of the Southern Bell Telephone and Telegraph Company had entered the case with the call the day before from Billy Vessels to Gerry Doyle, division security manager. It was Doyle's thirty-eighth birthday and two FBI agents were in his office on another matter when Vessels called. Doyle had served as an FBI agent from 1956 until he joined the telephone company in 1961. Vessels had explained guardedly that Robert Mackle's daughter had been kidnaped and requested that the company tap the telephone. The two agents in Doyle's office knew nothing of the case. Doyle telephoned Fred Fox, assistant agent in charge, wondering if it was legit, as he put it, or if he was being spooked. Fox assured him it was legitimate, and told him that he could have the assistance of the Miami bureau's "sound man," special agent Bill Heist. As no one wanted telephone company trucks rolling around the Mackle neighborhood, Doyle and Heist set up a listening post in a quiet basement room of the MOhawk or the six-six exchange central office building of Southern Bell, situated a mile away across a street from fraternity houses at the University of Miami. Every telephone in the MOhawk exchange fed into the central office and there Doyle and Heist identified a pair of wires for the telephone in the Mackle home. With an external speaker and a Magnetcorder tape recorder, they could record and hear all conversations simultaneously. That was the easy part. The tracing was more involved. Most of the Bell system's equipment was designed so that the calling party controlled the system; that is, the dialer sets off a series of impulses that race electronically toward any given number. Once the phone was answered, the apparatus locked and the technician knowing where to look could figure out in the banks and rows of equipment from where the call was being made—so long as the calling party stayed on the line. Obviously, a kidnaper was not going to stay on the line very long. By means of a little device which looked like a clothespin, a common electronic component known as a diode trap, however, the process could be reversed; that is, so long as the party receiving the call didn't hang up, the technicians at a central office could still discover from where the call was made. This generally worked fine within an exchange, say from one MOhawk number to another MOhawk number. Calls from other exchanges and other trunks made things much more complicated. The little clothespin-styled diode traps were needed for all incoming trunks. In the case of Miami, that meant installing nearly five hundred diode traps at fourteen additional central offices all over Dade County.

That would take manpower—and did. Under the circumstances, though, motivation was no problem and the telephone company assigned in excess of twenty men to the task. Doyle soon realized he had another problem. He didn't have nearly enough diode traps in Miami. (The company executives, conscious of public relations and images, preferred not to use the word "trap" publicly. Publicly and euphemistically, the diode traps were called merely line-identification equipment.)

To get more diode traps, "I cried wolf," said Doyle. The Florida Highway Patrol provided superb delivery services. Troopers picked up the boxes of diode traps from the district offices as far north as Orlando and sped them to the southern tollgate of the Florida Sunshine Turnpike. There telephone company trucks waited for transfer. In the early afternoon of Wednesday, December 18, Doyle learned of Father Mulcahy's call, and the monsignor for the Church of the Little Flower, Peter Reilly, gave him permission to tap that line, too. Doyle made arrangements for men to work around-the-clock in a stand-by tracing capacity at the fourteen other central office buildings in Dade County. Normally the buildings remained unmanned after eight o'clock at night. Tonight they wouldn't. The FBI also wanted the WATS line into the Mackle home converted into an ordinary exchange line with a separate number to enable them to telephone the downtown FBI office and elsewhere if need be. That was no problem.

So night came—eight o'clock, nine o'clock—and Robert Mackle changed into his white clothing. The pants were a little too long. Jane, protected by family and friends, not comprehending fully, was asked to hem up the trousers. She complied. "I wondered why he just couldn't roll them up." The sight of Robert pacing nervously in the game room, garbed in hideous white, struck Dr. Lauth as terrifying, and he turned away and said nothing. FBI agent Kusch sat on the couch dressed exactly the same, conspicuously quiet. "We'll decide about Lee when we get the call," said Inspector Shroder, trying to keep open his options.

Agents John R. Ackerly and Donald R. West waited in the basement of the MOhawk or six-six exchange with two telephone company security men, Doyle and Jack Campbell, and at the Church of the Little Flower, Father Mulcahy sat uneasily before a television in the lobby of the rectory with two other priests, tense and alert in expectation of a second telephone call.

The FBI had instructed him to ask the kidnaper three questions. They were typed out and lying beside the telephone.

"What was Barbara wearing on her feet when she was kidnaped?"

"What is the signal to drop the money?"

"What is the nickname of Barbara's grandmother?"

Father Mulcahy had no idea what the correct responses should be. The kidnapers, of course, should know of their own knowledge that Barbara had left the Rodeway Inn wearing black woolen socks. It was unlikely that any sort of an impostor trying to collect the ransom money would guess that.

The response to the second question would have to come directly from the persons who wrote the ransom note; ". . . When you arrive at the pickup site you will know it by a signal of three short flashes repeated continuously from a flashlight directed at the windshield of your car. When you see the signal you will stop the car and immediately take the suitcase toward the light. The light will be mounted on top of a box. . . ." It was almost inconceivable that anyone unfamiliar with the note could provide that information. The third question, if answered, would establish that Barbara was alive and her kidnapers could communicate with her. It was extremely unlikely that anyone outside the immediate family knew the nickname of Robert's mother, "Garmee." As a baby twenty-eight years before, Elliott Mackle's first son couldn't pronounce "Grandma." It had come out "Garmee," and that's how she was known within the family. No one else called her Garmee.

Very few of the one hundred and fifty agents assigned to the Miami FBI office slept the night of December 18–19. In anticipation of any possible need, they were assigned patrol districts and in unmarked radio cars they were scattered throughout the metropolitan Miami area. If Robert Mackle had but a single minute to leave the house after the kidnaper called, it might be much too late to dispatch cars to any particular location from the central FBI headquarters at 3801 Biscayne Boulevard. Put them out ahead of time. It was as simple as that. The FBI wanted to keep the Lincoln under surveillance, a highly discreet surveillance, to be sure, in the initial stages of the dropoff, and be able to assist from close quarters if necessary. Miami, unlike so many older compact American cities, sprawled out all over creation, and the sheer fact of geography made the problem formidable. All agents received very explicit instructions: Do not intervene. Do not interfere.

Under no circumstances, unless their orders were countermanded by unforeseen emergency, were they to get close enough to arouse any suspicion whatsoever. If that meant staying out of residential neighborhoods, stay out. The FBI cars would have to remain on the primary thoroughfares where cars would normally appear late at night. Nowhere else. There would be no attempt to arrest anyone. Again, the orders were specific: Allow the kidnapers to pick up the suitcase and allow them to leave unhindered.

All agents, of course, were expected to describe and take license numbers of all vehicles in the vicinity of the pickup site, once it was known; but again, they were to do so surreptitiously, inconspicuously. Don't get caught. Don't get burned. The life of a girl is at stake.

The FBI had already taken one precaution to make sure its agents didn't appear suspicious. Late in the afternoon some FBI secretaries and the girls in the steno pool were told they would be needed Wednesday night. When the agents took up their surveillance throughout the city late that night, most were accompanied by decoy dates.

Other police agencies in the metropolitan area, the Miami Police Department, which patrolled the city, and the Dade County Department of Public Safety, which retained jurisdiction in the unincorporated areas of the county, as well as the smaller police forces of twenty-five other municipalities, were not notified specifically. It would have meant notifying approximately four hundred men in no way connected to the crime. The chance of public dissemination would increase markedly. Additional police were not wanted nor needed. To attempt to notify other police agencies once the drop site was known also seemed to be an unnecessary risk. The payoff operation would already be in progress.

In the den and game room of the Mackle residence, Inspector Shroder and Billy Vessels read over again for perhaps the thirtieth time the instructions: "Sir, your daughter has been kidnapped . . . We have tied into several of the possible means of communications that you have with the police and we feel that you will be unable to contact them without our knowledge . . ."

Bravado? Boast? Bluster? Or were the kidnapers listening to police radio calls? It would be a simple matter to install a shortwave radio in a car and monitor the standard police radio frequencies.

Frank and Bobby Mackle both asked the same questions: Couldn't the kidnapers pick up the transmission from the microphone hidden in the air-conditioning vent of the Lincoln? Couldn't they monitor the FBI's short-wave frequency?

"No," said Inspector Shroder. "Not even the Russians can break this frequency."

"Not even the Mafia," deadpanned agent Kusch.

Billy Vessels believed the kidnaping had to be committed by a genius, and he thought of what he had read years ago about the Loeb-Leopold case, a crime committed eight years before he was born. Richard A. Loeb and Nathan F. Leopold, Jr., both sons of millionaires, both brilliant teen-age youths professing a belief in the superman philosophy of Nietzsche, had cold-bloodedly murdered a fourteen-year-old boy, Robert Franks, in Chicago in 1924, and devised an elaborate scheme to make the victim's unknowing father drop the ransom money from a passing train. But before the drop, their plan went askew. A workman found the boy's body in a culvert. To Billy Vessels, still rereading the ransom note, the kidnapers had to be led by some sort of demented genius. ". . . Contemplate, if you will, the position into which this puts you. . . ."

"You know, Billy," said Inspector Shroder, "this is a petty crook."

Vessels would never forget the remark. "My mind was working 180 degrees in the opposite direction."

The ransom note had declared, ". . . we will call you at your home after midnight to advise you of where you must go to deliver the money . . ." and everyone was keyed to the hour of twelve. The call would come at midnight. "It became sort of a bewitching hour," said Vessels.

At 11:30 P.M. the congregation in the den and game room—the three Mackle brothers, Bobby, Billy Vessels and Dr. Lauth, and six FBI agents, a dozen men in all, realized that Jane Mackle was in the kitchen. She knew only the amount of money. No one had told her about the drop or the call expected in thirty minutes.

"I was just cleaning up, putting the roast beef in the refrigerator, and I guess I startled them."

"What are you doing here?" someone asked.

"I told them things had to be straightened up. And Ed, I guess, got rid of me. He ushered me out and he gave me another shot in my arm." For the second straight night she would lie in a Demerol-and-Sparine-induced sleep, fully clothed on her bed upstairs, a blanket carefully tucked around her shoulders.

The windup eight-day clock over the red telephone in the den showed twenty, fifteen, ten minutes until midnight, and everything was ready. Bobby would take the suitcase and go out through the sliding glass doors on the poolside to the garage and put it on the back seat of the Lincoln. An agent would roll up the sliding overhead door. Road maps were out. They would pinpoint the site for Robert before he left. If indeed Robert made the delivery. Agent Lee Kusch, his white golf cap now on, stood waiting, aware that Robert had announced flatly that he was going himself. Agent Coutre appeared depressed. He would not go in the trunk with a shotgun. That much was definite. The black minute hand moved upward and everyone kept glancing at his own watch. Five minutes until midnight, four. The short-wave-radio speaker in the game room fell silent. Everyone was ready. FBI cars had situated themselves strategically throughout the county. There was no need to say anything.

"It was like *High Noon* waiting for the damn telephone," said Vessels. "We were rendered completely helpless. The only thing we could do was wait. We were at their mercy, their command, and we had to wait and react to their demand."

"I still didn't know if Dad was going or not," said Bobby. "Dad was scared to death and so was I. I was terribly worried about him. He was shaking."

"I'm going to get lost for sure," said Robert Mackle.

The black minute hand crept upward across the hour hand and then pointed upward as one. It was midnight.

I've Bungled It

In the den of the Robert Mackle home, December 19, the red telephone—the instrument of contact, command and survival—remained silent and unused.

"Billy," said Robert Mackle quietly, "I know they've killed her."

Fearful of the terrible burden of delivery thrust upon him, Robert Mackle feared far more that the kidnapers would fail to call and that neither he nor the FBI would be able to do anything. He was determined to obey explicitly the instructions of the ransom note—if he was afforded the opportunity, if the telephone ever rang. He would do everything humanly possible to comply.

The minutes lengthened. Frank Mackle reread the ransom note, scrutinizing it again. ". . . we will call you at your home after midnight to advise you . . ."

"*After!*" he repeated. They didn't say how long after. After could mean one o'clock, two, three, anytime. It was anyone's guess. His mind, as others, had fixed on the single word midnight and the crescendo of anxiety had been a false one.

"I expected the call within five minutes after twelve o'clock," said Robert Mackle. "We had all read the thing. I thought it said shortly after midnight. Or immediately after midnight. It did not, of course, say that, and after we realized it, we felt a little better. It was left completely open." Suddenly, the telephone rang.

Inspector Shroder slipped on the headset earphones. Robert Mackle, his hand trembling, grasped the receiver. He let it ring once, twice, and as it started to ring a third time, he picked it up and answered.

It was a long-distance operator with a collect call from Hot Springs, Arkansas. Would he accept the charges?

"Yes."

"I know where your daughter is," a man began.

"I was pretty shaken," said Robert Mackle, and he began to tell the man of his desperation, his willingness to do anything to get his daughter back.

"I don't want your money," the man said, and his voice had a put-on quality, a cockiness about it. "I don't want your money," and he rambled on somewhat incoherently.

"I could see Rex writing on a prompt card for me," said Robert. The inspector wrote a singe word, "Dope." Shroder suspected the caller might be a drug addict. He wondered also if he might be an alcoholic.

"He kept saying he didn't want money," said Robert Mackle, "and I said, 'If it is medical assistance you need, if it is a political position, anything you need.'

"I told him I was a brave father, I'd do anything if he would just return my daughter. There must be a spark of good in you or else you wouldn't have made this call."

"I'm tough," he said. "Don't talk to me about being good. I'm tough."

The conversation ended inconclusively. The party hung up. As instructed, Robert left open the receiver momentarily. Frank had his hand over the cradle of the telephone so his brother couldn't hang up. But the elaborate system for tracing had been engineered for calls within Dade County, not Arkansas, and Gerry Doyle, the telephone company security chief who listened and taped the conversation in the basement of the MOhawk center building a mile away, had already had the chief operators trying to trace the call more conventionally by toll ticket. It seemed unlikely that the caller was the true kidnaper. The manner differed radically from the previous calls to the home the morning of the crime and the call to the priest. Yet who knew for certain? He might be involved.

He might know something. He might be a part of a group. The FBI went to work immediately to find him and put him under surveillance.

"About fifteen minutes later he called again," said Robert Mackle, "and he told me, 'I guess you kind of touched me. I guess there is some good in me. Oh, I'm a tough guy.'

"And he told me my daughter would be coming home on a Delta flight arriving in Miami at five fifty-three tomorrow afternoon. He said she would leave Memphis and would be interchanged at Atlanta. But this was going to cost money. He said he didn't want to put up his own money."

Somewhat abusive and threatening, he demanded a "couple of hundred for expenses." Robert Mackle thought he meant a couple of hundred thousand dollars.

"Hell, no," said the caller. "It'll probably cost me $500."

"I'll give you the $500," said Robert Mackle.

There was a long dissertation about payment of the money; how it should be made; how the office in Coral Gables was closed because it was late at night. "And he told me to put it in cash and wire it. He gave me his name as Robert J. Ward," said Robert Mackle. "I told him I would." Deliberately and coolly, he dragged out the conversation.

At the MOhawk exchange building Doyle had operators trace the call. While Robert Mackle kept the man on the line, the FBI learned the call was coming from a pay booth inside a small bar named the Bowler's Lounge, on Third Street, the main drag in the mountain town of Hot Springs. Three FBI agents, summoned abruptly from a Christmas party, drove immediately to the lounge. The caller had left. Agents quietly ascertained that a man in his twenties named Ward, Henry Lee Ward, not Robert, had been drinking beer there during the afternoon and evening, and had made two long-distance telephone calls. He had told the barmaid he expected to come into a lot of money very shortly. He didn't say how. Ward, not a bad-looking young man who had been in trouble with the law for car theft, worked as a kitchen helper in a restaurant. He had driven home that night to his grandmother's house. All night the three agents waited outside Grandma's house, keeping it under surveillance.

About nine o'clock the next morning Ward would drive an old dilapidated Dodge around town in the vicinity of the Western

Union office. There would be one dollar there waiting for him from Robert Mackle. Ward never collected. Agents, convinced he was in no way connected to the actual kidnapers, took him into custody, and eventually, on July 29, 1969, after pleading guilty, a U. S. District Court judge sentenced him to five years' imprisonment for having, in the language of the law, "transmitted, in interstate commerce from Hot Springs, Arkansas, to Coral Gables, Florida, by means of telephonic communication, a message containing a request and demand for ransom and reward for the release of Barbara Mackle who had been kidnaped and who then was being held for ransom, in violation of Title 18, United States Code 875."

There was another call that night, and again the tension mounted instantly at the ring, and this time it was a man from Long Island who identified himself and announced that he knew who had Barbara Mackle. Jabbering away, it was soon apparent the man was not stable. Inspector Shroder scrawled on a prompt card the word, "Crank."

"I know who has got your daughter," the caller said.

"Will you please tell me?"

"Well, you ought to know."

"The police?" ventured Robert Mackle.

"Yeah. And they kidnaped me for a year."

"Well," said Robert, wanting to get the man off the line. "That's all right. The FBI is on this case."

"The FBI!" he exclaimed. "You don't know what you are doing. The FBI kidnaped my mother and father in 1926 and I haven't seen them since."

"Everyone laughed," said Frank Mackle. "Under the circumstances, it was like laughing at a wake."

Robert Mackle, a man deeply protective of his children, by any normal standards, a respected and successful businessman, a man accustomed to an orderly and regulated life of work and rest, quick to laugh, content, would later try to analyze his feelings, and he would grope for words.

"This horrible fear. This horrible longing. It is such a constant thing. You know Barbara is some place. You don't know where she is. You don't know whether she is alive. Whether she has been harmed. Whether she is out of her mind. And all these things go through your mind. And constantly. Even when people are talking to you, they go through your mind. They are always there. They are with you constantly. And there isn't any way to explain. No way. My daughter, my whole family, are so close. And you just can't visualize or comprehend the agony. There is just no way I can describe it. There is no way it can be described. The only thing I can say is the loneliness. It is you and your thoughts. You know everything is being done that can be done. This is a consolation but it doesn't touch what I am trying to say. It doesn't touch the hours of walking and looking and staring out the window and seeing nothing. Or trying to sit down. Or trying to come to grips with things. They just tear you up inside. There isn't any mental torture like this. I can't conceive of any torture like it because of all the unknowns. There are many, many tragedies. Automobile accidents, sudden deaths, things of this nature where you know there is a person in a hospital and he is critically ill or dying or dead. You know these things. It doesn't take away the anguish, but you know. You know everything is being done. But here you had no known quantities whatsoever. You know that you are able to pay and that you have the money and that you are willing to pay and this doesn't help at all. You ache. You hurt. You feel it in your heart and mind. I couldn't honestly believe that Barbara was dead. I felt that some way we would get Barbara back. I was worried about her mental condition. I was worried about her physical condition, both from the point of being molested and from the point of her illness when she was taken. Those things, the flu, illness, can become desperate so quickly. If I could just get to her. But where was she? Is she cold? Is she feverish? Is she out of her mind? Does she have any water? It is just all the horrors you can imagine. This is probably the worst thing anyone ever goes through.

"The closest thing to come to it—and I've thought about it a long time—would be a mother who receives a telegram that her son is missing in action. I think this is the closest thing. That, of course, is under war conditions and a lot of other conditions. The plane was shot down. It was over enemy territory at the time. There was a parachute or there wasn't a parachute. There are certain basic things you know. Then you are hoping against hope that someone is alive or is a prisoner of war. And that would be terrible, but this, this is much, much worse. We knew one thing. We knew a man with a gun took Barbara. My wife had seen the hemline of her nightgown as he took her out the door. That was the only thing we had positively. And there is no way of describing what you go through."

"Every time the telephone rang it was a traumatic experience," said Billy Vessels. "We had all prefixed on midnight—or four or five minutes after midnight—and we all thought this is going to happen. And when it didn't happen there was a great letdown.

"Later on we tried to laugh a little bit. It was pretty hollow. Frank is on the board at Notre Dame and they were kidding me because Frank and I had gone to the Oklahoma game together at South Bend that season and Notre Dame won forty-five to twenty-one, something like that. We were all so tight and wound up. Nobody could stretch and go to sleep."

The trivial conversation surfaced in eddies, calmed, died, as the hours crept, and the twelve men in the Mackle home waited and waited impatiently, restlessly. At 3:47 A.M. the telephone rang.

Inspector Shroder quickly slipped on the headset again. On the third ring, Robert Mackle picked it up.

"Hello?"

"Robert Mackle?"

Robert Mackle knew instantly he was talking to the kidnaper. The voice struck him as cold as hell. There were no formalities.

"Yes," he said.

"You will proceed down Bird Road to Twenty-seventh Avenue. Take a right on Twenty-seventh Avenue."

"Just a minute. How do I know who I'm talking to?" Robert Mackle could see the prompt card Inspector Shroder held. "Identify," it said.

Inspector Shroder had realized Robert Mackle would be under tremendous emotional pressure during the telephone conversation. He had told him he would hold up prompt cards just as an off-camera assistant would on a television show.

"You know it," spat the kidnaper, ignoring the question. "Now . . ."

"How do I know Barbara is well?"

"You don't, but you'll have to take the chance. Now . . ."

"Twenty-seventh Avenue?" Robert Mackle asked.

"And you'll go to Fair Isle Street."

"Fair Isle Street?"

"Fair Isle. You know where it is?" the kidnaper asked.

"No."

"It's on the right off Bay Road."

"Right off Bay?"

"And you go the . . . as far as you can up Fair Isle Street to the right toward the bay, and you'll come to a wall. If you look down the causeway, the bridge, over the wall, you'll see a blinking white light. You'll put the money in the box, which will have a light on it, gently, and close the lid, and you'll turn around and leave. Is that clear?"

"Yes," said Robert Mackle nervously. It wasn't clear at all. Bay Road? Did the kidnaper mean South Bayshore Drive? He was thinking of his daughter.

"Is Barbara all right?"

"She certainly is."

"Would you . . . would you do something for me? I'm a broken father, believe me, I've done everything that you . . . you could ask. Would you release her completely?"

"We will release her. Don't worry."

"And I go down which way on Twenty-seventh Avenue, south, or . . ."

"You take a right."

"A right on Twenty-seventh," Robert Mackle said. "Okay."

Again, it wasn't clear at all. The kidnaper meant for Robert Mackle to make a right turn off U. S. 1 onto Twenty-seventh Avenue. If Robert Mackle was to find Fair Isle Street once he was on Southwest Twenty-seventh Avenue, he would have to make a left turn at South Bayshore Drive, not a right.

"And down Fair Isle?" Robert Mackle asked.

"That's right, okay."

"Till I run into a dead-end street. I'm trying not to . . . I'm trying to get it . . . to a dead-end street."

"You've got it now, that's right."

"And I'll run into a . . ."

"You'll run into a wall at the end of a bridge."

"All right, fine, I'll do everything you say."

The instructions were not good. They could be understood only if studied carefully with a map. They were easily misinterpreted.

"We had the various maps," said Robert. "The maps weren't very good. They were road maps, and I was thinking Bay Road.

I had never heard of a Bay Road. He was trying to say South
Bayshore Drive. Bayshore Drive, I know. Bay Road could be anywhere."

"We were trying to find Fair Island on the map. It was damn
difficult to find on a miserable small-scale map," said Frank Mackle.
As land developers, the Mackles were accustomed to working with
big oversized maps. "We were trying to outline the street to Fair
Island with a heavy pencil."

For a frantic and hectic moment, Robert Mackle tried to study
the map. "Oh, there it is," he said, as someone pointed. He hurried
toward the back door. It was just that fast.

"Now whatever you do, don't touch the antenna!" an FBI man
said.

There was no doubt about agent Kusch. He would stay. No
one would go in the trunk either. This wasn't the way the FBI
wanted it but it was the way Robert Mackle wanted it.

"Whatever you do, don't let anyone stop you," Billy Vessels said.
"Everything is going to be fine."

Vessels was worried that someone not connected with the kidnapers would try to rob him during the ransom drop. With all the
publicity, any reasonably astute thief might well decide to follow
anyone leaving the Mackle home in the middle of the night. The
FBI had considered the same possibility.

They would watch Robert as closely as they could without interfering with the drop. "Don't let anyone stop you and everything
will be all right," Vessels repeated, patting Robert on the shoulder.

"I picked up this suitcase and carried it out the sliding glass
door on the poolside and took it into the garage," said Bobby.
He put the green suitcase on the back seat.

"Good luck, Dad," he said. Vessels had rolled up the overhanging
garage doors. Robert Mackle inserted the key from a brown leather
key case, turned the ignition, shifted to reverse, and backed out the
Lincoln Continental on to San Amaro Drive. The car had little more
than two thousand miles on the odometer. The only distinguishing
mark was a Tropical Park "Turf Owner" sticker on the lower left
front of the windshield. Vessels stood in the driveway a minute
watching as the Lincoln moved to Bird Road, then turned right. In
thirty or forty seconds, he saw a blue-and-white Cadillac moving
on Bird Road in the same direction. He hurried into the house to
tell Inspector Shroder.

Alone in the Lincoln, the concealed microphone picking up his conversation, Robert Mackle kept reporting his location. The Granada Presbyterian Church on the left, the Coral Gables High School on the right at LeJeune Road. In his rear view mirror, he saw the headlights behind five or six blocks. He reported that too. He need not have. Agent Wayne Swinney and Fred Frohbose, agent in charge of the Miami office, were in the Cadillac behind him. They were so far back they weren't certain they were following the Lincoln taillights until they heard by radio Robert Mackle reading off the street locations. They didn't want to get too close.

The FBI had twenty or so cars cruising specific sections of Dade County and because the agents wanted to have their gas tanks filled at all times, they had kept pulling into service stations throughout the night and buying a gallon or two or a dollar's worth at a time. When the run began for the drop, the FBI ordered six cars to take up positions and keep crisscrossing in the general vicinity of the site, but a mile to two miles away. No one, except agents Swinney and Frohbose, was to be allowed east of South Dixie Highway, which was U. S. Route 1, well lit and fairly well traveled even at four o'clock in the morning. A neighborhood of darkened homes ten blocks thick shielded Fair Isle from U. S. 1. Other agents established a second outer ring of cars much farther back in the expectation that Robert Mackle would be directed elsewhere, perhaps upstate to Jacksonville, Ocala, or some place closer to Atlanta. There was as little radio conversation as possible. At the bureau's radio desk on the second floor of its downtown headquarters, agent Pruit Klinkscales remained silent. Inspector Shroder called signals from the game room of the residence even though the headquarters equipment was far more powerful. As all cars could hear Mackle himself, there was very little reason for anyone else to say anything.

"We were following Robert on the maps, street by street, as he called them off," said Vessels, then in the game room.

It was some moments after Robert left that Frank Mackle realized suddenly how close Fair Isle was to Everglades School for Girls. Barbara had attended the school. Robert had delivered her there a hundred times. Although the school was on the west side of South Bayshore Drive, it was only two blocks from the turnoff at Fair Isle Street. The information would give him his bearings. The inspector ordered a car to intercept Robert and tell him, then quickly he reconsidered. Robert was getting too close. There might not be time. If the kidnapers detected any sort of surveillance, they might run. He canceled the order.

"No one thought to relate it to Everglades School at first," said Frank. "The map didn't show the school. And, initially, the conjecture had been that the first place Robert would go would not be the final place. Gradually it became rather obvious, particularly after Robert left, that Fair Isle was the place." There, he surmised, Robert probably would see the flashing light on his windshield and the light mounted on a box on the causeway. It would be isolated enough. There were no telephones around. No one would be in the vicinity at that hour of the morning. Certainly the kidnapers would be able to see a car approaching. Inspector Shroder, unfamiliar with the geography because he was from Washington, relied on the judgments of the local agents, St. Pierre and Kusch, and they were in agreement. This looked like it would be it.

On the map, Fair Isle appeared as an elongated, perfectly rounded white oval on a chorographic blue of Biscayne Bay. It was at the very edge of the mainland, connected by a private causeway. Directly to the north about a half mile was Mercy Hospital, a three-hundred-bed institution set back several hundred yards from the street traffic. To the south on the mainland lay the Coral Reef Yacht Club, the Biscayne Bay Yacht Club, an abandoned United States Coast Guard Air Station where two-engine Albatrosses used to waddle dripping wet out of the bay onto concrete ramps, and finally, a little more than a mile from Fair Isle, Dinner Key. The city of Miami had an office complex on Dinner Key and there was a marina near there and three hundred and seventy private boats docked to five piers.

Fair Isle lay three and three quarter miles due east of the Mackle home in Coral Gables, and the kidnaper's instructions, which reflected the most logical street approach by car, measured just under five miles.

Although only ten minutes from downtown Miami, Fair Isle had stubbornly defied progress and development for more than forty years. It was born from a sandspit and pumped-up bay bottom in the early 1920s when its owner, Louis Kloeber, wanted to turn its twenty acres, four and a half feet above sea level, into a plush housing development similar to other residential islands between

Miami and Miami Beach. But a hurricane in 1926 wrecked his dream, destroying bulkheads made from old railroad ties. Two Miami financiers, Harold Landfield and Joseph Weintraub, owned it for more than twenty years. They constructed an 800-foot two-lane concrete causeway across the bay from Miami at a cost of $250,000 in 1960. The causeway pitched upward several feet in elevation and curved northward from the mainland so that someone on foot in the center of the causeway could not be seen from the Miami side. The financiers had won zoning approval for high-rise apartments but the land, priced high and covered with Australian pines and sea grapes, remained uninhabited. It proved to be a mecca for boaters, fishermen, picnickers and assorted vagrants who left it littered with beer cans.

Paul Lynch, an attorney with money who managed his own investments, lived at the northern edge of the Miami entrance to the causeway. His property was walled off—as was an old two-story home at the southern edge of the causeway. Attorney Lynch had little use for the nocturnal riffraff, as he put it, which used the street between the two homes that led to the causeway. He had two dogs, a big black shaggy and frisky cur and a cairn terrier, known as Eartha Kitt. Eartha Kitt was a good barker.

Until 1966 only a wire fence kept motorists from driving onto the causeway and sometimes vandals tore it down. On the Fair Isle side, the causeway ended abruptly five feet above the sandy shore, and several vehicles, including a police car one night, hung their front wheels over the edge. In the year before, the new owners had built a forty-two-inch wall eight inches thick at the entrance so that Fair Isle Street dead-ended between the two homes.

The Lynches referred to it as "the alley" and it looked like one.

Landfield and Weintraub, the two financiers who owned Fair Isle, had once made an overture to the Mackles for sale of the island. Someone from the Mackle company had looked it over. It was fine property, but nothing that coincided with their interests. Robert Mackle had never seen the property.

As he drove toward Fair Isle from Bird Road, he took U. S. Route 1 northward to Southwest Twenty-seventh Avenue and turned right, the blinking ping-ping-ping turn signal so loud on the dashboard that the radio transmitter broadcast the sound to the game room as the plucking of the string of a banjo. To his right he could see a Royal Castle, an all-night hamburger emporium, and he knew he was a block off a well-lit boating supply yard of a firm which professed not to live up to its name, Crook and Crook. At an avenue named Tigertail in the Coconut Grove section of Miami, he slowed as a red light turned green, and he kept driving straight until he intersected with South Bayshore Drive at Dinner Key. He was a mile too far south and he didn't know exactly where the bridge to Fair Isle was. He turned right. It was the wrong way. At Dinner Key he saw a couple of fishermen ready to board a boat. He stopped the Lincoln, leaving the engine running, and hurried over.

"Is there a bridge over to an island around here?" he asked.

"Oh, yeah," said one of the fishermen. "But you can't get to it from this side, you have to go over this way," and he pointed south. He sounded as if he knew what he was talking about. He did not. He was pointing in the wrong direction.

Robert Mackle, already under severe pressure, tried to follow the fisherman's directions.

"So I started off in absolutely the wrong direction. I was going into Coconut Grove and I knew that just couldn't be right. It had to be the other way. So I turned around and came back." Robert Mackle knew there were four other islands just off the mainland, all smaller than Fair Isle and all uninhabited, but he couldn't see them in the darkness and he couldn't identify them, and he certainly couldn't see a bridge anywhere. There was only one bridge. Of that he was certain. Fair Isle had to be farther north.

As he drove back on South Bayshore Drive, acutely aware of the passing time, streets intersected from the bayside to his right, and along those streets he could see the darkened homes, some built in the Florida boom of the 1920s. A block or two to his right, bulkheads ran along the water's edge. He kept trying to read the white lettering of the green street signs, Crystal View Court, Vista Court, Ah-We-Wa Street, and at Crystal Court he swung to the right. It just had to be about there.

"There wasn't any bridge there and I couldn't see any flashing light. I drove another block north and looked again."

Here the beams of his headlights caught a low white retaining wall, an abutment blocking the street. He saw no bridge. He didn't see a street sign. Hurriedly, he drove westward to South Bayshore Drive again.

A block farther north he came back again to a pier this time, and suddenly, his heart pounding, he realized his tires were off the pavement into sand. Sand sparkled in the headlight beams. "That really panicked me. I just couldn't believe I would get stuck."

He reversed and his tires touched pavement again and he knew he would get out, but where was the bridge? Where was it? Where? Where? He didn't know where else to look. The time was running out.

He could read a street sign for East Fairview Street and on the next block West Fairview Street. But neither led to a bridge to Fair Isle. He groped in a labyrinth of blackened streets on a black night.

"I can't find this place!" he cried, his voice cracking. "Look," he said, grasping for control, "I'm going back south to South Bayshore Drive."

He turned south again and driving much slower than the posted 40-mile-an-hour speed limit, he strained to see the Fair Isle Street sign, the round concrete curb markers unseen, the bus benches unseen, "Monkey Jungle 22 Miles South," "Tan Dark as Can Be with Sea and Ski." He kept identifying his position so his listeners would know where he was, the Coral Reef Yacht Club, Merrill-Stevens Dry Dock Company, Waverly Arms Apartments.

He returned to the marina at Dinner Key. He knew that a bait-and-tackle shop remained open practically all night. As he pulled up, he saw a man with keys in his hands. Robert Mackle stopped and jumped from the car. In the Mackle game room the radio went silent.

"I'm looking for a bridge across to one of these islands," Robert Mackle said. "Do you know of any island other than Fair Island which has a bridge?"

"No, sir. Ain't but one island around here that's got a bridge to it."

"Are you sure?"

"Yes. It's up that way," and he pointed northward exactly where Robert Mackle had searched in futility moments before.

Frantically, he climbed back into the Lincoln, the undelivered suitcase still on the back seat, the kidnaper's threat reverberating through his brain. Time had run out. The time limit was gone. The kidnapers would run.

With the windows up, Robert Mackle cried aloud into the concealed microphone. "I need help," he cried.

"I'm desperate. I can't find this place. I can't find it! Somebody has got to come help me. I don't know what I'm looking for. I need help!"

In the game room of the Mackle home, Elliott, Frank, Bobby, Inspector Shroder and the agents, and Billy Vessels suffered almost the same feeling of desperation. They had followed him on the maps. They knew how close he had been. He had to have been right there. He had to.

They had already discussed the possibility of an agent intercepting the Lincoln. But Robert wouldn't know the agent. Maybe Vessels could intercept. If the kidnapers actually knew what Robert Mackle looked like, they might recognize Vessels, too. Inspector Shroder knew he had to make a decision immediately. Or should he just let Robert try again?

"I'm lost. I need help! Somebody has got to help me!" His plea crackled in strained distortion from the speaker.

Suddenly, Billy Vessels could take no more. "Let's go!" he said, and he grabbed agent Edward J. Putz. Wordlessly, Elliott Mackle gave Billy the keys to his car. It was a red 1968 Cadillac, parked in the driveway close to the street. Vessels and Putz ran out the front door, oblivious to anyone who might be watching, and seconds later the Cadillac screeched into motion. Vessels accelerated and the car raced down deserted Bird Road at 70, 80, 90 miles an hour, then slowing slightly, tires again screeching, he veered northward on U. S. 1. Vessels was going so fast he was afraid he would miss the turn at Southwest Twenty-seventh Avenue. He was running red lights.

He also was blaming himself. "God damn it! We should never have let him go by himself. I knew better."

The Cadillac screamed through the night. It would take them at least three to five minutes to find him. There was no FBI radio equipment in Elliott's Cadillac. Vessels and agent Putz were not in contact with either Robert or Inspector Shroder and the cordon of FBI cars, lying back, waiting.

The agents in the cars had heard everything, Robert Mackle crying for help, and they fought to keep their own emotions under control. One young agent, Warren R. Welsh, knew the neighborhood extremely well. He had once lived within four blocks of the drop site. And a few minutes before, he was told he should drive north on South Bayshore Drive. A secretary from the office, Jackie Marks, sat in the passenger seat, playing the role of his date.

As agent Welsh reached Bayshore another car came toward him. It wasn't the Lincoln. He saw a man driving and a woman in the front seat. He recognized it as a Ford or Mercury and suddenly he saw the front license plate. It was from Massachusetts. He knew that a man and woman driving a Volkswagen station wagon with a Massachusetts plate had asked about Barbara Mackle on the Emory campus just before the kidnaping. He was positive the car was from Massachusetts. He caught part of the tag.

Agent Welsh broke his radio silence. Someone had to verify that number. It could be crucial. At the same time he knew he couldn't turn around. That would be too obvious.

Agent Ralph Hill, an old hand in the bureau and one of Miami's most reliable men, drove into the area from farther south and he spotted a black Ford. The driver seemed as if he was looking for something. As agent Hill approached, the Ford slowed and made a U-turn. Without changing his speed, agent Hill caught the full license number.

"We thought for certain the Ford was following Dad," said Bobby, listening in the game room. And we knew Daddy couldn't make the payoff. We thought at first Billy was the only shot. Billy had to get Dad in order that we could even make the delivery. Then, when the Ford showed up, the FBI knew they had to stop Billy.

"It was at this point they gave instructions to intercept Billy. Stop him. If they couldn't intercept, ram him. Ram him." Young Robert Mackle envisioned a catastrophic pile-up of speeding cars. "I thought there would be a hell of a wreck."

The telephone line in the game room was open to FBI headquarters downtown and some of Inspector Shroder's commands would be repeated from the more powerful equipment with a few seconds lag. He wasn't positive he could be heard broadcasting directly.

"And this Massachusetts car just dropped off," said Bobby, "and they quickly countermanded the order. They gave the orders to let the Cadillac get through." Robert Mackle, his panic now controlled in the desperate loneliness of his car, knew nothing of the Ford. He never saw it. "I'm going north as far as Mercy Hospital," he said, "and I'm going to turn around and I'm going to take every little street. But I still need help. I don't think there is anything down there."

In the Cadillac, Vessels and agent Putz raced northward along South Bayshore Drive and they realized they were near the intersection of Fair Isle Street. Vessels slowed down. The street lights were a block apart. "I was stopping and looking at every street sign and trying to find Robert."

One sign was missing. Vessels thought it must be Southwest Seventeenth Avenue. He and Putz had stared at that map at the house so long they knew the correct order. As they slowed again, they saw a double street sign, "Fair Isle St." "S. Bayshore La." Lane! Lane! Not Drive, not the main thoroughfare. Was this the Bay Road the kidnaper meant?

In the distance, perhaps three or four blocks away, Vessels saw headlights and recognized the Lincoln coming north. So he sped south and he stuck out his hand, waving frantically, trying to stop him. And Robert Mackle didn't see him at all. He was exploring the side streets, one by one.

"I wasn't thinking about being seen by the kidnapers. That never crossed my mind. I had to get to him. And then we saw him again about six blocks north," said Vessels.

Straddling the white center line, Vessels raced straight toward him and slammed on the brakes and stopped in the path of the Lincoln, pinning Robert's tires to a six-inch curb at Halissee Street, almost upon the iron water spigots in someone's front lawn. Vessels leaped from the Cadillac, wordlessly abandoning it to agent Putz, and threw himself into the back seat of the Lincoln.

"Get going!"

"Billy. I can't find it! I've bungled it."

"Turn here," Vessels commanded, and they were on West Fairview Street, and then, turning right again they were on Fairhaven Place. All the damn names sounded alike.

From crouching on the back floor, Vessels could see as they drove the outline of tall palms, a three-story apartment building, the old boom homes, an inlet, sailboats stiff and still, and my God, where was it? "This is not it." He told Robert to drive around the block and this time he saw again the double sign.

"This is it! Right here!"

The Lincoln pointed east on Fair Isle Street. He drove straight, ignoring the Fairhaven Place intersection from the left and crossing South Bayshore Lane. The street seemingly narrowed between two homes and dead-ended into a low retaining wall. Even in the glare of the headlights, it was impossible to see a bridge or causeway beyond—or anywhere.

Robert stopped the Lincoln perhaps thirty to forty feet from the wall. High walls from the two homes on both sides left the car in a chute more or less. It would be impossible to turn around. He would have to back out.

"Billy," cried Robert Mackle. "I've already been here."

"This is it. Take the damn thing! Just get rid of it," Vessels whispered, and he flung himself to the floor. Robert reached over into the back seat and grasped the handle of the suitcase and yanked. A half million dollars bounced heavily off Vessels' head. Robert pulled it into the front seat.

He left the front door open purposely. He wanted the inside light to be on so anyone looking could see he was by himself.

Vessels flattened himself on the floor mat, and he was frightened. He thought of his two sons. He thought how easy it would be for someone to walk to the car window and fire a gun. He had never felt so helpless in his life.

"I kept listening for something. I couldn't hear anything. I heard Robert leave and then nothing."

"I walked up to the wall and couldn't see any flashing lights anywhere. I couldn't see a bridge. I couldn't tell if there was water on the other side or not. I lifted the suitcase and gingerly let it down as easily as I could until I felt it rest on something solid. I knew it was firm. Everything was pitch black."

As his eyes adjusted, he detected a difference between the blackness of the water and the faintly lighter black surface where he put the suitcase.

"That's all I could see. I looked for the box and I couldn't find it. Then I saw something metal over to the right. It looked like a metal cylinder and it immediately flashed in my mind that it was scuba diving gear. I caught a reflection of something metal, I know. The stars were out. It could have been a metal pipe."

For a second he stood there, then he pivoted and walked hurriedly back to the Lincoln.

Vessels didn't hear him coming. Abruptly, the door slammed.

"Billy, there wasn't a light. I didn't see anything."

"Let's go!"

Robert Mackle backed out the Lincoln. The time was somewhere between 4:30 and 4:35 A.M. The kidnaper had called nearly an hour ago.

Vessels waited several blocks until he sat up. "All the way home Robert was belittling himself. He was pretty hard on himself," he would remember.

"It is not your fault, damn it. It's their fault," said Vessels, and the anger within him rose.

At a red light he leaned over the front seat and said, "Why don't you let me drive?"

"No. I'm all right."

Agent Edward J. Putz, who had raced to the site with Vessels in Elliott's red Cadillac, had hurriedly returned the car to the home. In the game room the waiting group, monitoring the FBI radio, knew that Billy had found Robert. They assumed that the money had been delivered. They should be back soon.

At 4:41 A.M. the red telephone in the den rang again. Agent St. Pierre quickly put on the headset and Frank Mackle answered on the third ring.

"Hello," said Frank Mackle.

"Mackle?"

"Yes."

"You missed. How come?"

"What do you mean I missed? My brother went with the money."

"Pardon me?"

"My brother went with the money."

"He did?"

"Yes."

"Did he go to Fair Isle Street?"

"Well, that's where he . . . that's where he thought he was going. We looked on the map real . . ." He didn't finish the sentence.

"There's an island, and there's a causeway out," the kidnaper interrupted.

"Yes, yes, I know, but we were looking on the map and we could hardly find the turnoff and he may have missed. We've been wondering why he hasn't come back."

"He's all right as far as I know. Now, let me tell you something. If he comes back without having deposited it in the right spot, tell him that it's halfway up the causeway on the right-hand side, the box, okay?"

"Halfway up the causeway?" Frank Mackle asked.

"Right, you have to go halfway out to the island, and put it in the box."

"Right," replied Frank Mackle. "Well, he's got the money and he's on his way and he just . . ."

"Yeah, he's probably pretty shook up," the kidnaper cut in.

"Yeah, he's shook up, and he probably just . . ." and Frank Mackle hesitated. "We've been expecting him back . . . back here."

"Okay. Well, I haven't seen him, so I'm going back to check now."

"I would think . . ." Frank Mackle began.

"Tell him there's no light on it, now."

"There's no light on it?"

"There's no light on it."

"All right. Well, I'm sure he's trying to find it. I . . ."

"I hope . . ."

"I . . ."

"I hope . . ."

"I thought this call perhaps was from him," said Frank Mackle.

"I'm actually pretty worried about Barbara. Our last report was that she was coughing pretty badly."

"Yeah. Well, he's coming with the money and he has a clear hand, nobody's interfering or anything."

"Good. Okay."

"So he has all the money and he's ready to go."

"Thank you very much," the kidnaper said.

"But he must not have found it."

"All right, now, we'll see you."

"Fine," said Frank Mackle, and he heard the line go dead.

The conversation amazed Frank. Only at first had the kidnaper appeared aggressive. This is what he had expected. He had been so curt with Robert the hour before and Bill O'Dowd on Tuesday.

"I had thought he would start threatening me and then when I explained he started talking so calmly so casually I could hardly believe it. It was as if we were drinking a cup of coffee together," said Frank Mackle, trying to analyze the conversation.

"When I first answered I heard my voice trembling, faltering, and I remember thinking quickly, let it tremble rather than control it. You know how conscious you are when your voice doesn't come out the way you want it. He may have heard this because he cooled off. I wanted him to know he was talking to the right person.

"He seemed to believe me and the amazing thing was he was willing to talk. He had spelled out in the note that he was aware of the time factor and he couldn't talk too long. I was trying to keep him on the line. I was wracking my brain to think of something else to say. I needed to keep my composure in case he gave us another address or something and I wanted to make sure we heard it right. But he didn't, of course, and he was so casual I almost expected him to say I'll see you later."

The conversation was not quite as long as Frank Mackle suspected. In the basement of the MOhawk center building, a telephone technician didn't have time enough to trace the call.

"We missed it," Gerry Doyle spat in disgust.

Either the complex diode-trap system wasn't functioning properly or the Mackle telephone was hung up too soon. An agent had held his own hand over the cradle in the den this time to keep Frank from hanging up.

"We traced it to a coin box in the FRanklin or 37 exchange," said Doyle. "It was right near the boundary line between FRanklin and HIghland and we figured it may have been from Mercy Hospital or the Holiday Inn at the Stuffed Shirt Lounge across from the entrance of Rickenbacker Causeway. But we didn't get it." There were no problems taping the conversation.

Two FBI agents in the basement, as well as Doyle and Jack Campbell, another telephone company security man, realized what had happened. Robert Mackle had finally made the delivery at the bridge to Fair Isle. And there, presumably unattended, sat half a million dollars in cash in a suitcase while the kidnaper telephoned.

"Hey, chief," dead-panned Campbell, "I think I'll go out for a cup of coffee."

The identical thought—not in jest—occurred in the game room.

"We knew that fishermen, picnickers and hippies and whatnot occasionally frequented Fair Isle," said Frank Mackle, "and we wanted to be sure the right man picked up the ransom, not someone else by accident."

From monitoring the radio, he knew that all the FBI cars had withdrawn completely from the site. No one would make any attempt whatsoever to stop the man or persons who retrieved it, Frank said.

Within five minutes of the call to Frank from the kidnaper, Robert and Billy drove into the driveway. They had taken a different route home through the still-quiet business district of Coconut Grove, west on Grand Avenue, seeing no one, driving past an all-night coin laundromat lighted and vacant, and a block of wooden shack row houses so close together the colored call them "shotgun houses" because a shotgun blast supposedly would go through more than one.

"Billy, I didn't make it," said Robert.

"You did," argued Billy. "That had to be it."

They parked in the driveway, ignoring the open garage door. They walked through to the back door, closer than the front, and Frank spoke immediately. "The kidnaper just called again. Did you leave it?"

"Yes. It was the only place I could find. Billy thinks it is the right place."

As they exchanged information, they began to feel better. Everything made sense. From the bridge of Fair Isle the kidnapers could have seen the Lincoln going up one street, then another, and realized Robert Mackle was lost. They probably had left the place to make the second call when Billy and Robert went back. They would find it there when they looked again. The mood changed to cautious optimism. "Someone from the FBI said they saw some flashing lights down there," Robert recalled later. Everyone drank coffee. Inspector Shroder said Robert and Billy should go back a little before sunrise, just as soon as daylight broke. They wanted to give them time. That would be plenty of time.

"Rex gave me a radio which would transmit and receive," said Vessels, "and he showed me how to use it. It had a 10½- or 11-inch antenna. The FBI kept referring to the suitcase as 'the package,' and he told me that just as soon as we looked I was to call car twelve, that was Fred Frohbose, and tell him whether or not it was still there."

This time Vessels drove the Lincoln. It took approximately twelve minutes.

When they stopped forty to fifty feet from the wall, they could see plainly in the breaking daylight the steel-railed causeway, slanting upward in gentle elevation and curving to the left, and Fair Isle off in the distance. Palms behind the walled yards on both sides hung outward above, obscuring to the left a "No Parking Any Time" sign. In the inexact past, vandals had scrawled assorted graffiti on the low retaining wall. Someone had blotted out the "No" to a "No Trespassing" sign and added in red paint to a "No Fishing" declaration "Or Homos." Below, printed in black, was the admonition, "By Police Order."

Outward on the bridge, perhaps three hundred feet away, they could see two young men fishing. Their presence startled both Robert and Billy. They walked hurriedly to the wall and looked over.

It was gone.

Excited, exhilarated, Vessels ran to the car and grabbed the radio.

"The package is gone! The package is gone!"

"And that cylinder is gone, too, Billy," Robert said a moment later. "It was right here and now it is gone." He was elated.

Still in his whites, feeling as if he must look like an intern, Robert Mackle quickly approached the two fishermen. Vessels, exuding confidence, felt as if he was playing Dick Tracy.

"Have you been fishing here very long?" Robert asked.

"A little while," replied a young man who worked as freight clerk for Braniff International Airlines.

"Could you tell me what time you got here? It is important to me."

"I would say ten minutes after six."

"It must have been pitch-black dark?"

"Yes, sir."

"See anyone around? Any boats? Anything unusual? Anyone?"

"No, sir. Not a thing."

Sunrise was at 7:02 A.M. and Mrs. Paul Lynch, who lived in the home to the north, let outside her dog, Eartha Kitt, just then, and she saw the men talking. Neither her dogs nor the dogs on the other side of the "alley" had barked much during the night, or if they had, she certainly hadn't heard them.

Agents Frohbose and Swinney pulled up behind the Lincoln, and then agent Welsh in a second backup car arrived. They hurried over to the wall. Agent Welsh looked back to make sure his girl in the front seat was all right. He went out to interview the two youths. Robert Mackle, immensely relieved, hopeful, showed the agents exactly where he had left the suitcase.

Then agent Swinney heard a blurp on his car radio. He walked back to find out what the chattering was about. What he heard stunned him. He couldn't believe it.

The others walked up to him. He turned to Robert Mackle. "There has been a shoot-out," he said. "There has been an apprehension and the money has been recovered. The money is at the police station."

"Oh, my God!" cried Robert Mackle

Vessels stumbled to the wall and wept.

Robert Mackle, sobbing uncontrollably, groped blindly toward the wall and slumped over. "My God, my God. They're going to kill my daughter."

Not Me, Officer

At the downtown Miami Police Department at seven o'clock that morning a green U. S. Trunk "Socialite" suitcase filled with twenty-dollar bills lay on a desk in the uniformed captain's office, and the two men responsible for its recovery, Paul Stanley Self and William Joseph Sweeney, felt—for the moment at least—that they had put in a good night's work. They had.

Technically, Self was in the wrong police station. He was a Dade County Sheriff's deputy and he worked for the Dade County Metropolitan Public Safety Department, not the city of Miami Police Department. Sweeney was a city man.

Both the county and city operated separate police departments, as did such suburbs as Miami Beach, Coral Gables, Hialeah, North Miami Beach and Homestead. At the eleven o'clock roll calls for the overnight shift eight hours before, the assorted departments listed a force of three hundred and ninety-three officers to maintain the domestic tranquillity for a metropolitan populace in excess of 1,130,000.

To these men, the night of December 18–19 was just another night. They had not been formally apprised of the kidnaping and what little they knew they had learned by way of radio, television and the press. The girl was kidnaped in Atlanta, wasn't she?

Deputy Self, a Mississippian, enjoyed his work. At age thirty he worked nights by choice. It gave a man a chance to think. He and another deputy, Charles Heller, patrolled Key Biscayne at night in separate vehicles. Their zone covered more than three miles of Rickenbacker Causeway with its nighttime fishermen forever leaning from the catwalks on the bridges, who seldom caused trouble, the privately owned Miami Seaquarium theater showcase, the University of Miami Marine Laboratory, two miles of public beach at Crandon Park, a zoo with one thousand three hundred and ninety specimens, and a community too small for a stop light. The county commissioners knew they would soon have to replace the Key's volunteer fire department, where a siren summoned the citizenry, and on this day of December 19, a deed would be filed at the courthouse for a $127,810 home at 516 Bay Lane. It was the first of several purchases by the President-elect.

About one o'clock that night, two hours after roll call, deputy Self drove into the Seaquarium parking lot, ignoring the darkened sign which identified it as the home of Flipper, an aging television celebrity who happened to be a porpoise. As he drove into the grounds he noticed two cars parked on the otherwise vacant lot. The occupants noticed his arrival and with their lights off they drove to the other end of the parking lot. Odd, he thought. Deputy Self remained where he was and radioed for deputy Heller. Heller came into the lot from another entrance directly upon the two cars and he discovered that they were FBI agents on an assignment. They would appreciate it if he would move along so they wouldn't attract attention. Both deputies moved along. Among themselves they tried to figure out why they were there. "Some nut had shot at a Greyhound bus on Tamiami Trail a few weeks before," said deputy Self, "and we had heard that he was supposed to have been seen on Key Biscayne. Because of Nixon and all, we figured that maybe that is who they were looking for."

About three-thirty deputy Self decided he wanted a cup of coffee. He could pick it up at the closest all-night restaurant, a Royal Castle on the Miami mainland, just a block off U. S. 1, a highway that kept changing names as it ran northward through Miami. South Dixie Highway, Federal Highway, Brickell Avenue and Biscayne Boulevard were all the same.

At the Royal Castle he paid the night man thirty cents for two coffees in paper cups, both with cream and sugar, and he carried them back to his car in a sack. Deputy Heller would want one.

As he traveled south again on U. S. 1, he turned eastward at the tollgate entrance to Rickenbacker Causeway, slow enough that he wouldn't spill the coffee. As usual, he glanced southward toward a blocked-off residential street known as Brickell Avenue extension.

Perhaps 400 feet away he saw a parked car.

Deputy Self stopped.

"Automatically, I knew it didn't belong there. I didn't recognize it." He had stopped at that precise place many times before, up over a curb on a grassy strip within a hundred yards of the circular Seaquarium advertisement where a small hidden motor powered a revolving twenty-foot fiberglass tiger shark. Deputy Self's patrol zone began at the tollgates to the causeway and the Brickell Avenue extension to the south was within the city, not the county. It was a logical place for him to pull over at the boundary of his beat and once, a year before, a homeowner in the neighborhood, Morris Rabinowitz, had seen him there, and walked over and explained to him that his home had been burglarized.

Rabinowitz worked for the Miami Diamond Center where his brother-in-law, Arthur Koff, always waited on the Robert Mackle family. Rabinowitz had returned home one night and found his home ransacked. Thieves had smashed down three doors inside the home. He wondered if deputy Self could keep an eye on his home? Self explained that he had no jurisdiction in the city, but that, yes, he would try to watch the house.

Brickell Avenue extension dead-ended at the entrance to the Rickenbacker Causeway. A year before the city had installed as a traffic barricade a line of pipes filled with concrete. They were painted a striped orange and black and they were spaced just wide enough for an emergency vehicle to drive through. Brickell Avenue extension ran parallel to the bay on the east, six hundred to nine hundred feet from the water. The pipe barricade made Brickell Avenue extension accessible by vehicle by a single street six blocks south. Consequently the fifteen homeowners on both sides of the street had become accustomed to an unusual degree of privacy and isolation. They enjoyed it. With the price of land rising, some of the homes on the bayside, old waterfront mansions built in the 1920s, were valued in excess of $200,000. There had been talk about eventual construction of high-rise apartment condominiums on the land, and one lot, 200 feet in width, had been so zoned, and the single home there had been abandoned. An assortment of vagrants would occasionally take refuge in the old home at night and their highly affluent neighbors didn't appreciate it at all. The old estate was soon to be torn down. The street itself was two-laned and separated by a palmed and well-kept median.

The property directly adjacent to the Rickenbacker Causeway, 700 feet in length and not quite equal in width, belonged to the city of Miami, and the plan then was to develop it into a park. As it was, it comprised a dense thicket, a sort of dry mangrove, elevated and sealed from the bay by a concrete bulkhead. Huge old banyan trees with their twisted aerial roots kept it shaded year round.

Ever since the jeweler had mentioned the burglary, deputy Self noticed the cars parked on Brickell Avenue extension. Generally there was only one, a yellow Rambler which belonged to a servant at one of the mansions. Everyone else, except for an occasional visitor, would park in driveways or garages.

Self looked again at the strange car parked approximately 400 feet from the pipe barricade. It was facing north toward the causeway and extremely close to shrubbery, off the pavement. He decided to check it out.

"I cut through the pipes and drove up. I could see it had an out-of-state plate and I figured it might belong to a camper. A lot of race-track people come south in November and December, I know, and I find a lot of them over at Crandon Park in the early part of the season. They just don't have a place to go. I figured the guy might be asleep in the car or camping in the woods."

Deputy Self stopped and inspected the vehicle. It was a 1966 blue Volvo station wagon with a chrome-plated luggage carrier on top. No one was inside. The doors were locked. The back was filled with clothing, suitcases, a trunk. It looked as if it belonged to a traveler.

He noted the license plate. P72-098. Massachusetts, 1968.

It was 4:05 A.M. and he picked up the microphone from the dash and identified himself as 72-B, and from his headlight beams he carefully read the license number. Was the car wanted?

A moment later a soft and pleasant female voice, the voice of the radio dispatcher, responded negatively. The Dade County Public Safety Department had no record of the vehicle. It was not wanted.

Deputy Self hesitated. It had to belong to somebody. It didn't belong there. That was for certain. It could belong to a prowler. But that wasn't his problem. He wasn't even in his zone.

With the microphone still in his hand, he depressed the button again and asked for his radio dispatcher to notify the city police. "Reference information," he said. He told the dispatcher he would wait "for a city unit" at the entrance to the Rickenbacker Causeway—and back to the shark he drove. He parked so he could see the Volvo in the distance.

Within a few minutes, probably about 4:15 A.M., Miami officer William Joseph Sweeney pulled up.

The two gentlemen knew each other.

When officer Sweeney pulled up Thursday morning, deputy Self said, "I brought you a cup of coffee." Self knew the coffee would get cold before he could deliver it to his partner back on the Key. Besides, the Volvo bothered him.

Sweeney, a dark-haired and solidly built man, not unhandsome, had joined the Miami Police Department eight years ago, and he accepted his rotating midnight shift every three months philosophically as a necessity of his profession. He was a New Yorker who moved to Miami as a boy of twelve when his mother wanted a divorce. He was now thirty-four, addicted to golf, and until he broke his left little finger a few years ago playing jai alai, he was physically as agile as he had been as third baseman for a MacDill Air Force Base team some years previously where he served as a B-47 mechanic.

Officer Sweeney decided he, too, would check out the Volvo.

Complying with the barricade, he drove his squad car around the long way, south on South Miami Avenue, which turned into South Bayshore Drive within a mile, and east on the single entrance street, Southwest Thirty-second Road. Brickell Avenue extension ended there at a famed tourist attraction, Vizcaya, a lavish and ornate museum estate built at the turn of the century by William Deering, a farm implement magnate. Officer Sweeney swung back toward the Volvo and the pipe barricade at the other end of Brickell Avenue extension. He saw no evidence of anyone up and about.

At the Volvo, he too took the license number, radioed his dispatcher to see if it was wanted, and filled out a yellow card for headquarters. He had yellow cards for "suspicious cars" and white cards for "suspicious persons." He could turn it in at the station when he went off duty at seven o'clock. He drove back to the pipe barricade.

Deputy Self, the more gung ho of the two officers, suggested that he and Sweeney look in the woods for the owner of the Volvo.

"That Volvo belongs to a couple of good-looking girls and they've got more coffee for us."

Both men realized the car could belong to a prowler. Officer Sweeney thought it much more likely that it belonged to a pair of lovers.

"Aw, let's leave them alone, Paul," he said.

With their two green-and-white police cars parked under the well-lit causeway entrance, directly in front of the pipe barricade to Brickell Avenue extension, the two officers stood there in the windless and calm 71-degree temperature and idled away the hour in conversation. Both could hear their radio dispatchers.

They saw three carloads of young ladies come across the causeway shortly after five o'clock. They wondered what they were doing out so late or where they were going so early? Off in the distance the Volvo still sat unmoved.

Francis A. "Mike" Calhoun, Jr., a suave, congenial, aggressive and successful real estate agent, a descendant of the American statesman, lived with his wife in a baronial old waterfront mansion at 3029 Brickell Avenue, just about 1400 feet south of the pipe barricade. His home once belonged to L. B. Maytag, Jr., the president of National Airlines. The home next door once belonged to William Jennings Bryan, the Great Commoner of the early 1900s who lost the presidency twice to McKinley and once to Taft. Calhoun's house sat well back from the street, its driveway flanked by huge towering Sabal palms, and Georgia-born Calhoun, a vigorous forty-two, who jogged fifteen minutes every morning, liked to quote his Negro handy man. "We is the only poor people in the neighborhood. You works for a livin'." Calhoun ran his firm from an office in his home where he had a cartoon, thumbtacked on the bulletin board, of two financiers in conversation, "The trouble with owning a big house, driving expensive cars and sending your kids to private school is that everybody thinks you have money." Some of his neighbors considered him the "unofficial mayor." "Others called me an upstart newcomer." At any rate, Calhoun cared deeply about the welfare of the neighborhood and as a civic-minded organizer he was quick to detect anything amiss.

He awoke abruptly the morning of December 19, suddenly aware of an outboard very close to shore. "I heard it very distinctly, put-put-puttering." He lay in bed listening, expecting it to fade away gradually. It did not. The engine cut off suddenly. It had to be stopping.

Calhoun bounded out of bed. It took him no more than a few seconds to slip on a pair of shorts, grab a handgun and arouse his dog, Boysie, a mongrel good at jumping walls. He raced down the stairs, turned off the single 100-watt yellow light bulb gleaming from his dock, and hurried outside and down the coral-rock stairs carved into the broad green lawn now dark and damp from dew.

"Whoever it was had to be using my light to get his bearings," said Calhoun. "There is not another light from the Rickenbacker Causeway to Mercy Hospital."

Calhoun's home was situated a mile and three-eighths northeastward of the Fair Isle Causeway. With the hospital land jutting out into Biscayne Bay, a boater would have to travel about two miles between the two points.

In the blackness Calhoun could see just well enough to reach inside his boat and flip on the battery for his Mercury 160 engine. It provided electrical power for a spot searchlight attached to his starboard cabin.

Silently, wordlessly, his gun in hand, Calhoun beamed the powerful shaft of light along the waterfront northward. It carried easily to the Rickenbacker Causeway 1400 feet away. Except for two lots, where the bay lapped naturally into sand and coral, concrete bulkheads lined the waterfront for a thousand feet. Even at high tide the bulkheads were too high to permit anyone to land from a small boat. The two lots without bulkheads lie adjacent to Calhoun's property to the north at the homes of a coffee merchant from El Salvador, Edward Wilson, who slept soundly, and George S. Black, who also slept soundly.

Calhoun, carefully directing the probing beam from the vantage point of his dock, spotted a small white boat beached on Black's property approximately 400 feet away.

"It couldn't have been more than a few minutes after the engine cut off. Whoever was there would have had to be blind not to see my searchlight."

Calhoun and his dog raced back to the home. He telephoned Black.

"George," he said, "you've got visitors."

George S. Black, a bulky and agreeable retired movieman, had long ago learned to take things in stride. For seventeen years he had worked as director and head of production for Louis de Rochemont in the *March of Time* documentaries. Once he directed the Faye Emerson show, the first lady of television. Black and his widowed sister, Mrs. Marion Vaccaro, lived in a spacious two-story home at 2999 Brickell Avenue which they had built in 1955. Black's dog, like nearly every other domesticated animal along the waterfront that night, seemingly slept through the excitement. His dog was Jack, a survivor of a Jack and Jill duo of uncertain breed, born under a porch in Ocho Rios, Jamaica, and smuggled into the United States as a pup in a straw handbag. Jack slept in the bedroom of his master. A poodle, Danny Boone, slept in Mrs. Vaccaro's bedroom, and the poodle had growled earlier. The paper boy, she thought. Both Black and his sister had telephone extensions in their bedrooms and the call from Calhoun awoke both of them.

Black, quite groggy, thanked his neighbor for the information, and flipped on the switch for the outside floodlights. To his surprise, they didn't work. Still, he wasn't overly concerned. The home was well protected. He thought about telephoning the police. He had called once before when vagrants smashed windows in the abandoned mansion next door to the north and he had to wait for an hour before an officer arrived. He thought the policeman got lost, and couldn't find his house. He wasn't about to stay up another hour and wait for the police again.

"If the boat is abandoned, let's put a claim in for it," said his sister.

Calhoun, persistent and anxious, waited five to ten minutes, and not seeing the floodlights, telephoned again and implored them to call the police.

Mrs. Vaccaro, listening from her extension, said, "You are right, Mike. Will you call the police for us."

"Yes, Marion," he replied, and he dialed the Miami Police Department to report the unwelcomed boater.

Officer Sweeney and deputy Self leaned against a squad car, still facing Brickell Avenue extension and the deserted Volvo about 400 feet south.

"Hey, look!" said deputy Self. "There's somebody."

From the light of a street lamp, both officers saw a figure in the median strip perhaps 500 feet away. He seemed to be walking toward the Volvo.

"Let's check him out," said Sweeney, and both men hopped into their cars. With headlights on, both cars cut through the pipe barricade at different points and approached accelerating, Self in the lane closest to the bay and Sweeney in the parallel lane ten yards away.

"I saw a second figure angling toward the Volvo from the median and he started to run across Bill's lane," said deputy Self. There was no doubt in his mind he had seen a second man, not the same man twice. "I was 500 to 600 feet away. He was carrying something. I couldn't tell what."

"This guy in a yellow shirt cut in front of me, running from the median, as I was coming up my side of the street," said Sweeney. "I made it there in twenty or thirty seconds and I was only twenty feet behind him."

The man fled between a hedge and the far side of a house into the blackness. "I drove across somebody's front yard."

Sweeney stopped within a yard or two of the corner of the house at 2800 Brickell Avenue, his headlights angling off into a vacant lot. In a rack to his right was a shotgun. On the seat lay a flashlight and a portable radio transmitter. In the split second before he flung open the door, he had to choose: Shotgun, flashlight or radio. He grabbed the radio.

"This is 961. I'm chasing a white male on foot. He's on Brickell running toward South Miami Avenue." He knew he would have help in a few minutes.

Deputy Self, hurrying up the other lane, saw Sweeney jump

from his stopped vehicle. He looked hurriedly for the second figure. He couldn't find one. He cut through the median and stopped on the other side of the front lawn of the same home. He radioed a signal 15, a backup-support call, and told his dispatcher, "Pursuing a subject on foot at Old Brickell Avenue near Rickenbacker Causeway."

"He was running like hell. I lost him," said Sweeney, who raced into the back yard of Marvin L. Duncan, a building contractor. It was too dark. If he would have stepped a few feet to the right, he would have fallen into an empty swimming pool.

Somehow, though, he caught a glimpse of the man climbing over a low concrete wall, jumping a hibiscus hedge at the rear property of another home a house to his left. The man ran along the side of the house toward the front on South Miami Avenue. Sweeney ran after him.

At this instant that morning, Richard Andrew Largen, garbed in his bus driver's uniform, was driving his 1962 Chevrolet toward downtown Miami on South Miami Avenue. He was on his way to work.

"All of a sudden this guy runs between the bushes, right in front of me. I didn't miss him by ten feet," said Largen.

Largen slammed on his brakes. It happened so quick he didn't have time to touch the horn. His car screeched to a halt and Largen sat there, his hands trembling. He had seen something that officer Sweeney had not. The fleeing man had a weapon.

"I just sat there for a minute. The guy running had a carbine and he turned around and looked back to see if anyone was following. That's when the policeman ran up. I got out of the car," said Largen.

Sweeney, searching intently, did not notice Largen's Chevy stopped in the middle of the street.

"I remember reading the street sign under the street light. I radioed the location. But I had lost him again," said Sweeney.

Then he saw him again, running this time more than a block beyond the oblique intersection of South Miami Avenue and U. S. 1 where Sweeney stood. He was fleeing northward on Southwest Twenty-eighth Road.

What the fleeing man apparently did not realize was that Southwest Twenty-eighth Road dead-ended at the end of the block. He was running straight toward a wire-link hurricane fence at the bottom of a steep incline. He was running straight toward a ramp entrance to a six-lane I-95 expressway.

The fence was four and a half feet tall. The incline behind rose fifteen feet. It gave Sweeney just enough time to catch up.

"The fence didn't slow him much. He went right over it," said Sweeney. "But I reached the fence just as he scrambled up the ramp to the top." For a second, he had him cold.

"Stop or I'll shoot!" Sweeney yelled.

Panting, out of breath, Sweeney held his service revolver at shoulder height over the top of the fence.

The man hesitated, paused, then pivoted slowly.

"Come on down!" Sweeney ordered. He thought he was surrendering. He had no intention of shooting him. He didn't want to shoot anyone.

And then, with a terrible swiftness, Sweeney realized the man had a carbine in his right hand. He had it behind him, as if he was trying to hide it. He seemed to raise it as he turned. Sweeney had already lowered his own weapon. When he saw the carbine, he thought he was about to be shot.

Without aiming, Sweeney fired twice quickly and threw himself to the ground, expecting a return fire. There was none. He looked up. The man was gone. He knew he had missed. He had fired high. He jumped to his feet, threw his radio transmitter over the fence, quickly climbed the fence, picked up the radio, and ran up the ramp.

Deputy Self heard the shots in the blackness of a vacant lot adjacent to the Duncan home now more than two blocks away, and he ran out to South Miami Avenue, his gun in his hand.

"Freeze!" he shouted.

And Largen, the bus driver on his way to work, stood in the street and raised his hands.

"Not me, officer," he said weakly. "He's over there shooting at the policeman. He was carrying a carbine."

"Bill! Bill!" Self shouted. He could see no one.

Bill Sweeney had reached the top ramp and raced across six lanes of expressway, just in time to see the man climb a second hurricane fence at the bottom of a ramp on the other side and run northward between two homes. He was getting away. He would be impossible to catch on foot.

Sweeney flagged down an approaching car on I-95 and commandeered it. "It was some guy in a Volkswagen on his way home from a party. He was bombed. I didn't think much about it at the time."

The helpful drunk apologized for not having a pistol with him. Sweeney had him drive off I-95 and around the block once, and by this time the tight woundup spiral of sirens echoed everywhere through the morning quiet.

"Police cars were coming every which way," said Largen, the bus driver. He decided he better get on to work. He didn't want to be late.

An arriving city officer told deputy Self that officer Sweeney was still radioing his location after the shooting. No one had shot him.

Deputy Self hurried back to his squad car. Both his and Sweeney's were parked still on Duncan's front lawn, lights on, doors open. He was glad to see them. He was certain he had seen two figures and, obviously, they had chased only one. He didn't want anyone to steal his police car.

Some of the neighbors were outside. Matter of factly, deputy Self announced, "Everything is under control. Stay inside."

A few moments later Sweeney returned to his squad car, too, and he immediately heard the dispatcher repeating a message about a boat landing in someone's yard at 2999 Brickell Avenue. He figured it was related to his chase. He knew he was close.

He drove up the block in search of the address, the numbers growing higher, and his headlights caught some luggage in the median strip. He kept on going. "I knew it wasn't going to run off by itself." No one will take it, Sweeney said to himself. He noticed the Volvo. It had not been moved.

Sweeney couldn't locate the house immediately. It was easy to overlook. So he turned around and came back and stopped by the luggage.

He could see there was a suitcase and a duffel bag. The exterior of the suitcase was moist to his touch as if from the morning dew. Since he and deputy Self first had seen the figure, a good fifteen minutes had elapsed.

Officer Sweeney radioed headquarters.

"I think I've found some evidence." There was no doubt in his mind what he had. Someone, obviously, had broken into a home and dropped the loot.

He opened the duffel bag first. There was a padlock on it but it wasn't locked. The duffel bag contained a pair of flippers for a skin diver, a snorkle, goggles, a steel tape measure, and curiously, two flashlight batteries. Everything felt wet. Peculiar, he thought. Why would a burglar go skin diving?

There was a name stenciled in white paint on the duffel bag. "Ruth Eisemann." It meant nothing to Sweeney.

As he stood there, Mathew John Horan, a city officer, pulled up. "I think that clown got away," Horan said. "Whatcha got there?" Horan was forty-one and from Long Island, and his fourteen years on the Miami Police Department had done little to alter his New York accent.

Self, the boy from Mississippi, arrived a second later.

"Come on, Willie," said Horan to Sweeney. "Open up that big airline job. Let's see what's in it. Maybe somebody left us some whiskey." He had his flashlight in hand.

Sweeney had the suitcase upright on the ground. He pushed down and slid open the catches, and opened it slightly, V-like. Money spilled out.

"Wow!" said Sweeney, and he stuffed it back.

He closed the suitcase and threw it on the hood of the squad car and opened it again wide, all the way.

"And we almost passed out," Horan recalled.

"It's got to be a hit on an armored car," he said aloud. "It looks real," said Sweeney in disbelief, "I don't think it is counterfeit."

They could see packets of $20 bills, all tightly bound with rubber bands, and they could read the blue identifying straps, "Burdine's," "Food Fair," "Wells Fargo."

The same thought occurred to the three officers almost simultaneously: Turn in the money immediately. Don't give anyone an opportunity to accuse them of theft.

"Look, me and you had better go to the station together," said Sweeney to Self. "We're in this thing together. And let's not get out of each other's sight."

"I'll lock up my car," said deputy Self.

"I'll follow you guys," said Horan.

As Horan and Self watched, Sweeney carefully locked the suitcase and duffel bag in the trunk of his police car. Sweeney drove. Self sat with him in front.

In the car they could hear the radio chatter of other city units in the area searching for the man with the carbine. The two cars stopped briefly so that officer Sweeney could point out to another officer with a German shepherd police dog the exact location where he had last seen the man. He didn't get out of the car.

From there they drove directly to headquarters.

"Jesus, that's a lot of money," said Sweeney.

"I sure don't know of any armored car robbery," said deputy Self.

Neither man, like officer Horan in the car behind, had any idea whose money they held.

The half million dollars locked in the trunk of the police car that morning constituted the second largest ransom payment in the history of the nation.

Only once before had kidnapers demanded and received a larger sum of money, and for years afterward two policemen who recovered part of that payoff were suspect. They went to prison for perjury.

This was the Greenlease case. Like the kidnaping of Barbara Mackle, a man and a woman had dug a grave for their victim before an abduction.

On September 28, 1953, Mrs. Bonnie Brown Heady, forty-one, an alcoholic divorcée, kidnaped a six-year-old boy, Robert C. Greenlease, Jr., from Dame de Sion School in Kansas City, Missouri. She told a nun she had come to pick up the boy because his mother had suffered a heart attack. As the boy was summoned, the nun and the kidnaper stepped into a chapel to pray. The boy was the son of Robert Greenlease, then seventy-two, an automobile distributor who had made a fortune selling Cadillacs.

Bonnie Brown Heady's accomplice, Carl Austin Hall, thirty-four, a wastrel heir and ex-convict who inherited and squandered a fortune, shot to death the child in a wheatfield only hours after the crime. They buried him under a blue plastic cloth in a shallow lime-filled grave in the back yard of Bonnie Brown Heady's home in St. Joseph, Missouri, forty miles away. Identifying themselves by the code name "M" in frequent telephone calls, they demanded $600,000. "Lady, he is alive," Carl Austin Hall told the distraught mother. "He is driving us nuts. We have earned this money." A banker, Arthur Eisenhower, brother of President Dwight Eisenhower, helped assemble the ransom in twenty- and ten-dollar bills, and the drop was made at Hall's instructions under a deserted bridge. Nine days later a prostitute in St. Louis became suspicious of the free-spending Hall and she tipped a police lieutenant, Louis Shoulders. Lieutenant Shoulders, a veteran of twenty-seven years on the force, and a rookie patrolman, Elmer Dolan, arrested Hall in a hotel room. There they recovered money. But, somehow, when it was counted, $303,720 of the original $600,000 had disappeared. Carl Austin Hall, confessed to the crime, insisted that he had spent only a couple of thousand and that he had stuffed everything else in two suitcases and a brief case and that he had them in his possession when arrested. Bonnie Brown Heady also confessed and the boy's body was found the next day. They pleaded guilty. On December 18, 1953, strapped to chairs less than two feet apart in the Death House at Jefferson City, Kansas, Bonnie Brown Heady called to her mate, "Are you all right, honey?" And Carl Austin Hall replied, "Yes, Mama," just before the fumes from cyanide pellets asphyxiated them. From crime to execution, eighty-three days had elapsed.

A federal grand jury investigated the missing money and indicted both Lieutenant Shoulders and patrolman Dolan for perjury the following spring of 1954. Shoulders insisted, even as a guest columnist for Drew Pearson, that he had remained in a cellblock interrogating Hall after the arrest. A district attorney said he left the jail for an hour. Witnesses placed him elsewhere. In separate trials, both officers were found guilty. Shoulders served nearly two years' imprisonment; Dolan one year and six months. Five years after the crime, the Senate Rackets Committee was still trying to find out what happened to the missing $300,000. Joseph Costello, a St. Louis gangland taxicab owner, pleaded the Fifth Amendment forty-seven times when asked what he knew about the money. Visibly nervous, Costello asked for permission to smoke when the counsel for the committee, Robert F. Kennedy, asked him if he kept a loaded pistol behind a statue of the Virgin Mary in his home.

It was after six o'clock when officers Self, Sweeney and Horan marched into the first-floor office of Lieutenant James H. Knight at the Miami Police Department. Sweeney plopped the suitcase on the top of a glass-covered desk and opened it.

"Christ!" said Lieutenant Knight. "Nobody leaves this room. Everybody stays right here."

Lieutenant Knight was the ranking officer in the station. The night-shift captain had already left. He wanted to get home a few minutes early.

The lieutenant listened to their explanations and began telephoning his superiors, Majors Newell Horne and Charles Gunn. They said they would be right down.

"We could see all those bands from Burdine's and I thought that maybe Burdine's had been robbed. But even Burdine's wouldn't carry money like that," said Lieutenant Knight.

The lieutenant counted the rows and made a guess: $400,000. For half an hour everyone remained in the room, telling and retelling the story. Deputy Self and officer Sweeney had agreed upon descriptions of their two suspects. The Yellow Shirt was the easiest: White male, about twenty-five years old, five foot eleven, light build, neat haircut, wearing long-sleeved yellow corduroy shirt—and a very fast runner. For the other, they decided he was a white male, forty years old, five foot ten, 220 pounds, heavy set, dark hair, wearing a dark business suit.

Someone suggested that they had better make sure that the Volvo didn't disappear. And what about the report of the boat landing at 2999 Brickell Avenue?

The ensuing commotion after the chase had put a small army of policemen in George Black's back yard, or so he thought. They congregated around a white 13½-foot open outboard with a 33-horsepower Evinrude motor, a Boston Whaler by make. It had a Florida registration number, FL 5146F. That could be checked.

Black tried to reach his neighbor Mike Calhoun. He had misplaced Calhoun's private unlisted telephone number and he had to call his answering service.

"It is most urgent he call me immediately," Black told the operator, and a few minutes later Calhoun returned the call. Calhoun said he would come right over. He asked Black to tell the policemen he was coming. He didn't want to be mistaken for a prowler and shot. He arrived a few moments later with his pistol and a walking stick, which was a cane with a concealed sword, a useful weapon for deterring yapping dogs while jogging.

"Why are you so late?" he asked the officer.

"We've been shooting people up and down the street," the officer replied, and Calhoun heard about the suitcase full of money.

"Probably some Cubans," suggested another officer.

"Why don't you ask the bum who lives in the woods?" said

Calhoun. "There is a hobo who lives on the city property adjacent to the causeway."

The officers trooped off. It reminded Calhoun of a scene from a Toonerville cartoon. He retired home to don his jogging attire.

Later that morning, with a police helicopter hovering overhead, Stephen Mark Riska, an unshaven and khaki-garbed eccentric skilled in the hacking and peeling of coconuts, surrendered himself. A scrawny little man of fifty-five, he owned a plastic tobacco pouch, a social security card, and lived the life of a recluse in his almost private subtropical jungle. He always ran from visitors. Exactly four years ago to the day at exactly the same place, a policemen had arrested him for vagrancy, and in the four years since, he had been arrested nine more times for vagrancy and served 195 days in jail. Sometimes he slept in a fleabag hotel in downtown Miami.

"Just been swimming here," he volunteered quickly to officer B. E. Morene.

"Then why aren't you wet?"

The officer searched his suspect. In Riska's plastic tobacco pouch he found twenty soiled $20 bills and two $50 bills.

"My life savings," Riska mumbled as the officer carefully counted the $500, before booking him at the jail an eleventh time for vagrancy. A judge would find him guilty four days later and let him off with "time served" and give him back his money.

Later that same morning Charles Price, the acting chief of police for Miami, would arrive at the station, sustain a barrage of inquiries about lack of co-ordination among law enforcement agencies, and declare, "Purely from an objective viewpoint, this was a marvelous piece of policework."

Then he added, "Of course, it may have been at the wrong place at the wrong time."

It was still some moments before seven o'clock when Inspector Francis Lee Napier, a tall, gaunt and tight-lipped survivor of ancient political wars within the Miami Police Department, meandered into the office and asked what all the excitement was about.

The second he saw it he knew. Kidnap. Atlanta. Miami. Mackle. Money. What else? He listened a few minutes and went upstairs to a private office.

He dialed the FBI. Fred Fox, assistant agent in charge, took the call.

"We've got a suitcase over here filled with $20 bills," he began.

Fox listened a moment. "Can you freeze it?" he asked, wondering if the information could be kept secret.

It couldn't. Practically everyone in the station already knew. A newspaper reporter was standing in the doorway downstairs looking at it.

Today Is Wednesday

I thought about dying again. I said to myself that this is where I am going to die. Three or four times I thought this is going to be my casket. I didn't think the word casket the first time, but later on I did. I said, yes, this is just about right. It could have been a little bit longer.

And when I got morbid I would think of who would find me. Who and when and how? Maybe it would be a farmer. Or maybe someone building something. In ten years? Twenty years?

I wondered what I would look like and whether or not they could identify me. I was hoping that Mom and Dad wouldn't be alive when they found me. Because I wouldn't want them to think that was the way it was. Maybe they would think I was shot or something faster. Anyway, faster.

When things really got bad three or four times, I said to myself, I'm going to end it now. I don't want to wait. If I am going to die here, I want to die now.

So I turned off the fan. It would be so easy. Just go to sleep. It wouldn't be any trouble. It would start getting hot and stuffy and I would suffocate.

Then I would get a hold of myself. What if they find me in time—and I'm dead already. And Mom and Dad and everyone finds out I've turned off the battery.

Then I would say, something is going to happen. Daddy is going to pay the money. Somehow, Daddy is going to find me.

I also thought about suffocating regardless of what I did. I knew there had to be an air intake above the ground and I thought, what happens if a squirrel or a small animal gets stuck in it? I knew I was really out in the sticks and there might be animals around. What if an animal gets curious and crawls into the air intake? I knew something had to be protruding above the ground for the air to reach me. With my hands I could feel the screens inside the box. But I didn't know if there were screens above too. What if there weren't? And then what if it snowed? Would the snow cut off the air?

I had plenty of time to think about kidnaping in general, too. When I was young I had always had sort of a fear of being kidnaped. I remember thinking about being up in my room and I was afraid someone was on the roof near my window. I guess a lot of young girls feel that way. I was scared, I know, and I got up once and turned the light on in the bathroom. The dark had always been my main fear. I don't know why. It just had been. I conquered it as I grew up, just naturally I guess. I remember thinking about being kidnaped when I was eleven or twelve years old, which I thought was clearly a little too old to be kidnaped even then. When I thought of it, I said, no, I'm too old.

The logical thing in a kidnaping, of course, is just to kill the victim. And especially in a case like mine where I knew I could identify them. I was the only one as far as I knew. I didn't think Mother would be able to identify them. So why wouldn't they just leave me here forever? Sometimes I almost lost hope completely. But I would never let myself dwell on things like that very long.

I thought about being blind. When I was a child I used to close my eyes and pretend I was blind. It was pretty scary. If anything had to be wrong, I would think I sure wouldn't want it to be my eyes.

I used to work for the blind with the Twenty Little Working Girls. That is a Junior Assembly-type thing, social, and I joined when I was in Everglades School for Girls, the tenth, eleventh and twelfth grades. They must take twenty girls a year because there are sixty or so members. And one of the things I did was to go to the University of Miami every week, in the library building there, and listen to the readers read for blind people.

I would sit in a little booth and listen to the tapes made for the blind and read what the reader had read to make sure he hadn't made any mistakes. The readers had to come for an audition, I know. They wanted a certain type of voice. I listened to tapes that were made for blind boys and girls going to school; a lot of science articles, and some of the technical words were difficult to pronounce and understand. One of the tapes, I remember, was about the American Revolution. Blind persons had put in special requests for articles and books and I had the names for the requests and the ages, too. Some were the same age as me, you know, late teens, and I wondered what it would be like, and as I lay there I related back. Now I knew. This is what it is like to be blind. You want to see. You are just so frustrated. You want to see and you can't. You can't see your hand in front of your face. And I thought, if they can spend their whole life like this, well, I could tolerate it.

In my mind I constructed the ransom payoff again and this time I contrived a Miami version instead of an Atlanta version. I thought the kidnapers would have trouble getting in touch with Daddy. We haven't had our telephone number in the book for five or six years. We were always getting telephone solicitations. Someone from Gulf American was always trying to sell us land. So this time the kidnapers had to call Uncle Frank. His number is listed. I remember I had the kidnaper saying, MACK-le, and Uncle Frank called Daddy and then drove over to the villas. I had Daddy in Villa 15. Before he got there Mother called and she said, Oh, Bob, Bob, I have to tell you what happened. And he said, Yes, Jane, I know. I made up all these fictitious conversations, trying to think of everything that they would say and do to use up time. And Daddy would say come on down to Miami, we have to pay them down here. Mother wouldn't want to leave Atlanta. She would say, No, I can't leave here. She is up here. But Daddy would convince her to go to Miami. I thought I hope they don't think that, but they probably will. They'll go to Miami. They had a discussion about calling the police and they decided not to. That's what I thought. This time I decided the kidnapers would want a little more money, $10,000.

Anyway, I remember thinking that Billy Vessels would get into it. I thought Billy Vessels would be there. He is pretty calm and I think I had Uncle Frank bringing him over. They calmed Daddy down. Billy Vessels, he calls my father uncle sometimes. Don't worry, Uncle Robert, we'll get her back all right. The man who said MACK-le had written down all the details. The payoff was going to be at Crandon Park on Key Biscayne, parking lot number two, and it was at night again. Everything happened at night. I thought that Uncle Frank would want to make the delivery and he would ask Dad if he was all right. Uncle Frank would be nervous, too, and he would say, I'm fine, I'm fine, and by this time Uncle Elliott was there, too. It was the three of them. Dad said, No, he was going to make it.

I decided that the payoff would have to be sometime Wednesday night, not Tuesday, the first night, and that was another reason for the delay. I knew something had gone wrong for Tuesday. In my mind I put the place just back of a building, the bathrooms there at Crandon Park, and I remembered it as a bluish-green-type building, cement. It had to be the next night, Wednesday, otherwise they would have come and found me by now. It seemed forever. I kept saying to myself—really, the whole time—today is Wednesday, today is Wednesday, today is Wednesday, and the payoff will take place tonight in Miami. That's exactly what I thought. I had Daddy with the money and he drove the Lincoln. Daddy doesn't drive very fast. When we go over a bridge, mother makes him drive in the center lane.

I had him going by himself to Crandon and this time there were two men waiting for him, just shadowy figures, one of them big like George, the man with the girl. I kind of thought of his eyes. He had eager eyes. I didn't have the girl there. I had some thoughts that maybe they had killed her if they were in an organization of some kind. Then I said, that's not right. But why didn't she come back? She said she would. But there were so many things they said that weren't true. I just couldn't believe anything. I just didn't know. Maybe she was my only hope. Daddy left the money, anyway, and he drove back to the villas at the Key. Billy was worried. Generally, he is very optimistic. He bubbles. So Daddy said I think it went all right, and Uncle Elliott and Uncle Frank and Bobby were all reassuring themselves just outside the villas by the ocean. So they all had to wait for the telephone call. The kidnapers had to count the money. That would take time. And I remember thinking the kidnapers would have to get out of Miami; they would have to get out of the vicinity because they knew Daddy would call the police right after he knew where I was, and maybe Daddy would ask them to let him speak to me. If they let me up to talk to him, I knew they would never bury me again. They would have to kill me. I was very angry with myself for not trying harder to get away. But I knew they wouldn't be coming back.

I had the kidnapers stop at a restaurant, not any one in particular, and make the telephone call to Daddy and they were all happy. And Billy Vessels would say, I told you everything would be all right. When they called, they said someone was with me up here. Then I had Bobby and Daddy flying up on the company plane. I gave them time to fly up, three hours almost, and I had the plane landing finally. And then they had to rent a car. Then they stopped at the K-mart on the way and bought a shovel. I invented traffic jams, little things. I remember I had them getting lost trying to find me because Daddy didn't know his way around here. Nobody did. In my mind, I kept building up and building up to the point where they should arrive. But I never had them actually digging me out. I kept thinking the car should be coming before long. I should be able to hear footsteps pretty soon.

But I heard nothing except that fan. Nothing. Not an animal, not a bug, not a clap of thunder. Nothing. I remembered that railroad track and wondered if I could hear a train. And I turned off the fan and listened.

I turned the fan off many times. I know the noise from the fan started to get on my nerves. I can't stand it, I thought, and I turned it off again and I began to feel the box get kind of stuffy again. I remember a couple of times thinking, oh, this is great, I'm falling off to sleep. Sleep is the only way to pass the time. It was so nice and I felt it get warmer.

Then I would think, if I fall asleep, how is the air going to get in? I might fall asleep and suffocate. So I would turn it on and it would get cold again, too cold to sleep.

I am sure I must have slept some but I can't remember how much. I guess I was fairly well rested before the kidnaping. I know I had slept a lot because I was sick with the flu. I can't remember ever waking up in the box and thinking I've been asleep. That never happened. At home I am always conscious of when I wake up. You know how your thoughts are kind of half there, half not, sort of dreaming. I can generally recall my dreams. I dream quite a bit at night. But this didn't happen. I remember telling myself, I've got to sleep, I've got to sleep, and maybe I did, but I can't remember it.

I started to count sheep. I had never done that before. It was the first time. I pretended to see a little wooden rail fence, a rickety one, and I had white sheep jumping, and I counted eight hundred or nine hundred.

Most of all it was the cold. The cold and the wetness. Every time I moved I felt wet. The dripping just almost drove me crazy. Every time I moved I had to rearrange the blanket. I was underneath it and I couldn't get air. And every time I opened it a little bit the cold and wet would come in. I was very cold. The blanket was wet by this time, too, and sometimes my feet were sticking out. My feet would come unloose from the blanket. My hips were sore, very much so. Every time I moved from one side to the other it was painful and I would try to move and lie in a way that it wouldn't hurt. I couldn't find a way. Every place hurt.

Sometimes I just got on my back and raised my knees a little bit. There was some bread there and it was sopping wet. Everything was sopping wet. Except maybe the chewing gum which they had left, and I very rarely chew gum. I don't like it. I know I had to breathe out of my mouth because of the flu. I had to keep my mouth open. I was never conscious of my fever breaking and I remember thinking I could get a lot sicker. I could get pneumonia. My nose wasn't runny. That makes me terribly nervous. It didn't run at all. They had left toilet paper which might have been used as Kleenex but it was also sopping wet. And with all that cold and wet I thought about clear water. In my mind I thought about a great big pitcher of water and how I would laugh and pour it and drink it and taste it. I just wanted to move; anything to move. I pounded in this position, and every time I pounded, the box shook enough that all the water, the droplets, fell. I pounded while on my back. I did this four or five times just as hard as I could to release energy. I was very conscious of what I was doing. I just wanted to move. Stretch. Anything. I wasn't able to kick with my feet. I tried that. The box was too confining. I kept tensing my muscles up.

I never put on the other blanket at the bottom. I got it with my feet and pulled it up one time and it was so wet and clammy that I pushed it down again. I kept thinking that I should be hungry. I should make myself eat. I am used to making myself eat. But I just wasn't hungry. I had three or four bites on an apple and that was enough. I didn't want to eat too much because I didn't want to go to the bathroom. I remember nothing appealed to me. I like candy and there was candy there. I had a caramel. But I didn't think of any steak dinners or anything like that. I just wasn't hungry.

I tried to determine whether it was day or night by temperature; not at the beginning, but later. I said this is Wednesday afternoon. It has to be daytime because it is warmer. When it is night, the earth is cold, right? And I'm not as cold as I was. And when I felt myself getting colder later I decided it was getting to be night. It might be eleven o'clock Wednesday night. No. It can't be that late. Today is still Wednesday. Today is Wednesday.

And the time came when I started to talk to God. Religion, I believe, is very personal. Everyone has his own beliefs in what kind of a God there is. Everyone has a different idea of God. I don't actually think of God as a person, but more as a power, a force, something greater than all of these things.

For a while, I was a kind of agnostic, I suppose. Not really agnostic. I believed in a God most of the time. It was more a kind of questioning about religion in general—about the necessity for organized religion.

And when I was down there I thought that, maybe I should believe more. Maybe I am wrong. I don't know. I only know how I feel. If there is a God, you can talk to Him yourself. You don't need someone else between you and God. And when I was there buried alive I thought about this.

I thought about a lot of things I never wanted or had time to think about before—about facing death, facing God.

It was hard for me to pray. I don't like to recite words. I never made any promises. Promises like people sometimes make.

I just started talking, as if God were there beside me. And I said, God, I'm not going to die here. I don't know what kind of feelings people have when they are going to die. But I know You are not going to let me die.

I said even if no one knows where I am, You know where I am. And I found this comforting, extremely comforting.

And after a while, the more I prayed, I said, yes, I know there is a God. Even though I don't believe in a lot of the other things, I know there is God. And I know He heard me.

Don't Be So Cruel

At 10 Rickenbacker Causeway on Virginia Key, adjacent to the Miami Seaquarium, Jack O'Donnell arrived at work at the University of Miami Institute of Marine Sciences at 7:15 A.M. Thursday. He was the dockmaster and his responsibilities encompassed the watch and care of the institute's nine vessels there. It was a bright sunny morning, the sky already a hard enamel blue, and the tide would be high in fifteen minutes. Even at high tide anyone intent upon entering the fenced six-acre institute grounds could wade on the sandy bottom alongside a seawall and walk up a launching ramp. The deepest spot wasn't three feet.

O'Donnell, a retired U. S. Navy chief gunner's mate, noticed immediately that someone had borrowed or stolen the institute's smallest craft, a fiberglass Boston Whaler. Its empty sixteen-foot trailer stood in the launching ramp.

"I wondered if the port captain had given permission to a student to take it out early," said O'Donnell. He telephoned his superior, Dick Gledhill, and Gledhill told him, "No, you'd better call the police."

O'Donnell called the police. While waiting, he noticed something else amiss. Someone had broken into a gasoline storage locker. Only two weeks before someone had stolen his entire ring of keys. But the key to the gasoline storage locker wasn't on the ring. It was on a peg inside a building.

Now O'Donnell could see that the hasp to the door of the storage locker had been pried off. The padlock was still intact. It appeared that someone had gassed up the Boston Whaler and taken off.

An officer arrived a few minutes later from Key Biscayne. He had been listening on his car radio to reports of the shooting and the chase at the entrance to the causeway. He knew a boat had been abandoned three miles away.

"How can you identify your Boston Whaler?" the officer asked O'Donnell.

"It's an old boat," said O'Donnell. "The spokes in the steering wheel are rusted out and broken. They've been taped up in two places."

The officer radioed the information to headquarters. He had his answer within a few minutes. Yes, the abandoned Boston Whaler was the same. It belonged to the University of Miami Institute of Marine Sciences.

The marine lab, as it was called, for years a tadpole to the university, had rapidly grown, despite the zoological impossibility, into a splashing and prestigious academic whale. With a staff of 473, of whom 271 labored directly in research, it functioned on an annual budget in excess of five million dollars. Its scientists immersed themselves in the esoteric glories of projects such as the role of calcareous green algae in sediment and the extracellular proteinases of marine yeasts.

In its pursuit of knowledge, the institute had somehow neglected to properly register its Boston Whaler. According to its registration, the craft still belonged to Robert J. Hurley, which it did not.

Dr. Hurley, an articulate, exuberant, and candid oceanographer—very much with it in his position as chairman of the division of graduate students at the marine lab—had sold the boat to the university two years before. As he shaved at home in Coconut Grove that morning, careful not to disturb his Van Dyke beard, three radios all tuned to the same station blared the helicopter-in-the-sky morning traffic report. The announcer had a sketchy report of police cars and traffic trouble at the entrance to Rickenbacker Causeway.

Unknown to Dr. Hurley, FBI agents would soon be all over his neighborhood, asking his neighbors if he owned a foreign car (yes, two), and had they seen a blue Volvo around (well, yes, the baby sitter might have had a Volvo).

As he turned onto the causeway, on his way to his office, he saw a police car towing a boat in the opposite direction. He looked at boats, especially Boston Whalers.

"My God! That's mine," he said.

Within a few hours that Thursday morning of December 19, the FBI would know exactly who it wanted for the kidnaping of

Barbara Jane Mackle. The Volvo and its contents provided a virtual treasure chest of information. Miami police, now fully aware of what had happened, had the car and boat in custody while FBI agents, accompanying deputy Self and officer Sweeney, explained the situation to U. S. Commissioner Edward Swan. He signed a search warrant.

Legally, the status of the Mackle kidnaping at this point was reduced to the heading on the warrant: United States of America versus one 1966 four-door square-back Volvo, dark blue in color, bearing license 1968 Massachusetts, P 72098.

The FBI in Boston quickly established the ownership of the Swedish-made Volvo. It belonged to George Deacon, a former employee of the Massachusetts Institute of Technology. He had purchased it through MIT's Federal Credit Union, which still held the mortgage. Records there indicated Deacon was now employed at the University of Miami.

An FBI lock expert had no trouble unlocking the vehicle.

Inside, strewn in the back rear luggage space with three suitcases, a Scotch-plaid carrying case, a big black metal trunk tilted upward with the word "Ruth" written in chalk, agents found a black zipper case. There they found a green motel key. It was for room 153, Rodeway Inn, 1706 Clairmont Road, Decatur, Georgia.

Stuck in a spiral University of Miami $.59 notebook was a stack of sheets of bonded paper, all blank. And upon close scrutiny somewhat later, an agent would detect distinct typewritten indentations on three separate sheets: "ROBERT MACKLE: Sir, your daughter has been kidnapped . . ." The paper had been used in a typewriter at the time the original ransom note had been typed.

Agents discovered pages 279 and 280 torn from the yellow pages of the Southern Bell Telephone directory for Greater Miami. Listed there were the names and numbers of Catholic churches. They knew the kidnaper had telephoned a priest.

They knew, too, that Jane Mackle had said the smaller figure wore a ski-mask hat during the abduction. In the Volvo they found a red knit ski mask with black and white stripes and a second green ski-mask hat with a yellow stripe. There was a roll of Red Cross adhesive tape, originally five yards, two inches wide. It had been used.

They found a box of Winchester shotgun shells, superspeed,

superbuckshot lead. Inside also was 30-caliber ammunition for a carbine.

Everything, obviously, tied in.

They found also an item that made them stop and think: A 20 c.c. multiple-dose vial of xylocaine hydrochloride. The small type on the vial said: "Only for infiltration and minor nerve blocks. Caution: Federal law prohibits dispensing without prescription."

And with it they found eleven detachable hypodermic needles, two glass plungers and syringes for a five cubic centimeter dosage and a ten cubic centimeter dosage.

Could the kidnapers have injected Barbara? It seemed quite probable. Why would they have xylocaine hydrochloride? And what would be the circumstances? Would they truly bury her alive in a capsule?

There was little doubt whose property they held. Besides the clothing for a man and a woman, packed separately, and dresses from a dry cleaner's draped over the front seat, agents found a checkbook at the Key Biscayne Bank with printed names, Mr. George G. and Mrs. Dorothy Deacon. The amount brought forward showed $364.10. There was a Miami address for the Deacons: 8401 Northwest Fourteenth Avenue. It was a trailer court.

Deacon, it appeared, had received an application from the U. S. Department of State for a passport. The application was blank. It had not been filled out. It had been addressed and mailed to him at the University of Miami, 10 Rickenbacker Causeway.

His traveling companion, undoubtedly, was Ruth Eisemann-Schier. In a black glossy purse, along with a lipstick, powder puff, green oversized sunglasses, a large plastic Band-Aid, agents found her billfold and three different passports, two from her native country, Honduras, one expired, and one from the United States, "Valid if presented before 23 August 1972."

There was her University of Miami student identification card, encased in plastic, and another card, signed by a security officer, which authorized her to be on the grounds of the marine lab after hours, and paper work, stamped University of Miami Graduate School, which indicated she had enrolled in four courses, 501, 502, 581 and 602, on September 10, 1968. A second outdated identification card in Spanish showed her as a student at the University of Mexico.

Ruth Eisemann-Schier, the last names sometimes hyphenated in her handwriting, sometimes not, sometimes just Ruth Eisemann, had lived in Washington, D.C. Her billfold held her public library card for the District of Columbia, a membership card for the Young Woman's Christian Association, a card designating employment at the Pan American Union with a Washington address on Nineteenth Street Northwest, her social security card, and bankbook from the First National Bank of Washington. The last entry, June 7, 1968, showed a balance of $655.56.

There was a second account book from the Dade Federal Savings & Loan Association in Miami. She had withdrawn every penny December 10, nine days before, $505.63.

In her billfold, too, was a Florida beginner's driving permit: Ruth, middle name (None), Eisemann, and a Miami address, 5901 Southwest Sixty-second Avenue. Race: White; Eyes: Green; Height: 5' 2"; Weight: 115; Date of Birth: Nov. 8, 1942; Sex: F; Color Hair: Brown, and Occupation: Student. She had taken five lessons at eight dollars each at the Blanco Driving School in Miami and the receipts were folded neatly.

There, too, in the billfold were business cards and addresses of a few gentlemen friends. Among them, in her handwriting, was "George 350-7425."

Two airplane tickets in the purse in the name of G. Deacon and A. Post were for flights scheduled Friday, December 20. G. Deacon and A. Post were to leave Miami on the 7 A.M. Delta flight 2Y to Chicago, then transfer to a Trans World Airlines, Inc., flight 195Y at 11:50 A.M. the same day. Destination: Las Vegas, Nevada. The tickets had been purchased for $285.60 Both were one way.

Who was A. Post? A third party to the crime? If Deacon had used his own name, why hadn't Ruth Eisemann-Schier? Or was A. Post, as the name might imply, simply fiction—a post instead of a person.

FBI agents, working rapidly, did not dwell upon all the possibilities and ramifications. They had four hard leads in need of immediate pursuit: Deacons' address; Eisemann-Schier's address; the University of Miami Institute of Marine Sciences, as well as Miami International Airport.

The Volvo, hooked up to a wrecker after transportation to the private basement garage of the FBI office, would very shortly produce other information, some significant, some trivial. Some of the bureau's Washington crime-laboratory experts were already airborne for Miami.

Deacon, it seemed, had left a pair of black pants, shoes and a belt in the back seat of the Volvo. Had he gone skin diving as the wet snorkle, goggles and flippers seemed to indicate? And why? Was he the man who called both Robert and Frank Mackle and instructed them to put the ransom suitcase in a box with a flashing light on the Fair Isle Causeway? Had he rigged the box to topple from the causeway into the bay? It seemed preposterous.

In the back of the Volvo the FBI agents found a handbook, *Shallow Water Fishing and Spearfishing,* a chemistry and physics text, forty-third paperback student edition, a book *The Seven Ages of Women,* a key case empty of keys, a poster advertisement of a party at the University of Miami with the drawing of a hypodermic needle and bubbling champagne glass, nearly a dozen bikini lace panties, a fluffy blue hair ribbon, shaving lotion and a six-cent postage stamp, and two one-cent stamps.

They began to catalog their find:

A woman's wig, binoculars, a portable radio, a Texaco Touring Atlas, a metal beer stein engraved, "George S. Deacon, MIT FBNML, 1966–1968," which stood for Massachusetts Institute of Technology, Francis Bitter National Magnet Laboratory.

They listed too: pair of tennis shoes, white jacket, white shirt, towel, two pairs of boxer undershorts, orange sweater, white sweater, pair of lady's orange shoes, lady's white shoes, white trousers, four jockey undershorts, six pairs of thin kid gloves, necktie, salt shaker, tape measure, T-square, pair of scissors, footpads, bottle of shampoo, chisel, hydrometer, five distress signals, mortar and pestle, electrical tester with wires, earplugs with wire, alarm clock, electric vibrator massager, pair of pliers, numerous mechanic's tools, flashlight batteries, and three boxes of color slides. The slides were of Deacon and others aboard a ship taken at sea.

From a Scotch-plaid suitcase agents removed a metal stamping device. The imprint stamp said, "Office of Registrar of Vital Statistics." Obviously, a man could use it to change his date of birth.

Inside the plaid suitcase agents also found flash bulbs, an unexposed film pack, a Polaroid Land Camera, model number

20, the Swinger, and seven exposed and developed photographs. They were à la *Bonnie and Clyde*.

One photograph showed George Deacon, nude, heavily bearded and beefy and fat, lying on his back on a bed, his hands propped up on a pillow, a flowered picture on the wall in the background. The photograph had been taken from the foot of the bed with a flash. His only attire was a policeman's visored cap, placed over his genitals.

A second photograph showed Ruth Eisemann standing in a provocative pose wearing only bra and panties, her head tilted. She looked very blonde. In the background were a man's clothing hanging in a closet and a bolt left unlocked on a door.

A third photograph had the bearded Deacon in a policeman's cap with a telephone in his hand, and a fourth was a good close-up of Deacon with a stove in the background. The other photographs were of Ruth, both dressed, one sitting at a table in a loose-fitting blouse and smiling, the stove again in the background, and the other of her standing.

If there could conceivably be any doubt of their involvement in the crime, a seventh photograph—taken as the number five picture in sequence of the film pack—made it certain.

The picture was of Barbara Mackle. A sign lettered "Kidnapped" was under her chin. Her eyes were closed. She looked as if she was dead.

The Polaroid film pack, the FBI knew, should contain eight photographs, not seven. One was missing.

In the ensuing hours, days, and months, FBI agents in scores of American cities and law enforcement officers elsewhere would piece together the fragmented lives of the man known as George Gary Deacon and his companion, Ruth Eisemann-Schier. They would interview in excess of five hundred persons whose knowledge and views of the man and woman contrasted and fluctuated in infinite rhythms and dissonance.

There was no symmetrical flowering of information. In scraps, slivers and chunks of fact and belief, the backgrounds of Deacon and Eisemann surfaced jaggedly.

Two agents began that morning with Dr. Hurley in his office. "They played coy fencing games for a few minutes," said Dr. Hurley. "I said, 'Look fellows. I can't play guessing games. If there is something you want, ask me and I'll tell you.'"

The agents asked if he would leave the room for a minute and let them use the telephone.

When Dr. Hurley returned, they told him they wanted Deacon and Schier for the kidnaping.

"And I gave the fuzz everything," said Dr. Hurley.

They kept open the telephone to the downtown FBI office and meticulously—and rapidly—they scrutinized every record they could get their hands on.

Deacon had gone to work for the marine lab at $8500 a year as a research assistant nearly six months before, June 1, 1968. He had listed his age as twenty-three.

Under education he had written that he attended Cobol High School in Cobol, Alaska, from 1954 to 1958. He said he attended Northeastern University in Boston the academic year of 1967–68. So where was he between 1958 and 1967?

Under "past employment," he said he worked for $3.50 an hour for the Channel Charter Service, Sitka, Alaska, from June 1958 to June 1960, listing his position as "operations executive." He said that his supervisor was J. Krist. The name meant nothing at the moment. It was a lead. Reason for leaving: "youth," he wrote.

From October 1960 until November 1966, Deacon said he worked for Research Associates, Cordilleras Road, Redwood City, California. He listed his supervisor as Gerhard Simon, another name that needed to be checked out. He listed his position as foreman and his salary at $10,000.

He said he had worked from December 5, 1966 until the present (early 1968) at the Massachusetts Institute of Technology National Magnet Laboratory as a research technician. He said he was paid $7500.

Was Deacon making $10,000 a year at age fifteen? Had he given up the position to start college at twenty-two and earn $7500 a year?

"Obviously, our people did not study this thing very carefully," said Dr. Hurley. As references Deacon listed on his application the names of four Ph.Ds at MIT. Under "special qualification," he wrote, typing, cryogenics, vacuum technology, drafting, and electronic design.

There was also space for "organizations belong to." Deacon wrote, "Not important."

"I guess I was the first to hear about him here in Miami," said

Dr. Christopher G. A. Harrison, a bearded geophysicist from Oxford, England. "A friend of mine at the National Magnet Lab at MIT, Henry Kolm, mentioned that he had a man keen upon becoming a marine technician. He said Deacon had been on boats and had great experience."

In Miami for a scientific cruise aboard a marine lab ship in early 1968, Dr. Kolm mentioned Deacon to Dr. Caesar Emiliani, a brilliant and quick Italian whose position as chairman of the division of marine geology and geophysics embraced employment. Dr. Emiliani knew he was about to lose his "chief," as he called him, a cruise co-ordinator. It was a job without any real future and Dr. Emiliani made that quite clear to every applicant. Except for cost-of-living increases, there was little prospect of advancement. It was a position a bright young man might want temporarily in which he could learn an enormous amount of marine geology useful in private industry. That was precisely why he was losing his chief.

"Deacon's references were excellent," said Dr. Emiliani, "but I didn't like to hire anyone sight unseen." He asked Dr. Mahlon M. Ball to interview him. Dr. Ball had to be at Woods Hole in Massachusetts on another matter and it would be no trouble for him to see Deacon at MIT.

"He struck me as an aggressive, hard-working kid, very ambitious and physically strong," said Dr. Ball. He interviewed Deacon while Deacon was drafting. "I talked to him about an hour. He didn't smoke or drink, he knew boats, and he looked just like what we needed. He looked good."

Dr. Emiliani concurred. Deacon went to work in June. "Any reservations I had about hiring him unseen evaporated very quickly once he was here. I was very much impressed with his drive. Tell him to do something—and he did it. He wouldn't come back and ask how. He learned very quickly. I liked his frankness. There was no pussyfooting around. He was a bit blunt, straightforward. He didn't butter up people. We were very happy with him."

Dr. Emiliani's secretary, Betsy Fast, a pretty young charmer, liked him, too. "He was brusque and businesslike." She kept track of petty cash. Because Deacon had to make certain all marine geological equipment was properly functioning and ready for the various cruises, he purchased all manner of inexpensive hardware. He accounted scrupulously for every penny spent, $279.48 in thirty-five entries. Deacon replaced Luke Baumgardner, who remained at the marine lab for Deacon's first three months. "He proved that he was extremely adept mechanically. Much of our work was semidesign on marine geological coring equipment and George was pretty much of a liaison man for me to the laboratory machinists. He was quite capable of transferring sketches into workable drawings," Baumgardner said.

"He had perhaps excessive energy, a little on the nervous side. Quite active despite his 200 pounds or so. He was quite concerned about his title and responsibilities, how he fit into the echelon of command. He wanted to be assured that he had a responsible position. He worked well."

The university did not pay Deacon's moving expenses from MIT. "It cost him quite a bit to make the move. He moved into an apartment, as I recall, and he had been there for two months, paying in advance, when he learned that the two men who managed it were policemen. He announced he didn't like the place and that he was moving out. He said he was moving into a house trailer," said Baumgardner.

Deacon had lost a $160 deposit at the Claridge Apartments. The two policemen, Gordon Groland and Howard Rachlin, weren't the least suspicious. "I was coming home from the midnight shift in my uniform once," said Groland, "and Deacon did a double-take."

" 'Don't mind me,' I told him, 'I live here too.' "

They remembered him primarily for one thing: His skill at ping-pong. Deacon had a ping-pong table, which he sometimes carried around on top of his Volvo, and at a pool party in July he had set it up and challenged everyone. One after the other, the apartment dwellers tried to beat him and failed. "He told us he had been a ping-pong champion in California," said Groland.

Baumgardner at the marine lab noticed that Deacon was unusually camera shy. "Whenever a camera came out, George would disappear," he said. "Normally aboard ship we take photographs of our operations, the equipment, methods, and techniques. But George just didn't like to have his picture taken and he so stated. I thought it was just a quirk."

When Baumgardner left his office in September 1968, Deacon fell heir to his private office, North 203, Physical Science Building, a small, well-lit room on the second floor with an acoustical ceiling, blackboard, bookshelves, desk, modern Royal typewriter, an old adding machine, and a Centrex telephone, 350-7425. A window gave him a view of the adjacent Miami Seaquarium, and off in the distance, beyond the blue-green of Biscayne Bay, the skyline of Miami. On his door he attached a comic strip from the Smith Family. The character Georgie had a hobo's pole and sack over his shoulder. Georgie was fed up with the world and leaving for Alaska.

Dr. Emiliani would escort two FBI agents to Deacon's office that first morning and they would find it stripped clean. He found Deacon's suspected role in the kidnaping "totally incredulous."

"I thought him incapable of anything remotely criminal."

To the contrary, Dr. Hurley, being interviewed in his office, was willing to believe Deacon could be involved in virtually anything. "In my private opinion, he was an obnoxious ass, an extremely difficult guy. Deacon was a distinctively highhanded and an arrogant sort of soul, perfectly willing to push his weight around. He had comparatively little patience with anyone; no respect for anyone."

Between August 26 and September 5, marine scientists at the lab had conducted a series of seismic-refraction experiments in the Exhuma Sound of the Bahamas, measuring the earth's undersea crust by timing of sound waves of explosives. Deacon, among other things, piloted a small boat between the firing ship, the *Pillsbury*, and the listening ship, the *Gerda*.

"As a boat driver Deacon had two speeds, stop and wide open. He would take the lines off the ship and throw the throttle into the dash. Obviously he had some skill, otherwise he would have creamed the boat at the onset. It was a pretty hairy performance to watch," Dr. Hurley recalled.

"At one point they hung up a cable on the bottom and rather than take a careful diddle to get the thing loose, they elected to use good old beef. Deacon hauled away on the damn thing, pulling the cable out of the housing and flooding and screwing things up rather successfully. This was in character for him. When in doubt, yank.

"He seemed to take the attitude that he didn't know what the goddamned scientists wanted, but if they wanted it, they would get it. He was beefy, sort of gone to blubber, and ran around there as hairy-chested as anyone can be with a great big knife on his belt. That sort of jazz.

"But he did his work. In a sense, he was a pusher. He would get all the gear together, all the people together, and get the crews out. It required a certain amount of abrasiveness and he certainly had the appropriate character."

The University of Miami Institute of Marine Sciences, like most academic citadels of research, served as a repository for considerable brain power. Deacon, an outsider newly arrived, found almost instant acceptance intellectually. No one questioned his mental abilities. As a scientific community, accustomed to the quest for exactitude and truth, personal eccentricities went largely ignored, his honesty unchallenged. Certainly no one gave Deacon's black bushy beard a second thought.

Arthur Horowitz, an outgoing and personable graduate student a year younger than Deacon, shared quarters with him on the seismic-refraction cruise and found him friendly and very willing to learn. Deacon read Horowitz's entire geophysics text.

"George had a tendency to be loud, demonstrative. He told some funny stories. He said he was on a fishing boat in Alaska and he and other fishermen tried to warn some hunters about bears. The hunters wouldn't believe them. So the fishermen slipped in at night and hung up a side of bacon on a tree near their camp. The place was crawling with bears the next morning. The way he told it, it was funny."

About two weeks after the voyage, Horowitz discovered his draft card was missing from his billfold. He thought he lost it. He looked everywhere. He even went back to the ship to ask if anyone had found it. No one had. Horowitz decided that he would pay a call on his draft board in the Bronx at Christmastime and personally explain. He didn't want to ask for a replacement by mail. He didn't want the board to think he had burned his.

Later that first day of the aborted ransom, Horowitz would hear that Deacon's blue station wagon Volvo had been found at the site. "Good heavens," he exclaimed, "somebody must have stolen George's car."

Geologists Ball and Harrison were also aboard the seismic-refraction expedition and Dr. Ball was impressed by Deacon's carpentry. "We needed a wooden bin for seven thousand pounds of explosives and Deacon help build it on the fantail, eight by four.

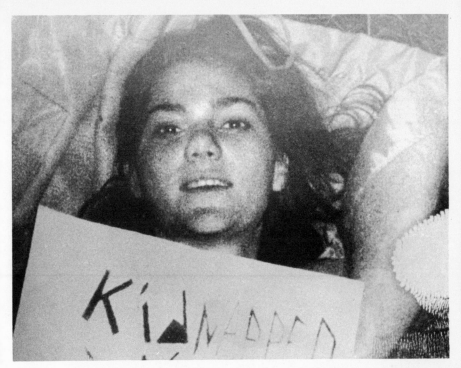

1. Gary Steven Krist took this photograph with a Polaroid Swinger a few moments before he buried alive Barbara Jane Mackle on a Georgia hillside on December 17, 1968. He mailed the photograph to the family as "proof" of the kidnaping. FBI agents found the camera in Krist's Volvo station wagon. (*Wide World Photos*)

2. This is the Coral Gables, Florida, home of the Robert Mackle family at 4111 San Amaro Drive. The kidnapers had buried a ransom note in a test tube under a rock near a palm tree on the property. The unaware gardener, Walter Powell, parked his truck in the driveway the morning of the crime. (AP *Wirephoto*)

Money Left Here

NOT PRIVATE PROPERTY
O.K. NO TRESPASSING
NO FISHING OR HUNTING

3. At 3:47 A.M. the second night after the abduction, the kidnaper telephoned cryptic instructions to Robert Mackle to leave $500,000 on a seldom-used causeway to uninhabited Fair Isle in Biscayne Bay in Miami. In the darkness Robert Mackle could not see the causeway. *(Miami Herald)*

5. Moments after his capture, Gary Steven Krist grimaced and fell unconscious as FBI agents Rex I. Shroder (left) and William Kittel (right) took him from El Jobean, Florida, to a hospital in Fort Myers. He was suffering from exhaustion. Krist still had in his billfold seven of the 25,000 twenty-dollar bills in ransom money. (*Wide World Photos*)

4. Twelve hours before his capture, Gary Steven Krist abandoned his boat on the Gulf coast of Florida at the approach of a Coast Guard helicopter. In this previously unpublished photograph, Krist is seen fleeing toward the treeline of Hog Island. An FBI agent photographed him from the helicopter. (FBI *Photo*)

6. The gravelike burial site attracted the curious and inquisitive to a forest in Gwinnett County northeast of Atlanta, Georgia. The pit measured nine feet in length, two feet nine inches in width, and three feet three inches in depth. The nearest road was up a hill 130 yards away. *(Wide World Photos)*

He just worked like the devil." Dr. Harrison had charge of the shooting operation, a technique new to him for studying the structure of the ocean bottom and he was extremely cautious with the explosives.

"George was doing the hard work. He was supremely confident. He was very energetic and if he botched something up, he bulled right ahead as if he knew all about it. If he had had a little more willingness to learn, he would have made a very good technician. He thought he knew everything and didn't mind telling you."

Kenneth Fink, one of the older graduate students a few months from his Ph.D. in geology, said that Deacon came to him to talk about improvements in coring techniques aboard ship.

"He had a lot of wild ideas. I tactfully tried to redirect him. Most of the things he suggested had been tried or were discussed in the literature. He was trying to pick everyone's brain the best he could. I felt that he was trying very hard to reach above his ability, trying to grasp the technical aspects of coring to enhance his image. But he certainly was friendly and he definitely was a hard worker."

On an earlier five-day scientific cruise that August aboard the *Gerda,* Deacon met a man he genuinely admired, Edmond Fisher. Fisher was a professional underwater photographer. Virile, independent, foot-loose and fancy-free, by reputation a ladies' man, Fisher excelled in his chosen field. Few skin divers anywhere took better photographs than Fisher. And, seemingly, he never lacked money.

"We stopped off at the Dry Tortugas and George and I palled around the island," said Fisher. "I'm not really a very friendly guy. But a comradery developed and we found a couple of chicks. Although George was anxious to be thought of as clever and intelligent, he was a likeable guy so far as guys go. He liked to tackle technical problems. He liked to walk into a situation which a Ph.D. might not be able to handle because the problem was unique and all his scholarly knowledge wouldn't be of much help."

In the course of their brief friendship, Fisher told Deacon about the time he was driving a motorcycle in Miami and a taxi driver forced him off the road. "I punched him and he swore out a warrant for my arrest and I had to go to court," said Fisher. "The judge fined me twenty-five dollars.

"George told me I should have never told my side of the story in court. Instead of telling my side, I should have said, 'Your Honor, I move for a dismissal for lack of evidence' because the only evidence was that of the accuser. It seemed like fairly good advice— offered too late. George told me he had studied law."

In Dr. Hurley's office that morning, with the telephone line open to FBI headquarters downtown, agents began also their investigation of Ruth Eisemann-Schier. Dr. Hurley knew well the circumstances of her acceptance into the graduate school. On a leave from the University of Miami in 1965–66, he had served as a deputy director of UNESCO's office of oceanography in Paris, France, and there he had become acquainted with Jose Suarez-Carbo, a Cuban scientist in exile, who later went to work for the Pan American Union in Washington, D.C.

"From Washington Jose wrote me recommending very highly this wonderful little girl, Ruth Eisemann, praising her to the sky and indicating she would like to come here as a chemistry major," Dr. Hurley said. "This was my first introduction. I wasn't impressed. She sent a formal application and she seemed imminently qualified. But, still, this didn't excite anyone."

Because of the marine lab's crammed quarters and limited budget, it accepted annually for postgraduate study only about thirty of six hundred applicants. Ruth's educational credentials appeared sound. On her application she listed her birth date as November 8, 1942, El Hatillo, Honduras. She had attended the Universidad Nacional de Mexico from February 1961 until March 1967, earning the equivalent of a master's degree in pharmaceutical chemistry. During her last year at the university she worked in the office laboratory of a Mexico City doctor. The months of March to October 1967 were blank as far as employment. During that time, though, she had enrolled in the Mondino School of Languages in Washington, D.C. and attended for twenty months, becoming fluent in German and French. Her native tongue was Spanish. She spoke English competently. From October 1967 until her application to the University of Miami, she had worked as a research biologist in the Pan American Union's department of scientific affairs.

"Then one day in the middle of the summer of 1968," several months after the marine lab had already accepted and rejected most of its applicants, "Ruth and her mother simply showed up here," Dr. Hurley said. "Ruth was well poised, very cool, self-possessed, wrists properly crossed, that sort of thing. She was pleasant enough."

In his position as chairman of the division of graduate students, Dr. Hurley inquired about financial support. "Frankly, I was curious. I tried to find out something about the family. I tried delicately to find out who were her antecedents? Who in the hell was going to support her here? I received perfectly polite and nebulous answers. I had the feeling the family had some money. She assured me that the Pan American Union would give her a fellowship. This was to occur in February—and, needless to say, February never came."

Prior to Ruth's appearance that day, another graduate student, just off the docks, had sat in Dr. Hurley's office and somehow he had left a splotch of asphalt on a plastic-covered chair. Ruth, wearing a sheer cotton dress that looked like her Sunday best, sat in the same chair. Her dress was a mess.

Understandably, Dr. Hurley and his secretary, Mrs. Lyria Blanchard, apologized profusely. Ruth managed it all quite coolly.

She was interviewed that day by Dr. Walter Drost-Hansen, chairman of the division of physical and chemical oceanography, and accepted for the fall semester.

"She probably would not have been accepted except that she was here," said Dr. Hurley. "I was a little surprised; not a lot. Her background looked good and she came fully supported. We didn't have to worry about money. At least this was our understanding at the time."

Some weeks later, before the start of the autumn semester, Dr. Hurley received a postcard from Ruth in Honduras.

"Cordial greetings from my wonderful small country. I hope that all my transcriptions are already at the graduate school. I'll be there at August 26. Did you get the black spots out of your office's seats? (Hope so!) Greetings to your nice secretaries. Kindest regards."

Dr. Hurley's secretary, Mrs. Blanchard, had taken an interest in Ruth since the first day she and her mother visited the marine lab. Mrs. Blanchard had been born in El Salvador and had lived in Nicaragua, two Central American countries bordering Honduras, Ruth's native country.

"The mother wanted to know the living arrangements," said Mrs. Blanchard. Ruth's mother struck her then as "an extremely demanding woman; German, nice, polite, quite civilized, but inwardly, sort of a demanding female." Ruth's mother was Mrs. Elfriede Eisemann-Schier, a widowed dentist from Catacamas, Honduras.

"I introduced them to Mrs. Anna Harrison, our receptionist," said Mrs. Blanchard. "I knew she rented rooms."

Mrs. Anna Harrison worked behind the counter in the main lobby of the Gilbert Hovey Grosvenor Laboratory, where on the walls a taxidermist's versions of a 376-pound blue marlin kept her company. She was a cheerful, blue-eyed, gray-haired grandmotherly woman whose father, Sir Henry Thornton, had been the first president of the Canadian National Railways. She was once married to a distinguished physician who had since died, and she had accepted the job as receptionist from an old friend of the family, Dr. F. G. Walton Smith, the director of the marine lab.

The Eisemann-Schiers, mother and daughter, arrived on a Sunday afternoon in July at the home of Mrs. Harrison to inspect the furnished room for rent. Mrs. Harrison lived in a modest three-bedroom two-bath house at 5901 Southwest Sixty-second Street in South Miami with a big malaluka tree in the front yard. She accepted roomers when her two daughters married.

For fifty dollars a month Ruth could have the room, and Mrs. Harrison would be glad to drive her to the marine lab at eight o'clock every morning. "They came by bus to look at the room. They had sandwiches with them and they picnicked at my dining room table. The mother inveigled me to drive them to a hibiscus exhibit in North Miami that afternoon. She was a very managing woman. She would talk you into a tight corner, then make you feel sorry for her. When I dropped them off at their motel, she asked me, 'Do you suppose you could keep a trunk for us?' It was the heaviest thing. It took all three of us to get it into the trunk of the car, and I didn't have the remotest idea of how I was going to get it out. A week later my son-in-law came over."

From August 26 until December 13, not quite four months, Ruth lived at Mrs. Harrison's house and studied at the marine lab, physical oceanography, chemical oceanography and marine geology. With the laboratory courses, she carried a normal load of seven credit hours, for which she paid $420.

On that Thursday after the discovery of the Volvo, as well as in the days and weeks to follow, the people who knew her groped for explanation.

"She seemed so demure, gentle-voiced, polite. She spoke four languages and I always spoke German with her," said Mrs. Lois Keith, secretary for a professor of marine biology and physiology. "Before she left she came by and wished me a Merry Christmas."

Initially she seemed lonely at the marine lab. Rene Weldo, a young Cuban boy who worked in the stock room, detected this. "She once said, 'I've been in Miami for two weeks and I never go out of the house because I don't know a soul in this city.' I introduced her all around and took her out to lunch. But there was something about her. You just couldn't get to know Ruth."

Because of her Spanish, she met Mrs. Sylvia Valdes, one of about eighteen Latins at the marine lab. Sylvia Valdes, a few years older than Ruth, held a Ph.D. in chemistry from Havana and supervised three other Cuban girls in an atomic adsorption project in a geo-chemical lab. "Ruth joined us for coffee a few times. She was rather friendly, nice and pleasant, and she was an optimist; not a pessimist. She could conquer the world. She had not had calculus and one of her professors ordered her to take it on the main campus. She said she thought she could study and learn it on her own. I told her she needed the course. She didn't take it. Once, I know, she skipped a class and had someone take in a tape recorder and tape the lecturer."

Sylvia Valdes began to question Ruth's academic qualifications. "She said she had her master's in chemistry and she didn't know some of the basic things. She would stay late to do her work in the lab, and the next morning I could see she couldn't possibly have made the correct measurements. I told her that she should study harder or she would flunk."

Mrs. Lyria Blanchard, Dr. Hurley's Central American-born secretary, noticed Ruth's academic problems. "She started out fine, but in November I received confidential information that one of her professors was going to have to give her a C as an interim grade. That is very bad news in graduate school. A C is almost an invitation to leave. I saw her, and I said, 'Ruth, what are you trying to do? You are not applying yourself.' She said she had not been feeling well. 'I am going to study very hard. I promise you that, Mrs. Blanchard.'"

Mrs. Blanchard and Ruth's landlady, Mrs. Harrison, took a detached interest in Ruth's social life. "She was very much infatuated with a young engineering student," said Mrs. Blanchard.

"She is too timid," Mrs. Harrison suspected at the time. "I don't know if the fellow knew it. He came to call and she was all a dither."

Ruth Eisemann-Schier wasn't exactly the shy retiring young lady that she appeared. While in Washington, D.C., one of her romantic attachments left her pregnant. She had flown to Puerto Rico and obtained an abortion.

Neither Mrs. Blanchard nor Mrs. Harrison, however, knew anything of her sexual promiscuity.

"If she had any greater proclivity for leaping into bed than normal, I probably would have caught wind of it," said Dr. Hurley. "She was quite discreet. She had not demonstrated an unlimited enthusiasm for rolling in the hay; at least, not any exceptional enthusiasm.

"She had a slightly canned smile, obviously part of her façade," Dr. Hurley said. "She cultivated the helpless female role. She had a strange way of rotating her shoulders. I think I could recognize her in silhouette at a hundred yards just by that mannerism. She seemed mild and meek and pleasant, very feminine. But put it this way. She was thoroughly conscious of being a female, and not a bad-looking female at that.

"Near the end of the first semester she was in my office talking about money. I suggested that she find some elsewhere because I couldn't do much about it. I had the feeling I was being manipulated to a certain extent; the fellowship hadn't materialized."

His supposition was correct. Ruth had not been promised a fellowship at the Pan American Union in Washington; at least, not to the knowledge of Jesse Perkinson, director of the union, whom she listed as a reference on her application to the marine lab. Dr. Perkinson had met Ruth once or twice in the hallway, he said, and that was about the limit of their acquaintanceship. She had applied for a fellowship, however, and in due course she might well have received it. The Pan American Union granted approximately five hundred fellowships annually. There was one good reason why her application had not been acted upon. "It wasn't completed," said Jorge Zamorano. "We never reached the point of grading her application. She had not yet submitted all the necessary documents."

She was remembered there as "vivacious," a girl who never lacked masculine attention.

This situation was not altogether different at the Institute of Marine Sciences. The mere fact that she was female made her conspicuous. There were only seven other girls classified as students. Ruth developed a friendship with the marine's only female postdoctoral fellow that semester, Diana I. Sanchez, a young unmarried biochemist of Spanish descent from Laredo, Texas, who was studying the toxin of the Portuguese man-of-war.

"I met her in September. She did not speak English well," Dr. Sanchez recalled. "She seemed like a very nice girl, very moral. She was a little daring as far as swimming was concerned. She was a strong swimmer."

During lunch breaks Ruth would sometimes dive into the swift currents of Bear Cut off the marine lab's dock. "Not even the guys in the lab would do that," said Dr. Sanchez.

"I told her it was very dangerous," said Mrs. Blanchard. "The current there is very bad and we have spotted many sharks there." Ruth didn't appear concerned.

It was Mrs. Blanchard's opinion that Ruth attached herself to Diana Sanchez like a flea to a dog. "It was a little disturbing. Diana didn't want to be her mother, but Ruth just didn't want to be alone."

Nonetheless, a fondness grew between the two women and they attended the play, *Andersonville,* together, double-dated, and made a trip to Kissimmee in central Florida. "This guy who she knew in Washington was coming down to a ranch around Orlando somewhere, and Ruth had another date in Miami she had to break. She told him a big story about going up to see a girl friend who was pregnant. I asked her, 'Why did you lie to him? Why didn't you say you were going with me? You didn't have to tell the guy that.' She was always going on these tangents, fantasy, just make-believe. She would make up the wildest stories. I knew she was lying. I asked her once why she did it and she said, 'Well, I guess I make them up before I realize it, and then I have to keep them up.'"

The lives of Ruth Eisemann-Schier and the man known then as

George Gary Deacon first crossed at sea on a voyage of the *John Elliott Pillsbury,* the marine lab's largest research vessel.

In the five years that the marine lab had owned the 560-ton, 176-foot *Pillsbury,* the ship had steamed 188,000 miles in scientific exploration of the southeastern Pacific, the Caribbean, Mediterranean, Black Sea and the Atlantic from Miami to the coasts of South America and Africa. It was built originally as an Army miscellaneous cargo vessel in the shipyards of Chicago in World War II, and in September 1968 it had the cluttered look of a floating laboratory, which it was, huge A-frames on deck, mobile platforms, labs both wet and dry, a deep-sea trawling winch operative at 42,000 feet, deep-sea coring apparatus, two hydrographic winches, a bathytermography winch, and a precision depth recorder and echo sounder with a range of six thousand fathoms. Because of the tropical heat, it was air-conditioned.

On September 23, the *Pillsbury* had sailed from Port Everglades in Fort Lauderdale with its usual crew of twenty-one and thirteen scientists from the marine lab; its destination, the western Atlantic; its objectives, multiple: collection of piston cores for stratigraphic analysis, collection of sediment for microalgate cultures, and collection of sea water for tritium analysis. One objective, listed last on the cruise plan, was to introduce new scientists to conventional marine-sampling procedures.

Among the new scientists were Dr. Diana I. Sanchez and Ruth Eisemann-Schier.

"It was not normal to take women to sea," said Jim Gibbons, the operating manager of the ship. "We had one hard and fast rule. Never allow one to go alone. They always had to go in pairs."

"With thirty-four persons aboard, the quarters were pretty close," said Gibbons. "And the longer we were out, the smaller they got."

Because of the scientific nature of the expedition, the ship, like the marine lab in Miami, was alive at all hours of the night. Besides the two crewmen always on duty in the pilot house, the scientists usually had nocturnal projects that kept them up. "It was very difficult to get any privacy," Gibbons said.

The two women aboard altered the shipboard routine. One able-bodied seaman from Pennsylvania, so dark he had once been mistaken for a black man in a tavern, gave up his habit of sunbathing in a jock strap.

"When you have thirty-two men aboard ship and a good-looking girl or two, they are going to be looked at," said Gardner G. Duman, the chief engineer of the *Pillsbury*.

"Ruth knew she was kind of cute and I think she didn't mind everyone knowing it," said Roy C. Dawn, the bosun. "She was polite enough. She would say hello. She certainly was well educated."

"Not all the girls we get are bright; she was," said Norm G. Cubberly, the chief mate. "But she wasn't awfully interested in working and she was a bird of many plumages. I think she had the biggest laundry on the ship." Cubberly had the impression that "Ruth definitely was looking for a little something and when George came along at the right time, she found it."

Apparently no one, though, noticed anything between Deacon and Ruth during the first six days of the voyage.

The second assistant engineer, Edward R. Clup, a crew-cut Dutchman from Indiana, positively disliked Deacon. "He was a tub of lard. I called him Big George, the way he put away the chow." Clup, who felt that the engine room belonged to him on his watch, had loaned Deacon a couple of small screw drivers which Deacon did not return. Clup confronted Deacon, "When are you going to give me back my tools?"

"He told me he'd already put them back, and I said, 'That's funny. There is a padlock on that tool box and the only key is in my pocket.' I'd seen sharpies before." Clup found his screw drivers hidden in a drawer the next day.

Duman, the chief engineer, got along well with Deacon. "He was sort of a tinker, always trying to improve things. He designed a clam-shell device with a spring release which we used for scooping up two or three cups of mud off the bottom in shallow water for samples.

"Deacon had a very alert mind, very practical—like a ten-dollar mouse trap."

Hendrick Miller, a muscular young man from Poughkeepsie, New York, worked directly with Deacon as a technician, lifting and fastening cast-iron weights to coring pipes. The weights weighed sixty-three pounds each, and working on a platform over a rolling sea wasn't the safest way to make a living. "George was devising a way we could keep the weights on all the time," said Miller. "There was no question he was very smart. I thought he was a genius.

"But he could never put a tool down gently," said Miller. "He would always toss it."

On the sixth day of the cruise, a Saturday morning, the *Pillsbury* arrived at St. George, Bermuda, for a long weekend, and Deacon and Miller went ashore and soon found themselves in the company of John F. Allen, a veterinarian on a postdoctoral fellowship studying whales and dolphin, and Diana Sanchez and Ruth. The one simple way to tour the island was to rent motor bikes. Ruth announced, however, she didn't know how to ride. Would anyone let her ride on theirs?

The bikes were Italian-made, chain-and-sprocket vehicles, designed girl-fashion without the bar, with pedals for pumping for going uphill; perfectly adequate, nonetheless, for maiming oneself going downhill on the wrong side of the road, which was the right side.

"Actually," said Miller, "they were just girls' bikes with little motors. You could lift one with one hand."

The Negro gentleman who rented them for five dollars a day disapproved of two on a bike. The bikes simply weren't built to take it.

"It was against the law to take two," said Diana Sanchez, and when Ruth asked her if she could ride, Diana said she was sorry. "George said it wasn't very nice of us to leave Ruth alone. But there was nothing else we could do."

"Ruth asked several of us if she could ride two on a bike," said Miller. "When she asked George, he said fine. Any time anyone paid any attention to George he was quick and obliging."

Thus began the romance of George Deacon and Ruth Eisemann-Schier, she clinging to him on a motor bike, the balloon tires squished almost to the rim under his 220 pounds and her 110.

Cubberly, the chief mate, said he saw Deacon in a white plastic helmet complaining bitterly to the bike renter. His bike wasn't tuned well enough.

Cubberly thought that Deacon rented and ruined five different bikes during those three days in Bermuda.

"I think it was five," said Miller. "They kept bogging down. Deacon was bragging about it."

On one occasion, Miller and Allen and Sanchez stopped with Deacon and Ruth near a lagoon for snorkeling. "We wanted to catch some small fish and we didn't have a net. George made a net out of a coat hanger and burlap sack."

Soon it became apparent that Ruth and Deacon preferred each other's company to touring the island. When the threesome took off the next day for Port Victoria, Ruth and Deacon decided they would rather swim.

As Miller pedaled his bike up the steep incline of a cliff, he could see two persons swimming out to sea in the magnificently clear water toward a rock outcropping.

"I bet that's George and Ruth," he guessed, and he stopped and looked through the telescopic lens of his camera. He was right. He waved and went on. Several hours later he noticed they were still lying together on the rock.

It wasn't until a day or two after the *Pillsbury* departed Bermuda that university scientists learned that Deacon had abandoned his last rented motor bike at Gun Powder Cavern.

"It was a little embarrassing," said Cubberly, the chief mate. "We sent a message to Dowling, the bike man, and told him we were willing to make good for it.

"Ruth and Deacon's affair was fairly obvious to everyone during the second half of the trip," said Cubberly. "The chief scientist had to tell him to knock it off. 'This is a ship. We're at sea for scientific purposes. If you want to play around, do it at home.'"

"I went to Dr. Bader," said Dawn, the bosun. "I usually try to walk around the ship and I saw a mattress, blanket and pillow out on the science deck, as we called it, and they'd been rained on. I told him I didn't care what his people did, that wasn't our business, but we have to take care of the equipment. I knew Ruth and Deacon were going together. On a ship, you know."

"It was not all that apparent to me," said Diana Sanchez. "I figured that something was going on, but I gave her the benefit of the doubt. There was no big deal to the mattress. Several of the guys took mattresses up there and looked at the stars."

Dr. Sanchez and Ruth worked different shifts. "I was eight to twelve; she was twelve to four," said Diana Sanchez. She thought it unlikely that Ruth entertained George in their shared female quarters while she was elsewhere about the ship.

One young crewman, though, one of the three unmarried men aboard, had no doubts whatsoever. Wandering about late one night, he came across Deacon and Ruth inadvertently in what he felt certainly was an act of fornication. He shrugged his shoulders and forgot about it.

Young Rick Miller surprised Ruth and Deacon as they were leaning against a box containing life rafts on an upper deck aft, and thereafter he purposely made a great deal of noise every time he went up the ladder. He didn't want to embarrass anyone.

Dr. Richard G. Bader, the chief scientist on the cruise, a geochemist and oceanographer, did not attach much significance to the Deacon-Ruth relationship. "I think I spoke to them on the bow on the day before we arrived home. I told them to be a little more discreet; that they should act like ladies and gentlemen."

The *Pillsbury* returned to Port Everglades October 7, ten weeks before the kidnaping of Barbara Mackle, and Ruth and Deacon ceased to attract attention as a couple. Except for a few seemingly chance encounters around the marine lab, they were seldom seen together.

Ruth's shipboard romance did not enhance her popularity among other postgraduate females at the marine lab. They considered her choice of a locale for a fling, aboard a scientific ship, just about the worst possible place. It was difficult enough for any girl to be accepted as a scientist. To allow a love affair to occur aboard the *Pillsbury* was inexcusable. "We all heard the stories about her fooling around on the cruise and it peeved me," said Nancy Maynard. Apparently Ruth realized how the other girls would feel. Although no one said anything to her, they noticed a distinct change in her behavior. "After the cruise I saw very little of her. She just wasn't around very often," Miss Maynard said.

Diana Sanchez noticed the difference too. "She avoided seeing me after the trip because she knew that I would question her. I could tell she was upset. I didn't want to pry too much. I knew she didn't want to go into details so I didn't press her."

Ruth seemed occupied with her grades and studies, and the demands of her mother from Honduras.

"I knew she was having trouble with her mother. I got this from Ruth. Her mother was quite domineering," said Diana Sanchez. "She got these letters from her and they were mostly like sermons. Fanatical. Ruth wasn't religious at all; although, she wasn't anti-religious."

"Her mother was making constant demands on her," said Lyria Blanchard, the secretary to Dr. Hurley. "She told me all she had in the world was $1500. She hadn't received the scholarship yet. She didn't know if she would be able to pay her tuition and buy books. Even used books cost more than a hundred dollars a semester. As time went by, her mother made constant and persistent demands; she would want this, want that, little things like clothing, make-up, odds and ends, one thing and the other. Her mother wanted a large plastic swimming pool and Ruth bought and mailed her one. Then her mother sent it back air express, collect. It wasn't big enough for her mother. Think of the shipping charge. Her mother wanted a five-hundred-dollar pool, the most expensive one. I felt sorry for Ruth."

Mrs. Harrison, the landlady, recalled the incident. "Her mother badgered her that the first one was too small. In every letter she was complaining. She insisted Ruth take the pool back to the store or resell it herself. Ruth was getting kind of fed up with her mother."

On December 9, Ruth took her last $500 from her Miami savings account and purchased the expensive plastic pool. She had it shipped to her mother in Honduras.

On the morning of the nineteenth, as FBI agents began to ask questions at the marine lab, no one had seen either Deacon or Ruth there since the previous Friday, the thirteenth.

Deacon's absence wasn't noteworthy. As long as he kept up with his work, which he did, he pretty well came and went as he pleased.

Ruth had made a production of her departure. On the previous Friday she had left gifts for Mrs. Harrison, the landlady, and her two grandchildren.

"She gave the children little stuffed animals with music boxes inside them," said Mrs. Harrison. "One was a Pooh bear and the other an alligator with a bee on his tail. They were both darling. She gave me an embroidered handkerchief. It was beautiful. I believe she had picked it up in Vienna a year or so before when she visited her grandmother in Austria.

"She had been discouraged about her bad grades, but she had just passed her troubles off lately. She seemed quite excited. She told me she was going to spend the holidays with a friend, Julie, at a ranch near Jacksonville. Julie's grandfather owned the ranch, she said.

"When I said good-by to her, she just had her overnight case.

She owned a big suitcase and said that her girl friend had come by for it the day before so that she wouldn't have to worry about it and she'd be ready to leave. She told me she would be back January 5."

Mrs. Harrison had seen Deacon bring Ruth home once after the cruise on the *Pillsbury*. "She told me he was very good to her. I thought to myself several times that I must ask what happened to Deacon, why she wasn't seeing him any more."

Mrs. Harrison had just returned from a hospital confinement for bronchitis and did not drive Ruth to the lab that last Friday.

She had asked Lee Hearn, a postgraduate student who worked in the same lab with Dr. Sanchez, to pick her up.

"It slipped my mind completely," said Hearn. "I lived close by. She called me at the lab and I drove back and picked her up. She was talking about this ranch somewhere in North Florida. She said she intended to do a lot of horseback riding. She told me she had an examination that Friday, Dr. Broida's class. She had borrowed my notes to study for it."

Ruth attended Dr. Saul Broida's general oceanography class that morning, but there was no examination. None had been scheduled. He had become quite concerned about her poor grade on the first test, October 18. "She seemed to be preoccupied. She wasn't studying. She wasn't doing her work. I talked to her about it and she said she was going to study harder. Every student says that," Dr. Broida recalled. On a second examination, November 18, however, Ruth improved immensely. Since the Friday class, Dr. Broida had found a Christmas card from Ruth in his university mailbox. It wasn't postmarked. Presumably, she had put it there herself that Friday.

The news of the stolen Boston Whaler and the finding of Deacon's Volvo at the site of the ransom drop circulated swiftly through the corridors and offices of the University of Miami Institute of Marine Sciences that day. And soon there was talk that a girl was involved in the kidnaping.

"I bet that's Ruthie," said Nancy Maynard, a postgraduate student.

"Oh, come off it," replied Diana Sanchez. "Don't be so cruel."

Tell God Too Much Going Wrong

At the wall at the Fair Isle Causeway, agent Fred Frohbose had tried futilely to console Robert Mackle at daybreak Thursday. Billy Vessels managed to pull himself together first.

"Fred," he said, "we will go back to the house. Don't worry about us."

They drove back in pit-bottom despair, shattered, destroyed, the father weeping. "It's all over," he said. "We've bungled it."

The first radio accounts from the police had not been accurate. Both men believed that someone had killed the kidnapers during a "shoot-out."

Slowly the anger began to well up in Billy Vessels. He possessed extremely limited information, but there was no doubt about the basic fact: the Mackles had placed complete trust in the FBI and something had gone wrong, tragically wrong.

"We had this understanding. We wouldn't play games with each other. We had to know all the facts; what was true, what was not true; what was real, what was not real," Vessels recalled later. "We placed 100 per cent trust in the FBI. They assured us that they would not under any circumstances interfere, they would never close in."

And with Robert Mackle crying beside him, he felt the FBI had double-crossed them. His anger exploded as he walked into the house.

"Some sonofabitch better start having some answers for me!"

"Rex Shroder came back at me just as strong," said Vessels. "He told us it wasn't the FBI's fault, they didn't have anything to do with it, no one knew very much at that time."

It took more than an hour for the facts to solidify at the Mackle home. At one point Inspector Shroder walked up to Robert Mackle and told him that the news was out. Newspaper reporters had heard about it. It would be on the radio.

Billy Vessels telephoned his wife. He wanted her to know he wasn't shot.

"I am at Robert's house," he said. "I am fine."

"Is anything wrong?"

"No," he said. "You might hear something. I'm fine."

Some moments later, after pulling together the pieces by radio and telephone and agents from the site, Inspector Shroder again approached the Mackle brothers.

"Now this is what we have," he began, and he laid out what he knew of the Volvo, the two names, George Deacon and Ruth Eisemann-Schier, and the chase, and the recovery of the $500,000. FBI agent Andrew A. Armstrong, Jr. transferred the money to FBI headquarters.

"I don't care about the money," said Robert Mackle. "We've got to get another contact." He had recovered from the initial shock. "We've got to let them know we had nothing to do with it. We have to tell them it was completely accidental, and that I have the money and I'm ready to deliver it."

At FBI headquarters agent Swinney tried to answer the incoming press inquiries. The switchboard operator had the callers stacked up and holding. Again and again, without direct attribution to the FBI, he tried to straighten out the misconceptions. Robert Mackle, he said, had nothing to do with the payoff failure and he wanted to do business with the kidnapers.

Jim Savage, a reporter for the Miami *Herald*, sat in agent Swinney's office listening, and after the fifth or sixth call, he stuck a piece of paper in a typewriter, and typed:

I had nothing to do with the action Thursday morning of the Miami police who tried to arrest you and recovered the money which I left for you.

I regret that you did not get the money because my only interest is the safety of my daughter.

I pray that you have not harmed my daughter. I did everything you told me to do, and I had nothing to do with the accidental appearance of the Miami police on the scene.

Please contact me again through any channel. I will do anything you ask so my daughter will be freed.

"Is this about what he said?" Savage asked.

"Fine," said agent Swinney, and he put quotation marks on the paragraphs. At the bottom of the page he signed Robert

Mackle's name. During the next twenty-four hours, the plea of
Robert Mackle would be read repeatedly over television and
radio and printed in the newspapers.

The Miami office of the FBI had its work cut out for it that
Thursday. Almost the entire 125-agent force found itself assigned
to the kidnaping. Besides the marine lab, details of agents converged on Miami International Airport. Nine agents would practically live there in the lobby of the sprawling airport for two
days, searching the faces of thousands of passengers who boarded
departing flights. Soon they would have photographs rushed to
them of Deacon and Ruth Eisemann-Schier, and they had the
description of a possible third suspect, the second man deputy
Self and officer Sweeney believed they had seen. It fit ten thousand
men. Other agents set up the watch at smaller airports where
someone might charter a plane. Agents rushed to the Trailway
and Greyhound bus stations, the Seaboard Coast Line Railroad
passenger station, and a detail of agents parked and waited at the
tollgates of Sunshine State Parkway for automobile traffic north.
The descriptions went out to all police agencies. The chance
that agents or anyone else would detect them in the enormous
outflow of traffic from the metropolitan area appeared remote; but
it was a chance that couldn't be overlooked. It might be the
only chance they would have. They simply did not know. Other
agents began asking questions at the twenty-six hospitals in the
county. Was anyone treated for a bullet wound? Officer Sweeney
just might have hit him. Did the Dade County medical examiner
have an unidentified body? Still other agents began a street-by-
street search of hotel and motel parking lots in the vicinity of the
drop site. What happened to the black Ford with the Massachusetts plate? Would Deacon try to rent a car since he had abandoned his Volvo? That was another possibility.

One lead dominated all others that morning. Deacon's address:
The Al-Ril Trailer Court at 8401 Northwest Fourteenth Avenue in
Miami.

If the ransom note was a ruse, couldn't Barbara be held in a
trailer? Could Deacon's trailer in Miami actually be the "small
capsule," "the box, fiberglass-reinforced plywood"?

Four cars of agents sped directly to the trailer court. Soon two
helicopters chomped the air overhead.

"And I thought nothing ever happened around here," said Frank Wales, a flabbergasted delivery-service truck driver who lived across a road from Deacon's blue-bottomed and white-topped forty-eight-foot trailer. He hadn't seen Deacon in a week.

"They didn't tell me why they wanted him, but they said it was real serious," said Cyril Hedrick, manager of the court.

A reflecting aluminum bauble sign, flickering in the breeze, designated the court as the Al-Ril, and by no standard could the Al-Ril be considered the most affluent of South Florida's trailer-court enterprises. It abutted a racially integrated neighborhood in one of the county's lower-income neighborhoods. The monthly rent for a space on the lot ran forty-five dollars. The Al-Ril took its name from its previous owners, Albert P. and Rilla M. Daigle. They had moved to Miami from Maine with an Al-Ril license plate.

Deacon had moved in during the summer after purchase of a repossessed trailer, and like the other seventy-seven trailers on the lot, it was "blocked up" on concrete blocks. He brought with him a wife, Dorothy, and two small sons, Adam and Vince.

Deacon's wife, Dorothy, was a slender dark-haired girl, quite intelligent, who had left for California with her children exactly a week ago Thursday. At least that's what she had told Diana Carmona, one of the few persons there she ever talked to.

Miss Carmona, a plump young girl going to Barry College, qualified as Dorothy's closest—and seemingly only—friend in the trailer court. They played tennis together. Occasionally she would baby-sit for them. Diana thought she was the only person in the court who had ever been inside Deacon's trailer. Nearly everyone knew who he was. He was the big guy with the black bushy beard who didn't have much to say, "very closed mouthed," "not very friendly."

"He was very cynical, kind of bitter," said Diana. "He resented having to live in a trailer. But he was very bright and I liked him."

Deacon, she remembered, venerated wealth. "The one man he admired was a man who had money, a real swinger. I think his name was Ed something. George thought I was a bad influence on his wife. He thought the woman's place was in the home."

Frank Wales, who lived diagonally across the road, had never had anything to do with Deacon. "I thought he was a crank. He always had his shades pulled down." Wales, a redheaded man of thirty-four with decided opinions, noticed that Deacon had a Massachusetts plate. "I'm from Framingham and I knew he should have a Florida plate if he worked here." He disapproved. Deacon kept an old U-Haul trailer with a Massachusetts plate parked by his house trailer, too.

Wales' younger brother, Ronald, also lived in Al-Ril and he owned a lime-green flower-decorated Volkswagen. Like Deacon, he wore a beard.

"When the FBI knocked on the door, I couldn't believe it."

"Barbara," he said to his wife, "it's Efrem Zimbalist, Jr. You open the door, not me."

Ronald, a muscular ironworker, often related the people he knew to others. Zimbalist was an actor on an FBI television show. Dorothy Deacon reminded him of Olive Oyle from the comic strip "Popeye."

Ronald Wales wondered about Deacon. "We called him 'the Deacon.' Working people work around here and he was home all the time. He had better than banker's hours." Wales was very much impressed with Deacon's carpentry. "Ironworkers and carpenters generally don't like each other on construction jobs, but the Deacon really built some sturdy shelves. A hurricane could have hit us, blown away the whole trailer court and those shelves would have stayed."

Others in the Al-Ril became quite aware of Deacon's carpentry. During the summer he had stayed up hammering until two or three o'clock in the morning. "I had to go over and ask him to stop," said Joe Donahue, an elderly retired neighbor. Deacon obliged.

"They kept very much to themselves," said Mrs. Vernard Powell. "Anytime they went away, he would come out and sit in the car. She would have to drag the kids. If they forgot anything, she was the one who went and got it. He didn't move."

Agents wanted to know if anyone had seen Deacon lately. One man had. This was Albert William Bischoff, a retired house painter from Elmhurst, New Jersey. He lived in the adjacent trailer. At seventy-three Bischoff had a full head of dark brown hair and the only gray was a stray hair or two in his eyebrows.

He had seen Deacon the previous afternoon, Wednesday, the day after the kidnaping. He had talked to him sometime between four and five o'clock.

"I didn't recognize him when I saw him at first," said Bischoff. "He had shaved. His beard was gone. I walked up to him and said, 'I didn't know who in the hell you were.'

"Deacon had his Volvo parked on my lawn and he had just finished washing it. It burned me up a little. I don't know why he didn't use his own lawn.

"He told me he shaved because he was taking off for six months. He said he was going out on the ocean for the university and that he was going out of the country. He said that a couple of times."

Bischoff's sister, Bertha, visiting for the holidays, overheard the conversation and asked Deacon, "What country?"

"Jordan," Deacon replied.

"He said he was going to have to store his Volvo while he was away at the upper ramp at the airport and I told them that was valet parking and that would cost him a fortune. He wanted to know if I knew anybody offhand who might want to use it while he was gone so it wouldn't be idle," said Bischoff. "He showed me how to open the hood. The catch was broken and he had a wire under the grille that you pulled and the hood opened." To Bischoff, Deacon seemed out of character that afternoon. A woman from a trailer nearby came out asking if she could borrow some paprika or seasoning and Deacon went into his trailer and obligingly offered her some from his own kitchen.

"I must have talked to him for ten or fifteen minutes," Bischoff told FBI agents. "He told me he would give me the keys to his Volvo today."

Agents would remain at the Al-Ril on shifts for several days, some sitting in Bischoff's trailer with a view out the window to Deacon's trailer.

As agents canvassed the Al-Ril, the manager, Hedrick, recalled his one major run-in with Deacon.

"When he moved in he had an air conditioner and I hooked it up temporarily, and changed 110 volts to 220. He said he would get heavy wire and do it right," said Hedrick. "I saw it a couple of months later and he had it hooked up in front of the meter so the meter wouldn't register. I got mad. He said somebody else did it. I told him I was going to fix it right and watch that meter for a month, then double his bill for the month he didn't pay. We had words and I told him he would pay up or I would get the cops and have him thrown off the lot."

At the mention of police, Hedrick recalled much later, Deacon had quieted down and decided to pay.

The mailman delivered the mail at the Al-Ril during the hub-bub and commotion that Thursday morning and there was a Christmas card for Deacon from his wife in California. It had a return address: 1931 Cordilleras Road, Redwood City.

She had written that she had a nice flight, and that the kids were adjusting.

Then, quite cryptically, she had added:

". . . By the time you get this you should be well on the road to wealth and excitement and glory. Remember you asked me if you couldn't go to bed for excitement? My first thought is 'isn't it exciting with almost every member of the opposite sex?' My second thought is 'yes but only because it is forbidden.' If everyone were a 'criminal,' you'd probably find the 'good Christian life' exciting. I accept what you are attempting; personally, it is not my way. I don't find social orientation exciting—like flashy cars, clothes. Of course if there weren't anybody like you in the world it would be a lot less exciting.

"No one has been around yet asking questions (December 16).

"The airplane ride was fun.

"I'll be reading and listening to the news. Good luck; be careful and brave and DON'T LET THE BASTARDS WEAR YOU DOWN! You are the only man I know who can do it."

It was signed, "My love. C."

The Christmas card to George Deacon, like the hundreds of letters addressed to the Mackle residence, had funneled through the U. S. Post Office Department's Biscayne Annex in Miami, a central distribution agency for nearly all incoming and outgoing delivery. Approximately ten million pieces of mail went through the annex daily. Postal employees on three shifts there sorted the Miami-addressed mail into nine hundred and seventy-eight letter-carrier zones. The mail for sixty-eight of those zones went to a Coral Gables substation during the night, and at six o'clock, Ed Nauman, carrier route man for route fifty-five, San Amaro Drive, arrived at the substation and began arranging his mail by sequence of address. He put all the Mackle mail aside. Ever since Billy Vessels and agent St. Pierre had telephoned Post-master Eugene Dunlap, postal employees were watching for it.

Before carrier Nauman had finished sorting, agent Benjamin O. Cantey, Jr., was there waiting. Everything was being handled as an intensified special delivery.

When agent Cantey picked up the first batch sometime after eight o'clock, he scanned the pile and stopped suddenly when he saw a plain white envelope with no return address. In capital letters someone had typed:

MISTER ROBERT MACKEL
4111 SAN AMERO DRIVE
CORAL GABLES, FLORIDA

Two five-cent stamps were affixed. The letter had been post-marked "MIAMI, Fl. Dec. 18 P.M.," which was the previous day. It could have been mailed from any one of eighteen thousand and seven public mailboxes in the Miami postal district.

Agent Cantey noticed that both Mackle and Amaro had been spelled incorrectly. When he held the envelope up to the light, he suspected immediately it was from the kidnapers. He hurried to the Mackle home.

The kidnaping of Barbara Jane Mackle struck a highly sensitive emotional chord across the breadth of America, and the telegrams and the letters, first in the hundreds and later in the thousands, began to pile up on the low, wide round table in the corner of the game room of the Mackle residence. By the morning of December 19, a great tide of messages flowed into the home of the missing girl.

Some were from Barbara's friends. Susan Bennett, a pretty little blonde who with Barbara always refused to raise her hand at St. Theresa School when the teacher asked who was going to be a nun when they grew up, wrote as Sister Susan Bennett, s.s.j., from a convent at Jensen Beach, Florida, and enclosed a line from Tennyson, "More things are wrought by prayer than this world dreams." "At a time like this, words seem to be inept, but again, there are times when words are all a person can offer," she wrote.

A telegram arrived from Tokyo: JUST HEARD OF THE KIDNAP-ING OF YOUR BEAUTIFUL DAUGHTER. WILL BE PRAYING FOR HER SAFE

RETURN AND ALSO THAT GOD'S LOVE AND COMFORT WILL BE WITH YOU AND YOUR FAMILY. GOD BLESS YOU. BILLY GRAHAM.

In Rock Sound, Eleuthera, the news caught up with Eve and Stuart Symington, a United States senator from Missouri. He telegraphed, THINKING OF YOU WITH ALL SYMPATHY AND EARNEST HOPE.

Through the Elliott Mackles came another wire: WE HAVE BEEN LIVING EACH HOUR AND EACH MINUTE WITH YOU. PLEASE KNOW OUR THOUGHT AND PRAYERS ARE URGENT AND SINCERE. MIRIAM AND JACK PAAR.

"I am a poor colored woman but I care for everybody," a woman from Midville, Georgia, wrote. "Tell God too much going wrong."

"I am no one important in the world," wrote a stranger from Bradenton, Florida. "My heart aches with yours."

"Dear Unknown Friends," began a woman from Cleveland, Ohio. "You will always be in my mind, heart, and daily prayers for the safe unharmed return of your daughter."

A spinster from Erie, Pennsylvania, wrote, "I have never been married, and I never had a child, but I can imagine what you parents are enduring. It must be unbearable."

A real estate executive from Miami Beach dictated to his secretary. "I hardly know how to express my feelings and those of my family concerning the agonizing and horrible experience you are going through. I seem to never get this matter out of my mind and I realize how terrible it must be for all of you."

"Our hearts and prayers are with you at this time. Oh, so very much," a judge and his wife wrote simply from West Palm Beach.

The cablegrams came from overseas, too. A constable in Victoria, Australia, perhaps thinking more of himself, suggested "establishing me in a small cottage." He promised to "smash the mighty Communist empire."

The messages and letters and telegrams knew no sectarian singleness, and the uncertainty and suspense of the plight of Robert and Jane Mackle rekindled memories of persons that they had not seen or even thought of in years. "Our youth was so carefree, you, Elliott, and I had such good times," wrote a woman from Birmingham, Alabama, "and to think that your daughter has to suffer this brings great sadness to my heart."

"Dear Bob," began another letter. "Although we have not met

since 1943 while at the Key West Naval Base, I wish to express my sympathy for the frightful incident of the kidnaping of your daughter."

At the Grace United Presbyterian Church in Spring Hill, Florida, a congregation prayed in silence, and in New Jersey, a man designating himself as a Jewish War Veteran made a donation to the Tal Hashomer Hospital in Israel for Barbara's safe return. At Villanova University in Pennsylvania, where Robert was well known, came a message of prayers and masses "of the six hundred priests and seminarians of the province for the safe and speedy return of your beloved daughter."

Neighbors just doors and blocks away, not wanting to interfere personally, also communicated by mail. "Words fail me."

One telegram, perhaps more than any other, touched Robert Mackle deeply. It was from the parents of a small boy whom he had never met.

OUR HEARTS GO OUT TO YOU. WE TRULY UNDERSTAND YOUR VIGIL AS WE DID THE SAME FOR TWO DAYS IN AUGUST. WITH GOD'S HELP AND THE FBI YOU ARE IN MARVELOUS HANDS. HAVE FAITH. WE PRAY FOR YOU AND YOUR PRECIOUS DAUGHTER'S SAFE RETURN. It was signed Mr. and Mrs. Stanely Stalford, Beverly Hills, California.

Stalford was chairman of the Fidelity Bank of Beverly Hills the previous August when a kidnaper, Robert Lee Dacy, posing as an electrician, took his four-year-old son from his home and fled in the family's Cadillac. Dacy demanded payment of $250,000 in ransom through an intermediary. Two days later, during a wild 90-mile-an-hour chase and gun battle, FBI agents rammed the kidnaper's car. They captured the kidnaper and retrieved the boy unharmed.

When agent Ben Cantey arrived at the Mackle home, he had the plain white envelope on top of the batch. "Here, this one, I think," he said.

Someone called for the flat-edge tweezers. Billy Vessels, seated in front of the low round table in the game room, reached into his pocket and gave the agent his small Swiss Army pocketknife with a scissor blade. Agent Cantey extracted a Polaroid black-and-white photograph.

It was Barbara.

The photograph was a close-up, her face only, her eyes open,

7. At the FBI laboratory in Washington, D.C., an agent photographed contents of the box in which Barbara Mackle was buried. She wasn't hungry during her eighty-three-hour burial. She had only a caramel and a bite of an apple. The kidnapers had dissolved tranquilizers in the drinking water in the plastic container with the molded handle (upper right). (FBI *Photo*)

8. On a bier borrowed from a funeral home, Sheriff Lamar Martin and his deputies wheeled the coffin-styled box toward the DeKalb County Courthouse during the trial of Gary Steven Krist. It weighed 231 pounds. It was eight feet long and two feet square. "It is well constructed," Krist said admiringly. (*Wide World Photos*)

9. Robert F. Mackle and Billy Vessels, a football Heisman Trophy winner who worked for the Mackle land-development firm, arrived at the court-house in Decatur, Georgia, to testify in May 1969. Vessels helped Mackle find Fair Isle in a first aborted ransom drop and delivered himself the $500,000 in a second drop. *(Wide World Photos)*

10. Seventy-eight days after the abduction, FBI agents found the Honduras-born Ruth Eisemann-Schier working as a carhop in a drive-in called the Boomerang in Norman, Oklahoma. She laughed as Floyd Parks, a deputy U.S. Marshal, escorted her from an arraignment in Oklahoma City. Moments before, she was blubbering. (*Wide World Photos*)

11. "Kidnaping? The only kidnaping I know anything about is Robert Louis Stevenson's," Gary Steven Krist said after a jury granted him mercy. "Crackle-barrel justice," he called it. Here he is taken from the courtroom after Judge H. O. Hubert sentenced him to the rest of his natural life at hard labor in a Georgia prison. (AP *Wirephoto*)

12. Two days after FBI agents found Barbara Mackle unharmed in a plywood crypt buried on a hillside outside of Atlanta, she made her one—and only—public appearance before newsmen. Above, her father and brother escort her from the television cameras. "I just feel wonderful," she said. "I really do."

the flash of the camera reflecting in her pupils, her even white upper teeth showing a trace of a smile.

A sign slanted under her chin with the single word, hand printed in angular letters, "KidNAPPED." The lower-case letter d had been filled in, emphasizing the Kid more than the upper-cased NAPPED. It appeared that she was lying on a blanket.

Inspector Shroder, holding the photograph by tweezers, asked Robert Mackle to look at it.

"Is that my daughter?" he asked, and later he would not remember that he had asked the question.

To him, seeing the satinlike background of the blanket, it looked exactly as if she was in a coffin. "It shocked me so bad and I had to turn away."

"Thank God she was alive when that was taken," he said aloud.

Also in the envelope was a 14-carat-gold ring with a mounted white stone and two small diamonds. Inspector Shroder handed the ring to Robert Mackle.

"Have you see this before?"

"Rex," he said. "That's Barbara's ring."

"How can you identify it?"

"It has an opal. That's Barbara's birthstone, and the two little diamond chips."

"Are you sure?"

"I bought it for her."

It had cost about seventy-five dollars. He didn't remember exactly. His daughter had never been ostentatious and she did not really like jewelry. The ring she liked.

Robert Mackle had purchased it as a gift for Barbara for her sixteenth birthday, four years ago. He had purchased it at the Miami Diamond Center from a salesman he knew personally, Arthur Koff. He had no idea that the evening before Arthur Koff had sold an FBI agent a suitcase which at that moment still contained the $500,000 ransom money.

Bobby thought about the futility of it. It struck him as illogical. They had already tried to deliver the money to the kidnapers. What was the purpose of the photograph and ring now? Bobby saw the photograph as a means to encourage his mother.

"I told Mom Barbara had a big smile on her face and that she was kidding the kidnaper," said Bobby. He was terribly aware of his mother's physical and emotional condition.

"We didn't realize he was exaggerating either," said Jane's sister, Ann Briggle.

Jane walked through the den that morning and looked at the fireplace.

"Where is the suitcase?" she asked Eileen McCaughan, a close friend who had been called to the home to help.

Eileen McCaughan did not realize that Jane knew nothing of the drop or the failure. She started to explain.

Ann Briggle stood behind her sister and put her index finger to her lips and shook her head, No, No, No.

"Everyone just clammed up when I came around," Jane Mackle said. "And Ed Lauth was giving me those antibiotic shots. My finger hurt so. It was absolutely raw, as if I were a cannibal, I'd chewed it so.

"I wondered in the back of my mind if Barbara were dead; whether we would ever see her again. I could see Robert and I watched him. As long as he stayed sane, I knew there was hope."

But something had happened, Jane Mackle realized. She turned to her sister. "Something is wrong, Ann," she said. "Bobby is in Barbara's room. The door is closed. I think he is crying."

In midmorning the FBI abandoned the Mackle residence as a headquarters. Too much was occurring simultaneously for adequate communication co-ordination. Inspector Shroder left the home for the downtown office. Several agents remained.

At the Brickell Avenue site where the kidnaper dropped the suitcase, Marvin Mathes arrived for work in his old Buick as a wrecker towed away the Volvo. Mathes, a jaunty middle-aged man with long sideburns, wore the green uniform of a City of Miami Park and Recreations Department groundkeeper. The red baseball cap was his. He cared for the city-owned property at 2900 Brickell Avenue, the abandoned estate next to George Black's home.

He recognized the Volvo immediately. It had been parked there the previous afternoon. He had worked for the city at the site for nearly a year and until Wednesday afternoon no one had ever visited the estate in the daytime.

"There was this boy and girl in that blue wagon," he said. "The man was a stocky fella. He looked like one of them football players. The girl was littler and she had dark hair. I didn't look at 'em too close. I don't like to look at people too close.

"They looked around the waterfront. They stayed down there about twenty minutes. Then he came and asked me what time did the park close. I said three-thirty. Then they got in that little blue wagon and rode away."

Mathes had noticed that the Volvo pulled a trailer. "There was some stuff and junk in it," he said. "Looked to me like life jackets."

The trailer had disappeared. It wasn't among Deacon's possessions at either the Al-Ril Trailer Court or the marine lab.

Chris G. Koutrobis, a young man three weeks out of the Army, suffered a few disconcerting moments that morning. His black Ford with a Massachusetts plate sat in the parking lot of the Waverly Inn Motel on South Bayshore Drive. Lost and in search of a friend's motel room, he and a girl had driven up and down South Bayshore Drive at four o'clock the previous morning—exactly at the time Robert Mackle searched for Fair Isle. Agents had spotted the car.

"There were six of them at my door and they thought the girl I was with was Barbara Mackle. They tried to convince me I really did it," said Koutrobis, a tourist.

The car had been registered in his mother's name in Dracut, Massachusetts, and in the brief few hours before it was straightened out, agents out of the Boston office had interviewed her at her home, her husband at work, and her married daughter and her married son at their places of employment.

Looking for leads, the Boston FBI also quickly checked out Deacon's past employment at the Massachusetts Institute of Technology in Cambridge. Deacon had worked there from December 1966 through May 1967, as a $140-a-week technician.

Emanuel Maxwell, Deacon's supervisor at MIT, described him as a man with a good head on his shoulders who thought he knew everything about every subject. "He was conceited. He thought what he didn't know wasn't worth knowing," said Maxwell, who was amused to see Deacon, the proud owner of a Volvo station wagon, oiling the lock instead of using graphite on it.

"He also considered himself an authority on marriage at age twenty-two," said Maxwell. "Nelson Rockefeller was running in the presidential primary and Deacon said he could never support him because of his divorce; he had no faith in a man who could make a mistake with the woman he married."

In Miami Thursday afternoon a young blonde in her mid-twenties, attractive, small framed, drove a Pontiac into the driveway of the home of Ruth's landlady in South Miami. She dashed into the home without knocking.

An FBI agent, parked discreetly down the block, was almost certain. Ruth Eisemann-Schier. He had the home under surveillance.

Hardly a minute later the blonde returned, holding the hand of a little girl about ten years old. The agent knew he had to stop them.

The blonde was Wynne Kieffer, daughter of Mrs. Anna Harrison. Although the news media had reported the finding of the $500,000, no one had yet publicly tied either Ruth Eisemann-Schier or the marine lab to the kidnaping. Mrs. Kieffer had listened carefully to all the newscasts. She had attended Coral Gables High School with Elliott Mackle, Jr. She had ridden saddle horses at the Southwest Riding School where Elliott rode and she had married a blacksmith who occasionally shoed race horses for the Mackles' stable, Elkcam.

"I was in a big hurry that day," she said.

"Come on, I'm late," she told her daughter, Terri Jo, who often visited her grandmother.

"I started up the car and as I was looking into my rear-view mirror this car pulled up right behind me. I couldn't back out. I thought some man wants to ask directions—and here I am in a big hurry."

"Get out of the car!" he said.

"He wasn't rude but by the tone of his voice I knew he wasn't kidding." Her heart pounding, Wynne Kieffer said, "What do you mean, get out of the car? No."

"Get out of the car. What is your name?" the man demanded.

"I could see he was unshaven. He had a coat and tie on but he looked as if he had stayed up all night."

"What is your name?" he demanded again.

"Why do you want to know?"

"I want to talk to you. Get out of the car."

Well, she thought, if he wants to know that badly.

"Wynne Kieffer," she said, thoroughly convinced that he wouldn't believe her anyway.

He identified himself as an FBI agent.

"And I didn't believe him. He was so determined. And just then two other men pulled up in another car—and they looked just like him. And I thought, oh, no, they're going to kidnap me. What would they want me for? I don't have any money."

"Terri Jo," she said to her daughter in the front seat. "You stay there. Don't move."

She stepped out of the car. The agent showed her his identification.

"I must have looked frightened and pale because the other two men who walked up were more relaxed. One asked, 'Didn't he tell you we're FBI?'

"Yes. But I didn't believe him."

They showed her a photograph of Ruth Eisemann-Schier. "She is blond. I am blond. She is five foot two. I am five two. We are both small framed."

"This is who we thought you were," an agent said.

"When they found who I was they were very businesslike."

"What do you want her for?"

The agents declined to explain.

"Come on," said Wynne Kieffer, laughing. "You can tell me."

In an exact flat tone, an agent replied. "You will hear."

From the driveway the agents went to the front door and talked to Mrs. Harrison. Where was Ruth? When was the last time she had seen her?

"I didn't know why they were asking," said Mrs. Harrison. "They told me it was just routine. I thought it must be a case of mistaken identity."

Ruth had left on the desk of her small rented room a copy of *Your Family Horoscope*, a twenty-five-cent Dell Publication handbook printed for people who believe the stars are trying to tell them something.

For whatever it was worth, the first chapter might well have said something about Ruth: "You delight in putting on different characters for different people. Others are completely mystified as to what you are really like." And on that particular date, with a half million dollars dropped on Brickell Avenue, the daily horoscope advised all Scorpios, Ruth included: "Drastic business or financial moves are outside the cover of supporting trends; postpone them."

Beside the booklet on the desk was a collection of swizzle sticks, mementos of an evening of night clubbing, and on her book shelves, side by side with technical works—a physics textbook and Goethe's *Faust* in German—stood a collection of comic books, *Casper the Friendly Ghost.*

Some of Ruth's clothing still hung in the closet, dresses brightly colored, soft in line and tending toward puffy sleeves and lace trim.

FBI agents would remain there long through the evening.

It had been a long and torturous afternoon for the Mackles. "We kept constantly trying to reassure ourselves without any really great belief," said Frank Mackle. "What the hell would he do now? He didn't have the money. He had to be running and he might get shot. It was purely in the FBI's hands at this point."

From the radio monitor in the game room they could hear the static-punctuated conversations, agents dispatched one place, then another, the feedback of leads and information.

"Elliott and I drove over to Villa 41 where the families were on the Key. They were frantic to know what was going on and there were so many conflicting reports on television and radio. We were getting it pretty straight on the FBI monitor," said Frank Mackle.

"So we got the family together. We felt it would hurt nothing to tell them what we knew. Elliott and I were both beat. I lay down and took about an hour's nap. It was the first time I had been to bed since Tuesday morning. I slept very soundly for an hour, but I wished I hadn't done it. I felt so darn bad afterward. I took a shower. I would have been better going on without that hour.

"Elliott and I got back in the car and went back to Robert. We were extremely discouraged. There was a lot of time to think. I was trying to put myself in the kidnaper's position. If it had been me, a reasonable thing to do would be to try to get some sort of immunity to get out of the country. He had one asset, Barbara. We knew he wouldn't tell us where Barbara was until he was clear. And I became convinced that this guy would get a hold of us again. I was convinced he would call again."

At the Epiphany Church in South Miami late Thursday afternoon, Father Joseph Biain sat in the living room of the rectory waiting for dinner at five-thirty. He was from the Basque province in Spain, where he had played jai alai in his youth, and during the entire five years he had lived in the United States he had served at Epiphany.

Father Biain knew Robert Mackle. At one time Robert had attended the 6:30 A.M. Sunday Mass at Epiphany and Father Biain had said that Mass. Father Biain had also read the evening newspaper. The black type across the eight columns on page one of the Miami *News*, declared:

MACKLE RANSOM PAYOFF FLOPS
POLICE STUMBLE ON KIDNAPERS

Father Biain had read carefully Robert Mackle's plea to the kidnapers. He mulled over the story and turned inside, and read also of the death that day at eighty-four of Socialist Norman Thomas. At about five-fifteen the telephone rang.

"I picked up the phone and someone was asking for advice. He wanted to know if he could speak to a priest and I told him I was Father Biain. And he said, 'Do you promise not to tell anybody what I am going to tell you now?' and I said, yes, of course, and then he told me he was the kidnaper of Barbara Mackle. He had some orders for Mr. Mackle. I didn't believe him at this point; not yet, but I listened. He told me to get in touch with Mr. Mackle and tell him to get the money ready again. He told me to tell him not to be so nervous, that Barbara was okay. He said that she was buried some place and he said something about a breathing device. He mentioned a battery. He said he couldn't guarantee that it would last for more than twenty-four hours. Physically, Barbara was all right. He told me all these things. He told me about the police interference and I told him I had read about it in the paper, and he told me to tell Mr. Mackle that we—he said, we—believed him, that he had nothing to do with the police. He told me to get Mr. Mackle's private telephone number and that he would call back at eleven o'clock, eleven o'clock tonight."

Father Biain began to believe his caller, yet not totally. Eleven o'clock? At eleven o'clock he would be in the monastery, not the living room.

And without thinking out the situation, he said the first thing that jumped into his mind.

"I might not be here at eleven o'clock because I have to go to the monastery."

"Father," the kidnaper said very slowly. "You had better be there. It is a very important message."

And Father Biain, realizing he shouldn't have said anything, gave the caller the night telephone number for the monastery. The conversation, the priest thought, had lasted perhaps eight minutes. Buried alive? A breathing device? It made no sense.

He related the conversation to Monsignor John O'Dowd. Monsignor O'Dowd telephoned immediately Monsignor Peter Riley at the Church of the Little Flower. Both monsignors knew the background.

Monsignor Riley drove directly to the Mackle home and in the presence of FBI agents related the latest message.

The Mackles were elated. "We felt we had another chance," said Robert. With the caller speaking of a burial alive, a breathing device, and batteries running out—information highly restricted —Inspector Shroder believed the probability excellent that the caller was indeed the kidnaper.

Agents rushed tape recordings of the kidnaper's two Thursday morning calls to Father Biain at Epiphany. The priest felt certain it was the same voice. The church and the telephone company quickly arranged to have the telephone there tapped also. Agents sat down to keep Father Biain company for the night. He would be there at eleven o'clock—or for how long it was necessary.

"I think the FBI called Washington," said Father Biain. "It would be all right for me to personally deliver the money, if need be." He would ask the kidnaper if he called.

Frank Mackle telephoned Epiphany from the Mackle game room. The red telephone in the game room had been a long-distance WATS line, but the FBI had converted it to a regular private listing for its own use. Frank Mackle gave that number to Father Biain. The priest repeated it back slowly and accurately.

Frank Mackle had been astounded by the kidnaper's demand for money.

"I just never thought he would call and try to get the half

million dollars again. It just never entered my mind. I thought he might try to make some deal to get away.

"But he wanted that money, period. I guess that's all he thought about."

The FBI was way ahead of him on the money. The $500,000 had been recounted and placed this time in the original blue Samsonite suitcase, the one that belonged to the banker's wife. The other suitcase might be needed as evidence.

As darkness fell, the vigil began again.

A Dragon in a Wagon

Charles Gullion listened to the news broadcast on his car radio as he drove home from work late Thursday afternoon. He was a painter for the Modern Paint Company in Miami, and that day he had worked on a high-rise apartment under construction in Hallandale north of Miami. He had followed the news of the kidnaping closely. In the past he had worked as a subcontractor on several Mackle projects, and somehow, that made the news a little more personal.

The newscaster spoke of the police chase and the gunfire, the $500,000 ransom money found in a suitcase, the abandoned boat and the Volvo station wagon with a Massachusetts license plate.

The mention of the Volvo struck him like a sledge hammer.

It couldn't be, he thought. And he knew it was. It had to be.

He had bought a trailer from a man in a Volvo with a Massachusetts license plate the night before, and now, as he thought back, he might have seen a blanket rolled up in the back of the Volvo. Barbara Mackle might have been rolled up in the back of the Volvo in that blanket.

Yet that seemed preposterous. He could be mistaken; maybe it was just a coincidence. "And frankly," as he acknowledged later, "I was afraid. I didn't want to get involved."

On the previous evening, Wednesday, Gullion, tanned, wiry and thirty-nine years old, had stopped at the Jewish Home for the

Aged Thrift Shop, a huge warehouse second-hand store at 7300
Northwest Twenty-seventh Avenue, not too far from where he lived
in a new two-family duplex apartment at 2987 Northwest Nine-
tieth Street. In his spare time Gullion often stopped at the thrift
shop to buy old television sets to repair and sell. Gullion knew the
assistant manager there, George Lucas. They were friends. Gullion
had seen this man in a Volvo parked at the front curb with a loaded
trailer. The man wanted to sell it. The thrift shop didn't buy used
merchandise from anyone; as a charitable organization, it accepted
donations for resale.

Curious, Gullion walked over and looked at the loaded trailer.
It was seven-thirty or eight o'clock. "He had some scuba diving
gear, a mask, mouthpiece, tank, weight belts, an extra valve, and
a couple of boxes of books, suitcases and stuff, and I skin-dive
a little so I asked him what he wanted for it," Gullion recalled.

"I think he said fifty or sixty dollars. I told him I would give
him thirty-five dollars. We didn't haggle. He said okay and I
asked him to drive his trailer over to my house and leave it in
my back yard. He said he would."

The Volvo followed Gullion home.

"There was this girl with this guy. At first I thought she was
a boy. She had on pants and shirt and her hair was up. When
she got out of the car, I could see by her figure that she was a
girl. He said they were going back to Boston and they had to sell
everything they couldn't take. The Volvo was loaded. I could see
that it couldn't take much else.

"I noticed her Spanish accent. I think she said I was cheap,
something like that. I said I didn't necessarily need the trailer.
She asked the guy what he thought. And he said, 'We've got to
get rid of it.'

"He had a shotgun, too. He wanted to sell it for thirty-five
dollars. He showed it to me. I think it was a single barrel. I'm
not sure. I didn't want it.

"They must have been at my house fifteen or twenty minutes. I
asked him if he had a clear title to the trailer. He said, yes, and
he gave me the papers. I could see they were made out to him,
George Deacon. He had bought it up in Massachusetts somewhere."

The trailer, a standard six-by-nine-foot open-top, two-wheeled
vehicle, had once belonged to the U-Haul Company, and its

original orange color could be seen under a second heavy coat of blue paint. The license was a 1968 Massachusetts plate, I 36-003.

"He was very calm and he was no dumbbell. He was pretty smart on electronics. He talked like an intellectual. He had some equipment there for bugging telephones. He said that he and the girl had to see somebody and they had to leave. I gave him the thirty-five dollars."

Gullion rummaged through his trailer, totally disinterested in three boxes of books. He found an expensive tape recorder in a black attaché case and took it into the house to his wife, Penni, an attractive woman of twenty-six from Kansas City. They had a daughter five, Charlene.

"I wondered if the tape recorder worked and I played it," said Penni Gullion. "It sounded as if some man was talking to his wife and kids on the telephone. So Charlene and I sat down and taped our voices. We erased part of his. We read from a book, *A Dragon in a Wagon*."

The title was not altogether inappropriate.

In the trailer lay a large green tarpaulin, big enough to cover a coffin. Deacon had left a collection of glass non-Pyrex laboratory test tubes, the proper size for a number-three stopper. The buried ransom note had been found stuck in a number-three stopper when a shovel broke a test tube in Robert Mackle's back yard.

Gullion noticed a tool kit containing nineteen bits and some men's clothing stuffed into a duffel bag. Someone had worn the clothing while painting. A light gray enamel paint had been splotched and splattered over the front of a shirt, a pair of trousers and a plastic apron.

Gullion went through his trailer, its contents meaning nothing to him in particular. He found an empty box which had contained a $49.95 two-way radio, an inexpensive sort of walkie-talkie, a Claircon Transceiver, model 15-150, manufactured in Japan. The serial number was stamped on the box.

Besides the scuba diving gear and two pairs of wet boots, one male and one female, the trailer contained rubber tubing, a cutting blade, a plastic pen, metal wiring instrument, and some day-old newspapers from Atlanta, Georgia.

Gullion glanced at a seven-column headline:

MOTEL COED KIDNAPPING HERE
SPURS NATIONWIDE ALERT FOR 2

He was more interested in a "couple of old suitcases," where he found "some junky clothes and a white outfit like you'd wear around a lab."

Besides the tape recorder, the black attaché case contained a spray can of deodorant and a pile of old letters.

"I wonder if he left this by mistake," he said as he gave it to his wife.

After Penni Gullion and her daughter tape-recorded *A Wagon in a Dragon*, it was bedtime for Charlene. Some moments later Penni Gullion began to read over the letters, feeling a little self-conscious. They weren't addressed to her.

They were addressed to a man in a prison in Tracy, California. His name was Gary Steven Krist. It appeared as if his mother had written them. They were postmarked Sitka, Alaska.

There were other letters, dated a year later, addressed to George Deacon in Massachusetts. They also seemed to be from the mother in Alaska. She had written him that some law enforcement authorities had been around asking about him.

"Hey, honey," exclaimed Penni Gullion, "this belonged to a crook."

To the Gullions, inspecting the contents of their newly acquired trailer that Wednesday night, it appeared that George Gary Deacon's real name was Gary Steven Krist—and that somebody, probably the police, was looking for him.

Penni Gullion felt uneasy. Shouldn't they call the Miami police? What if he came back? Were the things in the trailer really his? Had they bought a trailer full of stolen property?

There was no doubt in Gullion's mind that the trailer lawfully belonged to Deacon. Deacon had given him the title. Besides, it was getting late. They could think about it tomorrow. There was also another reason Gullion wasn't particularly eager to telephone the police. He didn't want to make trouble for his friend at the thrift shop, George Lucas. Lucas had had his troubles with the law.

Now it was Thursday evening, twenty-four hours later, and Gullion kept listening to the news broadcasts. And he thought again about that rolled-up blanket in the Volvo.

About ten o'clock he made up his mind. He dialed the Miami office of the FBI. Haltingly, he began to tell the agent who answered the telephone that he knew something about the Mackle kidnaping.

"I think the kidnaper's real name is Gary Krist," he said. "He's got an alias. He says he is George Deacon. That's the name he goes under. I think I bought his trailer last night."

Within ten minutes two agents were at his front door.

At the thrift shop that same night, George Lucas had closed up and gone home at nine o'clock. Lucas was a shy, nervous man with seven kids, a blue suit, a pair of white socks—and a past.

Eighteen years before, a judge in Kimberly, Alabama, had sentenced Lucas to prison for one year, nine months and nine days for passing four bad checks valued at about $250. It wasn't much of a jail. Lucas walked off.

In the autumn of 1968 his past caught up. The Jewish home and its thrift shop inaugurated a new policy: It asked its employees for fingerprints. Lucas complied. Back from the FBI in Washington came the report: Wanted for unlawful interstate flight to avoid confinement after conviction.

The thrift shop people, horrified about the whole thing, prevailed upon Miami attorney, Richard B. Stone, to fight extradition. Lucas became a celebrity of sorts. Reporters interviewed him. He had his picture taken with his wife and seven children. He put on his blue suit and white socks and appeared in the state capitol, Tallahassee. Florida Governor Claude R. Kirk, Jr., left the extradition papers unsigned.

As the assistant manager of the thrift shop, Lucas knew Deacon by sight.

"About a month before, he and that little girl walked in here just like ordinary customers and they bought a used double bed. Sold it for twenty-five dollars. They had that Volvo with the Massachusetts plates and he tied the bed on the luggage carrier up top," said Lucas.

"Then about a week ago they came back again and bought some suitcases, six, seven or eight of them. And they tied them up on that same wagon.

"Next time I seen them was that Wednesday night. He'd shaved his beard. I didn't say anything about it. That was his business. But I knowed him on account of the girl and the wagon. She was in jeans, dungarees, and she looked so young, she looked like fourteen or fifteen.

"He wanted to sell the stuff in the trailer. I told him we don't buy from people coming off the street. We only accept donations.

So he walked in here and dumped on the floor an old bag of clothes, a black leather jacket and a white plastic helmet. He said, 'I'll donate them to charity.' "

Penni, Gullion's wife, telephoned Lucas at home. It was after ten o'clock. She explained that the FBI agents wanted to talk to him.

"They wanted to know if Deacon left me a black leather jacket and a policeman's cap. I didn't know nothing about a policeman's cap."

Lucas had given the black leather jacket to a friend. "Some guy who comes into the shop all the time." He retrieved it from his friend and took it to the FBI agents at Gullion's. "I told the FBI I didn't mind helping, co-operating any way I could. But I sure didn't need any trouble."

The past of George Deacon intrigued agent Joe Yablonski far more. Was Deacon in fact Gary Steven Krist, an escaped inmate from California, as the letters seemed to indicate? Agent Yablonski radioed the information to his office. The Miami office had an open line to Washington.

In the FBI files in Washington, clerks quickly pulled the fingerprint file and the so-called rap sheet on Gary Steven Krist, born April 29, 1945, Aberdeen, Washington. Copies of the same file, FBI number 924 598 D, lay in steel cabinets in police stations all over the state of California.

Krist was a wanted man. He had escaped from prison in California in 1966.

Although he was then only twenty-three years old, his rap sheet ran back seven years. Normally, the criminal acts of a fifteen-year-old boy would not come to the attention of the FBI. But Krist's had. His first entry, July 29, 1961, was for an arrest in Pocatello, Idaho, after an escape from a juvenile delinquent institution in another state, Ogden, Utah.

The information was sketchy, incomplete; yet the FBI could see at a glance that Gary Steven Krist had been arrested at least seven times for car theft, once for burglary, and had escaped three times.

Was Gary Steven Krist the same man as George Deacon?

In Washington, the permanent records contained the fingerprints of approximately 82,000,000 persons, including everyone convicted of a felony in the United States. In a matter of minutes, there was no doubt whatsoever.

The fingerprints of Gary Steven Krist were identical to those of George Deacon. Deacon's real name had to be Gary Steven Krist.

Inspector Shroder had re-established the game room of the Mackle residence as a command post late in the afternoon Thursday. After questioning Father Biain, no one doubted the validity of the new contact. Now, again, it was a matter of waiting for the call. Everyone keyed to the eleven o'clock call-back time.

"We were trying to figure out what we would say when he called back," said Frank Mackle. "This time we weren't going to just accept whatever he said, but strike a bargain with him. We were prepared to say, all right, we have done everything you have asked, now, by God, you do something to evidence your good faith. We were trying to formulate this so as not to antagonize him; put it on an intellectual basis. Apparently, he was that kind of a guy. At least he wasn't a wildly threatening guy."

Inspector Shroder emphasized another possibility. Every crook and hoodlum in Florida knew about the availability of a half million dollars in a suitcase. Would someone—other than the kidnapers—try to intercede? Would someone else telephone with instructions?

"I was going to take the eleven o'clock call," said Billy Vessels. "Rex Shroder and I were going over this. What would I say? The key word was assurance. How do we know? I was to assure him that we didn't involve the police; that we showed our sincerity this morning. What assurance do we have about Barbara?

"I was thinking I would have to take the initiative away from him," said Vessels. "In essence, tell him we did our part; you know we want to co-operate. We want Barbara back. Let's do it right this time. We wanted him to be very clear about the instructions. Make him be clear."

No decision had been made about who should deliver the money. There had been very little overt discussion.

"Dad was ready to go," said Bobby, "but physically, he was much worse than the night before. He had had no sleep."

Inspector Shroder had not expressed an opinion. What if the kidnaper demanded that Robert Mackle—and no one else—deliver the ransom money? The original note had specified Robert Mackle. They would cross that bridge when.

Brothers Elliott and Frank did not want to see Robert try again. "It wasn't ruled out. We were just preparing ourselves to react," said Frank.

At Epiphany Church, Father Biain waited anxiously. He had the private unlisted number to the red telephone in the game room and, if the occasion arose, he would suggest that he make the delivery. Two FBI agents waited with him. His conversation would be taped in the basement of the MOhawk exchange building.

At 10:35 P.M.—twenty-five minutes too soon, the monitoring apparatus rang in the basement of the MOhawk exchange building, and agent John R. Ackerly realized instantly the call was not to Father Biain at the Epiphany Church in South Miami. Instead, it was 443-3889, the Church of the Little Flower in Coral Gables.

Father John C. Mulcahy had not been more than a room or two from the telephone since he had taken the call from the kidnaper the previous day and returned from the Mackle home. He was edgy. He and two other priests were sitting in the living room watching the Dean Martin show. The hour before, they had watched a kidnaping on television. On a Bob Hope special Santa Claus had been kidnaped.

When the telephone rang, Father Mulcahy bolted from his chair. If it was the kidnaper, he wanted to make certain—absolutely certain—that he understood everything perfectly.

"Hello?" he said.

"This is the man who called you earlier about a very important matter, if you remember . . ."

"Uh huh," said Father Mulcahy. He recognized the voice instantly.

"Okay. I have another important matter to relate to you . . ."

"Uh huh."

"Under the same conditions. Do you accept the conditions?"

"Yes. I certainly . . . Is this the kidnaper?"

"Yes."

"Well, this . . . I didn't follow the conditions as you know—indicated last time because . . ." Father Mulcahy started to explain.

The kidnaper cut him off. "All right, then, this is most urgent. You must tell Robert that . . ."

"Robert who?" Father Mulcahy asked nervously.

"Mackle, of course."

"Uh huh, yes."

"About that new pickup site . . . It's 2.2 miles on the left side of the road."

"Just a moment, now. I want to get this right now."

"You got that?"

"Just a moment."

"Are you ready? Hello?"

"Yes," the priest said. "Two point two."

"Yes. On the left-hand side of the road on SW Eighth Street."

"On the left-hand side of the road," the priest repeated.

"On Southwest Eighth. That's Highway 41."

"On Southwest . . . Southwest Eighth Street."

"Going west and it's 2.2 miles past the Little City Trailer Park."

"Little City. Again, now, 2.2 . . ." the priest said.

"Past the Little City Trailer Park, going west, it's on the left-hand side of the road."

"Little City . . . Little City Trailer Park," the priest said.

"Right," the kidnaper replied.

"Trailer Park. Going west."

"All right. And tell him that . . . he'll see a little road down there."

"Pardon me?" said Father Mulcahy.

"He will turn left, across the divider strip, and he'll see a little road. He's to go to the very start of the little road."

"He's to go . . . say that again."

"He's to go . . . to go to the first part of the road. Just go into the road and stop. Right? And leave the suitcase."

"Now, in other words, he goes on Eighth Street, two and a half . . . 2.2 miles past the Little City Trailer Park."

"Yes, uh huh, fine. Okay."

"Now, what happens after that?" the priest asked.

"Well, there's . . . there's a way to turn left there."

"There's a left. The first turn on the left?"

"Oh, you'll see a little dirt road."

"I'm—yes," said Father Mulcahy.

"You just go to the very start of the road. Deposit the . . . by . . . and leave, okay? Just put it out on the side of the road."

"Put the bag and leave?"

"Okay."

"Yes. I have that now. Just a moment. I want to . . . because this is important. Uh, he's to go 2.2 miles. Begin at the Little City Trailer Park."

"Right."

"Going west?"

"Right," said the kidnaper.

"On Eighth Street?"

"Right."

"Okay, now. He's to . . . The thing is I'm not clear as to when he's to make the left turn. When he sees the dirt road?"

"Now, because there is only one place to make a left turn at this point."

"At that point he makes a left turn?"

"That's right," the kidnaper said.

There was a pause.

"Hello?" said Father Mulcahy.

"Yes."

"Is there a dirt road there? Is that right?"

"Yes. There is. I've got to hang up now."

"Yeah, okay. And then he leaves . . ."

"That's right."

"And does he leave the bag right there?"

"Right. Right out on the side of the road.

"Okay. Good-by," said the kidnaper.

"Fine. Okay. Good-by," said Father Mulcahy.

The priest had kept him on the line more than three minutes. There was no doubt in his mind that he was talking to the same person who had called the day before.

"I couldn't keep him on any longer," said Father Mulcahy. "He was rushed. I could detect this very clearly in his voice. And he was quite nervous."

Father Mulcahy hurried out the door to take the message to the Mackles. It would take him a few minutes.

Agent Ackerly, also convinced the voice was the same as the man he had heard twice before in conversations to both Robert and Frank, immediately telephoned the game room. He gave them the new drop site. He told them Father Mulcahy was on his way over.

"We felt we had a little time," said Robert Mackle.

The caller, if he was the kidnaper, had not set a hard deadline on delivery. He had not said specifically that Robert should make the delivery.

Nor had he mentioned a white suit, a flashing light on a box. It seemed much simpler.

"Dad said something about the white suit," said Bobby, "and then there was a discussion—which Dad wasn't a part of—about just dumping a half million dollars out on a dirt road for some guy we weren't certain about."

Inspector Shroder caught the nuance.

Bobby heard him say, "What do you think about delivering the money?"

"The discussion didn't seem like it was going in the right direction," said Bobby. "There wasn't any argument. But I could see that it might develop."

In a firm voice, young Robert declared, "If it increases the chance of getting Barbara back by one percentage point, we have to take that chance."

And that ended that.

"I remember my son walking up to me and saying, 'If we are going to get Barbara back . . . She is depending on you,'" said Robert. "And Bobby said, 'Daddy, give him the half million.'"

"I said, 'Bobby, there's no question about that. I am not hesitating at all. I'm hesitating only to see if we get another call. At the other place, Epiphany. If we have two calls, we have one contact.'"

What if they delivered the money as instructed only to have someone call Epiphany at eleven o'clock? Couldn't they be dealing with two men?

They could wait until eleven.

"The FBI wasn't absolutely convinced it was the right guy," said Frank Mackle. "We figured we could wait until eleven before we reacted. This guy had been punctual on everything else he did. We figured we could wait until ten or fifteen minutes after eleven—and then decide."

Father Mulcahy arrived and repeated the instructions.

"They were pretty clear this time," said Robert. "No Mickey Mouse about it this time. Apparently this guy wanted to get it right. He wanted to make sure we understood."

As the minute hand approached eleven o'clock, one decision had to be made: Who would make the delivery?

Frank Mackle felt that perhaps he should make the delivery. Bobby felt the same. "But I didn't trust myself. I was damn sure I wouldn't be able to find it," said Bobby. He felt even stronger about his father. From a mechanical standpoint, thought Bobby, it was not an exceptionally difficult place to find, although it was a good deal easier to miss than Fair Isle. "Dad had missed the night before because he was too keyed up emotionally. After another night without sleep and the added traumatic effect of the last twenty-four hours, I felt that he had little chance of locating the payoff point. For similar reasons, I felt that my chances of finding the rendezvous were significantly less than someone who was not as personally involved.

"Uncle Frank and I got Dad aside," said Bobby, "and I said, 'Look, Dad. You're in no shape to deliver the money. You missed it last night. We were lucky. This place is forty times harder to find. I don't think you should go.'

"Then I said, 'Let Billy go. Let him wear his regular coat. We aren't playing games. We are not trying to say it's you, Dad. Just let him drop the money and go.'"

Bobby looked at Vessels. "I could tell he wasn't thrilled with the thought. He was tense. He was scared, I know.

"Billy isn't as close to this thing as we are and he isn't going to make the mistakes that you or I would," said Bobby.

And Billy Vessels, listening in silence, feeling in his own mind that Robert simply could not be allowed to go, nodded affirmatively.

"Yeah," he said.

Inspector Shroder spoke up quickly.

"What about someone going with you? In the back seat on the floor under a blanket?"

"Fine," said Vessels.

This time there was no vital time element. Vessels, Inspector Shroder, and agent Lee Kusch, who would hide on the back floor, carefully studied their maps.

Vessels copied down the instructions on a plain white piece of paper. "I'll keep this on the front seat with me," he said.

The same rules as the night before applied. FBI cars, now already converging toward holding areas, would keep away from the exact drop site, and they would not interfere. "They weren't going to come in and lasso anybody," said Vessels.

On the map, Vessels plotted out his route. "Now this is what I'm going to do," he said, and he showed Inspector Shroder and agent Kusch how he could swing toward the Riviera Country Club near the Mackle home, drive up a private road, a path almost, obviously not a thoroughfare, and into a parking lot near the club tennis courts. No one, he knew, could possibly follow him without becoming extremely conspicuous.

Then, and only then, would he drive the nine and one half miles west-northwest to the drop site.

Agent Kusch, his .38-caliber revolver in his hand, crawled into the back seat of the Lincoln and sprawled out, humped over the drive shaft uncomfortably. Someone put a blanket over him. Vessels put the blue suitcase on the passenger side of the front seat. An agent rolled up the overhanging garage doors and Vessels backed out slowly to the white center line of San Amaro Drive. He could see the FBI cars ready to block off any traffic. It was 11:25 P.M.

"I was very conscious of talking; the radio in the vent. I was overly loud. Very distinct, hollering more than talking, trying to be very explicit."

He kept glancing into the twelve-inch rear-view mirror attached to the front windshield. He made his no-follow test at the country club and proceeded west on Bird Road.

He had driven the street an uncounted thousand times before, and never had he been so tense, so acutely aware, and he kept thinking, don't mess it up, get the money there, don't let anyone stop you.

And suddenly a bell rang and two red lights started blinking at a single railroad track across Bird Road.

Christ! he thought. This is all I need, and he accelerated. "I wasn't about to stop." He never saw the headlight of the train. He didn't look back.

A moment later he reached the Palmetto Bypass, an expressway curving around the bulk of the metropolitan area, and he drove northward up a ramp into a sparse flow of traffic.

"This car came up behind me and didn't pass. I was nervous and I thought I was being followed. It looked suspicious."

Very loudly, he expressed his belief into the hidden microphone. Agent Kusch remained silent on the floor.

An FBI car soon pulled in directly behind them, cutting off the car following.

At Tamiami Trail, once an Indian trail through the Everglades from Tampa to Miami, Vessels turned off the bypass and drove westward. He still had more than five miles of straight and flat four-lane highway, U. S. 41. Street lights lighted the first two miles.

No one at the Mackle home had paid too much attention to the weather when Vessels left. It was a warm night, 71 degrees, and the sky was clear; certainly no threat of rain. At midnight the southerly winds, very light at three knots, went unnoticed. The air, though, was unusually moist, and the conditions were perfect for development of ground fog. Before daybreak visibility at Miami International Airport would be a mile.

As Vessels drove toward the Everglades, past the Goony Golf Miniature to his left, he started running into patches of fog, low patches, hugging the pavement at first, and then almost obliterating the signs, "$100 Fine For Throwing Trash."

The black hood of the Lincoln caught the reflection of the mercury street lights overhead, one after the other, darting, vanishing, darting.

The Tamiami Canal ran parallel to Tamiami Trail on his right. A steel guardrail and Australian pines blurred at the edge of the pavement.

All the streets intersected perpendicularly on the other side of the trail, beyond the median and the two eastbound lanes, and as the fog piled up in patches, it became increasingly more difficult to see. Vessels slowed to 35, 30 miles an hour, well under the "Max Speed Cars 55" sign for night driving.

He stared into the night. He caught a glimpse of H 'n H Liquor Bar, "bait and tackle," and a lighted Pepsi-Cola sign. There were no homes, no houses, only the edge of the Everglades, a spaciousness, emptiness, designated on the maps merely as Water Control Conservation Area Number Three.

"I couldn't find that Little City Trailer Court," said Vessels. He knew he had overshot it.

Again, loudly, he announced to his unseen audience, "I've missed it. I'm going back and try the run again."

He slowed, found a turnaround through the grass median strip, and drove eastward toward Miami again. He thought about flipping on the window wipers for the fog. But he wasn't certain where the control knob was. He had driven Robert's Lincoln only once before and he kept thinking he didn't want to touch anything that might interfere with his hidden radio transmitter.

As he U-turned, he suddenly saw the red Mars light of a police car.

"Oh, my God. Not again," he said.

Then, addressing the air-conditioning vent, he said, "If there is a car in the area, tell the fool to stop! Get him out of here."

Looking through the rear-view mirror, the fog lifted momentarily, he could see that a police car had stopped a semitrailer truck.

Back toward Miami he drove, and this time he saw clearly the Little City Trailer Court. He hadn't seen it on the way out because a light bulb on the sign had burned out on the east side. A bulb on the west side burned brightly.

He U-turned again and began the run a second time, closely watching the odometer for the 2.2 miles. He drove in the left passing lane, slower and slower. There was no traffic.

At two miles exactly by his odometer he saw a paved turn-through between the eastbound and westbound lanes of the Trail, and across off the pavement, a telephone pole—and the dirt road he thought he was looking for. A stop sign faced the other way.

The closest structure was the H 'n H roadside bar, a half mile east toward Miami. Westward into the Everglades "Betty and Johnnie" advertised air boat rides at a Phillips 66 two and a half miles away.

"I go off at an angle. It is real foggy, eerie, and there is a sharp little dropoff. The road is dirt and coral rock. I've got my brights on. And all these bushes are on my left. And I'm thinking somebody might be in the bushes."

The road, a narrow two-laned swath of whitish clay strewn with hunks of coral, ran directly south into uninhabited nothingness of the Everglades parallel to a canal to Vessels' right. The road jagged slightly to the right off Tamiami Trail. Vessels did not notice the canal. He did not see a six-foot embankment. He drove twenty yards, maybe thirty, the Lincoln jouncing over the rough surface.

"All of a sudden there was this car in front of me. It startled me. It caught me completely off guard. It was twelve or fifteen yards ahead, stopped, facing me. Its lights out. I must have been going five miles an hour, not much more than that. I hit the brakes hard. And I just stared for three or four seconds. I was afraid to say anything into the mike. The bushes were right outside."

He turned off the engine of the Lincoln. He left the headlights on.

And, deliberately, the anger and the belligerence rising in his throat, Vessels stepped from the car, sliding the suitcase across the seat under the steering wheel. Unconsciously he left the door ajar. A back inside light cast shadows forward. Agent Kusch lay motionless under the blanket.

Vessels walked forward, now perfectly calm—and defiant.

He put down the suitcase in the middle of the road, turning it broadside in the headlight beams, thinking, here it is, here it is, take it.

For three or four seconds he stared at the other car, the fog smothering the blackness in the diffused glare of the headlights. He said nothing. He heard nothing. He saw no one, only the grille of the darkened car.

"Then I turned around and walked back to the Lincoln."

Looking straight ahead, he started the engine and he backed slowly out. There was no space to turn around. In backing out, Vessels forgot about the slight jag in the road.

Suddenly the impact of steel upon steel startled him. His back bumper had rammed a post with a sign, "Private Property."

Quickly he pulled forward a few feet, negotiated the jag, pulled onto the Miami-bound lane of the trail and sped away.

"The package is dropped!" he shouted. "The package is dropped!"

"I'm heading home. Lee hasn't said a thing," Vessels recalled. "It's even foggier and I'm going thirty or thirty-five, I'm looking through the rear-view window and I am telling them about a car being there. It passes me. It is a yellow Ford, a convertible, not the one I saw.

"And then this other car comes up behind me at a high rate of speed. It is really going. And I think this is the one."

"This is the one!" he shouted.

"Get the license number!" agent Kusch yelled from the back floor.

But it was too late. The car pulled away swiftly and Vessels, maintaining his speed, could see only that it was a Florida plate, beginning with a 1, a Dade County car. "The second he gets by me, he starts blinking his right blinker," said Vessels. "It keeps blinking and blinking for more than a mile. I'd say a minute. And I think he is trying to signal something. She is here. Barbara is here. Somewhere on the right. This is the thing that enters my mind."

He tried to time the blinking by his watch. It was too dark. He had the location. From Southwest 117th Avenue inward into Miami somewhere beyond the Coral Park Center, a shopping area at Southwest 97th Avenue.

Agent Kusch remained under the blanket until the Lincoln reached the Mackle home. Inspector Shroder debriefed Vessels in the living room, the Mackles listening. Two agents took notes.

Vessels had never paid much attention to automobiles. He hardly knew the new models, one from another. He told Inspector Shroder he thought he had seen the grille of a 1963 Chevrolet at the site. He didn't know for sure.

The grille would haunt him for days to come. "It was like a nightmare. It became an obsession. It really bugged me. All I could see wherever I went were grilles of automobiles."

Vessels had made the drop within a few minutes of midnight. At approximately 12:30 A.M., with Vessels still answering questions at the Mackle home, the FBI dispatched a car to the site.

The report came back moments later: "The package is gone." "And then the waiting game began," said Frank Mackle.

Within another half hour there was a flurry of excitement over the monitor radio. A man and woman in a Rhode Island car, behaving suspiciously in the opinion of FBI agents, were driving along Tamiami Trail in the city of Miami. The couple furtively checked into a motel.

Vessels and Dr. Lauth drove to the motel so that Billy could look at the car. It wasn't the one. Agents discreetly made a few inquiries. Their momentary suspects had reason, perhaps, to sneak into a motel, but their names were not Krist, Deacon, Eisemann or Schier, and they in no way resembled them. Agents also spotted the yellow Ford convertible that had passed Vessels on his return trip. It belonged to a night nurse at a convalescent home.

The blinking light of the car that sped past Vessels puzzled the FBI. Could it have been the kidnapers? From the dirt road at the drop site, which was unmarked Southwest 132nd Avenue, they almost certainly would have used the Trail to get away. They could have driven five and a half miles east to the Palmetto Bypass, then gone either north or south, or directly into the city. West from the site would take them to either the Gulf coast or a turn north on U. S. 27 four and a half miles away.

Vessels felt the blinking light had to be significant. Could someone have thrown a note from the window?

The FBI was taking no chances. Thirty to thirty-five agents with flashlights assembled at a darkened Texaco station at Tamiami Trail and Southwest 97th Avenue between 2:30 and 3 A.M. They moved methodically forward along the northern edge of the Trail. For a mile they picked up every scrap of litter, paper, cardboard and trash they could find. They examined every bottle. There was no note.

On the map Robert Mackle had noticed the distance between the drop site and old Tamiami Airport. Driving a mere three miles, the kidnapers conceivably could charter a small plane and fly across the Gulf of Mexico to the Yucatan Peninsula, which was close to Honduras, Ruth's native land.

Agents already had the airport under surveillance. They had also determined that neither Ruth nor Krist apparently knew how to fly; at least neither had ever mentioned it at the marine lab. But if there was a third man, he could be a pilot.

By this hour, 4 A.M. Friday, December 20, 1968, the city edition of the Miami *Herald* was on the streets, the headlines proclaiming:

TWO MEN AND A GIRL HUNTED
IN BARBARA MACKLE KIDNAPING

Ruth was not identified by name. Deacon was. For the first time, he was identified publicly in the third paragraph of the main story as an electronics expert at the University of Miami Institute of Marine Sciences. The third man, supposedly seen by the two officers during the aborted first ransom drop, was described only as a "heavy-set man about forty."

Vessels had seen no one at the second drop.

Exhausted, emotionally drained, Vessels accepted a sleeping pill from Dr. Lauth, and downed a stiff Cutty Sark and water. "I was barely able to get up the stairs to Bobby's room."

Glued to the door of Bobby's room—at a child's height—was a sticker from Boy's Town, Nebraska, a girl carrying a boy piggy-back. "He ain't heavy, he's my brother," she was saying. Barbara had stuck it there ten years before. Vessels entered the room and collapsed and slept.

In the game room downstairs, Robert Mackle read again the last sentences of the ransom note:

"Within twelve hours after you deliver the money you will receive another phone call advising you of your daughter's whereabouts. A letter will be sent also to insure the finding of your daughter."

Could he believe it? Every fiber of his body ached in uncertainty.

Just a Try-out Deal

Mrs. Marguerite Yessman, a secretary for the Deltona Corporation, and a French Canadian who once had typed Barbara's French papers, read George Deacon's name in the newspapers Friday morning—and remembered it.

Deacon, as he identified himself, had telephoned her Monday, November 11, 1968. "He was very polite and he wanted me to mail him the annual report. He told me to mail it to him at the University of Miami Marine Institute on Virginia Key."

The annual report, a twenty-page illustrated brochure, listed the company's financial status, total revenues, net income, total contracts receivable, total assets, and stockholder's equity. Mrs. Yessman might not have remembered the day except that on the radio news at home that evening she had heard a research diver for the marine institute, Berend H. "Ben" Joost had drowned. The diver, a thirty-four-year-old man with a family, developed an air embolism at a depth of 165 feet while installing an under-water acoustic cable near Fowey Rock Light off Miami. The Yessman family had owned a boat and knew well the location.

"About two weeks later George Deacon called back again, very put-out, impatient, and told me he had never received the report. Then I remembered the drowning the same day and I mentioned it. And he said, 'Wasn't that a sad thing.'"

Mrs. Yessman told Deacon she mailed him the report. He suggested that perhaps someone down the hall at the marine lab had received it. Could he have another? There was a discussion about whether she addressed it correctly to Virginia Key, where the lab was situated, or Key Biscayne, the island adjoined by a bridge at Bear Cut.

"He started to spell his name, George, G-E-O, and I told him, he didn't have to do that, my husband's name is George."

George Deacon gave her a complete address. He did not, though, spell Rickenbacker. Mrs. Yessman remembered that she had to look it up. She thought about having one of the company messengers stop by the marine lab on a trip to Key Biscayne Hotel but she said nothing. He had not been polite. The mail would do just as well. She mailed him a report—a second time.

Gary Steven Krist, quite obviously, had wanted to make sure that Robert Mackle could raise half a million dollars.

Another possible fragment of Krist's planning came from the memory of Mary Lou Braznell. She was married to Charles W. Braznell, a cousin of Jane.

After the FBI identified Deacon as Krist and distributed wanted flyers with photographs for both Krist and Ruth that Friday, Mrs. Braznell remembered the night of November 27. Robert and Jane Mackle had celebrated their twenty-fifth wedding anniversary that night with a party for friends at the Key Biscayne Hotel.

"We arrived about an hour late," said Mrs. Braznell, "and as we walked into the lobby this man with the beard and this girl were leaving. They left in a blue sort of bus." To the Braznells, the couple obviously did not belong.

Had Krist and Schier coldly familiarized themselves with their victims three weeks before the crime? Barbara had not attended the party. She was at Emory.

Throughout the day Friday the pieces began to fit together. The great overwhelming concern was Barbara. Where was she? Was she in fact buried alive? Was she already dead? The man and the woman who knew, the FBI believed, had to be Krist and Schier, and gradually, an investigation that had kept in excess of a hundred agents at labor almost continuously for three days and three nights began to isolate their precise acts.

Although the FBI felt compelled to honor Robert Mackle's request that the kidnapers be allowed to collect the ransom without interference, the bureau believed the capture of Krist and Schier now would be the best possible means to locate Barbara. Someone would talk. Someone always talked.

The FBI tracing, though, was not instantaneous. Twenty-four hours had lapsed since the aborted ransom drop and the discovery of the contents of the Volvo. Where was Krist? What had he done besides telephone Father Mulcahy and pick up the money a second time, if indeed he was the one?

The intense news coverage, some of it none too accurate, reflected the public interest. The Miami *Herald* published in excess of nineteen columns of type and pictures on the kidnaping that Friday, more than two full pages, and the FBI received scores of leads from citizens.

Some persons were extremely reluctant. George Fischer was one. A nervous and timid young man who lavished his attention on the care and upkeep of his automobile, Fischer worked as an interoffice mail-room messenger boy at the marine lab.

On his way to work at 8:05 A.M. Thursday, the morning of the first drop, he stopped for a red light at U. S. 1 and Southwest Twenty-second Avenue, at the corner of the Florida Bible College. This was eleven blocks northwest of the first drop site on the Fair Isle Causeway. Ruth Eisemann-Schier stood at the curb.

"I recognized her right off the bat. I knew she worked in the lab," said Fischer. "She looked kind of dazed. Her legs were all scratched. She had this sheet, rust colored, wrapped around her like a poncho. I was going to ask if she wanted a ride to work. But she looked so dirty I decided not to."

At the change of the light, Fischer drove on. No untidy passengers were going to ride in his polished and immaculate automobile.

He was positive of his identification. The girl couldn't have been anyone else.

If he was correct, a supposition could be made: The police action at Brickell Avenue probably forced Ruth and Krist to separate. Miami officer Paul Sweeney had chased a man across the entrance of I-95 about 5:35 A.M.—two and a half hours earlier. The two points were a mile and a half apart.

Soon the FBI had confirmation on the separation. Both Ruth and Krist, they discovered, had been seen at the Florida Bible College at 2100 South Dixie Highway—six hours apart. Krist was asking for Ruthie. Apparently, they had selected the Florida Bible College—of all places—as a rendezvous site.

The Florida Bible College, a three-building non-denominational institute of higher learning for four hundred students, believed in the Bible as the inspired word of God, absolute in its authority, complete in its revelation, final in its content, and without any errors in its statements, and its teachers there preached that Satan was a person and the author of sin. In four years a young man or woman could earn a bachelor of arts degree in Biblical Education.

Linda Fontaine, a dark-haired sophomore, nineteen years old, had arrived from her home in Fort Lauderdale for a seven o'clock class that Thursday. She was early and she parked her car in an unpaved parking lot beside a huge banyan tree and took a nap.

"I awoke about six forty-five and there was this girl sitting under the tree. She had cut-off jeans and a white sleeveless blouse and it was torn, I think, and she was very dirty and dusty. I thought she might be a hippie. She looked like she might be spaced out, high on pot or something. She had kind of a glassy look."

To Miss Fontaine the visitor appeared to be an appropriate candidate for salvation.

As a Bible student she had in her purse several fold-out tracts, small blue pamphlets emblazoned with a single question: "Am I Going to Heaven?" "Find Out Inside," the tract said at the bottom of the first page, and inside there was an eighteen-point check list. The proper answer, explained on page three, was "faith in the Lord Jesus Christ alone can save you."

"I walked up to her and said, 'Hi,' and I gave her a tract and I said, 'Have you ever seen one of these before?' And I told her how if a person trusts in Christ to get to Heaven, it is a free gift. Christ died and paid for our sins and all we have to do is believe.

"She had a nice smile on her face, but she didn't look like she was comprehending me. She said, 'Thank you.' She wasn't very responsive. She had an innocent face and big eyes. She looked about seventeen years old. She never got up. She just sat there."

Linda Fontaine left for her seven o'clock class. Her teacher, however, did not show, and after a ten-minute wait, Linda and several students walked to a nearby donut shop. "I saw her again on the sidewalk," she said.

This time the girl wore what Linda believed to be a red shawl over her shoulders. Later the FBI would suspect that Ruth had snitched a red sheet off a baby's crib from the Bible college's unlocked nursery.

At 12:45 P.M. that day, Linda, her boyfriend, and the Reverend Thomas H. Davis and his wife, Simone, sat in the chapel of the church. "Tommy," as he was known by his students outside of class, taught Hebrew and Greek and Minor Prophets of the Old Testament. For eight and a half years he had been a policeman on Miami Beach. He was thirty-one and a man of firm conviction. He was also a weight lifter, capable of a bench-press of 375 pounds.

"I was telling them about this girl," said Linda Fontaine, "and from the front of the church a man walked in, a real grub."

The man started down the nineteen pews of the aisle. Now halfway down he halted, seemingly he changed his mind, and cut through the pews to a side door.

"Boy," said Linda Fontaine in jest. "They would make a beautiful pair."

Tom Davis arose and followed the man outside. "This guy just looked to me like he'd got out of jail, he had makeshift clothes, a gray flannel suit, his pants were ripped on the inside right leg. There was something black underneath, like he was wearing another pair of pants or a skin diver's wet suit."

By the time Davis caught up, the man had entered the back seat of a Yellow taxicab, parked on Secoffee Street, facing east right beside the banyan tree.

"I asked him if I could help him," said Davis. "He said he was looking for a girl friend, or something like that. He was a smooth talker. I asked him what her name was, 'Maybe I can help you.' He said Ruth Eisemann.

"I wanted to find out who he was so I introduced myself. I reached through the window and shook hands. He told me his name was Bob Denver. I noticed he had a Band-Aid and scratches on his hand."

Both Linda Fontaine and Tom Davis identified photographs of Ruth and Krist for the FBI.

Much later Mrs. Marilyn Nelson, a reservations clerk for Northwest Orient Airlines, would also identify photographs of Krist.

Shortly after Krist left the Bible College, he walked into the Northwest office at 301 Northeast First in downtown Miami. "He came in about one-thirty or two o'clock and said he wanted a refund on his wife's ticket to Chicago. He said something about his wife being sick. Right away I thought, what a bad guy this is. But there was no reason why I couldn't refund the ticket."

Mrs. Nelson could see that the tickets, made out to Mr. and Mrs. Schultz, had been purchased the night before, December 18, at Miami International Airport for flight 729, Miami to Chicago, 7 A.M. Obviously, they had already missed it.

"I gave him a refund check for $58.28 for his wife's ticket. He didn't even ask me to cash it. He kept pacing back and forth."

After he left, Marilyn Nelson walked into the back office and told another reservationist, "There was something funny about that." She couldn't put her finger on it. No one, just no one, ever booked Miami-Chicago on Flight 729, unless they were connecting west. Flight 729 made two stops, Fort Lauderdale and Tampa. A passenger could catch a non-stop out of Miami much later and arrive in Chicago at almost the same time as 729. She fished Krist's airline envelope out of her trash basket and tossed it up on a file. About three-thirty that afternoon Donald J. McGarry, the desk supervisor for Northwest at Miami International Airport, telephoned Mrs. Nelson.

The same guy, Schultz, was there. He had been there the night before. McGarry had checked his baggage through to Chicago. He had lost his baggage claim tickets. Mrs. Nelson examined the envelope she had fished out of her trash basket. Stapled inside were the baggage claim numbers. She read them to McGarry.

"I sold him the tickets about ten o'clock the night before," said McGarry. "I remember he gave me two one hundred dollar bills. He and this girl were together. They weren't leaving then, but they wanted to check their baggage. I noticed the bags were heavy. He said he had some scuba gear in them and I asked him if the tanks were empty. He said they were."

McGarry noticed that his customer was limping that afternoon. "He told me that he and his wife had an automobile accident on the way to the airport and that he hurt his leg and she was in the hospital; that's why they missed the seven o'clock flight. He wanted to cash in the other ticket."

Krist, under the name of Schultz, redeemed that ticket for $77.70. He had purchased it under a family plan, which accounted for the lower price of "Mrs. Schultz's" fare.

McGarry asked his customer for identification and Krist produced his identification: George Deacon. McGarry questioned it. Why wasn't it Schultz?

"He told me his father had been in trouble and it only costs you twenty-five or fifty dollars to have your name changed," said McGarry, "and that's why he went under the name Deacon. To protect himself."

When McGarry eventually heard over a radio, the names Gary Steven Krist, "alias George Deacon," "it hit me just like a bolt of lightning." He telephoned the FBI.

The FBI already had agents in the airport. "They were here in a minute." McGarry had teletyped the baggage claim numbers to Chicago and the two suitcases had been returned. They did not contain any scuba-diving equipment. They would be watched for days on the chance that someone would want to retrieve them.

Agent William F. Beane, controlling much of the investigation from the downtown headquarters, made a few assumptions: On Tuesday morning Krist had seen the want-ad message in the *Herald* that the money was ready. This was faster than he had expected. It speeded up his timetable. He and Ruth would want to flee early Thursday morning after the ransom drop, not Friday morning as previously planned. They would not need the G. Deacon and A. Post Delta tickets that they had already purchased for Friday morning. So Wednesday night at the airport they bought two more tickets, this time Northwest instead of Delta. When the ransom drop aborted Thursday morning, Krist had the Northwest tickets in his possession. The Delta tickets he lost in the Volvo. He cashed the first Northwest ticket because he needed cash. On the way to the airport or perhaps after he arrived he heard of Robert Mackle's plea to contact him again. The afternoon Miami *News* was on the street with Robert Mackle's plea in black oversized type—above its masthead. So Krist decided to try again. He had redeemed the second Northwest ticket because he still needed cash. He would have to get another car. He might want to rent one.

Friday, agents began to check the two hundred and twenty-seven different locations listed in the Yellow Pages of the telephone book where a driver could rent or lease an automobile in the metropolitan Miami area. They began with the bigger agencies near the airport, Hertz Rent A Car, Avis, National Car Rental.

At noon Friday an FBI man interrupted Ray Hoadley's lunch. Hoadley worked for Merlin Rent-A-Car near the airport in Miami Springs. The FBI agent showed him three photographs of Krist, alias Deacon. "Have you ever seen this man?"

"I recognized him immediately," said Hoadley. Krist had rented from him a lime-green two-door 1969 Ford Fairlane about four-thirty the previous afternoon. Krist had given his name as George Deacon.

"He showed me his driver's license. Everything seemed very legitimate. He wanted me to call the University of Miami and verify his employment. I didn't bother."

Krist had bargained about the price. "We usually ask for a fifty-dollar deposit," said Hoadley. "He said he only had thirty-five. I let him have it for thirty-five. A Yellow Cab driver came in with him."

The FBI quickly issued an all-points bulletin message to every major police agency in the southeastern United States. Besides the description of the car and license number 1 E-24848, the bureau described physically both Schier and Krist, and warned police, "Krist may be heavily armed. Consider extremely dangerous."

Agents soon had the Yellow Cab Company driver, Harold Shofner, a part-time cabbie who lived for years as a chicken farmer in Colombia, South America.

"I picked him up on the upper ramp at Miami International Thursday afternoon. He told me his car had flipped over and he had straddled a fence. Said he hit a construction ditch and he needed to get another automobile. I could see that he was hurt. He had difficulty getting into the cab." He noticed that his fare had not shaved for a day or two.

Cabbie Shofner had first driven Krist to Budget-Rent-A-Car System. "They wanted him to take a car for a minimum of a week or something. He didn't want to. That's why I drove him to Merlin Rent-A-Car."

FBI agents failed to locate the taxi that had waited for him earlier that day at the Florida Bible College. By law, cabbies were required to record times and places of all fares. Sometimes they were careless.

Friday morning the FBI received another lead on Krist. He had been treated in the emergency room of Jackson Memorial Hospital Thursday night before his identity became public. He could have been there as late as ten o'clock—only thirty-five minutes before Father Mulcahy received the instructions for the second drop.

Dr. Burton H. Cohn, a young resident physician in surgery, heard the name Deacon in a newscast as he drove home Friday morning after a twenty-four-hour sleep-in shift at the hospital.

In the county's largest hospital, the emergency room treated an unrelenting conglomerate of man's miseries, often inflicted in violence. Usually Dr. Cohn treated seventy to eighty patients a shift. He seldom paid much attention to names.

But the name Deacon he remembered.

Alone, Krist had walked up to a front desk receptionist, Margie C. Baker, and given his name as George Deacon at 6:23 P.M. She made out a chart for him and logged the time. He listed his wife Dorothy as his closest relative and gave his Al-Ril address. He told Mrs. Baker he had a laceration of his "private area" and an abrasion of his knee. He said he had fallen in a hole. As he was a walk-in patient, obviously not in any dire urgency, she told him to please be seated, a doctor would see him as soon as one was available.

He waited for more than an hour until a nurse, Maria Richardson, escorted him through the swinging double doors to a trauma room. She took his temperature. It was normal. He gave her his age as twenty-eight. Dr. Cohn saw him some time after eight o'clock. It could have been after nine.

Krist told him he had tripped in his yard and sustained a laceration of his left scrotum by falling on a pitchfork. Dr. Cohn, accustomed to farfetched explanations, didn't press the question. He noticed his patient's disheveled appearance and a heavy one or two days' growth of beard.

He sewed five nylon sutures to the wound, a superficial triangular laceration of one centimeter involving the skin only, and noticed that Deacon also suffered from a fungus infection of the groin. Dr. Cohn also dressed Deacon's right knee. He probably would have never remembered the name Deacon except that his patient seemingly went out of his way to try to impress him with his knowledge of medicine. Deacon struck Dr. Cohn as intelligent—and arrogant.

Dr. Cohn instructed Deacon to return to the hospital to have the stitches removed in eight days. Deacon said it was impossible; that he worked at the University of Miami marine lab and that he would be at sea and nowhere near a medical facility. Dr. Cohn gave him a small suture removal kit and told him how to remove the stitches, a simple procedure.

As Deacon, Krist had been to Jackson Memorial Hospital once before. After the *Pillsbury* cruise to Bermuda he had appeared at the hospital with the flu. On the back of a motorbicycle rental form, he had written his symptoms. The Univeristy of Miami picked up the bill. The school had a billing arrangement with the hospital.

"Do you want me to bill the university, Mr. Deacon?" Ray Duey Coquet, the cashier, asked him late Thursday night.

"Don't bother," he said. "I'll pay for it. I think they'll have enough problems today because of me."

FBI agents tended to disbelieve the pitchfork explanation. The fact that he said he had fallen into a hole, however, worried them. To bury someone, obviously, a person digs a hole. They suspected, though, that he had probably cut himself when he leaped the sharp-edged hurricane wire-link fence running from Miami officer William Sweeney.

FBI agents Frank Smith and Fred Doerner returned to the marine lab Friday morning, parking their car near a sign at a fenced dock, which declared more convincingly than any beware-the-dog sign: "Extreme Danger. Large Trained Sharks Will Attack Any Sound Source. Authorized Personnel Only." The agents wanted to know more about Krist. Could they develop any leads to his whereabouts? Where did he work at the lab? Could he have left anything behind?

The marine lab owned nine government-surplus trailers which served as private labs for scientists and storage. Krist, as Deacon, had the exclusive use of one such trailer, a standard road-size eight-by-eight-foot steel-bodied vehicle thirty feet long. Once it had belonged to the U. S. Marine Corps.

Now it was on concrete blocks. Someone had stenciled in black paint: "J.O.I.D.E.S." for Joint Oceanography Institute's Deep

Earth Sampling, and underneath, "routine analysis lab." This was Deacon's.

Robert W. Thornhill, the graying bifocaled supervisor of the service department for the lab, knew it all too well. Thornhill supervised a staff of twenty-eight carpenters, plumbers, machinists, electricians and painters who worked year-round for the scientific personnel of the lab. Forever they were building devices and apparatus for experiments, aiding the researchers, scholars and academicians anyway they could. This was their job.

Deacon and his trailer had given Thornhill a few unpleasant moments. "He was kind of overbearing, pushy, and he had to have everything done yesterday. He wanted a power outlet hooked up to his trailer. We didn't get it in fast enough to suit him and he complained."

Deacon, alone of the lab's research assistants, had attached a padlock to his trailer. This had come to Thornhill's attention some weeks before when an air-conditioning repairman tried to get in and couldn't. "I asked him to take it off. He did," said Thornhill.

The agents wanted to see the trailer the moment they heard about it. They were in Dr. Hurley's office asking him if he knew anything about the construction of a fiberglass box.

Mentally, both agents were keying to the ransom note ". . . Barbara is presently alive inside a small capsule buried in a remote piece of soil. . . . The box is waterproof and very strong—fiberglass reinforced plywood—and she has little chance of escaping."

Could Krist have built the box or the "capsule" at the lab?

"Box?" Dr. Hurley repeated. "How big a box?"

"Big enough to hold the body of a young woman," one of the agents replied candidly.

Beginning to comprehend, Dr. Hurley informed the agents that high-level lab technicians such as Deacon, were, in fact, expected to build boxes. The marine lab built and used seventy-five to a hundred boxes a year, all sizes, plywood and fiberglassed for waterproofing. They needed them for specimens, keeping anything from a fragile gulper eel to a lemon shark, sometimes alive, sometimes dead and preserved. An eighty-foot flume, used for study of corrosion, poked from the marine-lab grounds into the bay and it looked like nothing so much as a long row of cheap plywood caskets stacked end to end.

And where did Deacon work? The trailer.

Dr. Hurley took a master key and unlocked the swing-out double doors. They stepped up and walked in. They could see the pale blue interior of a deserted lab, a vacant lab-type table, book shelves empty of books, and the litter of construction labor on the hard pine floor—scraps of plywood, work gloves, electric bits, a screw driver, pieces of fiberglass cloth.

They smelled a heavy odor of resin. On the floor the agents immediately detected splotches of an epoxy glue in the outline of a rectangular box—a box large enough to contain the body of Barbara Mackle.

Agent Smith stared at the outline disbelievingly. He had read and reread the ransom note, and thought it hideous, and he had hoped against hope, and suddenly there was no doubt in his mind. It had to be true.

FBI interrogations at the lab would confirm the suspicion.

"Sure," said Thornhill, the supervisor. "George had permission to sign out material for himself." Thornhill thumbed a pile of requisition forms, searching for the "G. G. Deacon" signatures. He found one requisition for twenty-four flat-edged wood screws, and he found another, dated six weeks before, for exterior plywood. "No one thought a thing about it," said Thornhill.

"He came to me with the dimensions for a box," said Donald Stewart, the carpentry shop foreman, a tall, slender craggy-faced man with sawdust on the lenses of his spectacles. "He didn't show me a drawing. Most guys do, but he didn't. I didn't ask." Stewart had an assistant, Lehtinen Kaufe, a Finn, cut the plywood. It was an AC exterior grade stamped Mount Baker. "I told George how to butt the ends so it would fit tighter and be easier to assemble," said Stewart.

"He asked me about fiberglassing to make it watertight," said George Destin, a painter. "The question he wanted to know was, was it durable? I asked him if it was going to be knocked around, handled in a rough manner, and he said yes. I told him epoxy resin was best. You mix a hardener with it. He seemed to know all the mixtures. He was a very intelligent boy but you always got the feeling he thought he was a little bit above you.

"He told me he needed a fan for cooling, something that would work on a twelve-volt battery for a week to nine days," said Forrest J. Andrew, a research associate in the machinist shop. "He said he needed it for underwater cooling purposes and I told him that with solid-state electronics he wouldn't need it. But he insisted he did. I spent five hours going through catalogues trying to find a lousy motor which would use very, very little current."

"He finally got a little electric motor from a hobby shop," said Joseph Patnode, the chief machinist. "He wanted to know how much air it would throw and we figured it out. He had a little airplane propeller and I put it together for him, fit the hole in the propeller to the motor shaft. I build instruments for everybody. He said it was just a try-out deal, it didn't have to be too good."

This had occurred about a month prior to the kidnaping. One day about that time Patnode walked up to Krist's trailer.

"What you doing, George?" he asked.

"Cleaning up this trailer. I'm going to make a shop of my own. Cost too much to have you make things."

"Can I take a look?"

"Aw, naw, just a lot of fiberglass in here now. You wouldn't want to go in."

Patnode didn't press him. Patnode recalled another peculiar conversation with Krist. Krist had once questioned him about developing a float that would pop to the surface upon an electronic impulse from a submerged box. They talked about using a strong plastic rope such as those used for water-skiing.

Krist had also questioned a lab electrician, Ray Goudet, about making a small light blink by flashlight battery from a two-hundred-foot wire.

Did this explain the kidnaper's demand to put the ransom suitcase in a box with a flashing light on the Fair Isle Causeway? Did he expect to pull the box off the causeway from a boat into the bay, then retrieve it by skin-diving? Had Robert Mackle seen a scuba-diving tank on the causeway at the wall? Did this explain the flippers and mask found with the $500,000 near the Volvo? Did this also explain the belief of the teacher at the Bible College that Krist was wearing a wet suit under his torn trousers?

Yet, why on earth would anyone make the collecting of a ransom so complicated? And what happened to the box?

The FBI, uncertain of the answers, soon had skin divers exploring the bay bottom twenty feet deep off the causeway. They failed to find a box. Could it have been shoved into the bay and floated away, too light to sink when Robert Mackle left the suitcase at the wall instead?

No one took time for leisurely speculation. Said Dr. Hurley, "The FBI was extremely concerned with the search for a warm body." Agent Smith was on the telephone to Inspector Shroder. He was positive. The kidnapers had indeed buried Barbara Mackle in a fiberglassed-plywood box.

The FBI did not convey this information to the family. It couldn't possibly serve a useful purpose. If the kidnaper kept his word to call within twelve hours after delivery of the money, the Mackles would know the truth very shortly. The time was approaching noon. If he did not keep his word, Barbara's survival would depend on whether or not anyone accidentally discovered her. Obviously no one had discovered her during the three days and three nights since the kidnaping. If he did not call, the chances were that she would not be found alive. In the collective mind of the FBI, the probability of finding her alive diminished every hour. It was quite possible that she was already dead.

Record checks in Utah and California would soon provide additional insight into the character of Krist.

As a boy of sixteen, Krist had served a year at the Utah State Industrial School in Ogden for theft, June 2, 1961 to June 4, 1962, and while there he was given a standard IQ test on July 8, 1961.

His score astonished the school. Krist scored 142. Undeniably, by the criteria of the psychologists, Krist ranked as a genius.

Over the years, the same test had been administered to 2764 young boys and girls committed to the institution. Eight others scored in the 130 to 139 bracket, which comprised three-tenths of one per cent. But no one scored as high as Krist.

Sheer intellectual ability in itself, of course, did not correlate necessarily with a man's guile or cunning. But the FBI knew it could not rely upon him to blunder about stupidly. The Bureau realized fully it was dealing with an extremely capable and dangerous criminal.

Additional information on his escape arrived from California. Twice Krist had been committed to the Deuel Vocational Institution in Tracy. At age eighteen, after car thefts in Ventura, Alameda and Oakland, Krist served one year from November 12, 1963 until December 4, 1964. He had been sent back the second time on May 20, 1966, convicted of the theft of two cars from a used-car lot in San Mateo. Police had arrested him January 6, 1966, and while awaiting trial Krist complained of stomach pains. He was taken to a hospital and escaped—only to be rearrested. When he arrived at the Deuel Vocational Institution May 20, he was under an indefinite sentence of six months to five years.

He escaped before his six months were up—November 11, 1966. His wife had visited him the day before.

At 4:35 A.M. that morning a tower searchlight caught two inmates going over a double fence.

Krist and Earl Melvin Harding, a twenty-four-year-old murderer serving life imprisonment, had sawed a single steel bar from the window of their first-floor two-man cell. They had left two dummies of stuffed clothing in their beds, squeezed out a nine-by-sixteen-inch opening, and replaced the bar so it could not be detected casually.

Workmen the day before had been painting a three-story building in the prison grounds. They had left a wheeled scaffolding near the building. Krist and Harding wheeled the scaffolding next to an inside security fence twelve feet high. A second outside security fence ten feet high surrounded the first fence.

The two men had found a twenty-foot-piece of lumber, a two-by-six, and placed it across the two fences, using it as a bridge. There they were, scrambling across the plank, when the spotlight caught them. A tower guard reached for his .38-caliber Smith & Wesson revolver and fired.

Harding, struck in the heart, fell dead to the ground. Krist, first across the plank, leaped to the ground and escaped.

So this then was the escaped criminal for whom the Robert Mackle family waited to call—brilliant, reckless, and warped.

Hi, Burgh!

You know how you try to make a situation better than it is? Well, I kept thinking to myself it is nice and cozy and warm here. If I were outside, I would be cold. This is warm. This is snug. What better place could there be than right here. If I were out, why, maybe something would go wrong and the kidnapers would want to shoot me. But here they can't. I'm safe here. I'm glad I'm here.

I really tried to talk myself into this. It didn't work for long.

I was cold and I was wet and I ached, but it just didn't help to think about it. I would turn off the fan from time to time just to stop the noise. It was getting to me. And then I would deliberately sing happy songs. I have such a bad voice that when I hear myself sing, I laugh. I really do. I felt silly singing, but it felt good.

Daddy and I used to sing together when I was young. There was one song I had forgotten almost completely. The only thing I remember is the ending. It ended, "Seattle, Washington, and Pitt." And when we finished, I would always add, "Burgh" for Pittsburgh, and Daddy would laugh. This was my big part—Burgh. This was when I was a kid, and after a while I started calling Daddy "Burgh." I would say, "Hello, Burgh," and he thought it was cute. I must have been four or five years old. This was my pet name for him.

I worried a lot about Daddy having a heart attack. I couldn't help from thinking about it. I could just picture Dad. He gets so nervous anyway. And I was thinking, I hope he calms down. I hope they give him some kind of pills to calm him down.

I kept thinking of other kid songs Daddy and I used to sing. They were corny, but they helped. "I've got a real good friend who is a ghost, don't mean to boast, but he is a pal of mine." Crazy little songs like that. "I'll sing you twelve holes, green grow the grass is grown . . ." Nothing popular, really. I don't go out and buy records. But I know "My Fair Lady" from the album, and I was singing "With a little bit of luck," and of course, all the Christmas songs, "White Christmas," the Bing Crosby version, and my mind was just wandering. A week or so before I got the flu, the Tri Delts sang for little black children in Atlanta, the First Atlanta Baptist Church, I think, I'm not sure, and the kids all joined in. And I was thinking of walking on the Emory campus with Stewart. Ice skating, and I remember he was falling down and I was laughing, and one time it was cold and we were just running at Lullwater, the president's home at Emory, tremendous grounds. And we were just running and playing tag and leap frog; childish things, but it was fun. And I was thinking of all the happy and fun things I could.

The twelve hours since the second ransom drop had come and gone. Robert Mackle sat in the vinyl-covered captain's chair around the Viking oak round table in the game room, and everything reminded him of his daughter. He sat in Barbara's chair. Agent Lee Kusch, unaware of the family's private seating protocol, sat in Robert's chair. It had long been the custom of the Mackle family to gather around the round table the first thing every morning. It was a ritual. As Robert, Jane, Bobby and Barbara awoke, when the children were home from school, each would pour himself a cup of coffee in the kitchen and then walk through the den to the game room and take his place at the round table around seven o'clock. There they would scan the sectioned morning newspaper and talk quietly as a family.

Jane Mackle liked to tell guests that the game room had been built around a pool table. Although this wasn't quite accurate, a brass-cornered green-felt billiard table, two pull-down lamps overhead, dominated the golf-course side of the huge oversized room. The six cues stood in their places on the rack on the wall, and Robert Mackle could recall the quick competitiveness of his daughter, the family pool shark, good enough at one time that she could beat her brother Bobby.

Robert Mackle could see the untrimmed Christmas tree in a corner. Underneath was his present from Barbara, already wrapped and delivered early.

In a flurry of excitement during the morning, the radio monitor in the game room reported the search for a tourist pulling a trailer with a box on it into the Everglades.

"It took forever to locate it," said Robert Mackle. "It was a man with a completely harmless box, but in my mind, it had my daughter."

With the FBI reports from Jackson Memorial Hospital and the University of Miami Institute of Marine Sciences, Inspector Shroder said he thought he had better leave.

Robert Mackle escorted him to the front door of his home.

"Bob," said Shroder, "my work is done here. I am going down to headquarters."

Then the FBI man grasped Robert Mackle by the shoulders.

"I'll be back," he said. He paused and smiled. "At the family reunion. Believe me, I will be."

Robert Mackle wanted desperately to believe.

"The FBI would talk only very reassuringly," young Bob recalled. He saw the twelve hours come and go and he became extremely depressed.

"I thought she was dead for sure. The contact time was up. I was going to wait until five or six o'clock and then break the news to Mom and Dad. I figured if we hadn't heard by then, that was it. I think Lee Kusch felt the same. When I got him off by himself, he would say only, 'There's hope.'

"The FBI thought Krist and Ruth had brought Barbara to Miami. She was in the Everglades somewhere maybe, and that after they got the money at midnight they would let her loose in the boonies, the boondocks, and that someone would find her wandering around in six or eight hours. Dad was saying he couldn't stand to wait. I told him they'd probably tied her up somewhere. There were several contradicting thoughts. We thought they might let her out of the car somewhere and she might be wandering around before someone found her. Then again we thought that maybe they had left someone in Atlanta to guard her. We thought that once the guy got the half a million dollars he would run and the people in Miami weren't about to cut in the guy from Atlanta. I couldn't see anyone stupid enough to just stand guard. The Bureau wasn't telling us everything either. This was apparent to me.

"I just couldn't believe the buried capsule bit. Enough air for seven days. It just didn't seem logical. Not only illogical, but inhuman. It was such a hideous thing to think about. Dad sat at the round table and said, 'When they get her out, she'll be a vegetable. If they get her out.'

"And I said, 'If anybody can stand it, Barbara can.' And I thought to myself, Dad's right. She's got to be a vegetable. I just couldn't believe anyone would bury her alive."

So instead, not admitting it fully to himself, Bobby believed his sister dead. And it was simply a matter of hours before the others would be forced to the same conclusion.

Some moments before one o'clock, Robert Mackle walked out to the patio beside the pool. Billy Vessels was there reading the newspaper, squinting in the sunlight. Even the patio of the Mackle

home had not offered complete sanctuary. Earlier a newsman from
London had walked across the golf course and found Vessels and
Robert there. Vessels had erupted angrily, denounced him as a
"vulgar vulture," and chased him away.

Now Vessels was relaxed, or as relaxed as he could be.

"Sit down, boss man," he said. "Let me get you a bottle of beer."

Robert Mackle nodded affirmatively. He hadn't had a thing to
drink or eat that he could recall. His mind remained on his
daughter.

"I kept thinking there must be something I can do. Something
other than deliver money."

He sat in silence and began to pray.

Suddenly he jumped from the lawn chair.

"What's wrong?" Billy Vessels asked.

"We're going to get Barbara back, Billy. Don't ask me how I
know it. I know it."

Three to four minutes later the red telephone rang in the game
room. Agent Lee Kusch grabbed it. "Yes, sir. Yes," he was speaking
to another FBI agent.

No one was allowed to use the telephone. It had to be held
open. "I'll keep everyone off," he said. He did not elaborate.

Robert Mackle looked at his watch. It was almost half past one.

In the Atlanta office of the FBI at 12:47 P.M., Trisha Poindexter, a pretty little twenty-three-year-old black-haired girl from
Rome, Georgia, was just about ready to go to lunch. The Atlanta
switchboard of the FBI, like the Miami switchboard, had received
scores of telephone calls from persons who wanted to be helpful.
They hadn't stopped since Tuesday.

Fifteen lines fed into the Atlanta switchboard, 521-3900, situated
on the tenth floor on the Peachtree-Baker Building. A half wall
and counter separated Trisha from a hallway.

"FBI," she answered.

"I want to give you some information on the Mackle girl," a man
said.

"Just a minute, please," said Miss Poindexter. "I'll give you to an
agent."

"No," the man said. He said it emphatically. "I want to give you
some directions on how to find the capsule. I'll give this to you one
time."

Trisha Poindexter had no idea who he was or what he was talking about.

"Don't switch the call. I'll give it to you," he said quickly. "I'll give it to you one time."

"I don't take dictation," the girl said defensively. She wanted to transfer him.

"That's okay," he replied.

"He was very precise," she recalled. "He didn't rush me. I couldn't tell where he was calling from. I was a little afraid to ask any questions. I thought he might hang up."

Unaware of the significance of the message, she began to write on a three-by-five-inch scratch pad.

"Out on I-85. Buford Highway. To Norcross. Stop light at Buford and Tucker. Proceed 3.3 miles from intersection. Small white house on a hill. Turn left. Dirt road a mile on right."

Then the man said, "Go up in there about a hundred feet in the woods."

"One hundred feet," Trisha Poindexter wrote.

"Do you have that?"

"Yes," she said, not certain at all that she had taken everything down correctly.

"Are you sure?"

"Yes."

"Bye," he said, and hung up.

Trisha Poindexter thought the voice "nice." Later she would describe it as "kind." "But he sounded as if he was in a hurry."

As she looked up, eager to leave for lunch at one o'clock, she saw agent Don Tackitt walking by.

"This guy just called in and gave me some directions on the Mackle case," she said. "He gave me some directions on how to find a capsule . . ."

Capsule!

A few moments later Trisha was in the office of Jack Keith, the acting agent in charge. Casually, very low-keyed, Keith said, "Trisha, what did this man say?"

She began to read her notes—and she froze. Suddenly she knew. She began to tremble.

Agent Keith sent her to the lounge for a cup of coffee. He wanted her to relax for a few minutes and then write out everything she could remember.

The agents of the Atlanta office of the FBI had found the license number of Krist's Volvo at the Rodeway Inn where he and Ruth had registered as "Dr. and Mrs. Johnsen Rarik, 73 Bickford Street, Boston, Mass., Mass. Inst. of Tech." and they had been able to trace some of their movements in the Atlanta area prior to the kidnaping. But they had absolutely no leads on the whereabouts of Barbara.

The one-hundred-agent Atlanta office had pulled in experienced agents from Albany, Macon, Columbus, Rome, Athens and Marietta, and all agents had attended the five o'clock briefing sessions each day. Hardly anyone truly believed Barbara Mackle was "inside a small capsule buried in a remote piece of soil" as the ransom note said. The discovery of the epoxy resin on the floor of Krist's trailer at the marine lab in Miami an hour or so before had not yet been disseminated through the Atlanta office.

Prior to noon, though, a dozen or so agents were scattered around Atlanta in a rough and loose perimeter in anticipation of a possible telephone call from the kidnapers to the Mackle residence in Coral Gables.

Agent Keith knew instantly none of his men were anywhere near Norcross in Gwinnett County, a small town of about 1500 about twenty-two miles northeast of Atlanta. He and a supervisor, John Reynolds, and four other agents left immediately in three cars. Traveling northwestward on I-85, they could see icicles clinging to the outcropping of rocks and the green signs designating Stone Mountain. Off onto the Buford Highway, known as U. S. 23, they drove past the Christmas-decorated Treasure Island Shopping Center, "Help Wanted" at the Bonanza Sirloin Pit, and a Dairy Queen with a sign, "Go Hog Wild, Try our Bar-B-Q." Traffic signs warned motorists: "Drinking? Here comes da judge."

Agent Keith had the radio dispatcher order all units to assemble at the stop light at the intersection of Buford Highway and Tucker Road.

Proceed three and three-tenths miles, Trisha had written.

In which direction? If the kidnaper had been more specific, Trisha had failed to write it down. She couldn't remember anything else.

Besides the four possible directions from the intersection, Keith saw a fifth road nearby. Anyone could be the right one. Agents hurriedly began to check them out, searching for a white house on a hill three and three-tenths miles away.

It was already approaching three o'clock. Almost exactly three and three-tenths miles from the intersection agents found a white house on a hill. They found a turnoff to the right. But they couldn't find a second dirt road a mile farther. And the wooded land there dropped toward a valley. Hadn't the kidnaper said "go up in there?" Wouldn't "go up" indicate elevation? No one saw anything remotely resembling a capsule. Unanimously, the five agents had a bad feeling about the site. They wanted to try other directions. They returned to the starting intersection.

This time the cars sped northward on Buford Highway. Again, they found a small white house on a hill at about three and three-tenths miles. A two-laned blacktop turned off to the left. McGee Road it was called, and it led to the city of Berkeley Lake where some seventy families lived around an eighty-five-acre lake. A railroad track cut across the blacktop not far from the house. Off in the distance was a box-manufacturing factory where some thirty men worked.

The cars raced west on McGee Road.

Red fireplugs, not yet connected, sporadically lined the edge of the road in the hope of future development and a tilted red-and-white sign advertised, "For Sale—Industrial Site. Kinsland Realty Company."

To the right a rusted three-strand barbed-wire fence broke for a dirt road one and one-tenth miles from the turnoff. The property belonged to Mrs. Mason I. Lowance, the wife of an Atlanta physician.

"This has got to be it," said Keith. He and four agents, Vincent Capazella, Robert Stokes Kennemur, William Colombell and Ralph Williams, abandoned their cars and took to the woods. The dirt road ended 130 feet from the blacktop at a junk pile near the foundation of a torn-down house. Strewn in disarray were an old door, trash, a child's rusted slicky-slide, a pile of flattened beer cans and a dirty old leather jacket which had once been issued by the Navy. The label inside said "electronically heated."

The agents searched for a hill, an elevation. "Go up in there. A hundred feet." And there was no hill. The road was the highest elevation. Hills, rolling and uneven, sloped off erratically in all directions. They looked everywhere within a radius of one hundred feet. A hundred feet couldn't possibly be correct.

Keith left the site to return to the intersection of Buford and Tucker highways. He knew he had to set up a command post. He could set it up in the grocery store parking lot. It was approaching four o'clock and he knew he wouldn't have much more daylight. He would have to send search teams on all five roads. He would have to cover every possibility. He knew that every piece of rolling equipment the FBI owned in the city of Atlanta would soon be in Norcross if it wasn't already. And he knew it might not be enough.

He began to think of a posse, asking other Georgia law enforcement agencies for help. He knew Washington would be thinking of the Georgia National Guard. He would have to re-evaluate the situation shortly. It would be much tougher at night. He wanted to get more men at the site while he still had time.

Jack Keith, a gray-haired man of fifty years who had worked for the FBI for more than twenty years, was not a man to panic. But as he raced back to his car, he felt perilously close to it. He was frantic and he knew it. They had to find that girl. She could be dying. She could be dying right now and if they could find her—now, now, now—they could save her.

Jack Keith prayed. He prayed for God to keep her alive. He prayed for himself. He felt his panic subside.

Vincent Capazella, a black-haired collegiate-looking young agent, his shirt soaked in sweat, stalked through the underbrush, the fading sunlight unable to penetrate the forest of tall Georgia pines. Capazella and a balding pink-faced agent with a fringe of gray hair, Robert Stokes Kennemur, had discovered the faint traces of a path down a sloping hillside, past a few flattened Budweiser cans. They had been in the woods searching fifteen minutes. They were about three hundred feet from the dirt road at the dump.

Suddenly Capazella stopped. He thought he heard something. "I hear a noise," he said.

Agent Kennemur, fifteen yards away, pointed toward the road. He could hear voices off in the distance.

Capazella shook his head. He pointed to his feet. He kicked the undermat of fallen leaves and pine needles and he saw red clay, the fresh red earth of Georgia. It was twelve minutes after four o'clock.

I heard a little rustle or something. It was the first time, absolutely the first time, that I thought I'd heard anything. I turned off the fan. And I didn't hear it any more. I was straining so hard to hear. And I held my breath for a second and listened. And nothing. I was kind of letdown.

But it had to be something; an animal or something. I just knew it.

And I started pounding. I didn't scream. I didn't say anything. But I clenched my fist and pounded as hard as I could. I wasn't taking any chances. I pounded and I pounded and the box shook and the droplets fell. I flung off the blanket and I kept pounding. I was getting very wet. And my hands were hurting. I pounded for maybe thirty seconds, a minute.

And I stopped to listen for a few seconds and I didn't hear anything. But I started pounding again. By this time I didn't think anyone was there. I thought no one is here; it is just my imagination. But I kept pounding anyway.

And while I was pounding I heard footsteps and then a man shouting.

"Barbara Mackle! Barbara Mackle! This is the FBI!"

Vincent Capazella scuffed the red earth again.

Both he and agent Kennemur hear three distinct knocks.

Capazella fell to his knees and he brushed with his hands. He could see distinctly a mound of earth.

"Barbara Mackle!" Kennemur cried. "Barbara Mackle! This is the FBI!"

Frantically, they uncovered the dead leaves, twigs, branches.

"I'll radio for help," agent Capazella said, and he began the hard run up the sloping hillside of the forest to the radio in the car more than a hundred yards away. In the desperation of the moment, he had forgotten that Kennemur had the car keys in his pocket.

Panting, he returned a few moments later. "I'll run," said Kennemur, a much older man, and he began the same dash.

Capazella clawed at the earth with his bare hands. From above him, tangled in the trees, came the heavy scent of honeysuckle permeating the air he breathed. The honeysuckle vines were still green, alive.

I smiled. I quit pounding and I had this great big smile on my face. I said, "Bobby!" I thought it was Bobby. And the man above said, "No, this is the FBI!"

I just couldn't believe it.

I didn't say anything. It was complete happiness. I can't describe the feeling. I didn't know if it was the FBI out there or not. I didn't care. There was somebody out there and they knew that I was here. A human being. Even if it was the kidnapers, someone was there. I didn't care who. Just so long as it was someone. I had never felt such a wonderful feeling of relief.

And he said, "Knock! Knock! If you can hear me, knock!"

So I was knocking. I heard some scraping around. I thought, the FBI? Great! But it didn't really penetrate. I was just so glad someone had found me.

I stopped pounding and listened and I heard someone say again, "Knock." He said, "Answer me. Answer me if you are all right."

And I shouted, "I'm all right!"

I didn't know what was going on. Something was going on but I didn't know what. I heard someone yell, "She is over here! Here!"

I could hear things, noises, scuffing, but it didn't sound like they were digging me out. I couldn't hear any digging. I thought, if they'll just get me out quickly.

And somebody said, "We're getting you out. It is going to take a little while."

Then I heard some scraping. I knew they were scraping away the dirt. They were behind my head. I kept thinking, here I am. I kept expecting the lid to open but it didn't. I wondered what was wrong.

Someone said, "Hold on! Hold on! We're getting you out."

I was just smiling the whole time, and believe it or not, I was trying to comb the dirt out of my hair with my fingers.

Agent Colombell, a brawny young blue-eyed lawyer from New Haven, Connecticut, whose car radio transmitter had blown from constant use an hour earlier, reached the entombed young girl a few moments later, and then there was Ralph Williams, Jack Keith and John Reynolds. Kennemur returned, carrying a bucket from the dump.

And with the site pinpointed precisely, men raced through the woods singularly and in pairs, Roger Kaas, Tom Renehan, Richard Fuggat, D. A. Hughes, Jack Leuck, William Donald Cockran.

Agent Leuck also found an old bullet-ridden bucket, once used for target practice, and he gouged and scooped the earth. Someone else ripped a branch from a small sweet gum tree and poked and gouged. And others were on their hands and knees, clawing, digging. The red earth had been packed firmly.

Agents had found two flexible, six-foot plastic tubes, buried just under the surface, running parallel, then protruding above. Keith grabbed one and yelled to Barbara Mackle.

It was the exhaust outtake tube. He could detect the faint flow of air. Barbara did not respond.

Agents could hear the hum of the fan as they dug frantically. They didn't know what it was.

"Answer me if you can hear me, Barbara," Jack Keith cried again.

And again, there was no response.

Colombell had the terrible feeling that she would die before they could reach her. Suddenly he could see his hand bleeding. A screw, protruding from a lid, had gashed his right thumb. Other hands bled.

They would need a screw driver.

"Get a tire iron!" someone yelled. An agent raced off to the cars now pulled into the dump and lining McGee Road.

Two fourteen-year-old boys on their bicycles from the city of Berkeley Lake, Sterling Honce and Ray Dickson, stopped along on the blacktop and watched the men running.

"We thought it was a whiskey raid," said young Dickson. They stayed out of the way.

Other agents were still arriving. Still others, contacted by radio, were buying shovels in Norcross. They were on the way.

One thought kept recurring in the mind of agent Kennemur. What would they find? Would she be stark-raving mad?

About eighteen inches under the surface, agents uncovered one end of the box. They could tell it was made of wood and that fiberglass cloth had been glued to its surface. It had been painted a marine gray. They could see it was about two and a half feet in width. With the tire iron and brute force, they tore off the top.

Instantly they knew they had the wrong section of the box. It had been partitioned off. They could see a small compartment and a 12-volt battery and the wires leading to a plywood partition wall. They could see where the flexible tubes connected. On the bottom was a small boat pump and the ventilating fan, encased in a painted and unlabeled tin can which looked as if it had once contained tomato or fruit juice on a supermarket shelf. The fan hummed much louder.

It took another four or five minutes to uncover a trap-doorlike lid, attached by four hinges, and screwed down with fourteen three-and-a-half-inch galvanized screws set about four inches apart.

It was thirty-two minutes past four o'clock in the afternoon.

For Barbara Mackle, it was dawn. It had been eighty-three hours till dawn.

I heard the prying, all sorts of sounds. I couldn't imagine what was taking so long. Then they were right over my head. I remember they unscrewed the screws. I could hear that. I knew exactly what they were doing. But I couldn't see any light.

I was getting very wet and I pulled up the blanket. The box was shaking. And then, finally, they opened the lid and the dirt was falling in, and I heard a loud, creeeeek.

And everything was light. I stuck my head out from under the blanket and it was so bright I blinked. And I saw hands reaching for me.

I sort of put my head up—and there were a whole lot of men, all of them looking down at me, bending over me.

And they were crying.

And I had this great big smile on my face. They were all around, and they were smiling too, I think, and I could see the tears in their eyes, tears and sweat.

I don't remember how I got out exactly. They pulled me out sort of under my arms.

Someone said, "We've got her," and someone else asked me, "How are you?"

I said, "Fine."

I tried to stand up. I kind of got up. They helped me. And I fell forward. My knees just gave way. They caught me and one of the men said, "She can't walk."

And here I was, grinning. I know I looked ridiculous, wet and dirty, and everything.

And they were standing there, just looking, and I could see that their hands were bleeding and they were perspiring. And they were still crying.

I said, "How is my family?" And Roger Kaas, he was one of the agents, said, "Fine, fine."

I said, "Will you please tell them I'm all right."

And he said, "They'll know shortly."

And this other agent, Bill Colombell, I found out later, picked me up and carried me, and he was having a hard time going through the woods. He was sort of panting.

"I'm heavy, aren't I?"

Another guy said, "Let me take her." He was a dark young man, bigger and brawnier, and he took me.

I asked someone, "What time is it?"

He said whatever it was, four o'clock, and I said, "In the morning?" and he said, no.

I said, "What is today?"

"Friday," he said.

"Friday?" And I just couldn't believe it.

And he said, "How long have you been here?"

I said, "Just as soon as they got me."

He wanted to know if anyone had been there. "Wasn't there anyone around with you?"

I said, "No. Nobody came back after me."

He didn't say anything. No one said anything. I could tell they were angry. They put me in the car, in the back seat, and the man on my right had tears running down his face. I thought something was the matter. I really didn't think he was crying for me.

I said, "Is there something wrong?"

And he said no, and he sniffed and he looked out the window, and then it sort of dawned on me, and I felt bad for even mentioning it.

It was really funny. They acted as if they were afraid to talk to me.

They were interrogating me and they seemed to feel a little awkward.

So I said, "You are the handsomest men I've ever seen." And they all laughed.

The man in the front seat said, "Well, now we know something is wrong with you," and I laughed.

They were using the car radio, telling everyone I was safe, and they were trying to find out where they should take me. The man on my right asked me if I would mind looking at some pictures.

I said, "Oh, no, no," and I was excited because I thought I could help.

Before I looked at them, he introduced himself, Roger Kaas. I said, "Cause? C-a-u-s-e?"

And he said, "No, Roger Kaas," and he introduced me to the two other men in the front seat, Mr. Keith and Mr. Reynolds.

And I repeated the names back, I wanted them to know I was all right.

Roger Kaas gave me the pictures and the kidnaper wasn't the first one. He was the second one. He had a beard on in the picture.

I said, "That's him! That's him! But without the beard."

And he said, "George Deacon."

I said, "Oh, you already know." I was disappointed he already knew.

He said, "What about these others here?" I looked through five or so pictures. There was only one of the kidnaper.

I was so full of knowledge, and I was really disappointed they already knew. I was excited too, I guess. They showed pictures of girls.

I picked out the girl right away. It didn't look much like her, really. I said, "The one with short hair. Ruthie," I said.

And he said, "Ruth Eisemann-Schier."

And I said, "You know her name too?"

I so wanted to help. I said, "Does that help? Have you got them yet?"

He said, "No. But we will."

And he leaned forward and talked to the man in the front seat with gray hair, Mr. Keith. He must have been in charge. And Roger Kaas said, "She has identified these two subjects."

Mr. Keith said, "Good. Great."

On the radio they were talking about the director, J. Edgar Hoover. Where should they go? We were already driving toward Atlanta. Roger Kaas said, "My house is close by. Why don't we go to my house?"

Then Mr. Cochran's name was brought up. He was another

agent. We were going to go to his house. We were driving west, directly into the sun. It was a great huge red ball, fiery red, and it was the most beautiful sunset I ever saw. The driver had to put down his sun visor and I know I didn't want him to. I thought, couldn't they leave them up. But I didn't say anything. I just sat and grinned.

A little later I asked where we were. I wasn't familiar with that part of Atlanta. Roger Kaas or someone mentioned a part of town, and I said, "Where's that?"

He said, "That's pretty far out."

And I said, "Yes, sir. The whole thing is pretty far out."

In the game room 669 miles south of Atlanta, the afternoon had worn heavily. Once, several hours earlier, the telephone rang and agent Lee Kusch again grabbed it.

"Get off the line!" he had cried loudly. "Damn it, get off the line. I don't care what you want. My instructions are to keep this line open."

The ring had startled Robert Mackle. He would jump at the ring of the telephone in his home for months to come.

Bobby had overheard the conversation. "Dad was encouraged by this. I didn't see how it could be encouraging. I thought maybe they'd found Barbara's body. It didn't necessarily seem a good sign to me."

He went upstairs. He went into Barbara's room, paying no attention to the pink carpeting, the ice-pink flocked wall, the canopy over the four-poster bed, the frilly white organdy around a table for the Princess telephone, and a dresser covered with Shalimar cologne, perfume, seeing nothing. He was convinced Barbara was dead; that she had been dead all along. There wouldn't be a telephone call. There wouldn't be a contact by letter either.

His uncles Frank and Elliott had begun to feel extremely discouraged too. They had waited and waited.

Frank Mackle was slouched upon one of the oversized couches in the game room adjacent to the red telephone. No one was talking. The room was silent.

The red telephone rang again.

And again, agent Kusch picked it up hurriedly. "Get off the

line. Please . . ." he began, and he stopped in midsentence. "Oh?
I'm sorry," he said. He gave the telephone to Frank Mackle.

"Hello," said Frank, suddenly tense, taut.

"I heard a male voice," said Frank. "Someone said, 'Mr. Hoover
is coming on the line.'"

He braced himself. He knew he would know in a second.

"This is Edgar Hoover," said the director of the FBI in a quick
staccato voice. "I have some very good news. Barbara is alive and
well. She will tele . . ."

"She is alive and well!" Frank Mackle shouted, and he could see
everyone staring at him, stunned, immobile.

"I was yelling and crying and screaming, and it was like a
second or a second and a half before anyone reacted." He was
gesturing wildly, his arm in the air. "And then everyone was coming at me like in slow motion. I could see Robert running for Jane.
And the whole house went crazy."

Jane Mackle would not be able to remember the instant she
learned of Barbara's safety. She would not remember that Robert
bounded up the stairs and embraced her and held her very
tightly. A mother's emotions broke in a throbbing joy. She would
remember that Frank was still on the telephone when she came
downstairs into the den, and she heard him cry, "Jane! Come
quick. They have Barbara!" It wasn't until days afterward that
she realized she still thought they were waiting for the second
contact.

"I was shook and crying," said Frank Mackle, "and I had to
compose myself because he was saying something else. He understood that I was telling others. He said Barbara is on her way to an
agent's house. He had the agent's name. He gave me a telephone
number and said we would be able to reach her at this number
in about fifteen minutes."

Sobbing, repeating back every phrase for accuracy, Frank
Mackle wrote down the number. "God bless you," he said. "God
bless you."

We got caught in traffic on the way in and I couldn't have
cared less. We were moving slowly and Roger Kaas had his arm up
behind me on the back seat. They were still a little uneasy.

I said, "You know, I don't allow a boy to put his arm around me
on a first date." And they laughed again.

He asked, "Do you know how much they asked?"

I said, "No. How much?"

He said, "Half a million dollars."

I didn't believe him. I kept saying, "Half a million dollars? Half a million dollars?" And I started laughing at myself. I thought, five thousand. Or ten thousand. I said, "Oh, no!" And they looked at me funny because I was laughing.

I asked them if Mom and Daddy knew by now and they said they'd been radioed. I asked where they were and Roger Kaas said down in Miami.

"Are they coming up?"

He said, "You bet they are."

We were driving straight into that big red sun, very red, the whole time, and I remember we were going through some very beautiful neighborhoods. We stopped at the home of Mr. and Mrs. Donald Cochran in Doraville, northeast of Atlanta. I got out of the car and I tried to stand up and I kind of went down to my knees. It really surprised me. While I was sitting in the car I felt fine. They caught me as I collapsed and I said, "I guess you'll have to carry me again."

Mrs. Cochran met us at the door. Roger Kaas, I think it was, carried me upstairs, and he asked me his name. I think he was testing me. I said, Robert Kaas, and he said, Roger. I'm always bad at names. There was a doctor there and he wanted to examine me right away.

Mrs. Cochran came in and she said, "Would you like for me to be here?"

And he said, "Yes. Let's get this nightgown off her."

That's when I first realized how grimy and dirty I was. I said, "Could I please have a bath?"

He said, "Let me examine you first," and he wanted to know if I had been abused in any way.

I said, "No. I wasn't," and he started giving me an examination. Mrs. Cochran was there and she took off my nightgown. The doctor listened to my heart and he said, "Are you sure you weren't abused?"

I said, "No. I don't want that kind of examination, please."

He took my pulse and my blood pressure and asked me, "Did you ever give up hope?"

I said, "No. I'm a terrible optimist."

He said, "That's good. Nowadays, they are hard to find."

He asked me to stand up and I tried and I started to fall again. He made me sit at the side of the bed. He told me I was dehydrated and asked if I would like something to drink.

I was so thirsty. I asked for a Coke, please, and Mrs. Cochran got me a king-sized one. I remember the Cochrans had a little boy and girl, and they were peeking around the corner. Then they scampered off.

The FBI doctor felt my forehead and said I didn't have a fever. He must have known I had had the flu. He said, "Do you have any aches or pains," and I said no. He asked if my head was clear. And I sniffed. It was a real shock, surprise. I could breathe.

He had me stand on the bathroom scales and with a sheet around me I weighed 110 pounds. I said, "Oh, no, I've lost all my weight." My normal weight was exactly 125 pounds, and because I was studying for the exams when I was sick, I probably was down to 119, something like that. And it is so hard for me to gain weight. I was really upset. The doctor told me not to worry; all I would have to do was drink some liquid.

I asked again if I could take a bath. So the doctor left and Mrs. Cochran helped me. Just about then the headman wanted to see me. I think it was Mr. Keith. He told me that Mr. Hoover was going to call and that my father was coming up to get me.

"Mr. Hoover?" I asked, and slowly I began to realize the enormity of everything.

Mrs. Cochran said, "You are a pretty important young lady, aren't you?"

And I just looked at her and she said, "You've been in the front pages of the paper for the past few days."

I said, "You're kidding," and she kind of laughed.

I didn't really want to talk to Mr. Hoover then; I wanted to talk to Daddy, and I wanted a bath. They sort of helped me into the bathroom. I didn't want to be carried. And then I saw myself in the mirror. I was so grimy. I don't know how I could have been that dirty. I had red clay under my fingernails and my hair, it was awful. Terrible.

Mrs. Cochran sort of scrubbed me. Then she said she would leave me alone for a second. She left and I washed a little more. I was still weak so I decided I was clean enough. She came back with a Coke and helped me into the bedroom. She asked me if I wanted some soup and I said, "That sounds delicious."

She said it was homemade. She sat there and talked, mostly

about her house, her children, and I told her how beautiful her house was. It was very deliberate on her part not to talk about me, not to ask questions, and the conversation was a little contrived, synthetic, and I appreciated it.

"You must be exhausted," she said. "I'll leave you alone so that you can sleep," and she left.

I couldn't sleep. I was so happy and so content. And I lay back and thanked God. I thanked Him for being with me.

A little later I wanted to go back to the bathroom. No one was there. I got up and I fell down again. I kind of blacked out. I never told anyone that. I sat on the edge of the bed a minute and I was okay.

I remember they kept opening the door and looking in. I pretended like I was asleep. I don't know why. I heard someone say, "She is fine, and her father is coming up."

The next thing Roger Kaas came in and he said, "You have a phone call."

They brought the phone over to the edge of the bed, and Mrs. Cochran went into another room and got me a robe. I think they had to move the telephone in. It didn't reach to the bed. I don't know how they did it.

I said, "Hi, Daddy."

But it was Uncle Frank. He said, "No. This is Uncle Frank." I said, "How are you?"

He said, "Just fine. How are you?"

And I said, "I'm just wonderful." He wanted to know if they were taking good care of me. I said a woman is taking very good care of me; I meant Mrs. Cochran, but somehow, he thought I meant Ruth. I didn't mean her at all. Anyway, Uncle Frank said, "There is someone here who wants to talk to you."

Their conversation was monitored. At the MOhawk exchange center in Coral Gables, FBI agents and Gerald Doyle, the telephone security chief, had listened and taped every conversation since Tuesday afternoon.

A few minutes earlier, before Frank had talked to Barbara, Robert had asked an Atlanta FBI agent if his daughter had been violated. The agent, controlled and precise and unemotional, replied, "No, sir."

With Barbara on the line, Frank gave his brother the telephone.

Robert, his voice quavering in emotional distortion, said, "Barr-baraaah? Barr-bar-aaah?"

"Sir?" she said, not positive that it was her father.

"Barbara?" he asked, his voice still cracking.

Barbara Mackle recognized her father.

"Hi, Burgh!" she said cheerfully. "How are you . . ."

And their unseen listeners in the MOhawk exchange choked up so badly they couldn't see. Doyle, a stranger to the family six hundred miles away, would never forget it. "God, was she cool."

Mother and Daddy were both on the telephone together and Mother started to cry. And Daddy said, "Jane! Jane! Stop it. Now stop it! If you can't talk to her, you'll have to get off the phone." And Mother said, "I just can't help it." Daddy said he would fly up to get me right away. The plane was waiting.

I was asking how everybody was, and Daddy would say, fine, fine, everybody is fine. We hung up and I went back to bed. Mrs. Cochran brought me another Coke and she was talking about her husband. When he came home at night, she said, he was so upset, so terribly worried, that he couldn't talk about it. She said everybody at the FBI office thought of me as their own daughter. She said she would let me try to get some sleep.

It was real funny. Here I hadn't slept in three days, or if I had I couldn't remember it, and I should have been totally exhausted and I know I wanted to go to sleep. But I couldn't. I could stretch out. Oh, it was so great. All the way, spread-eagle. It felt so good. The box with all the stuff in it probably was five or six inches too short. And now I could stretch out completely; now that it was over, and already it was kind of like a dream. Like it didn't happen. That soon, really. I couldn't think about the morbid parts of being down there. I was thinking, am I really here? I was so happy and content.

I wondered when Daddy would be here. I kept thinking, where are they? Why aren't they here? And then I said I am not going to play that game again. Every time the door opened I thought it would be Daddy. I once crawled down to the bottom of the bed to look at the clock across the room. I'm nearsighted and I couldn't see it without my glasses. I forget what time Daddy arrived.

Dr. Lauth came in first by himself.

And he said, "So here is the troublemaker." He was always joking.

I asked him where Daddy was. He said he was the doctor; he wanted to see me first.

I said, "Dr. Lauth. I've lost ten pounds. Can you give me some Get Fat pills?"

He had been the family doctor for years and he used to always give me Get Fat pills to help me put on weight. They never did work. He laughed and told me not to worry. He took my blood pressure and examined me and then he said there is someone here who wants to see you. I knew it was Daddy.

I was sitting on my legs on the bed, sort of a kneeling position, and he came in and he started to hug me.

And I pushed him away and said, "I told you, you have an expensive daughter."

He was always telling me that. He just laughed and he hugged me a real long time and he didn't let me go. He didn't cry. I didn't either, except that there might have been a few tears in my eyes.

Mrs. Cochran came in and I introduced her to Daddy as my second mother; after all, she had told me I was everybody's daughter. Daddy thanked her for taking care of me.

Then Billy Vessels came in. He came in and I said it is good to see you again, Mr. Vessels. Around the house everyone calls him Billy. When I speak to him, I call him Mr. Vessels. He said we're going to have a hard time getting you out because of all the reporters. I thought he was kidding. I thought he was putting me on.

I needed clothing and Mrs. Cochran gave me her fifteen-year-old daughter's clothes. I put on a miniskirt. It looked like a mini mini, it was so short, and I was very conscious of it. She gave me her blue coat with a fur collar on it, and I had my own purse. That was the only thing of my own. They brought it from Miami. We walked downstairs and the house was full of agents. I don't know where they all came from. They all turned around and looked at me and I was thanking everybody. The company plane was waiting at the airport. We got into an FBI car and I was in the back seat and they asked me to put my head down. It was ridiculous and I was laughing. Roger Kaas drove very fast, real wild, I thought. It was like the kidnaping. Exactly.

When we arrived, all those people and reporters were waiting and I thought, this is for real. Daddy was saying, smile for the photographers, and he was laughing at me because I wouldn't believe him. Billy Vessels turned around and told me to keep my head down and walk straight to the plane and if anybody calls my name, don't turn around.

I remember getting out of the car and all the lights went on and the flashes and everything. It was the first time anything like that ever happened. It was kind of a shock.

The pilots, Mr. Raymond Anderson and Mr. Ed Wilson, welcomed me aboard. Mr. Anderson had me sign the autograph book on the plane because I was a celebrity. He said, "We have a new celebrity." I'd flown lots of times before and it was all kind of funny. We took off right away.

Friday night, as the Deltona Corporation's two-engine prop jet Beachcraft, N-962-M, winged southward from Atlanta, about thirty newsmen gathered on a lawn across San Amaro Drive from the Mackle home.

In one way or another, they represented nearly every major news outlet in the nation, the gentleman from the New York *Times* included—as if to answer in page-one headlines his newspaper's editorial commentary the morning before on the Nixon reappointment of Hoover "who at 74 and like Ole Man River just keeps rolling along. Who else" the *Times* had asked, "has been deemed worthy of holding the same public office since the Coolidge administration?"

On the two previous nights, the FBI had asked newsmen to leave. They had complied. Those were the nights of the two ransom drops. The news pack, for that is what it was, had begun gathering again as early as ten o'clock Friday morning and their presence was not exactly a welcomed contribution to the domestic tranquillity of the neighborhood. Previously, a neighbor had driven a group off his lawn by the abrupt employment of his yard sprinkler system.

Friday they had duly reported the arrival and departure of FBI men, the Western Union messengers, a bouquet of pink and white carnations from the Lance Flower Shop, and counted the four dish towels and a round peach-colored tablecloth hanging on the line in back.

United Press International had broken the story of Barbara's recovery out of Atlanta at 5:15 P.M., and in Miami, where the Mackle family was extremely well known, the story unfolded with an unusual degree of dramatic impact. The supposed clinical detachment of the Miami *Herald* newsroom, for example, dissolved in an uproar when a copy boy, Ed Sehon, watched the UPI bulletin move and shouted across the newsroom, "She's safe!"

To avoid the pack on the lawn across the street, Robert Mackle and Billy Vessels had departed by a back door. They hiked across the golf course to a waiting car at the same time that Elliott, Dr. Lauth, and several agents diverted reporters by leaving from the front door in different directions.

With Barbara and her father together in Atlanta, Frank, Elliott, Bobby and Neil Bahr, a Deltona executive, came out the front door into the glare of camera lights at 10:30 P.M., their eyes reddened and bloodshot. Their jubilant feeling couldn't hide their fatigue.

Frank acted as a spokesman.

"This is the happiest moment, I'm sure, in my brother's life."

Barbara, he said had told him, "'I'm fine. I'm fine, Uncle Frank.' We've sort of lost track of time," he apologized.

He was still somewhat uncertain of the facts. "I believe Barbara told her mother she was very well taken care of by a woman," he said. "I do not know if she was buried alive."

There was no doubt in his mind on the role of the FBI. "The FBI did such a tremendous, tremendous job," he said. "It's a great revelation to me to see what a great organization it is."

Someone asked when father and daughter would be home.

"How long are they going to cry together?" Frank Mackle replied. "Then, they'll start making plans."

Janet Chusmir, a *Herald* reporter, managed to reach Bobby. "This will be the best Christmas we will ever have," he said simply.

The newspaper would soon be off the presses again, the "Loved one, Please Come Home" want ad still in type, with an eight-column banner on page one:

BURIED ALIVE, BARBARA SAFE

Also, on page one, would be photographs of Gary Steven Krist and Ruth Eisemann-Schier with the caption: "Have You Seen This Pair?"

As we were flying home, Mr. Vessels began to ask some things about it, and Daddy got mad, well, not mad, irritated, and he said, no, no, let's not think about it.

Dr. Lauth interrupted him and said, let her talk about it if she wants to, and I guess I wanted to a little. Mr. Vessels was asking if anyone took care of me, the food, things like that, if they hurt me, and Daddy said, "Oh, let's forget about it. Let's not talk about it."

Dr. Lauth sort of puts up with him, you know, and he said, "Bob, do you want a tranquilizer or something to calm you down?" Daddy needed it a lot worse than I did. I think they had a drink. Daddy just sat there and looked at me. I was so conscious of him looking at me. And then he said, "It is sort of a long flight back, why don't we take a nap." He must have been absolutely exhausted. Both he and Billy Vessels went right to sleep. Matter of fact, they both snored. Dr. Lauth asked me if I didn't want to get some sleep and I remember closing my eyes, but I didn't sleep.

We landed at Miami International where all the private planes land. The company keeps the planes at the Opa Locka Airport, and I guess that's where all the reporters and photographers were waiting. Daddy said all the reporters knew our number, sixty-two Michael, and we had heard that someone had sent up a plane to follow us in. Anyway, no one was there at Miami International. When we stopped, a big jet was idling there with its bright lights on and the fumes were everywhere, and Billy Vessels went over and made them turn out the lights. We didn't go through the terminal. We walked around Concourse One where the planes are serviced. I had to rest a few minutes. Daddy went ahead and got a taxi. We wanted to go to the Miami Heart Institute on Miami Beach. Dr. Lauth had already made a reservation for me in the intensive care unit. He made the reservations for both Mother and me. We were to be Mrs. Reilly and Joan Reilly. Daddy told me that Mother and Bobby were there waiting for us. The taxi driver couldn't speak English very well. He had a Cuban accent and he drove one of those airport-only area cabs. He wasn't supposed to drive to Miami Beach. This was his third day of driving. The driver was saying he could be fined if he drove to Miami Beach.

Dr. Lauth reached across from the back seat and gave him a prescription blank and said, "Here. I'm a doctor. This is an emergency."

Billy Vessels gave him ten dollars and told him not to say anything. I don't think he had any idea who we were.

I saw Bobby first. He was grinning and he was coming down the corridor in the hospital.

And he said, "If it isn't my long lost sister. Hello, little sister." He is always calling me little sister.

"I see you lost your sun tan, little sister," he said.

I asked him, "Aren't you going to give me a kiss?"

He came over and kissed me on the cheek.

We were outside Mother's room. They had sent her over to the hospital a few hours earlier. Daddy said, "Somebody is here, Jane."

And Mother looked bad. She looked terrible really. I've never seen her like that. I really thought something had happened to her. She started crying hard, very hard, and she hugged me. I said, "It's all right. It's all right."

And she said she didn't think she would ever see me again. She wouldn't let go. And Daddy said, "Now, Jane. Be quiet. She is here and everything is fine."

A little later I whispered to Daddy, "Does Mother know anything about the box?" He said, "No. We'll tell her tomorrow."

Bobby was telling me all about the newspapers. He said the first day we were rich. The second day we were millionaires. The third day we were multimillionaires. And, now, the fourth day, he said, "You are an heiress. And if you are an heiress, I am an heir. Hello, heiress." We were all laughing and joking.

The nurse came in to give me a shot. She thought I was Joan Reilly, like the chart showed. Dr. Lauth told me not to tell anyone. She took my blood pressure, and while she was taking it, she said, "Isn't that awful about poor Barbara Mackle."

And I said, "Oh? I heard they found her."

She said, "They did? How is she? How is she?"

I said, "She is just fine." She gave me a sedative and I went to sleep immediately. It was so wonderful being home. And being alive.

He Didn't Wave

Barbara Jane Mackle was entombed in her plywood crypt for approximately eighty-three hours and thirty minutes—nearly four days and three nights.

Even before the agents found her, the FBI in West Palm Beach, Florida, received a telephone call about Gary Steven Krist.

Norman "Dix" Oliphant, forty-five, deeply tanned, a Kansas-born boat dealer with a cleft chin and the friendly outgoing manner of a good salesman, felt a little peculiar as he telephoned the FBI office in West Palm Beach a few minutes before four o'clock Friday afternoon.

"Look," he began apologetically, "this is D & D Marine Supply, all this may be crazy, but I think I might know something about the Mackle kidnaper. I just sold a boat to a guy who paid me in twenty-dollar bills. He had a car rental from Miami."

Oliphant knew nothing of the second ransom payoff. The information had not been released publicly. But he had read about the first aborted drop and Robert Mackle's plea to the kidnapers to contact him again.

"Did you happen to get the license number?" the agent asked.

"Yeah," said Dix Oliphant. "I think my partner Dave got it," referring to David Reip, the other D in the D & D Marine Supply. A moment later he read a number, 1 E 24848.

"Stay exactly where you are," the FBI agent replied. "We'll be over in a minute."

"And they came around the corner on two wheels," said Oliphant.

His customer, clean shaven, wearing pressed trousers, white shirt and boat shoes, his hair neatly combed, had walked in about 8:30 A.M. that Friday.

"Looked as if he just stepped out of a bandbox," said Oliphant.

The customer said he wanted to look at a boat that would go forty miles an hour. He wanted to do some water-skiing and wanted something that would really go.

Oliphant showed him two or three boats and then an Orlando Clipper, 16-foot outboard, a Nassau runabout. The customer wanted to know if the seats folded out and made beds.

"Yes," said Oliphant.

"That's got a convertible top, great. I'll take it out," the customer said.

Oliphant recalled: "Just bingo, 'I'll take it.' That's not too unusual though. We have a lot of impulse buyers."

The customer wanted to know how soon the boat would be ready. "In an hour?"

Oliphant told him it would take at least three hours to rig it up.

"A boat is not like an automobile. You can't buy it and drive off," Oliphant said.

The customer picked out an eighty-five-horsepower Johnson motor. Oliphant asked for a deposit as a binder while he rigged the boat up. The customer gave him a fifty-dollar bill. Oliphant also wanted to get the customer's name on a title application so he could get him a Florida boat registration number. He gave him an application and told him where to sign so the bookkeeper could notarize it.

"This was the only time he showed any nervous reaction," said Oliphant.

His customer wadded up the application and put it in his pocket and said, "I'll sign it later. Don't worry about that now."

"No, we can't do that," Oliphant said. "I can't put the boat overboard until we give you a number, until you sign and we notarize it."

Oliphant gave the customer a second application.

Krist signed the application "Arthur Horowitz, 13414 S. W. Ninth Avenue, Fort Lauderdale," the name of the man who "lost" his draft card.

Oliphant provided a number for the boat, FL 2883 AK.

He saw his customer's identification—the draft card—for Arthur Horowitz.

"I thought he was a rich Jew kid from Fort Lauderdale. To me he looked Jewish. Maybe just out of college with a pocketful of money; a young attorney or someone. He spoke very intelligently. He was well educated. He knew something about boats. I got the impression he was a Sunday boater. I thought he was twenty-five or twenty-six years old."

Krist was in and out three or four times while Oliphant was rigging the boat. He had to install the electrical system, put the motor on back, put in the battery, the lights, everything.

Krist said he needed camping equipment. Oliphant sent him to the Spencer Boat Company. When he came back he had a big Igloo cooler, a pair of binoculars, a ten-power spyglass, a good portable radio, radio directional finder, thermal blanket, sleeping bag, a hand battery lantern, a packet of tools, a five-gallon plastic water container, and "enough charts to go to Timbuktu."

Oliphant noticed there was no water-ski equipment. He said nothing.

Oliphant sold him two fifteen-gallon fiberglass tanks. Krist asked if they would take him to Bimini without running out of gas.

"If you want to go to Bimini," Oliphant said, "run to Fort Lauderdale, fill up, and then go. Don't try it from West Palm Beach because if it is rough and you slow down you'll never make it."

Bimini, the closest island in the Bahamas to the mainland, lay about fifty miles east of Fort Lauderdale.

Krist said he had more shopping to do and left Oliphant again.

Oliphant's oldest boy, Doug, a charter-boat captain, came by and began looking through the marine charts.

"All those cardboard tubes sticking out made the box look like a porcupine."

Doug pulled out each chart, unrolled it, looked at it, then rolled it up and slipped it back in the tube. There were enough charts to go from the Keys up the coast to Savannah, Georgia, and on the Gulf side from Fort Myers to Pensacola. There were long-range charts for everything in the Bahamas, all the out islands.

"I don't know where this guy is going but he sure is going somewhere," Doug observed.

Oliphant's younger boy, Mickey, home from junior college for the Christmas vacation, was helping rig the boat. He was up front putting in the instrument panel and hooking up the steering. Suddenly he blurted out, "Boy, this is a screwy deal. Wouldn't this be funny if we were rigging this up for the Mackle kidnaper?"

"For Christ's sake, Mickey. Don't be ridiculous," Oliphant retorted.

Mickey went down to the Hut, a hamburger place nearby. "He was laughing and telling everyone there we were rigging up a boat for the Mackle kidnaper," Oliphant said.

The man Oliphant knew as "Mr. Horowitz" returned again shortly after twelve noon. He announced he was ready to go.

"Give us half an hour to forty-five minutes," said Oliphant.

"I've got a few telephone calls to make and I'll be back," his customer replied.

This time when he returned, the mate on Doug's boat saw him get out of a Yellow Cab.

"He'd had that rental Fairlane all morning. I knew Dave would get its number. We always get a number if something looks a little funny. This Horowitz had a Navy duffel bag with him, some commander's name written on it, and my porter, Willie Harris, stowed it for him up underneath. He had a couple of little laundry bags, too. He paid me $239.64 in $20 bills. With the $50 bill before, that made $289.64, and he said he would pay me $2000 more—the full price—if he approved it after we water-tested it. It was on a trailer waiting for him. I thought he was going to give me a certified check.

"I took him down to Currie Park and we put it in Lake Worth. It was exactly two o'clock as I put him overboard. While I was parking, he cranked it up and was sitting under the wheel ready to go. I knew he knew what he was doing the way he handled it. He backed out and I said, 'You've got enough water now, you can let it go.' And he kicked up the throttle and away we went.

"He took it around a channel marker buoy there in Lake Worth, and he said, 'This is great. No cavitation.' That's when a propeller is turning bubbles instead of water; when the boat won't perform properly on a sharp turn. Dig a hole we call it, cavitating.

"We weren't out more than five or ten minutes. He said he'd take it. We were just idling, coming back to the ramp, and he reached inside his white shirt. It was just a regular white dress shirt, short-sleeved dress shirt. He didn't have a necktie if I remember correctly.

"He pulled out a brown paper bag. It looked like an ordinary pint grocery bag, a number-two size. He handed me a bundle of twenties. They still had the bank band on them. He said, 'You'd better count it.' I counted it and it was exactly right, a thousand dollars. He gave me another thousand-dollar bundle and I gave him the receipt. I'd made it out at the boat ramp. He said, 'You might as well have the bag,' and he gave it to me. He brought me back and lit out. That was the last I saw of him."

Krist had taken off in a southerly direction—toward Fort Lauderdale.

Dix Oliphant returned to the boatyard, flapped the two bundles of twenties, and announced, "Now that's the way to sell a boat, ain't it?"

"My boy Mickey was upset. When he heard about those twenties, he told me it might really be the kidnaper. I'd better do something. I told him not to be ridiculous.

"And then it began to gnaw on me. Why would a guy from Fort Lauderdale buy a boat in West Palm anyway? Lauderdale and Miami are a lot more competitive. If he was looking for a price, why here? And then there was the two-year warranty on the motor.

If something went wrong, he'd have to bring it up here instead of seeing someone closer in Fort Lauderdale. Something was crazy. I knew something was wrong."

Dix Oliphant walked up to his bookkeeper, Edna Brandon, and said, "Don't ring this up. Just put it in petty cash." He looked up the telephone number of the FBI. Just then the phone rang about another matter.

It was nearly an hour later, almost four o'clock when Dix Oliphant called.

In fairly rapid order, the FBI was able to trace the movements of Gary Steven Krist in West Palm Beach.

He had first been seen there about 8:30 A.M. Friday when he walked into the Army and Navy Salvage Store a block from the D & D Marine Supply, Inc.

"He came in here and he wanted to buy a duffel bag," said Bernard Sheer, the owner-manager. "He told me it had to be durable. It was going to hold stuff that would take a beating.

"I'm right across the street from the Saint Vincent de Paul Catholic Church Store and I'd picked up a duffel bag over there. They're hard to find. Anything that looks GI over there I get it out of their hands. He also bought a couple of blue laundry bags and a screw driver and a pair of pliers. He must have been here thirty minutes or so. We got to talking boats, and he told me he wanted to buy one. I put my arm around him and took him outside and pointed him at the D & D sign. I told him to ask for Dave. Dave gets a lot of nice trade-ins I told him, and he could find a nice cream puff in there."

Bernard Sheer noticed one distinctive mannerism of his duffel bag customer as he walked to his lime-green Ford Fairlane. "He walked with a pronounced limp."

Krist had driven nineteen blocks south to the Dixie Court Hotel and registered as Arthur Horowitz. Mrs. Harriett Kessler, the desk clerk, logged the time at 9:30 A.M. He paid for the room with a $20 bill. Krist said he just wanted to take a shower. A bellboy, Roosevelt Bynum, showed him to his room number 302, and carried his luggage, a heavy blue suitcase. Krist tipped him two dollars.

Within fifteen minutes, Krist left the hotel. Rosemary Alts, the chambermaid, would later find the shower unused, the towels in the bathroom seemingly untouched. The only evidence that anyone had used the room was a tissue in the toilet bowl and the removal of a water pitcher from the dresser to the sink.

Krist had tried to leave by a back fire escape. But the back fire escape did not lead to a back door. The only way out was through the lobby. "I saw him and I showed him the front door," said Andrew Roseman, another bellboy. "I carried his suitcase for him. It was pretty heavy. He said he had radio equipment, an amplifier or something, and that he had to go out on a job. I put it in the trunk of his green Ford. He tipped me two dollars."

Why had he checked into a hotel room? Perhaps he simply had not had time to inspect the $500,000 since he picked up the suitcase at midnight the night before. Quite probably he needed to take out enough money to pay for the boat and his supplies.

From there he apparently drove to Spencer's Boat Company, where he purchased the marine charts and camping gear. Krist paid clerk Lee Senuick in cash, $346.41. He gave him eighteen $20 bills.

Krist then drove his Merlin-Rent-A-Car Fairlane to the Allright West Palm Beach, Inc., Parking Station and asked to "store it" for ten days. He paid the attendant for ten days in advance, $15. The time clock showed 11:30 A.M., Friday, December 20.

When FBI agents located it at 6:35 A.M. the next morning, they would impound it and search it and find locked in the back trunk the blue Samsonite suitcase which Billy Vessels had delivered at the second drop. It was empty. They would also find in the Fairlane a road map, an empty shopping sack from a Zayre's Department Store, newspapers, a claw hammer, pliers, and a screw driver. FBI agent Patrick A. Philbin also found two styrofoam coffee cups from a Burger King. The coffee still sloshed in the lidded cups when a lab man from Washington picked them up.

From the Allright parking lot he apparently had taken a taxi to the vicinity of the Dixie Market, a small independent grocery owned by Mrs. Dixie Guethle, whose pappy named her Dixie in Louisiana in 1890 when she was the twelfth and last child born and he had "run out of names."

"We seen someone come in and use the pay phone on the pillar in the store," said Mrs. Guethle. "It might have been Krist," she said later. "We have a suspicion it was him." Conceivably, Krist picked up the brown paper sack there. No one recalled waiting on him.

When the kidnaper telephoned the Atlanta office of the FBI, 404-521-3900, he gave the long-distance operator the West Palm Beach number of TEmple 2-9616, the phone in the Dixie Market. Doyle, the telephone security manager, would locate the toll ticket the next day. Krist had talked for one minute and forty-four seconds. It had cost him $1.30.

Within a few minutes after agent Robert Schachner began to question Dix Oliphant, three buttons of the telephone in the D & D Marine Supply lit up simultaneously. He had on the line his office, Miami and Washington. Within thirty minutes, the first Coast Guard search and rescue helicopter lifted. Its mission: Locate an Orlando Clipper, 85-horsepower Johnson outboard, white hull and top, turquoise deck, two fifteen-gallon gas tanks aboard.

Before nightfall the Coast Guard would have another helicopter airborne and two cutters searching the ocean and the Intracoastal Waterway between West Palm Beach and Fort Lauderdale. But the sun set at 5:35 P.M. There wasn't enough time. The search would have to begin again at daylight, and obviously, if Krist ran all night they would have considerably more territory to cover. The boat description went out to police agencies all along the coast.

Agent John S. Atwater had the night duty at the West Palm office and he snoozed at his desk beside his telephone. He awoke during the night with a sudden thought: Instead of going north or south along the Florida coast or eastward toward the Bahamas, could Krist have gone west across the state through Florida?

The peninsula of Florida measures about 110 miles in width between the Atlantic Ocean and the Gulf of Mexico, and agent Atwater realized, as would most Florida boaters, that a boat could travel westward across the state through the Okeechobee Waterway, a serene passage of pastoral beauty. Krist, he surmised, could have run northward from West Palm Beach the thirty miles to the St. Lucie Inlet, then looped around the town of Stuart in the St. Lucie River and started southwestward through the waterway. The U. S. Army Corps of Engineers had built it years before, an indirect result of two great hurricanes in 1926 and 1928 which caused severe flooding of Lake Okeechobee and took 2800 lives. President Herbert Hoover first ordered the construction of levees and floodgates to contain the lake. Lake Okeechobee, an Indian name for "big water," was a remnant of a shallow sea, forty miles long, thirty miles wide and fifteen to twenty feet deep. Its 7000 square miles made it the largest fresh-water lake solely within the continental United States. Krist, agent Atwater reasoned, might try to run across it and follow the channel markers across the southern route to the town of Moore Haven, where he could go inland again on the Caloosahatchee Canal and on to Fort Myers and the Gulf coast. He might stop at any of the scores of little fishing camps or the marinas at Port Mayaca, Pahokee, Clewiston or Moore Haven. Atwater picked up the telephone and began calling local sheriff deputies he knew personally. At Clewiston, a town of 3500 on the southern rim of the lake, he spoke to Sherrill Price, a chief deputy for Hendry County.

About eight o'clock Saturday morning, as Coast Guard cutters and aircraft began a methodical search of the Florida east coast, deputy Price stopped by the Clewiston Marina.

"Bill," he asked Vyron Grant Vancil, "you seen a white Orlando Clipper with a 85 Johnson?"

"Sure have," said Vancil, a slow-talking, opinionated gent who had worked as deputy sheriff in Beaumont, Texas and a state trooper in Illinois for twelve years before an automobile accident disabled him. At sixty-four, he "just lived here" at his brother's marina.

Vancil had gone to bed early Friday evening. Krist had arrived about eighty-thirty and asked at a trailer at the marina if he could buy gasoline. "A lady in another trailer brings him down to me and I got up and put on my clothes," said Vancil. "We walk together about a half block to the gas pumps. I have a stiff leg and he noticed it. He said, 'So you've got a bum leg, too.' He was also limping. He said he'd hurt his driving or something.

"Well, I serviced his boat for him and he wanted to know if I've got anything he can take extra gas in. I sold him two five-gallon cans and I think he had a Coke. He stepped down from the dock on to the ice box in his boat and it caved in a little. He said, 'That thing is not supposed to do that. It is supposed to stand 300 pounds. I only weigh 250 pounds.' The bill came to about $14. When he paid me he gave me a $20 bill and he said, 'Sure is good to have a rich mother.'"

The remark struck Vancil as inappropriate. Hell, he thought to himself, I spend a twenty now and then and I don't have a rich mother. He let it go.

Briefly, the two men discussed the Okeechobee Waterway locks between Clewiston and Fort Myers. "I told him they closed at ten o'clock every night and he sure would have to hustle or he wouldn't make the next one. He said he had something to hustle in."

Krist sped away westward at full throttle.

Sheriff deputy Price just couldn't believe Vancil knew what he was talking about. He left Vancil for a few minutes and returned with a copy of the Miami *Herald* with Krist's photograph at the bottom of page one.

"That's the guy. I'm positive," said Vancil, and he would repeat his story reluctantly a few hours later when the "Glory Grabbers," his terminology for the FBI, interrogated him. Long before the interview, though, deputy Price and the FBI had the same thought: Had Krist made it through the locks?

There were four locks in the 155 statute miles of the meandering waterway between the Atlantic and the Gulf, one on the east side of Lake Okeechobee and three on the west side. Depending upon the lake level, winds and tide, a boater would be raised fifteen feet and lowered fifteen feet as he made his way from the ocean to the Gulf.

Krist had entered the first lock, the 50 by 250 foot lock at St. Lucie, at 5:10 P.M. Friday.

"He said he was going from Miami to Lake Okeechobee," Lawrence Shrout, the lock attendant recalled. "He said he thought he might be going around the lake, that he'd been working hard and steady and was going to take a little vacation.

"I threw him two lines, but he only took one. He wanted to know how to take care of two at the same time. He told me it was the first time he ever came through a lock."

Shrout followed the usual procedure: Using a long pole with a clip-type clothespin at one end, he handed down a paper form to be filled out. U. S. Army Corps of Engineers, it said, and there was space for the boatman to write his name, his address, and the name and registration number of the boat.

Shrout read the name as "Art Hoywirtz," apparently an error in deciphering Krist's penmanship. The boat had no name, but "Hoywirtz" had written a false registration number, FL 2085A. He put down his address as 841 Southwest Twenty-third Street, Fort Lauderdale. Shrout accepted it. He knew nothing of the different address Krist had given Oliphant earlier that day, 13414 Southwest Ninth Avenue, Fort Lauderdale.

Shrout raised the water level, opened the lock and Krist went on his way at 5:25 P.M. toward the twenty-two miles southwest to the lake.

After the stop at the Clewiston Marina, the Orlando Clipper arrived at the western edge of the lake and entered the Moore Haven lock in the Caloosahatchee River at 9:40 P.M.

"He didn't have his ticket with him," said Ray Thielen, the attendant. "It is normal for a man to make out a ticket and keep it all the way through. He said he'd thrown his ticket away because he didn't expect to come this far. He said he thought he would just come to the lake and go back to the Atlantic, but he enjoyed it so much he wanted to go on."

Thielen thought the explanation reasonable. "He was just like a fellow on a pleasure trip. I noticed he didn't have any fishing gear."

Thielen gave him a new form to fill out, instructing him to keep a copy for his passage through the next two locks. Krist wrote his name as "A. Horowitz" and his address as 8401 Southwest Ninth Avenue, Fort Lauderdale, the third different address he had written since he had purchased the boat.

At 9:50 P.M. he was on his way west again.

He didn't travel much farther that night. The next lock at Ortona, sixteen miles west, closed at ten o'clock, and somewhere between the two locks Krist apparently had to anchor or camp to spend the night. In all probability, it was the first prolonged sleep he had had since the kidnaping the previous Tuesday, four nights and four days before.

Cornelius Pugh arrived for work at the Ortona lock a few minutes before six o'clock Saturday morning, December 21, and he moved the lake-bound traffic first before he paid any attention to the Orlando Clipper waiting in the upper pool.

Krist, unshaven, his beard beginning to show, told Pugh he had lost his trip sheet. Pugh routinely handed him another one. This time Krist wrote his name exactly as he had the night before, "A. Horowitz, 8401 Southwest Ninth Avenue, Ford Lauderdale." He gave his destination as Fort Myers. Pugh let him into the lock at 6:55 A.M., and out at 7:15 A.M. Again, Krist took off at full throttle.

Forty-five minutes later he arrived at the W. P. Franklin lock at Olga, thirty-two miles away. The attendant, Clyde G. "Chuck" Clayton, let him into the fourth and final lock at 8 A.M. And Krist again said he had lost his trip sheet. Clayton gave him another one.

This time he listed his name as A. Horowitz and put down a slightly different address: 810 Southwest Ninth Street, Fort Lauderdale. He wore wrap-around sunglasses and he was listening to a green radio with a directional finder. He gave his boat number accurately—FL 2883 AK. Lock keeper Clayton, who handled up to forty craft a day, lowered Krist out of locks at 8:10 A.M., not the least bit suspicious.

Deputy Price's detective work came to light in the West Palm Beach office of the FBI shortly after nine o'clock. His information set off an urgent spree of telephone calls to the three locks west of Lake Okeechobee. Had a white Orlando Clipper gone through? The three lock attendants talked to each other by radio, compared notes and confirmed among themselves what the FBI already suspected: Krist had to be free of the Okeechobee Waterway.

He could have hardly selected a more cumbersome escape route. Waiting for the locks, identifying himself and his boat repeatedly, hung up over night, channeled for miles in a canal only fifty feet wide, Krist would have been a sitting duck to any sort of organized force that could have found him. Yet, quite obviously, he had succeeded. For sheer brazenness—or sheer stupidity—it rivaled his act of the day before, the purchase of the boat with $20 bills pulled from a brown paper sack.

Where was he now? Where was he going?

He could be in the town of Fort Myers. Or he could be somewhere still on the Caloosahatchee River with its abundant and playful porpoises, headed out into the Gulf of Mexico. Or he could be beyond San Carlos Bay, traveling either north or south.

If he managed to get very far south, equipped as he was, he could get into the Ten Thousand Islands. There, or farther south into Lostman's River, he would be extremely difficult to find. The count on the islands was a modest one. There were no adequate charts. They comprised one of the last regions in the continental United States which literally had not changed appreciably since the days of piracy on the Spanish Main.

The FBI diverted its east coast search toward Fort Myers. An agent in Miami telephoned the Tampa office, a hundred miles northwest of the Olga Lock, to notify the agent in charge.

Joseph F. Santoiana, an imposing and distinguished man, had teed off at the Carrol Wood Golf and Tennis Club at seven o'clock that morning with a non-bureau foursome. He was on the twelfth hole when a golf buggy rolled up with a message. "Urgent. Telephone your office." At the clubhouse, he made the call, listened a moment, then sent the buggy back for two other golfing agents he knew were on the course, William A. Sullivan and Lucien Hudson. He raced to the office on the sixth floor of the federal building in downtown Tampa. The others followed later.

They had no precise idea of where Krist was but they knew they wanted to go south in a hurry. An agent telephoned the U. S. Coast Guard search and rescue station at nearby St. Petersburg. Could they have a helicopter immediately?

Another agent, John R. Brett, joined the displaced golfers and they opened an office vault, grabbed three machine guns, a shotgun, and a set of handy-talkies. They sped to the nearest Tampa airfield. An H-52 turbine jet chopper, its blades flailing the air in a chomp-chomp-chomp roar, settled gently as they pulled up. They were up and away in a minute, not quite sure where they were going.

The twin-engine Grumman Albatrosses out of the Opa-Locka Coast Guard Base in Miami were already in the air when the FBI learned that Krist had crossed the state. Agent Smith, grayed and a little roly-poly, was on a flight to Bimini, Cat Cay. Smith was the office Santa Claus. He had already rented his suit for the Saturday afternoon Christmas party for children. His flight was already out of radio contact. Agents Edward James Tully and Ed Putz were aboard the other flight and they had been diverted to the Gulf coast.

They flew along the Intracoastal Waterway north of Fort Myers, their eyes pressed to borrowed binoculars of the Coast Guard. Everytime they spotted anything resembling a white Orlando Clipper, white bimini canvas top, turquoise deck, the Albatross would swoop low and circle. Everyone waved back.

At 10:30 A.M., while flying at about 500 feet at the mouth of the Caloosahatchee River and San Carlos Bay, they spotted what they thought they were looking for—the configuration of an Orlando Clipper, the right colors.

Again the Albatross swooped low, this time eighty feet off the water at 115 knots. They saw a lone white male. He had a blue jacket.

He didn't wave.

Why wouldn't he wave? Everyone else did. They were almost certain. They radioed the location. There was not much else they could do. At this point, there wasn't much Krist could do either. His craft sped northward in the Gulf of Mexico now, just off the shell-famed islands of Sanibel and Captiva.

For a mile, five miles, ten miles, almost fifteen, he raced along the coast at full throttle, a rooster-tail wake streaking behind. High above, the Albatross made lazy circles in the sky.

Two Lee County deputies, George Hartwig and Jim Rimes, gave chase in a swift and powerful police boat. The craft skipped and pounded the Gulf at great speed and gradually they began to cut down a gap of several miles. But suddenly a bailing plug broke and they had to give up, their prey unsighted from the water.

Krist veered toward the mainland through Redfish Pass into Pine Island Sound, and careful to keep to deep water, avoiding Jug Head Shoal, he continued to speed northward through Boca Grande Pass and into the openness of Charlotte Harbor—sixteen, seventeen miles from the initial sighting.

Effortlessly, the Albatross watched from the sky. If ever an albatross hung from the neck of a mariner, Krist had to know it that Saturday forenoon of December 21.

Lieutenant Commander Duane Coppock chattered constantly into his cockpit microphone. In the third floor of the Miami FBI office agent Swinney tracked Krist on a huge marine map. He had the open telephone line to the Kidnap Desk in Washington, where other agents studied the same map, U. S. Department of Commerce's Coast and Geodetic Survey, number 1255.

In the southbound Tampa helicopter, agent Santoiana wore a headset and he could hear the transmissions of the Albatross. At 100 knots at 500 feet, they were closing in fast. They should see them any minute.

Krist had reached the northern end of Charlotte Harbor, where the mouths of the Myakka and Peace rivers join, when the chopper, hugging the horizon, flew toward a fixed swing bridge over the Myakka at the town of El Jobean.

Suddenly, they could see him. In all probability, Krist spotted the chopper even a few seconds before; for abruptly, he swung his Orlando Clipper into a 160-degree turn. He piloted straight for land. Within a minute, he ran aground in the sand flats of the closest island, Hog Island.

And ironically, perhaps, Robert Mackle had once owned Hog Island. The General Development Corporation had owned it when the Mackle brothers managed the firm.

Hog Island had a certain primeval beauty. Uninhabited, probably never inhabited, certainly unaltered by man, it lay in a mostly submerged jungle of mangroves and swamp—an irregular outcropping of tangled subtropical vegetation two and a third miles long and two thirds of a mile wide. The alligators, the water moccasins, the flamingoes and a hundred other creatures of the wild held the proprietary rights, and the orchids bloomed wild. At high noon a man could sometimes see no farther than five or ten feet in front of him. All but impenetrable by man, the warm water of the bay gushed and swirled in at high tide at a depth of three to six inches everywhere except a rim of land three feet above sea level on the northwest shore. At low tide Hog Island was muck and mud and mosquitoes.

From the Albatross and the still-approaching helicopter, agents could see Krist abandon his boat, its motor still running. Carrying a small satchel, he jumped from the boat, and wading and stumbling, he ran through the shallows at low tide, trying desperately to reach the cover of the tree line before the helicopter caught him. He kept looking up over his shoulder.

Seconds before he reached the dense undergrowth, the helicopter roared in low, thrashing the water, and the four agents, their weapons in their hands, recognized Krist clearly. They held their fire. The FBI wanted him alive.

Krist disappeared into a swamp jungle. It was 12:05 P.M.

If Hog Island offered refuge to a fugitive, it also imprisoned him geographically. The closest town was El Jobean, a hamlet of four hundred situated a mile and a half northwestward. El Jobean took its name in 1924 from a debonair New England real estate visionary, Joe Bean. Mr. Bean envisioned a metropolis with orange trees growing on every lot. The profits from the trees, he thought, would make taxes unnecessary. He died a poor man. The Myakka Cutoff, a narrow and shallow flat less than five hundred yards wide at some places, separated Hog Island from the mainland to the northeast, and this was the most likely route of escape. But assuming that Krist could make it across the Myakka Cutoff, there was nothing but marsh and mangroves—and Alligator Bay—for another six miles before he could possibly reach the outskirts of the well-kept and carefully planned community of Port Charlotte, population 15,000. The Mackle brothers had planned and built it.

The manhunt had begun almost instantly.

Within a minute after Krist vanished into mangroves, the chopper settled in low, the water spraying fiercely under its rotating blades, and disgorged agents Santoiana, Sullivan, and Hudson. They had to jump fifteen feet into knee-deep water.

They were the first of about eighty-five agents to converge on the site that afternoon. They ran cautiously toward the tree line, men garbed in golfing attire, carrying machine guns, and they quickly discovered what would become terribly apparent in the ensuing hours: A man could be five yards away and impossible to see.

Despite the handy-talkie communication to agent Brett in the hovering helicopter, the three agents couldn't even find each other after a few minutes. It was that thick.

The FBI needed help and it needed it immediately. It needed a posse of local law enforcement agencies; it needed also the knowledge of men who knew the terrain, the region.

Sheriff Jack Bent of Charlotte County, notified of the search shortly after twelve noon, made his twenty-three full-time and twelve auxiliary officers available just as soon as they could be contacted, which in a small town and county, wasn't long. Prior to 1:15 P.M. they had road barricades established at the only seven roads anywhere near Hog Island, some of them as far as ten miles away.

Even before Krist had run aground on Hog Island, FBI agents were aboard an 82-foot Coast Guard cutter headed southward out of St. Petersburg. That afternoon Coast Guard planes and helicopters—and in some instances privately chartered craft—ferried agents to the Charlotte County Airport from Miami, Tampa, Jacksonville, and Savannah, Georgia.

Sheriff deputies from Lee, DeSota, Sarasota, Highlands and

Hardee counties, as well as twelve Fish and Game Commission Wildlife officers and four Salt Water Conservation officers, converged upon El Jobean. Approximately fifty Florida State Troopers, and uncounted numbers of auxiliary troopers, sped toward the site from both north and south on U. S. Highway 41, and downstate on U. S. 17.

As the afternoon wore on a grim army of three hundred men assembled. Inspector Shroder and Sheriff Bent set up a command post at the Lazy R fishing camp at the site of the bridge in El Jobean. Two Coast Guard helicopters, then a third chopper from MacDill Air Force Base, lifted and deposited agents and others onto Hog Island. An armada of two dozen vessels, everything from a luxurious yacht to small runabouts, also ferried men across.

It wasn't exactly the smoothest of operations. Ed Pikulski, the owner of the Lazy R, told one of the first groups of agents that they could borrow his boat. He neglected to say anything about tightening a clamp for the motor. They took off in a roar and Pikulski watched helplessly as the motor plunged into the river.

The men who left the Lazy R clean and neat and returned later bone-tired and filthy comprised a strange and incongruous legion. Some wore bright red and yellow ribbons around their throats for identification. Others tied bands around their foreheads. Others had white handkerchief arm bands. They didn't want to shoot each other. The FBI distributed scores of photographs of Krist. Nearly everyone crossing to the island at least knew what he looked like and the clothing he was supposed to be wearing: A blue windbreaker over a white shirt, dark pants, tennis shoes.

By late afternoon, agents, now outnumbered nearly three to one by other law enforcement men, tried to fight their way through the mangrove swamps in a semblance of order. Their lines kept breaking and vanishing.

A barefoot agent, who had lost his shoes, cradled a Thompson submachine gun in his arm. A gentleman with a Stetson hat and rolled-up pants legs carried a rifle with a sniper scope. He was in his stocking feet. His garters showed. He had lost his shoes, too.

Those who had arrived the earliest were easy to recognize. The longer a man had been there the more slime, muck and mud clung to his clothing. Some seemed encrusted in a black vile-smelling ooze. Generally the later arrivals came more appropriately dressed, heavy boots, hunting jackets, shotguns.

Agent Irwin Frank Davis had been among the first to arrive. He had been in Fort Lauderdale on the Atlantic side when the FBI learned that Krist had been seen on Lake Okeechobee. He had raced across the state as fast as he could on a toll road, Alligator Alley, and arrived at El Jobean on radio instructions as the Albatross and Coast Guard helicopter circled Hog Island off in the distance. He and two other agents promptly commandeered a small motorboat. They didn't know precisely what was going on but there was no doubt where the action was. Trying to get across the mud flats, they went aground twice and a couple of fishermen nearby, seeing men in neckties splashing into the water, gawked at them in wonderment.

Agent Davis was the first man to reach Krist's grounded Orlando Clipper, its smoking Johnson 85 still idling, its propeller screw digging a furrow. He boarded the craft about 150 yards offshore as two agents started for the island and began to look around. In a storage space in the bow, he found a GI duffel bag, its top carefully folded. Stenciled in black paint on the side was the name "Arthur A. Verner, Comdr., USN 77456."

Commander Verner had been assigned to SHAEF, Supreme Headquarters, Allied Expeditionary Forces, in London, England, in 1944, before the invasion of Europe, when he first received and stenciled his duffel bag. After the war he had become a professor, head of the school of Foreign Service at Georgetown University, then a vice-president of the Kelly Springfield Tire Company in Cumberland, Maryland. In October 1968, he had retired and moved to Delray Beach, Florida, and given away the extra clothing he knew he would never need again. The duffel bag went with them. Someone had picked up everything for the Saint Vincent de Paul Catholic Church Store—which just happened to be across the street from Bernard Sheer's Army and Navy Salvage Store in West Palm Beach.

Agent Davis looked inside and found two smaller blue drawstring laundry bags. Opening them, he could see stack after stack of $20 bills. They would total $479,000. Every bill had been recorded and rechecked at the First National Bank of Miami the previous Tuesday. Gary Steven Krist had had possession of the money for just about thirty-six hours.

Agent Davis stuffed the duffel bag back where he found it, and became, for the first time in his life, a boat pilot. He cut off the engine, managed to get the craft into deeper water with an oar, restarted it, and spent the afternoon ferrying agents and deputies from El Jobean to Hog Island. It was dark before he took time to formally account for the evidence.

Not a shot had been fired all afternoon.

By late afternoon the locals had eleven bloodhounds on Hog Island. But they proved almost useless. FBI agents, stalking through the mangroves for at least three hours, had made it almost impossible for a dog to stay with a scent. The incoming tidal flow confused things even more and the dogs, pulling at their leashes, kept twisting themselves up in the clawlike aerial roots, sinking to their bellies in the goo and the muck.

It had been a frustrating few hours for Milton Buffington, one of the "dog men" for Charlotte County.

By trade, Buffington was a butcher at the U-Save Supermarket. With seven checkouts, the U-Save was the largest store in Punta Gorda, and there "Butch," as he was known, sold porterhouse steak for $1.38 a pound. He owned four dogs and his best two, Bellstar and Suzie, he thought, were as fine as any two bloodhounds anywhere. He was an auxiliary deputy. The county paid for the dog food, rabies shots and veterinarian expenses and he gave his time and dogs for nothing. He and his two dogs had returned from Hog Island by Coast Guard helicopter.

As night fell the bloodhounds at the Lazy R at El Jobean yapped and bayed, and when they fell silent, the creaking of frogs and the incessant chirping of crickets and the sounds of the night competed with the walkie-talkies, the car radios. The air was alive with calls for more flashlights, searchlights.

The Florida State Patrol had brought in gasoline-powered generators with dual searchlights, and they were transported by airboat to the rim of the high land of Hog Island. Shafts of light poked and probed the blackness.

For a while an Albatross showered the island with flares, brilliant two million candlelight globs of light parachuted from 2500 feet. They lit up the sky for three minutes each, burning out abruptly just before landing.

Helicopters chomped the air sporadically, each with its two landing lights blazing, a bright "hover" light pointing straight down, and a fourth mobile spotlight shifting from the cockpit.

But the active search gave way almost completely to a holding operation.

"We're operating on the assumption he is still there," said Sheriff Bent. "I don't see how he could have gotten off the island. I know I couldn't. The most we can hope to do at night is to keep him confined. It's impossible in there. The mud is like glue."

Inspector Shroder concurred. He had some of his men billeted in a nearby Howard Johnson's Motel. They would try to get a few hours of sleep and start again at daybreak.

John Shannon, the chief deputy for Charlotte County, opened up his jail in Punta Gorda. He could sleep seventy-one men, he said. His jail cooks had already made and dispensed 360 sandwiches. Police had already made the rounds of homes in El Jobean to tell residents, as if they couldn't see all the commotion, that they should take the keys out of their parked cars.

As the night passed, the aerial surveillance slacked off, then stopped altogether. There weren't anywhere near enough flares for lighting the entire island all night and those they had might be needed if someone actually spotted him. Four airboats, small craft propelled by airplane engines mounted high in the sterns, skimmed around the island at irregular intervals.

The noise and the lights actually seemed to be more harmful than useful. Or so thought Richard McLeod, the "major" of the Charlotte County Sheriff's office. He was thirty-four, Florida born, tanned and weathered, and a highly accomplished hunter and fisherman who considered himself "just a cracker boy." Everyone called him Mac. As early as eight-thirty Mac had been unhappy about "all the damn noise from the gasoline generators."

"I had to shut one down so I could hear."

McLeod and Buffington, the butcher with the useless bloodhounds, had both gone home for supper, then returned to El Jobean, and caught an airboat ride out to Hog Island on a coffee and sandwich run. On the northwestern rim, six FBI agents had set up an overnight camp. They shared the island with a million mosquitoes.

"If Krist is gonna try to get off the island, he's gonna have to make it across the Myakka Cutoff," said McLeod. "That's his only way."

He thought that perhaps Krist could see the lights at El Jobean. He might try to get there to steal a car. "That's his only chance."

McLeod and Buffington—"Mac" and "Butch"—bid the agents
adieu, and plodded around the northern rim of Hog Island. They
found a little land out of water, sat down—and waited.

They waited for well over an hour, two hours. There was no
moon. A stationary front had stalled across Central Florida and
the winds kicked up fitfully, making the low 60-degree tempera-
tures feel cooler.

McLeod listened to the sounds of the night. Occasionally a
snook or red snapper would jump and smack the stillness. He
could hear a coon scramble along the water's edge now and then.
Varmints, he called them. He had been a coon hunter all his
life.

Sometime after eleven o'clock, the two men heard off in the
distance the distinct sound of movement, a gentle splashing, then
silence, wading again, then silence. "That's no coon," whispered
McLeod.

If they could hear him, he could hear them, McLeod reasoned,
and wordlessly they waded offshore into deeper water up to their
chests where they could move more freely without fear of detection.

McLeod carried an old Army carbine over his head. Buffington
had a .38-caliber pistol and a six-cell flashlight which he kept
turned off.

They had devised a plan. They would wade parallel to the
island in the deeper water, slowly, quietly, until they were about
even with the noise, then come ashore. When they hit the high
ground—two or three feet above the water line—Buffington would
turn on the light. They'd stay about thirty feet apart. "If he
opens fire, one of us should get him," said McLeod. Each man
had six children. Neither forgot it that night.

"We'd hear him wade awhile and stop and listen, then wade
some more," said Buffington. In the deep water, they kept moving
toward the source of sound.

Then, at about fifteen minutes after eleven, an airboat cranked
up at the FBI camp about a quarter of a mile away. "I guess he
stopped completely," said McLeod. For four or five minutes they
could hear only the distant sound of the engine. Then it was
quiet again.

For another thirty minutes, the two men waited in silence and
darkness.

Finally, he began to move again, much closer now, wading, silence, and wading. And then nothing.

They were perhaps thirty yards offshore. They thought they were about even with him.

"Okay," McLeod whispered, and the two men waded ashore, the water level dropping, highly conscious of their own motions and unavoidable splashing.

Buffington, his .38 pistol in his right hand, turned on his flashlight with his left. He took maybe three or four steps, his left arm extended, swinging the light in an arch back and forth.

To his right, ten feet away, Gary Steven Krist crouched motionless in a tangle of mangrove roots. The beam caught him. Another few feet and they would have walked right by him.

"Mac! Here he is!" blurted Buffington.

McLeod, fifteen feet the other side of Krist, leveled his carbine. "Stand up!" he said. "Put your hands on your head! And don't move!"

Krist stood up. He put his hands on his head. He said nothing. Hooked on his arm, Krist had a gray metal satchel. McLeod took it away from him.

"Handcuffs, Butch," he said to Buffington, as he ran his hands over Krist searching for a weapon. In Krist's right hip pocket, McLeod found a sheathed hunting knife. He took it.

Buffington gave McLeod the flashlight and manacled Krist's wrists behind his back.

"I have rights," Krist said.

The remark surprised McLeod. Suddenly he remembered the little white card in his billfold, printed instructions on the rights of a man arrested, as prescribed by the United States Supreme Court in the Miranda decision.

"So I took my billfold and used the flashlight and read to him his rights," said McLeod. "I told him he was under arrest and he didn't have to say anything, and that anything he said we could use against him, and that he had a right to counsel and we'd get him a lawyer if he couldn't afford one."

"He didn't do nothing," said Buffington. "He just obeyed what we said."

"Let's go," McLeod ordered.

With a gun to Krist's back and Buffington tightly gripping the handcuffs, Krist was marched along the sand flats.

McLeod had his hands full. He had the flashlight, his carbine, and Krist's satchel, which he did not bother to open. It contained a tube of Crest toothpaste, a jar of brushless shaving cream, a compass, a ten-power telescope, a packaged pair of jockey underwear, a wash rag, two Nestlé chocolate candy bars, $2.71 in change—and eighteen bundles of twenty dollar bills, $18,000.

McLeod stopped for a moment. He took a four-inch-barrel .38-caliber pistol from his holster, wet from an hour's submersion, and pointed to the sky and fired three times.

"You might as well shoot me," said Krist. "I'm a dead man anyway."

The shots echoed through the night, and as the three men waded into deeper water, they could hear the engines of airboats cough to life and race toward them, their lights blazing.

Krist, exhausted, suffering from exposure, badly bitten by mosquitoes, had eluded his captors for almost twelve hours. McLeod and Buffington had found him at 12:10 A.M. Sunday. In his billfold, which was yet to be taken from the pocket of a zippered blue and hooded windbreaker jacket he wore, were seven $20 bills, moist and sandy, as well as the receipt from the D & D Marine Supply for the purchase of the Orlando Clipper and Arthur Horowitz's stolen draft card. He wore rubberized blue pants and tennis sneakers, no socks.

As they waited for the approaching airboat, Krist said, "I'm tired. Can I have a drink of water?"

"We don't have any. When we get back," McLeod replied.

The first airboat, containing Sheriff Frank Klein of neighboring DeSota County, several of his deputies and an FBI man with a walkie-talkie, skimmed toward the waiting men, slowed and stopped, the propeller feathered.

In the glare of the lights, the FBI man radioed exultantly to El Jobean, "We've got the man and we're bringing him in." It was 12:28 A.M.

Krist again asked for a drink of water. A deputy gestured toward the brackish swamp water, "Drink that, you son of a bitch," he said.

Book of Ruth

On Saturday, December 28, 1968, almost a week after the capture of Gary Steven Krist, the FBI put Ruth Eisemann-Schier on its list of "Ten Most Wanted Fugitives." She was the first woman to receive this recognition since the Bureau established its wanted list in 1940.

Nine days had elapsed since the aborted first ransom drop when George Fischer, the postal messenger clerk at the Institute of Marine Sciences, had seen Ruth, disheveled and grimy, standing at the curbside near the Florida Bible College about eight o'clock as he drove to work.

Fischer had not been the last person to see Ruth in Miami. Sometime before ten o'clock that same morning, Peter Spillis, a senior partner in the firm of Ferendino, Grafton & Pancoast Architects, noticed a young woman knocking on the sliding glass door at the rear of his office at 2575 South Bayshore Drive. Spillis, who would not realize whom he had seen until he recognized her photograph in a newspaper several days later, could not understand the young lady. She spoke Spanish. He spoke Greek and English. He prevailed upon Jose Seito, an associate architect, for translation, and Seito ascertained from the girl in Spanish that she wanted a taxicab. He ushered her from the back door to the front lobby where Mrs. Margaret Golden sat as a switchboard receptionist.

"She was so shabbily dressed that I was alarmed," said Margaret Golden. "I called her a Yellow Cab. She sat in front of me for fifteen or twenty minutes. She had on white culottes and a blue-and-white striped shirt with a scarf around her neck. She had on tennis shoes. Her hair was frosted, cut short, but starting to grow out. It was dark at the roots. She was blond on top."

Margaret Golden left her switchboard for a coffee break shortly after ten o'clock and Diana Leviner filled in briefly. "She acted a little strange, I thought," said Diana Leviner. "She spoke to me in English. She said she had been on a boat with some friends and that she had decided to go on home." Because of the yacht basins nearby, Diana Leviner accepted the explanation without question. The architects' office was situated about eight blocks from the Florida Bible College—and five blocks from the drop site at the causeway to Fair Isle. Presumably, Ruth had walked from the Bible College in the direction of the drop site.

The Yellow Cab arrived after 10:30 A.M.

"She was the same girl I had seen earlier at the Bible College on U. S. 1, all dirty and wearing a red sheet of some kind," said the driver, Donald C. Berry. "I recognized her right off. She'd cleaned herself up. She had on a beige playsuit, a slit pants-skirt, and a pair of tennis shoes. She said she wanted to go to the Greyhound Bus Station.

"She said she was going to North Carolina to see her aunt. I noticed her accent and she told me she spoke several languages. I told her I wished I did, everyone should down here."

Berry delivered his passenger to within a block of the Greyhound Bus Station in downtown Miami. He had to stop for a red light and Ruth, whom he identified by photographs a week later, said she would get out. She paid him $3.10 and left. Berry turned a corner and drove on. He did not see Ruth go into the bus station. He let her out about ten minutes to eleven.

If she went into the bus station, FBI agents missed her. They had been there waiting.

Quite possibly, though, she had caught a bus and they simply had not recognized her. Approximately two thousand persons moved through the station daily on thirty incoming and thirty outgoing buses.

In the days and weeks and eventually months after the kidnaping, FBI agents attempted to find and interview everyone who knew Ruth. Sedulously, they tried to trace every person she had known in Miami and Washington, no matter how casual the acquaintanceship. And from every person interviewed, agents asked for other names. Who else knew her? Who else might she have known? Could anyone have aided in her escape? Where could she have fled?

She couldn't have had much money—if any—on the morning of the first drop, the FBI believed. Her purse and billfold had been found in the Volvo. Except for a $655.56 balance in the First National Bank of Washington, D.C., untouched since the previous June and now closely watched, the FBI could find no other source of money for her. She had withdrawn all her money from her Miami account on December 10, presumably for purchase of the plastic swimming pool for shipment to Honduras to her mother.

Yet she had changed clothing and washed between the time she had been seen at the Florida Bible College and the architects' office. Had someone helped her? Had she made contact with a third party? Did she have money enough with her to buy clothing? Could she have stolen the clothing off a clothesline?

The FBI wondered also if Krist and Ruth could have been in contact by radio on the morning of the first drop. This seemed feasible. From Krist's U-Haul trailer which he had sold to George Gullion, FBI agents had taken a box which had once contained a two-unit walkie-talkie. The price tag was still on: $49.95. Where were the two units?

Thirty agents canvassed, house by house, the Brickell Avenue neighborhood where officer Sweeney chased a kidnaper. At the corner of Southwest Second Avenue and Twenty-ninth Road, agents found a partial answer to their question. A homeowner there had found one unit. The serial number on the unit matched the number stamped on the box left in the U-Haul. Mrs. Charles E. Foster had found it among her dwarf carissa in a flower bin while searching for her morning newspaper after the first drop, and she was a little embarrassed about not notifying the FBI earlier. When she gave it to her husband, a high school band director, he had depressed the transmission button and broadcast jokingly, "Hello, kidnaper. I've got the money. Come in, kidnaper."

So where was the other one? The FBI wondered if Ruth had possibly pawned or sold it. A check of all pawn shops came back negative. The newspapers ran an appeal for help in finding it.

It wasn't until February 20, 1969, two months after the crime, that the second unit was found. A schoolboy eleven years old, Gene Beckham, found it in a vacant lot just off South Dixie Highway—less than 150 yards from the Florida Bible College. Young Beckham and his brother, Robert, Jr., thirteen, were on an "exploring expedition" of a thicket which they knew by the code name P.O.P.—for "place of pits"—when they found it in the weeds, along with a weathered and rusting pair of binoculars. They called the police immediately.

To the FBI, it seemed probable that Krist and Ruth had thrown away the units separately prior to the time they were seen at the Florida Bible College.

So could they have met each other somewhere else? There was one reason to think they might: The two Burger King coffee cups left in the rented Ford Fairlane which Krist parked at the Allright parking lot in West Palm Beach.

Then, again, couldn't the two cups be a deliberate ruse on his part? He would have realized no doubt that sooner or later the car would have been traced directly to him because he had used his George Deacon driver's license. Another explanation might lie in the fact that he needed coffee—and plenty of it—to stay awake. He couldn't possibly have had much sleep between the time of the abduction at four o'clock Tuesday morning and his purchase of the duffel bag early Friday morning in West Palm Beach.

FBI laboratory men scrutinized the car, vacuuming the insides for possible evidence. Fingerprint experts established positively that Krist had touched the car. His prints were all over it, inside and out. But Ruth's were not. There was no physical evidence whatsoever to indicate her presence in the car.

The FBI pursued every lead it could think of. Some of Ruth's friends were interviewed, reinterviewed, then questioned a third time. Agents questioned the crew of the *Pillsbury.* The Bureau explored the possibility that Ruth, multilingual as she was, had lost herself among the migrant workers who moved north through Florida, harvesting winter vegetable crops, the citrus groves, and sugar fields. Her dialect wouldn't attract attention. Workers came from Mexico, Puerto Rico, and Cuba, and they overlooked slight language differences. They probably would not have read English-language newspapers or paid much attention to news broadcasts either. Her appearance as an unmarried woman, though, probably would arouse curiosity sooner or later, the FBI felt. Inquiries were made. The response was negative.

The FBI suspected Ruth might try to return to Honduras or re-enter Mexico, and personnel of the Border Patrol, the Immigration and Naturalization Service, and the Bureau of Customs were asked to be particularly watchful. Law enforcement officers in Mexico and Honduras quietly conducted their own investigations on the chance that she might try to contact someone she knew for help.

Police in Catacamas, Honduras, where her mother lived, could find no one who had heard from her. Ruth's mother went into seclusion in the days after the crime.

On January 10, 1969, though, she wrote a letter about her daughter, affixed three stamps to it, and mailed it special delivery express. She addressed it simply: Barbara Mackle, Coral Gables, Miami, Florida, U.S.A.

And in a precise and slanting script, she wrote:

"Catacamas, Jan. 10. 69,

"Dear Barbara:

"I am Ruth's mother. Doctor Elfriede Schier.

"When the shocking news reached me, I just could not believe it to be true. . . .

"For twelve days and nights I did not sleep or take a complete meal—I just could not. I only prayed and cried and prayed. . . .

"Ruth had suffered a lot in her 26 years, lost her father when she was three years and soon afterwards her sweet baby sister Erika. Werner her brother had been her special love as he was living 15 years blind and paralyzed and she nursed him and fed him with a spoon. Werner died 18 years old. So Ruth grew up loving and caring for her blind brother and she is indeed very unselfish. Ruth never took advantage over anybody . . .

"The evening Ruth was to leave from Tegucigalpa for Miami Ruth and myself had been invited for dinner at the American Consul, Mr. Hubert Buzbee together with Mr. and Mrs. Donaldson and their two daughters. Mr. Buzbee also came to the airport to say good bye to Ruth. I felt so sad when Ruth left and ever since I had been so depressed as if I had felt unconsciously that some terrible event was coming. . . .

"When Ruth was with me and anything she did turned out wrong, she immediately said, 'Mámi, forgive me!'

"Now, that only God knows where she is—alive or dead—I want to do the same in her place:

"'Barbara, can you forgive Ruth?'"

In due course the FBI had the opportunity to read Mrs. Schier's letter, and the question arose: Would she make a public appeal to her daughter to surrender herself?

Jeremiah O'Leary, a crew-cut gray-haired man of military bearing who looked more like a Marine Corps colonel (which he was) than a newspaper reporter for the Washington *Star* (which he also was), flew to Honduras to find out.

He found Dr. Schier. She consented to an interview while she drilled an Indian's teeth. In late January, O'Leary filed his story:

CATACAMAS, Honduras—The adobe house of Mrs. Elfriede Schier is like any other in this Central American backwater, except for the long, black funeral dress hanging inside by the front door.

The dress is for the last rites of Ruth Eisemann-Schier . . .

The 59-year-old Mrs. Schier was shocked by the news—and wept and prayed after she heard it. She also began to prepare the black dress for Ruth's funeral.

The mother's dependence on God's will dominates her life. An extraordinarily religious woman, she owns seven Bibles and believes in God's counsel by revelation.

It is for this reason that Mrs. Schier, who came here from Austria in 1939, refuses to contemplate making an appeal to Ruth to give herself up. "If God wants Ruth to surrender herself, He will tell her to do it; if He wished me to plead with her to turn herself in, He will tell me," she said.

The closest Mrs. Schier has come to an appeal is in a few lines written as an introduction to what she said will be a "Book of Ruth." The lines say: "Ruth! Ruth! Ruth! Show yourself to me, frightened little rabbit in hiding. You must need me but how can I help you if I do not know where you are."

It was on December 13 that Ruth sent a Christmas card to her mother, what Mrs. Schier said was the girl's last communication with her:

"Remember mother, dear, this greeting it is bringing love, not for just a day or even a year, but love to last a lifetime." Mrs. Schier said her daughter signed it, "Ruth, Erika and Wernerli," the names of all three Schier children, including two who died some time ago. . . .

Her German-born husband, Ruth's father, was a poet and a journalist named Werner Eisemann. He died of a gunshot wound in Tegucigalpa, Honduras, on August 11, 1945. There is speculation that Ruth's father died by his own hand, though murder is a common crime in Honduras.

Mrs. Schier has many things to do to preoccupy her now. . . .

There is the black dress for Ruth's funeral. Mrs. Schier said it is a dress she brought with her from Austria as a newlywed refugee in 1939. She said she is going to have to shorten it because Ruth is such a tiny girl.

The FBI also speculated on Ruth's possible death. In the case of Ruth Eisemann-Schier, a high-priority investigation, there were absolutely no fresh leads.

Could Krist have murdered her? Had he killed her after the second drop so he wouldn't have to share the $500,000? If she had been in the rented Ford Fairlane he would have had ample opportunity on the trip from Miami to West Palm Beach. Some of the back roads—and even major thoroughfares northward—ran through swamp and cypress country as isolated as the Everglades. A body might go unfound for years.

What had happened to Krist's weapons? Both Jane Mackle and Charles Gullion, the U-Haul trailer man, thought they had seen Krist with a shotgun.

At the chase after the first drop, officer Sweeney and the bus driver on his way to work thought they had seen him with a carbine. In the Volvo, FBI agents had found ammunition for both a carbine and a shotgun. Neither weapon had been found.

The FBI could not precisely account for all of Krist's movements between the time he had rented the Ford in Miami and parked it in the Allright lot in West Palm Beach. Allowing mileage for the trip to Jackson Memorial Hospital and the trips back and forth in West Palm Beach from the different stores, the odometer still registered about sixty miles too much.

This could be explained by the different routes available to him from Miami to West Palm Beach. The mileage would have varied, depending on whether he had driven north on U. S. 27, the Sunshine State Parkway, U. S. 1, U. S. A1A, U. S. 441, I-95, or any combination thereof. A mistaken turn, not unlikely in his physical condition, could have also put on the unaccounted mileage.

But suppose he used those miles for a back-road murder. FBI search parties checked every back road they could find in the vicinity of the second ransom drop on the routes north. They found nothing.

Briefly one afternoon, agents thought they might have an answer.

On February 26, two Canadian tourists on a snake hunt discovered a badly charred human skeleton in the wilds of the Everglades off a dirt road about fifty miles west of Miami.

Someone had bound a body with about twenty wire coat hangers, stuffed it into a wooden trunk, doused it heavily with gasoline, and set it afire. The fire burned so fiercely it scorched trees twenty feet away. The body burned so badly that at first police could not determine its sex. Metal fasteners from a bra were the first indication. The Dade Country Medical Examiner's office determined that the skeleton was that of a relatively small, mature white female.

But homicide detectives realized immediately that the fire had occurred quite recently. The scene reeked of a strong odor of burning and gasoline, a factor which time would have abated. They found light ashes. Any sort of wind would have blown them away.

Agent Michael E. Crane, then running the investigation in Miami, obtained Ruth's dental charts and X-rays from a Washington, D.C. dentist, Dr. Angel Rivera, and they were submitted to Thomas C. Carlton, an oral surgeon in residence at Jackson Memorial Hospital for comparison. Dr. Carlton examined the skeletal remains of the woman known as case 69-501. He found one lower molar missing. The remaining molars were intact.

He issued a report: "I am able to state with complete certainty that the remains are not those of Miss Eisemann-Schier, since four molar teeth are shown missing in Miss Eisemann-Schier's chart, whereas only one molar (mandibular first right molar) is missing in the remains identified as M.E. 69-501."

Gary Steven Krist, the one man who might logically provide some answers to the whereabouts of Ruth Eisemann-Schier, had sulked in silence in the days after his capture. He had refused even to admit his identity as George Deacon.

When the airboats nosed to the launching ramp at the Lazy R fishing camp at El Jobean, the posse of armed men crowded forward and a hundred hands reached out to help. The flash and glare of cameras and television lights caught Krist kneeling in the prow, his hands cuffed behind him, exhausted, drenched. He grimaced, his face distorted as in pain, and hung his head.

Sheriff Frank Kline and FBI agents quickly led him to a waiting yellow car and drove him directly to the Lee Memorial Hospital in Fort Myers. In the back seat, Krist fell unconscious. The FBI wanted him seen by a physician immediately. It wanted also to establish positively his identity.

An agent spit on his handkerchief and rubbed Krist's hands in an attempt to examine the prisoner's fingerprints in the back seat of the now moving automobile. Krist's hands were too grimy. There was another way to establish identity. The man the FBI wanted had five sutures in his left scrotum. No one gave a damn about Krist's dignity. He was unzipped and examined. There was no mistake. To say the least, it was an unusual method of identification.

At 10:45 A.M. the next morning, a Sunday, U. S. Commissioner George Swartz held a hearing in Krist's hospital room. Lucid, rested, garbed in a two-piece gray hospital gown, Krist waived his right to counsel, signing his name, and writing the number "12" for school grades completed and "one year of college" on a form provided him. Commissioner Swartz read him the complaint on why he was being held. He was charged with violation of U. S. Code Title 18, Section 875 and 1201—the federal kidnaping statute. The formality did not call for a plea. Although Krist signed his name on the waiver, he refused to admit he was George Deacon. Commissioner Swartz set bail bond at $500,000, a sum that seemed a pardonable coincidence under the circumstance. The FBI then transported Krist to Miami. As a federal prisoner, he was lodged in an isolation cell in the Dade County Jail at 4:47 P.M. Sunday, December 22, 1968.

A desk sergeant scrawled in a notation: "Hold for U. S. Marshal."

Gary Steven Krist was born, seven pounds and seven ounces, April 29, 1945 in Aberdeen, Washington, a date memorable in the history of World War II. It was the day Italian partisans hanged the dead body of Benito Mussolini upside down in the public square of Milan. He was the second son of Arline and James Kimberly Krist, an introverted and disabled fisherman who moved the family to the village of Pelican, Alaska, population 135, not far from Sitka. Krist was a boy in trouble. At fourteen he stole a boat. At fifteen it was a car he didn't know how to drive. At twenty it was two guns from the Stanford Sports Shop in Palo Alto, California.

Another youth, Herbert Lee Jacobson, was arrested with him. An old police record contained a curious notation: "Krist said that

he and Jacobson wanted to commit a robbery and kidnap someone."

Jacobson. Jake and the Boys!

The FBI checked it out. They proved that Herbert Lee Jacobson was working in a sheet-metal shop in San Francisco at the
time of the crime. Jake hadn't seen Krist in years.

In the months that Krist waited in jail before he was eventually
brought to trial in Decatur, Georgia, law enforcement afforded
him the distinction of a constant sentinel. At the Dade County
Jail, two FBI agents took up posts in a small corridor outside his
cell every eight hours. One agent read; the other watched the
prisoner. In Georgia, where Krist was taken January 25, 1969,
similar non-FBI procedures were established at the Fulton County
Jail in Atlanta and the DeKalb County Jail in Decatur.

In these months Krist's moods and dispositions varied extensively,
and on occasion he talked of himself, his childhood, his supposed
mental aberrations, the crime of which he was accused, Ruth,
and murder.

Perhaps more than anyone else, Bernado M. Perez, a young
FBI agent born of Mexican parents in California who had once
studied for the priesthood, first managed to induce Krist to talk.
Perez, a perceptive man who expressed no judgments on evil
or virtue, ignoring the good guy-bad guy, white hat-black hat
syndromes of keeper to captive, guarded Krist five times. Seemingly, he established a genuine rapport with the prisoner. Krist
would later repeat much of his conversations to others, even
television and newspaper reporters.

Some of his statements were undeniably true. Others were
demonstrably false. And some defied precise analysis: "I know
I am a pathological liar. I can't understand why I lie."

Krist implied that he knew where Ruth was. He said he would
not "fink" on her. Let her remain free when she is young, he said,
she can serve her time later—if anyone ever finds her. Krist
surmised that Ruth could be a very successful prostitute. She is
very strong physically, he said. In his opinion, she would not be
hiding in the Cuban colony in Miami. He said she spoke dis-
paragingly of Cubans. He said he personally had never mentioned
marriage to her. He said he did not know her until the Bermuda
cruise on the *Pillsbury* and had not spoken to her the first three
days. He said they established a "mature relationship" with fre-

quent sexual intercourse both in Bermuda and aboard the ship. He described her as very intelligent and very clever, and a young girl who likes to appear innocent. He said he loved her. He said he also loved his wife and that insofar as he was capable of the emotions of love, he loved both Ruth and his wife equally. He said his wife understood everything about him "except the important things." Ruth, he said, would react as an elephant: Run at full speed as long as necessary, stop and wait, and then quietly get caught and lose.

Krist said he thought "Ruthie," as he often called her, was now probably in Argentina. He said she spoke some Portuguese. He said that they had planned to go to South America together where they wouldn't be gypped. He said that they both, he and she, had an interest in archeology and the ancient ruins there. A half million dollars, he said, wouldn't go very far; it was not that much money. He said it would have tided him over for a little while, but that he would have had to come back and "do it again." Someday, he said, there will be no money—"just plastic cards for everything."

When Krist spoke directly of the kidnaping, he almost always referred to himself in the third person. Occasionally he would forget and an "I" would slip from his tongue, but generally he would refer to the perpetrator of the crime simply as "the kidnaper." It was always singular.

Krist was adamant in his belief that the "kidnaper" in no way endangered or jeopardized the life of Barbara Mackle. This person, he said, knew himself very well. He knew that in certain situations his reactions became irrational, animalistic, and that to forestall this dilemma, the kidnaper made voluminous plans; he thought of everything. "Then he panicked." Krist said the kidnaper "captured himself," running like an animal. In the kidnaper's anxiety, said Krist, the kidnaper had not slept; fatigue influenced his actions. Krist allowed how the kidnaper "erred" when he bought a boat with twenty-dollar bills. He said that the act illustrated the kidnaper's panicky state of mind. Krist marveled, though, at the thought of filling the boat with sand and dirt and sinking it. If the kidnaper had *done* that, he said, the police would have wasted two or three weeks looking for it. Cashing in the two airline tickets, Krist said, was another illustration of the kidnaper's state of panic. "This was his weakness." Krist said the kidnaper had been running on instinct.

Krist, adroitly performing his mental gymnastics, went on to discuss the Fair Isle Causeway as a drop site. He said the island side was well protected from possible gunfire from the residential side. He said it would be much safer for the kidnaper if the depositor had to walk out on the causeway to put the money in a box. By lining the inside of the box with metal, the range of any sort of electronic homing device hidden within a suitcase would be impeded if not completely destroyed, Krist said. And a metal-lined inner box, he said, could easily be disposed of. Biscayne Bay, he noted, was full of scrap iron. He also acknowledged that he had learned welding in prison in California. He spoke vaguely and ambiguously of preventing pursuit. If the kidnaper had wanted to, he could have put a hand grenade under a police car, Krist said.

The revelations, fact or fictional, came in long and meandering conversations. Krist's thoughts and words often trailed off in mid-sentence, incomplete, hanging. At times he appeared quite aggravated; at others, willing to discuss logic and metaphysics, cosmology. Sometimes he would quote passages from the Bible. He said he admired the writing in the Bible, especially some of the "horny" parts. He said he believed in God but that he had his religious "hangups," his voice trailing off. He declined to elaborate. He said he joined the church at age nine and that at age fourteen he became extremely interested in religion, reading everything he could. He said he had no religious preference.

He said he learned about sex in the Elmer Gantry tradition at age nine with two daughters of a minister, both older than he, in a choir loft. He described himself as a sexual athlete throughout his youth. Sex, he said, was the only thing that kept his attention, and that he was at it very regularly. He said it did not matter to him if a woman climaxed. He said he had engaged in homosexual activities, but did not consider himself a homosexual. He said he did not find the experience repulsive.

Krist said that he had taken 200-milligram tablets of LSD on eight occasions, and once in Bermuda, he took a 600-milligram dosage, which produced hallucinatory angels and made him black out. He said he considered marijuana no more serious than alcohol and that he had once distilled marijuana and consumed it in scotch whisky.

Krist said he admired most the self-reliant man, the woodsman, Thoreau, the man, the real man, who could live in the woods alone, and he mentioned the fabled and legendary Paul Bunyan. He said he had become something of a wild-West buff.

Even when talking about himself, Krist appeared to be rather impersonal, his listeners felt. They described him as fatalistic, intent. Krist said that he had been lonely all his life. Intellectually, he was a near genius, he said, scoring 148 on one I.Q. test. He said this had made him extremely egotistical and this exaggerated his schizoid personality. While incarcerated at the Deuel Vocational Institute in California, said Krist, he had read extensively of psychology and psychiatry, everything on the library shelves, and that he had become convinced that he was a schizoid-paranoid personality.

He said that he was in desperate need of psychiatric treatment and wanted to be helped. Of course," he said at one point, "I am smarter than most of them." Krist said his schizoid-paranoid personality was due to heredity, that it had developed in his formative years, and that he saw the same symptoms of rejection of affection in one of his own boys. He said he had been violent as a child. He said he had seriously beaten his playmates. And he said he could feel the fits of violence coming over him.

During these episodes, he said, he was very dangerous and that he might attack any innocent bystander. The violence, he said, gave him a feeling of release. During these episodes, he saw himself as another person, he said. He was both actor and audience. He said he saw himself as if at the end of a long tunnel, knowing that he was doing wrong, yet unable to get his own attention.

"I am very dangerous at these times," he said. "I see anyone close to me as a threat to my safety."

During one such episode, a guard at Deuel Vocational Institute awoke him, he said, and he attacked the guard savagely and would have killed him except that other inmates pulled him off.

The agent who first heard this comment said nothing, aware that if necessary, the incident probably could be confirmed or denied. Much later R. M. Rees, the associate superintendent at

Deuel, would examine Krist's prison record and find his lone refraction of rules: Talking too loud while watching television in the recreation room.

Krist said that prior to the kidnaping, he had controlled himself for fifteen months. He said that he suffered terrible nightmares and in both day and night he heard things, animals growling at him. He said he was tormented by audio and video hallucinations from which he could not escape. He said he once saw a man standing in place on the steering wheel of his car and he was terrified; he knew he was driving, he knew he was having an hallucination, yet the man was standing there and he, Krist, could not escape.

Reluctantly, or so his interrogator believed, Krist also spoke of having a vision of two angels. "I know this sounds silly," Krist prefaced, and then he told of an intense light and haze of halos and sparks. He said the creatures spoke to him. He said he did not wish to divulge their conversation.

"My mind is slowly deteriorating," Krist said. "If I am sane by the time I am thirty, I will be very fortunate."

At one point, he said, "I may be insane now, but I am fully aware of the difference between right and wrong." He said he knew the tenets of the Judaic-Christian culture.

The FBI man who heard him say this marked his words well.

Later Krist told him not to worry that he was going to make any incriminating statements. Any statements made in jail, he said, could not be used against him. The FBI man said nothing.

In the course of his conversation, Krist spoke of four different murders.

He said that when he was about fourteen years old he had a homosexual experience with a man sixty-five years old. The man, Krist said, was a hermit. One night during the winter they were crossing a bridge, Krist said, and he became frightened and terrified. He said he kicked the man's legs from under him, and the man plunged off the bridge to his death. He said the body was found four or five days later and it was assumed that he had fallen accidentally. "Until this day no one knows I murdered him," Krist said.

Krist said he had murdered a young girl in California when he was about nineteen years old. She was approximately the same age. He said the girl told him "'my father is going to kill you for what you've done to me,'" and that he, Krist, panicked and struck her several times with his fist in her abdomen and knocked her down a ravine. She was still alive, he said, and he climbed down the ravine, choked her with his bare hands, and piled rocks on her body. He said he was never questioned.

The third murder supposedly occurred in his youth after an "escape." He had fled from the Utah State Industrial School in the summer of 1961. Krist said very little about the circumstances; merely that he had picked up a homosexual, whom he described as a "sissy," and killed him during a violent fit. He said he left the body somewhere near the Utah-Nevada line.

The fourth murder he wouldn't talk about at all.

"There was one other person," he said. "I don't want to talk about it."

Could he have murdered Ruth Eisemann-Schier? His inference seemed clear.

Perhaps a few facts could be established. Where was Krist when he was fourteen years old? Had a man sixty-five years old fallen off a bridge? What about bodies in California and the Nevada-Utah line?

On February 12, 1959, when Krist was fourteen years old, the body of Antone H. Simmonsen, a never-married halibut and salmon fisherman, was found face down in a creek bed 200 feet under a bridge in Pelican, Alaska. Tony, as he was known, was a blue-eyed man of ruddy complexion who supposedly had a heart condition. He had been born in Norway. He was sixty-five years old. The townfolks had last seen him two nights before, Tuesday, February 10. He had been drinking heavily in a saloon and he had complained of feeling very tired. He left the tavern staggering at 11:30 P.M. A narrow bridge crossed high over a shallow creek a quarter of a mile away. Ice and snow underfoot made it hazardous. A ten-foot section of a shaky hand railing had broken about ten days before and had not been replaced.

Only the red rubber heels of Simmonsen's boots protruded above a cake of ice when he was found. His glasses and fur-lined cap were missing. He wore no gloves. In his billfold was $171. His pocket watch had stopped at 11:40 P.M., presumably ten minutes after he left the tavern. When found, his forearms were tight across his chest, his hands clenching inward. To the town's registered nurse, Mrs. Janie S. Bann, his death seemed to be an obvious heart attack. There was no autopsy.

Krist's parents rented an apartment at 106 Finn Alley in Sitka at the time, several islands and almost a hundred miles south. They often fished out of Pelican and they often lived there on their boat. In 1969, the police chief in Sitka could find no one who remembered exactly where the Krists had been at the time.

Without further investigation, it was impossible to determine the truth or falsity of Krist's superficial Alaskan confession. Undoubtedly, every young boy around Pelican and Sitka would have heard of the death. Had Krist merely embroidered upon the facts? Or was he, as he professed so ambiguously, a murderer?

The California death was a different matter. There was little doubt that Helen Ann Crow, once a mental patient, had indeed been murdered. Under a pile of rocks her badly decomposed body, garbed in a light blue dress, black lace bra, panties and rubber thongs, had been found south of San Diego on October 3, 1964. An autopsy indicated fractures of the throat. She had been dead for a month to six weeks.

Krist, however, could not possibly have killed her. He was an inmate at the Deuel Vocational Institute more than four hundred miles away for the eleven months prior to her death. He had to be lying.

Krist's vague reference to a murder along the Utah-Nevada border conformed somewhat to the discovery of a skeleton on July 27, 1967. Nevada Highway Department employees found a fully clothed skeleton of a man about ten miles west of Wendover, Utah. A pathologist estimated the date of death at three to five years before, 1964 to 1962, cause unknown. In 1961, young Krist had run away from the Utah Industrial School at Ogden, Utah. He had been caught in Caldwell, Idaho. Conceivably, if the pathologist's time element was not accurate, Krist could have known something about the death. To the FBI, it appeared possible but unlikely.

Yet, if Krist's "murders" were all contrived nonsense, why had no one anywhere come forward with any valid information on Ruth?

As agent Perez first heard the confessions, he sat in a straight-back chair, leaning up against a wall across the narrow corridor from Krist's cell. At times Krist would lean back on his bed and drape his pants over his head. A rational animal needs a certain amount of privacy, he said. Take that away, and "you would destroy me completely."

Krist had fixed a sign to a wall. "Any Donations of Reading Material Will Be Appreciated." When agent Wayne O. Taylor casually copied it one day, Krist angrily took it down, tore it into pieces, and flushed it down the commode.

He told agent Perez he had to read to blot out his hallucinations.

"And if you had to do it again, would you do it the same way?" Perez asked.

"Yes, I probably would," Krist replied. "My mind has deteriorated that much." He had forgotten his third-person method. "Sooner or later he would panic," Krist said, picking it up again.

And then, for the moment, he gave up. "I would be egotistical enough to try it again—and try to control myself."

Krist's wife, Carmen Simon Krist, a slender, underweight woman of twenty-two with a quick intelligence and long dark hair, knew very little about Ruth Eisemann-Schier, her whereabouts, or her role in the crime. But she knew a great deal about her husband.

"I knew what he was when I married him. I went into it with my eyes open. The children and I are happy and nobody has to sing any sad songs for me," she said a few months after the crime in Redwood, California, and she looked terribly unhappy, gaunt, easily mistaken for a woman much older. For a while, before she reconsidered, she had talked freely and publicly.

Although she never said anything that proved preknowledge of the crime, she made statements that opened up considerable conjecture.

She said Gary would have been "clever enough" to have employed the use of the social register in selecting a victim. He might have checked a dozen or more prospective names, she suggested, obtaining addresses from the blue book, then inspecting the homes by driving around them. He could have seen a college insignia on the rear window of an automobile, Carmen Krist said.

Five names from the top of page 288 of the 1967 Social Register of Greater Miami, the publisher, Mrs. John Northen Jackson had listed:

MACKLE, MR. AND MRS. ROBERT FRANCIS (*Mary Jane Braznell*)

4111 San Amaro Drive, Coral Gables 33146. Tel. 665-7242
Summer: 1201 White Pine Drive, Hendersonville, N.C.
 Miss Barbara Jane; Mr. Robert Francis, Jr.
Clubs: Riviera (CC); Cotillion (Miami)
Coll. Mr: Wash. & Lee U. Coll. Mrs: Duke U. Cruiser: "Elk-cam"

In the months before the kidnaping, the Mackles kept a two-year-old green Mustang in the driveway and garage of their home. On the back bumper was a parking sticker: Emory University.

Carmen Simon met Gary Steven Krist at a roller rink in Red-wood, California, the home of her parents, on December 13, 1964—four years to the day that he would put her on an airplane in Miami and send her home with their two small sons, then about eight months old and two years old. "We were very much attracted to each other right from the start. We were together almost constantly until we eloped and were married by a justice of the peace on March 26, 1965."

Gary, she said, was the most fascinating man she had ever known. "When he wants to turn it on, he can charm the birds right out of the trees.

"He was out on parole when we were married. We lived to-gether for three years, except for the times he was in jail." She said he was a "good father and a kind husband, very considerate. But I think he realized I was the wrong woman for him. He didn't quite know how to handle that."

During their marriage, Carmen studied at San Mateo Junior College, where she received excellent grades, and later took a course in IBM key card punching. For a while she worked in the library at Stanford University.

Her husband, she said, was a man without friends. She de-scribed him as "highly intelligent" and "aggressive." She said he could have been anything he wanted to but was held back by his prison record. "He could have been a doctor, even an astronaut," she said.

"When he got put in prison the first time after we were mar-ried, I thought it wouldn't happen again. It did. I said the same thing the second time. Now there's a third time."

Gary, she said, "told me several times the dream he used to

have about kidnaping someone to make a lot of money." It was just a childish dream and he had forgotten it, she said.

"Gary wanted to do a lot of things but he was frustrated because he didn't have much money," said Carmen Krist. "He wanted to own a ranch and machine shop and be his own boss. He doesn't want to lead a mediocre life. He wants to be remembered. He always wanted to make an impact on the world he lives in. And he likes nice clothes and cars. And probably more women."

Carmen Krist said she detected a noticeable change in her husband when he came home from the Bermuda cruise on the *Pillsbury*. He wanted to know if it was possible for a man to love two women. Not unnaturally, she was suspicious, and she asked him if he had met another woman. He denied it.

Sometimes he would not come home for several nights. Once she checked to see if he was on the *Pillsbury*. He wasn't. She tried to find him in several bars and couldn't. She became depressed and cried a lot.

The week before the kidnaping, "he told me he just didn't love me any more. He said he wanted a two-month separation. He told me to live 'as if I am dead and see how you like it.'"

Carmen Krist said her husband also talked of "making a big score"; $100,000, $500,000, or a million dollars; she had kidded him about "inflation getting pretty bad." She knew that he had a partner in some "scheme to make a lot of money."

But, apparently, it never dawned on her that this particular person was a woman. Krist spoke of his partner as a "foreigner." He said his partner had several passports and connections in Mexico and knew a lot about drugs.

He said that he no doubt would be making a "big score" sooner or later and that he would probably be in Las Vegas. There was no doubt in her mind that he would send her some of the proceeds.

On the night of Friday the thirteenth, December 1968, Krist took his wife and two small boys to Miami International Airport. He had purchased one-way tickets by mail. It was about eight o'clock. The plane didn't leave for another two hours. He appeared extremely restless and impatient, and he left his wife and family about an hour before the flight. It would be the last time he would see them.

She would move temporarily into the two-bedroom, frame cottage of her parents, Mr. and Mrs. George Simon, in Redwood, and write three days later, ". . . I accept what you are attempting; personally, it is not my way . . . You are the only man I know who can do it."

The kidnaping of Barbara Mackle did not surprise Carmen Krist at all. She was shocked only that her husband had run off with another woman.

"I knew he had the intelligence needed to carry out such a plan," the UPI quoted her.

She told the Miami *Herald*, "I do not know the woman they say was involved in this thing with him. It comes as a great shock to me. I never heard of the woman. I do not want to talk about her."

A reporter asked her one other question: Did she have any feelings about Barbara Mackle and the suffering to which her husband subjected the Mackle family?

"Not really," she said. "I have thought more about what Gary went through than anything else."

On the Sunday of Krist's capture, Barbara made her first—and only—public appearance before newsmen and television cameras. It lasted one minute and twenty seconds. Except for her testimony in a courtroom much later, she would neither write nor say anything publicly about the crime until publication of this book.

Barbara had been at the Miami Heart Institute in Miami Beach for a little more than thirty-six hours. She felt much stronger. With Dr. Lauth as an escort, she walked fifty feet to a small patio in the sun where Robert, Frank, Elliott and Bobby waited quietly.

Barbara wore an aqua-blue silk-and-lace gown and peignoir, and white scuff slippers. Her make-up consisted of a touch of mascara, no lipstick.

Her father read a brief statement he had prepared. "Our first and deepest thanks—those of myself and Mrs. Mackle, our son and our daughter, Barbara, are to Almighty God, who in His infinite mercy has seen fit to return our beloved daughter safely to our family."

Barbara, quite obviously, was expected to say something.

"Barbara," her father said hesitantly, "these friends of yours out here just wanted to know that you were all right . . . They wanted to see you, and so on. How are you feeling?" He felt a little awkward.

A slightly quizzical expression crossed her face. With just a hint of a Southern accent, she said, "I just feel wonderful, and I just . . . just want to thank everybody for their prayers and for their concern for both myself and my family . . . and thank you, everybody. I just feel wonderful, I really do."

"That's just great, Barb."

Her father gestured toward the photographers, telling her they'd like some pictures.

"But don't become a ham," he said to his daughter.

Barbara leaned in close to her father.

"Is there any particular side, Barbara?"

"No, Daddy!"

Her uncle Frank wanted to know if he could be her business agent.

The press conference, if it could be called that, was quick, light, and as replayed on television in millions of homes across the nation—touching.

The letters, cards, telegrams and messages came by thousands in the days and weeks thereafter.

A man from Vanceburg, Kentucky, wrote, "It is heartening to see a businessman stand up in front of millions of people and give testimony to God."

"While I am writing this note," said a woman in Healdsburg, Georgia, "the tears of gratitude are rolling down my cheeks."

"Please forgive me for writing like this when we haven't met," began a housewife in Kensington, Maryland. "We have worried, cried, prayed and waited with you these past terrible days listening with horror and disbelief to the news."

"We have lived on Alhambra Circle for twenty years and remember Barbara coming by to talk to our basset hound Buttercup," wrote a Coral Gables lady. "We have prayed for her safety and we thank God our prayers have been answered."

"I don't know you folks but I prayed so hard my heart almost broke," an Avon, Connecticut, woman declared.

A Christmas card came from John Maguire, a schoolteacher who once told his pupils how they must learn to control themselves and how a man being tortured could divert his thoughts by pretending to build a house of brick. "My thoughts have been with you," he wrote.

"It is Christmas morning and the world is full of joy," wrote a widow from Washington, D.C. "The news is of the flight of *Apollo* and the return of the crew of the *Pueblo*, but somehow my thoughts keep turning to you. Please pardon this invasion of your privacy."

From New York City, a stranger wrote, "You must have been extremely proud of your daughter for her implicit faith in her father's ability to be able to cope with any situation, no matter how difficult."

The mail arrived from the Philippines, Pakistan, India, Indonesia, Lebanon, Switzerland, Norway, England, France, Brazil, Peru, Puerto Rico, and especially, Vietnam.

A young man from Turkey composed a love letter. "Oh, Barbara, Don't hurt my feelings. I need you so much. I am longing to be near you."

Scores of Barbara's friends at Emory University, where her sorority sisters often called her by her last name because there were so many Tri Delt Barbaras, tried—and tried not—to put their feeling on paper:

"Hi Mackle. What exciting times we live in," wrote Emily Balz.

"Thank your parents again for the cough syrup," wrote her roommate, Ramsey Owens.

"See you next quarter," said Burnley Bainbridge and Lisa Sintow.

Mrs. Herbert Woodward, the mother of Stewart, wrote from Charlotte, North Carolina, "Surely now we know the real meaning of Joy to the World."

And from the office of the dean of students, Ruth R. Montgomery wrote, "As though you have nothing else on your mind, dear Emory still hangs two final examinations over your head."

The fact that Robert Mackle had raised $500,000 led some persons to believe that he was a man of unlimited wealth who could correct all the wrongs of the world. The Mackle family, which for years had given to charities in a systematic manner, received an incredible number of letters from persons beseeching them for assistance.

A Brooklyn man said he needed $2358 for three hundred lessons at a Berlitz School of Languages. A gentleman from Canton, Ohio, wanted money to visit his sister's grave in Germany.

In Raiffeisenbank, Germany, an inventor needed only $50,000 for his revolutionary plastic turbine. An apartment dweller on West Twentieth Street in New York, displeased with his landlord, wanted Robert Mackle to fix his leaky roof. A missionary among the Bantus in South Africa needed a Cadillac.

Others weren't without an edge of humor: "As your so-called host," began a note from Ben Rabinowitz, the manager of the Rodeway Inn in Decatur, Georgia. "You are a very brave girl, I get nervous in a phone booth," wrote a man from Schenectady, New York.

Some few letters dealt with the kidnapers. Dr. Henry King Stanford, the president of the University of Miami wrote:

"There is one aspect of the tragedy which leaves me with a heavy heart. I cannot divest myself of the realization that, among the thousands of employees at the University of Miami, there were two miscreants of such evil and diabolic mentality that they would perpetrate such an act upon so innocent a girl and her family. I regret deeply that we had in our employ persons of such criminal makeup."

And some were not only moving but personally philosophic. L. B. "Buck" Walker, the chairman of the Florida State Racing Commission, wrote:

". . . Bob, I had a great personal tragedy in my own family, and not being as fortunate as you, I lost my daughter, therefore I know and have felt the anguish and suffering that you and your wife were exposed to. So often, I think, people such as you and I take our position in life, and our way of life, for granted until a tragedy of this sort happens, and it is only then that we realize how very much we have to be thankful for and to what degree we must depend upon a power higher than this world for the answer."

Inquire Within

On Wednesday, March 5, 1969, a bleak, damp and miserable day in Oklahoma City, Oklahoma, a young blonde of twenty-five, Jean Price, casually opened a thick manila envelope. She was a fingerprint classification technician for the Oklahoma State Bureau of Investigation. The envelope contained a stack of fingerprint cards from the Central State Hospital in Norman, Oklahoma, submitted as a part of a routine employment application procedure.

Sometime after ten o'clock that morning Jean Price picked up an employment application form of a Donna Sue Wills, white female, age eighteen. Routinely, unhurriedly, she checked the name in an index card system. Negative. The Oklahoma State Bureau of Investigation had never heard of a Donna Sue Wills.

So, in the jargon of her specialty, she began to "class it up," as she put it, noting the inked impressions of loops, ridges and whorls on the fingerprint card.

The number seven finger, the left index, seemed to be easily identifiable, Jean Price thought as she detected an ending ridge, a forking ridge or a dot. She walked over to the rows of metal filing cabinets which contained about 1,250,000 cards, all properly organized for comparison purposes. In a moment, she pulled out a card.

"I almost fainted," she said.

There, in large capital letters, read: "WANTED BY THE FBI." Underneath was the name: Ruth Eisemann-Schier. She recognized the name instantly.

Suddenly trembling, Jean Price hurried to her desk for a magnifying glass. "I tried hard not to get excited."

She began the comparison, one by one, the prints of Ruth Eisemann-Schier and Donna Sue Wills. Her heart pounded. She was positive.

She turned to her supervisor, Paul Boyd. "Mr. Boyd," she said, "would you come and verify this identification for me?" She spoke as calmly as she could.

When he walked over she jumped up and let him sit at her desk. Boyd saw the names. Silently, he scrutinized the two cards. "This is it," he said.

He grasped both cards and hurried across the room to the office of Tom Puckett, a graying former Army man who ran the fingerprint section.

"We have a positive identification," the supervisor said curtly, thrusting forward the two cards. Puckett looked hard once, rose to his feet, and grabbed his raincoat. Carl Tyler, the director of the Oklahoma Bureau of Investigation, would notify the Oklahoma office of the FBI by telephone as Puckett delivered the cards in person. He was on his way.

The FBI office in Oklahoma City had suffered the embarrassment of unwanted national attention a few months before, not for professional fault, but for social indiscretion. There had been a somewhat boisterous cocktail party at an annual convention of the Oklahoma Sheriff's and Peace Officer's Association at the Sheridan Hotel, an ancient downtown fixture of the oil town, and a complaint had reverberated to the director's office in Washington. Eight agents found themselves reassigned. The complaint, oddly enough, had originated in Norman, Oklahoma—where Ruth Eisemann-Schier had submitted to fingerprinting.

The new agent in charge, John W. Burns, a hulking giant of a man, had "come south" from Butte, Montana, for the winter. He telephoned Washington immediately. The response was totally predictable: Go. Seven agents piled into two cars and left promptly for Norman. The FBI did not notify any local law enforcement persons in Norman. It could do without any help from Norman, only nineteen miles away.

The two cars sped south on I-35 early that afternoon, past the turnoff to the Will Rogers World Airport. From the expressway agents could see the oil well pumps, skeletoned green steel dinosaurs, nodding up and down. Yes. Yes. Yes.

Seventy-nine days before, the Thursday of the aborted first ransom drop, Ruth Eisemann-Schier had boarded a Greyhound bus at the downtown bus station in Miami a few minutes before two-fifteen in the afternoon. She had purchased a $42.60 one-way ticket to Houston, Texas—1244 miles from Miami. In Sebring, Florida, later that afternoon, 164 miles north, a passenger on the bus suffered a heart attack. An ambulance removed him to a hospital and the bus driver, aware that a report would be filed with the General Fire and Casualty Company, took the names of all his passengers. Ruth gave a fictitious name. At 11:30 P.M. Friday, after thirty-three hours on the road via New Orleans, the bus arrived in Houston. Ruth immediately took a room in the Houston YWCA. On Saturday, running low on money, she moved to a less expensive room at the George Hotel and began answering help-wanted ads in the Houston newspapers. On Sunday she appeared at one of the six Felix Mexican Restaurants in Houston, seeking employment as a waitress, kitchen help, anything. She spoke Spanish. She said her name was Irma Hilga Sanchez. A cashier showed her a want ad for a live-in Latin-American maid in one of Houston's more discerning residential neighborhoods. Ruth prevailed upon the cashier to telephone for her.

"She lived with us for six weeks," said Lois Woolfolk, the attractive Junior League wife of Robert M. Woolfolk, a chemical engineer. "We never suspected anything."

As Irma Hilga Sanchez, Ruth kept the Woolfolk house and cared for the two Woolfolk children, Frank, eight, and Robin, two and a half, a beautiful dark-eyed, dark-haired child. Only the first day, after Robert Woolfolk drove to the restaurant and interviewed her, was he concerned. She couldn't provide any reference. She explained that she was from Laredo and that her father had become an alcoholic. That was why she had left home. She said she was twenty-one. She said her mother died when she was a child. She made a favorable impression and Robert Woolfolk asked her if she had a Social Security card. Ruth said that hers had been stolen. He told her that would be no trouble. Social Security could issue her a duplicate. "Then six hours later Irma came to my husband and told him she had lied about the Social Security card. She had never had one. She said she lied because she was afraid we wouldn't accept her."

The Woolfolks found the new maid unassuming, quiet, and excellent with the children. They paid her thirty-five dollars a week and gave her room and board. She never wanted to go anywhere. She never dated. She watched a lot of television with the children and she read. "I would drive her to the library; that's the only place," said Lois Woolfolk.

In late January Robert Woolfolk's mother was visiting the home one day. Her name was Ruth. Lois Woolfolk called her mother-in-law from the kitchen. "Ruth!" she called.

Irma Sanchez responded. "Did you call me?" she asked.

"No," said Lois Woolfolk, a little puzzled. Her maid appeared flustered.

During Ruth Eisemann-Schier's stay at the Woolfolks, another incident occurred that would later give Lois Woolfolk pause. "I was dressing one day and Irma answered the doorbell and told me that three men were at the door. They said they were Christian Scientists. I asked her to please tell them I wasn't interested. About thirty minutes later Irma asked me if Robin was with me. She wasn't.

"I thought she was with you," said her maid.

The two women quickly began to search through the house. They couldn't find the child.

"Irma," said Lois Woolfolk, her panic mounting, "the men who came to the door, did you let them in the house?"

"No."

"Did you lock the door?"

"No."

And then it struck her. "Oh, my God," said Lois Woolfolk. "What if they took her?"

She hurried across the street to look in her neighbor's swimming pool, then another neighbor's pond. She asked her maid to look at the schoolyard nearby, and Ruth Eisemann-Schier, a graceful runner, ran as fast as she could.

The mailman drove up and Lois Woolfolk, fear in her heart, asked him if he had seen her daughter. He had not. He began to search, too.

"I ran back in the house to call the police and just then I saw a wiggling under a pile of dirty clothes in the laundry room. Robin had spilled a box of detergent and she knew she was in trouble and she was hiding."

The mother embraced the child. Just then Ruth returned from the schoolyard. She saw Robin and burst into tears and for an hour she blubbered.

"She cried and she cried and she cried. She promised she

would never let her out of her sight again." Lois Woolfolk thought her maid's reaction extreme. Ruth Eisemann-Schier, perhaps feeling vicariously a mother's anxiety over a lost child, had witnessed herself an episode that could have only reminded her of the crime she had committed.

The Woolfolks attached no significance to the fact that their maid seemed unusually camera-shy. She would turn her face away when anyone started to take snapshots. They did not relate her behavior to the return of a role of film from the camera shop, blank because somehow it had been fully exposed to light. Nor did Robert Woolfolk pay any particular attention to her hesitant response when he suggested that she might get a driver's license so she could drive the family's old MG for errands for his wife. Texas required fingerprinting for licensing.

Nearly the entire time that Ruth Eisemann-Schier lived in Houston, Lois Woolfolk was deeply involved in a Junior League project. She was chairman of a costume committee for the league's charity ball, and day after day she was busy sewing costumes for a stage production. She had turned her guesthouse into a costume headquarters.

As the date for the charity ball approached, February 7, 1969, Lois Woolfolk had Ruth help with the sewing, and one afternoon in the guesthouse, one of the ladies on her committee, Betty Grey Finch, began to talk of the Mackle kidnaping. Betty Finch's parents, Mr. and Mrs. James Grey, lived in Hendersonville, North Carolina, where the Mackles had a summer home, and they knew them. Betty Finch remembered seeing Barbara as a child in North Carolina.

"We talked about how weird and strange the whole thing was, what a horrible thing it must have been for Barbara Mackle. Irma just sat there in stony silence. She left us at her first opportunity."

It was the Saturday morning after the charity ball, with Lois Woolfolk feeling that she had survived her "hour of need," that Ruth said she wanted to visit a friend in San Antonio. She said she would return Monday. The Woolfolks took her to the bus station for the 197-mile trip to San Antonio, and bought her a round-trip ticket on February 8. In San Antonio she wrote a letter to the Woolfolks which arrived Monday. "She said she had to go on to Laredo, Texas. Her friend had told her that her father had cancer; that's why he was drinking so much, and she had to go home and take care of him. She had left all her things here. She said she would be back to get them when he was better."

After mailing the letter, Ruth exchanged her return trip to Houston for a one-way ticket to Oklahoma City, paying the difference for the 467-mile trip. On Sunday, February 9, she checked into the YWCA in Oklahoma City as Lisa Wandernberg. For two nights she shared a room with an eighteen-year-old girl named Donna Sue Wilks.

Donna Sue Wilks had just taken a job with the telephone company in Oklahoma City. She had quit school the week before when the University of Oklahoma mailed home her grades to her parents. They were not good. Ruth stole Donna Sue Wilks' identification papers from her purse, which included baby photographs and her birth certificate, dated March 11, 1950. On Tuesday, February 11, she took a bus to Norman, a town of 35,000 known primarily as the site of the University of Oklahoma. A college town, any college town, appeared to Ruth to offer sanctuary, familiarity yet anonymity. She had lived most of her life as a student. She knew the role. She knew the part.

And by unreasoned fate, pure chance, Ruth had selected a sanctuary which could not have had more meaning for Billy Vessels. For the University of Oklahoma was his school. There, years before, Vessels had forever imprinted upon Oklahoma football fans the glories and triumphs of the ritualistic autumn violence at Owens Stadium.

Vessels' unforgotten fame lay recessed in the mind of John Mayberry that February. Vessels' sister, Bobby Jean, had taught Mayberry English in high school in Clairmont, Oklahoma. Mayberry's uncle, John Denbo, had married her. To Mayberry, she was never Mrs. John Denbo, but always "Billy Vessels' sister." She had died of an unsuspected congenital heart condition years before and Mayberry had attended the funeral. He remembered Billy Vessels, "my idol, the man I worshiped, standing there on the front porch at the funeral with his hands jammed in his pockets and he didn't talk to anyone." Mayberry had never seen him again.

Mayberry owned a big old rooming house at 739 Chautaugua Street on fraternity row in Norman. The neighbors included an assemblage of Theta Pi's, Kappa Kappa Gamma's, Delta Upsilon's, and Sigma Alpha Mu's. Mayberry's house, which had once belonged to a fraternity, provided inexpensive shelter for twenty students in seventeen rooms and one apartment. In keeping with the Cleveland County Housing Code, his roomers, mostly graduate students, shared four commodes and four showers in five bathrooms in a big three-story red brick home on the corner. In deference to Mayberry's age of thirty, a demarkation line of trustworthiness according to the caprice of the day, his tenants called him mister. Mr. Mayberry had purchased the home five years before for $34,500 and remodeled all but two rooms.

The cheapest room in the house, an unremodeled one just a few steps off a landing between the second and third floors, had just become vacant. He hung a rental sign outside. "Inquire Within."

It wasn't much of a room, ten by fourteen and a half feet, with a bed with a saggy mattress, a chest of drawers, coffee table, small bookcase and study desk, all painted black, and a single stainless-steel blue upholstered chair. Mayberry had painted the room blue and brought over from his own house a serviceable blue-gray rug which fit well, looked good and passed as carpeting. The purple-inked mimeographed "special notice" in the desk drawer reminded his tenants that "pictures, calendars or objects of any kind, shape or form will *not* be attached to the walls, ceiling or doors for any reason," and if so, "this constitutes damage." The room had a number. Number 13.

Mayberry, blue eyed, crew-cut, the genuinely eager salesman, noticed a girl at his rental sign. She looked like a student. She said she was. He asked if she wanted to see the room. She said she did. She was eager to take the room.

She noticed the room number.

"Are you suspicious," Mayberry asked. The girl grinned. "Do you want me to change it?"

"Well, no," she said. "That will not be necessary."

Mayberry thought she spoke with a distinct German accent. He asked where she was from.

She told him essentially what she would tell everyone else in Norman who asked. Her name was Donna Sue Wills. Ruth had changed the Wilks to Wills. She said she was from Edmond, Oklahoma. Her father was very strict. He was a fireman. He drank too much. She was an only child. Her mother was dead. She had to care for an invalid stepmother. Her stepmother had been paralyzed by meningitis for ten years. They were both from Germany. They always spoke German. She had no money. She needed a job, any job.

Never was this offered as an extemporaneous recitation. She merely answered questions, volunteering almost nothing.

"You certainly were in a captive situation," said Mayberry, "you being the only child and everything. It must have taken a lot of thought to leave."

Donna Sue Wills nodded. Mayberry changed the subject. He explained the rent payments. She must pay forty-five dollars for the first and last months of the semester; plus a thirty-dollar-deposit damage fee. That would be $120 in advance. She said she didn't have that much money. Could she pay the first month and the deposit fee? Seventy-five dollars? Mayberry accepted. She gave him eighty dollars. He gave her two dollars from his billfold and wrote an I.O.U. for the other three.

"Everybody liked her," he would say later. "She never scoffed at anything you would say. She called me John. 'John,' she said, 'I need a job. I can do anything, housekeeping, cooking.'" Mayberry's college roomers, dwelling in a communal society where everyone left his door unlocked and where the mail lay unsorted on the hallway newel post, quickly took note of the new girl with the German accent.

"Who is the new chick?" asked John Ray that first day when he spied her, as he put it, when he came "just bop-bop-bopping along." Ray, age eighteen, a classic of freshman self-confidence, slim, spectacled, bright by the standards of the composite entrance test, considered himself a "realist," a "philosopher," and a pretty good businessman. He had made $178 selling *Redbook*, the *Ladies' Home Journal,* and *Good Housekeeping* magazines the year before as a B-flat cornet player to pay for new uniforms for the Duncan High School band.

Landlord Mayberry was a little reluctant to introduce Ray. He had accepted him as a roomer because Ray's older sister, Beverly, a graduate student studying library science, lived upstairs. Mayberry had already had to speak to the lad about displaying on his window shade a nude John and Yoko Lennon record album.

"What girl?" Mayberry asked.

"The new chick," Ray said again.

"Oh," he conceded. "That's Donna Wills."

"When I knocked on her door and introduced myself I told her I'd be glad to help her get settled any way I could," said Ray. To his surprise, she called on him that evening. She said she needed sheets for her bed. Ray eventually would want to sell to the press the story of his gallantry for $500. He settled for $25. He was insulted when a newspaper rewrite man asked him if he was sleeping with her.

It was nothing like that at all. That first night she just "sat on the couch." "The lights are real low and I'm putting my head on her lap," Ray reminisced. "She was unhappy and mixed up. She said she had no one to talk to, no one to care for her, nowhere to go, no way to get there, and no job to make a living. She said, 'I'm going to starve.' So I made her some peanut butter sandwiches and she wolfed them down." She borrowed a pillow and sheets for her bed that evening and thanked her host profusely. "I tried to kiss her but she wouldn't let me," Ray said.

Donna, as he knew her, visited him in his room on four or five occasions. He had hung things by wires from the ceiling of his room: A coiled punk "incense burner," an ash tray, a Constitution of the United States imprinted on a lamp shade, and a psychedelic poster of a rock group, Canned Heat. A life-sized mat depicting Cupid and Psyche in embrace covered a dresser. "Greek mythology," Ray explained to Donna. He had intended to take her to a movie the second night but it rained hard. "So we listened to a record, the Mothers of Invention 'Freak Out,' 'Suzie Creamcheese.'" Ray also played for his date a Canned Heat rendition of "Fried Buggy" where the voice of Scott McKenzies began, "If you're going to San Francisco be sure to wear some flowers in your hair." "Donna told me she wanted to go to the Haight-Ashbury district where she could be a hippie. I told her not to. I'm a member of the Establishment, you know. I'm against Communism. She told me she had lost in love. Her father was a drunkard who wanted her to marry a nice German boy. She didn't want to and that's why she ran away from home." Ray kissed her twice before she departed. When he kissed her, she began to cry. "It shook me up."

Ray never quite realized he had encountered an older woman. "She told me she was eighteen and it was just one of those things.

It didn't quite fit and then it all smoothed out. Her wrists were very small. I could reach around them with my thumb and index finger." Donna, he said, had obligingly read his palms and deemed him fortunate in matters of the heart. "But she said I had overcome those traits by intellect."

Ray contemplated a romance until his Anglo-Saxon upbringing and heritage—small town Oklahoma, the Methodist Church, and the Republican party, not to dwell upon the therapeutic virtue of B-flat cornet playing, made him think twice. "A psych major upstairs, a veteran from Vietnam, told me, 'That girl is looking for a husband,'" said Ray. "She needed security and all that stuff. Wow! He really scared me. I wasn't afraid of her, I was afraid of the situation. It might have been a bad scene." Right then and there young Ray decided to be a friend.

In her role of poor little college girl, burdened by language, Ruth conveyed convincingly her one all-consuming need: employment. Her plight was soon known to the other roomers.

William Joseph Westerheide, twenty-three, matured in the chaos of combat in Vietnam, lived on the second floor and dated young Ray's older sister, Beverly, a dark-haired concerned young woman on a diet. "Donna spoke as if she thought everything out in German, then translated back to English," Westerheide said. Temporarily, he loaned her as a blanket a warm camouflaged lining from a poncho, issued by and unreturned to the 27th Regiment, Third Battalion, First Marine Division.

"I wondered how anyone could be dumped in this world and be so naïve. She was so scared and worried, not making enough money to live by, afraid of everything."

Among themselves, the ex-Marine and Beverly Ray began calling each other "Ma" and "Pa." Donna, an unquestioned eighteen, was their long-lost "illegitimate daughter." They searched the want ads for employment for her. Similarly, landlord Mayberry sought employment for his tenant. His wife unsuccessfully tried to find her work at the university.

In his paid-for Datsun sports car Joe Westerheide took her to a Howard Johnson's to apply as a waitress. "On the way back, she started to cry, as if the whole world had crushed her."

"She had hardly any clothes at all," said Beverly. Beverly owned a neutered male Siamese cat, Fuzzy Bug, and one day Fuzzy Bug scampered down the hallway, down the stairs, and took refuge in Donna's closet. Beverly retrieved the animal. "What clothes she had were all brand new. I wondered about that. How could she just be off the farm? Her clothes didn't look like a farm girl's clothes. She had a shrimp-colored miniskirt, not too short, a few flowered blouses, girl's jeans, pale blue bells, a pale blue sweater. But I didn't think much about it at the time."

On several occasions Donna visited Beverly's room.

"Oh, fish!" Donna exclaimed the first time. Beverly, unaware of her guest's oceanographical background, blithely exhibited her collection in a bubbling tank. "This one looks like he is catching the ich," said Beverly, uncertain of the species or ailment, if any. "Fuzzy Bug ate one," she said. Donna Sue Wills said nothing. If by nature, Beverly had been a woman of distrust and suspicion, rather than the slightly plump and congenial coed that she was, she might have recognized the telltale traces of the fugitive.

"She always took forever to answer her door. I never saw her without her fall on. I have a fall and I noticed hers. When she wanted to take a shower, she always had a towel piled on top of her head."

Most of the tenants believed Donna was enrolled at OU. Beverly knew better. She worked in an administration office and out of curiosity looked her up. "I couldn't figure it out. I thought maybe something was wrong with the records.

"She was so upset—and so frightened. I thought maybe she was younger than she said she was and that she had run away," Beverly said. "I offered to take her to a Catholic priest I knew. You know, she was Catholic, and Catholics have charities, and I thought a Catholic charity might help her.

"I picked up the telephone one day and dialed. She kept crying, 'No. No. No.' The line was busy. She told me her room felt just like a prison."

Through the want ads, dutifully clipped by John Ray, Donna Sue Wills eventually found employment as a carhop at a drive-in restaurant at 1808 North Lindsay Street in Norman.

Prophetically, the name of the restaurant was the Boomerang.

The Boomerang thrived on a college crowd clientele. On its marquee, a curving yellow boomerang sign, the management exhorted its patrons to "Support Your U.M.O.C." referring to a college-boy contest for "Ugly Man On Campus." The drive-in had a reputation for good cheap food and quick informal service.

The most expensive item on the wall menu, painted orange with a jumping kangaroo, was Number Three: "One Fourth Pound Hamburger with Chili and American Cheese, 75¢." The Boomerang's abundant trade had not gone unnoticed, and within a mile the competition had set in, a McDonald's, Taco Boy, a Pizza Hut, a Roy Roger's Roast Beef, and a Lum's. The Colonel Sander's Kentucky Fried Chicken, with its spiraling rooftop bucket, was right across the highway.

Lewis Armstrong, the manager of the Boomerang, hired Ruth on Monday, February 17. "She said she was taking some night courses at OU and could work in the afternoon. She was having some financial difficulty. She said she needed some way to feed herself. I was desperate for help and I said fine. I gave her a W-4 form to fill out. She filled out everything except the Social Security number. She said she would have it the next day."

The next day Donna Sue Wills took from her purse a worn and smudged Social Security card. Lewis Armstrong could see it had been folded three times. She read him the number 446-52-0643. He didn't see the name—nor the erasures and typing changes. She had borrowed John Ray's Sears, Roebuck and Company typewriter the night before and his instruction book, "Learn Touch Typing in Four Easy Lessons." It had taken one.

As a carhop, Ruth managed quite well. "She never lost money, never mixed up orders," said Armstrong, the manager. The owner, Robert Lehman, casually took note of the new help. "Just a sweet, innocent girl, very cute, long brunette hair and a baby face. She was very unassuming—meek, almost." As all carhops, Donna started at a dollar an hour plus tips.

Among the Boomerangs' daily clientele were two officers of the Norman City Police Department.

An FBI wanted poster for Ruth Eisemann-Schier, one of 275,000 distributed in federal buildings, post offices and police agencies across the land, had been thumbtacked to a station bulletin board. Neither officer recognized Ruth. Her only disguise was the fall hairpiece. She wore no make-up.

At the Boomerang, Armstrong kidded her about her accent. "I told her she sounded like Zsa Zsa Gabor—that same funny accent."

The rooming-house boarders would see Donna around campus as if walking from class to class. She told several tenants she was taking French, a language in which she was already fluent.

Nearly every evening Donna would walk over to the big red brick Student Union, find an empty chair in Beard Lounge, and watch the Huntley-Brinkley newscast.

In the lounge of the Student Union on Saturday, February 22, Ruth met an unusual young man named Arthur Halloran, a senior from Lawton, Oklahoma, majoring in business administration. She had been sitting beside an Indian exchange student and moved to a couch next to his. Later, after they had struck up a conversation, Ruth said she had moved because the Indian smelled bad. Halloran was twenty-six years old and compared to young John Ray, Ruth's first suitor, he was indeed a man of the world, having known previously several "bubble-headed" German women. To an interviewer some weeks later, Halloran would say that he was a private detective who had helped break up a 350-person dope ring, that he had polished off six karate experts who attacked him, and that there had been "five—no, excuse me—seven" attempts on his life, including somebody who shot at him across a theater. Some of his missions, he said, were so secret the police didn't know. He was safe from the underworld, he said, because of documents he had secreted in a safety deposit box.

Ruth, as Donna Wills, and Halloran hit things off fine. He found her "very warm," "affectionate," and possessing a "flawless body." They took up housekeeping after a fashion in his apartment. She made him thin crepes filled with jelly, and they washed their clothes in togetherness at the laundromat. He complained that she put in such small loads it cost him three or four times as much money as it should. They also had a dispute at a grocery store over whether to buy plain wieners or the special smoked ones that cost "five times as much." Halloran lived on a low budget. In his opinion she was extravagant.

Halloran, a student of ESP as well as the more prosaic pursuits in the OU business school, had a premonition about Donna. He felt she didn't really want to stay in Norman. Donna had applied for a job as a nurse's aide at the Central State Hospital and she seemed agitated over the procedures. He assured her everything was routine. Still, he felt that she would soon be leaving. She had mentioned California. When he told her about an older woman he was dating, Donna told him to keep on seeing her.

It was Mayberry, the landlord, who first suggested to Donna

that she apply for work at Central State Hospital, a mental institution for 1200 patients on the edge of Norman. He liked the girl. He told her she could make $2.45 an hour at the hospital. The hospital employed about a hundred and eighty students, most of whom worked 3 P.M. to 11 P.M. so they could attend the university.

Donna had applied on February 13, even before she received the carhop job. "Donna Sue Wills," she had printed in pencil on a standard application form in the almost sterile second-floor office of the personnel director, Mrs. Bea Campbell, a pleasant matronly woman. Ruth said her age was eighteen. Mrs. Campbell looked closely. "That was our minimum. I looked to make sure." She was sure.

Previous employment: "None," wrote the applicant. Any serious illnesses? Any mental illness? Any relatives employed at Central State Hospital? The answers were negative.

Assuming the altered identity of Donna Sue Wills, Ruth gave her birth date as March 11, 1950, Oklahoma City.

She said she had attended "Tulsa G School," and "Bishop McInnish H.S." She circled the "12" for grades completed.

The form had one other standard question: "Have you been charged with or convicted of any law violation other than traffic violation?" Again, the applicant printed, "No." A parenthetical notice declared: "Records will be checked."

The applicant impressed Mrs. Campbell. "We will probably notify you for an interview in a week or so." Ruth had listed her address as the rooming house and used John Ray's telephone number.

The notification came February 26. Could she be at the hospital the next day? Enthusiastic, eager, almost rhapsodic, she said she would.

Ruth Eisemann-Schier did not meet that day Dr. Hayden H. Donahue, the hospital superintendent. He was an imposing man. Thick, convex lenses distorted the appearance of his eyes, making him more owlish and awesome than his position as the budget-conscious treasurer of the American Psychiatric Association might suggest. In 1948 Dr. Donahue had cared for the mentally ill at a Veterans Hospital in Little Rock, Arkansas. During his tenure there a deranged man had wandered off. The wanderer did not know his own name. To the embarrassment of the Veterans Administration, no one could find him anywhere, the hospital, the police, his family. No one. About a year later Dr. Donahue moved to a new institution and position, supervisor of the Arkansas State Hospital. Geographically, it wasn't much of a move. "It was just across the Arkansas River. And there, making my rounds one day, I found him, my missing patient."

Right then Dr. Donahue decided it wouldn't happen again. He established a fingerprint-identification system, a practice since adopted elsewhere in institutions unconcerned with that "due process of law nonsense." Dr. Donahue, aware of the sensitiveness of the mentally ill, didn't confine the procedure. "I just said everybody. I didn't want to embarrass the patients, to pick on them."

If Ruth Eisemann-Schier felt a sudden tightening of the noose around her neck that day as she accompanied a small band of other applicants for a "purely routine" fingerprinting, it wasn't apparent. Logically, she might have excused herself to go to the rest room, professed illness, or in one fashion or another, fled. Possibly Dr. Donahue would have been notified. He might have deemed it suspicious. He might not have. The situation never arose. Ruth Eisemann-Schier submitted to the fingerprinting, saying nothing, realizing full well what could happen.

At 2 A.M. that very night, Ruth heard a knock on the door. Her caller wouldn't go away. He kept rapping.

Upstairs Joe Westerheide, as well as a few other night studiers, realized what was happening. A slightly inebriated scholar, the roomer in number 4, had selected 2 A.M. as the hour to express his longings for Miss Wills. He had an argument with his own girl. As spurned suitor, he carried a bottle of wine to Donna's door. Terrified, she declined.

"She was absolutely petrified," said Westerheide.

"I had never seen in my life anyone so frightened," said Beverly Hays. The next morning Donna said she had behaved foolishly. "Wasn't I silly?"

"I wondered how could anyone be so dumb," said Westerheide. "Here a guy wakes her at 2 A.M. with a bottle of wine and she doesn't know what is going on."

In the administration office of the State Mental Hospital that Friday, Saturday, Sunday and Monday, the fingerprint card of Donna Sue Wills lay in a box on a filing cabinet. There was no hurry. The clerk always waited until she had a good-sized stack before mailing them. Early Tuesday she stuck them into an envelope addressed to the Oklahoma Bureau of Investigation and left them for the mailman. For five days—Friday until Tuesday—Ruth Eisemann-Schier did nothing. Armstrong, the Boomerang manager, noticed her nervousness. "But I've never met a woman who wasn't nervous," he said, discarding the thought. "Aw, come on," he cajoled. "Smile for me, won't you?" She smiled.

On Tuesday Donna Sue Wills told Armstrong and Karen Larimore, another carhop, that she intended to go home to Edmond to visit her father. "An uncle," she said would meet her in Oklahoma City and drive her home Wednesday evening. She would be gone a few days. Could Karen give her a ride to the Greyhound Bus station in Norman after work Wednesday? Karen said, sure.

Little Miss Wills, everyone's friend, was on the run. She had waited until Wednesday—payday.

"She was awful anxious," said Armstrong. "I paid her about one o'clock and she wanted to know if she could run over to the Safeway and cash it. She wasn't off until 5 P.M. I told her to wait." She didn't wait. As Armstrong "took care of the spuds," his carhop hurriedly walked over to the supermarket, cashed her check, and returned. After the deduction for Social Security, she had sixty-two dollars for two weeks' work.

Earlier that Wednesday she had stuffed her worldly possessions into a drawstring red vinyl bag. She put the bag in the trunk of Karen's car along with a purse she had stolen from Julie Lynn Ferguson, a pert and bouncy coed of twenty-one. Julie Ferguson had used the rest room at the Boomerang the day before and laid her purse on a ledge. It had disappeared. Inside was a little flask containing Elan perfume, a Sheffield watch and a Vantage watch, and a package of vitamin-mineral pills for her puppy, a spitz, "Punkin," because "puppies are supposed to need vitamins and when it's your dog, vets can sell you anything." Her purse contained identification papers and her Oklahoma driver's license.

Strangely enough, Julie Ferguson knew a little something about the girl who stole her purse. "When she first arrived on campus several weeks ago, she came by the Yorkshire Apartments where I live. My roommate and I were looking for a third girl to move in. I didn't talk to her, but my roommate decided she didn't like her looks. She told her she had found another girl already," Julie Ferguson said.

Ruth Eisemann-Schier, alias Irma Hilga Sanchez, alias Donna Sue Wills, was about to become Julie Ferguson.

Before she left that morning, she cleaned out the dresser drawers in room 13, stripped the bed, neatly folded the bedding, and wrote three notes on scrap yellow paper.

One was to John Ray, the freshman. "Dear Johny," she wrote, spelling his name wrong, "I did not have time to wash your sheets. I am sorry. I leave some soap. Thanks for everything. Donna." Young Ray would eventually find his note under a small box of energized Oxydol.

To Joe Westerheide, she tucked a note into a paperback she had borrowed, *English for Everyone.* "Joe," she wrote. "I am so sorry I could not say goodby. I'll always be thankful to you! Donna."

The third note she left atop the bedding with the room key: "Please Mr. Mayberry, Return the blankets to Beverely and the sheets to Johny with an oceanful of thanks. I thank you all, from the bottom of my heart for being so nice to me, Sincerely, Donna."

At 1:30 P.M. at the Boomerang that day the telephone rang, and the owner, Robert Lehman, answered it. A male voice asked to speak to Donna Sue Wills. She had never received a call there before. Lehman had her paged and he overheard her conversation. "I will see you at seven o'clock," she said.

Much later some newsmen would attach great significance to this telephone call, suspecting that Ruth Eisemann-Schier had been contacted by a mysterious "flight pal."

The fact was that landlord Mayberry telephoned. He had not inspected the premises. He knew nothing of the notes. "But it was March 5 and she owed me March as well as the last unpaid month," he said. "I give all my tenants a five-day grace period. Her time was up. It was raining that morning and I had missed her. I asked her if she needed an umbrella. She said, 'No. I'll be back at 7 P.M. I'll see you then.'"

The two FBI cars reached the Central State Hospital in the early afternoon. Tom Puckett, the chief investigator for the Oklahoma State Bureau of Investigation, accompanied them. Dr. Donahue sat in the cafeteria for a late lunch. Had he hired Donna Sue Wills? Was she there? It took him a few minutes to check the records. The FBI asked for her address and within ten minutes agent Burns suspected the worst: She had run. There were the empty drawers, the good-by notes.

Agents hurriedly began asking questions. A roomer, Anthony Thomas DeMicco, a stocky black-haired young man, said Donna might be at the Boomerang. Would he please accompany them?

"Well," said DeMicco, "sure."

At five minutes after three o'clock March 5, 1969, agent Burns's car halted in the driveway of the Boomerang at a stop sign, bent previously by an errant motorist. It wasn't the proper parking place for drive-in service.

At the glass side door inside the Boomerang at the carhop counter, agent Burns saw a girl in orange tennis shoes, orange slacks, a white turtle-neck blouse, and a white vinyl coat with brass-plated buttons.

The girl looked up.

The car doors flew open and three men were on their feet. Wordlessly, the girl pushed open the door and walked out to meet them.

"Are you Donna Sue Wills?" agent Burns asked.

"Yes," the girl said.

"Are you Ruth Eisemann-Schier?" he asked.

"Yes."

He started to tell her she was under arrest. "We are from the Federal Bureau of Investigation," he began.

"Yes," the girl said. "I know."

Poor Sport

Ruth Eisemann-Schier confessed to the kidnaping of Barbara Mackle.

She talked freely of the crime from the time of her apprehension until well beyond March 19, 1969, when she wrote a letter to Robert Mackle. FBI agents questioned her for several days and she made a long formal statement which she modified, then remodified.

She made another two-part statement in the presence of her own lawyer in her native tongue, Spanish.

There was no third party to the crime. She and the man she knew as George Deacon—the two of them and they alone—committed the crime, she said, and the FBI, after analysis of its massive investigation, came to the same conclusion.

Most of Ruth's statements would be corroborated clearly and completely. Except for a distortion of her own role and a few errors in memory, she told the truth.

She cast herself as an innocent, helpless in her love for Krist, dominated by his will. He called her a "poor sport" and threatened her with ugly words, she said.

Her only concern, she professed, was Barbara. She wanted to crawl into the box and stay with Barbara the entire time, she said. George wouldn't let her. She was always "acting on his instructions."

From the Boomerang drive-in in Norman that Wednesday afternoon, FBI agents took Ruth to their headquarters in Oklahoma City. In hackneyed and appropriate terminology, the press would soon quote one unidentified source: "She is singing like a canary." She was.

Her demeanor, then as in the days ahead, alternated irregularly from distraught and profuse weeping to inappropriate giggling and a grin that can be described accurately as silly.

In the early evening hours agents took her before James L. Gullett, the United States Commissioner for the Western District of Oklahoma. While sobbing she munched chocolate-covered peppermints. Gullett set bail at $500,000. He postponed an identity hearing until 1:30 P.M. the next day, allowing how this was "no run-of-the-mill case." He announced he wanted to appoint a highly competent lawyer to represent her. He did. He appointed James H. Harrod, a former Oklahoma County attorney. During James Harrod's tenure as county prosecutor from 1961 to 1965, he broke open an Oklahoma Supreme Court scandal by taking testimony from N. S. Corn, a Supreme Court judge serving time in a federal prison. Harrod's investigation led to the removal of five other judges.

Attorney Harrod, responding like any good defense lawyer, wanted his client to remain silent. Ruth, high-strung, emotional, never involved previously in criminal matters, wanted to blurt out everything. Attorney Harrod soon filed a motion in a federal court asking that the FBI be prohibited from further interrogation while she was "under sedation and without her full mental capacity to respond." Ruth had been so upset a doctor gave her a tranquilizer and medication for her stomach.

The day after the arrest Attorney Harrod held up the identity hearing for ninety minutes. He demanded that the government provide a stenographer and it took a while to find one. He had interviewed his client for three hours and five minutes, and after all the crying and sobbing, he said, "I don't think the girl feels like she's done anything wrong. In her mind, she's only guilty of stealing that purse."

A standing-room-only crowd jammed into the commissioner's small hearing room, including seventeen young prep-school ladies from the Miller School For Girls. Ruth, seeing everyone looking at her, fidgeted and said, "It is terrible—all of the people, people against me and me, alone." She waited for the hearing in the privacy of the U. S. Marshal's office.

"I'm nearly dying," she said, nervously toying with a coat button.

The hearing was brief. Ruth, her face flushed and mottled, hung her head and big tears rolled down her cheeks and off her chin. They could be seen falling to the floor.

At the close of the hearing, Commissioner Gullett disclosed that the government was taking "extraordinary precautions" to keep Ruth from committing suicide.

The FBI had informed him of the uncertain nature of the death of Ruth's father. Furthermore, agents had interviewed scores of persons who knew her during their seventy-nine-day search for Ruth and one suitor had mentioned that Ruth once talked about taking her own life. The FBI was uncertain of the context. Was she kidding? Was it to intimidate him? No one wanted to take any chances. Ruth was held in a woman's jail ward with plenty of watchful company.

On March 14, a week later, Commissioner Gullett conducted a removal hearing necessary before Ruth could be transported east. The FBI had quietly requested that a nurse be present. The evidence would include the kidnaped Polaroid photograph of Barbara, and agent St. Pierre of Miami would read into the record the ransom note. Ruth had professed she had never seen it. The FBI believed her. Agents weren't certain how she would react.

When St. Pierre began to read, Ruth started sobbing. As he continued, she fainted. Gullett recessed the hearing temporarily. They laid her out on a court bench. The nurse gave her a whiff of ammonia.

Attorney Harrod said she would "stand mute" to the charges against her. He questioned the validity of the hearing because the government had only telegraphic copies of the warrants from Florida; the originals had not yet arrived. He protested the amount of bail. The commissioner told him that if he felt that the $500,000 was exorbitant or excessive, he could ask for a bond-reduction hearing. At the word "excessive," Ruth nodded her head vigorously, saying, "I believe, I believe." She dabbed at her eyes with Harold's handkerchief.

Two days later, March 16, Attorney Harrod consented to let his client make a confession in his presence. She wanted to. By this time she was willing to put more of the blame on Deacon.

Ruth had already made a full confession to agent William F. Beane who flew to Oklahoma City from Washington, D.C. the day of her apprehension. Agent Beane knew the case extremely well. He had worked in Miami during the crime and had since been transferred to the bureau's Kidnap Desk in Washington.

He had interviewed her extensively over the course of several days and extracted, in the opinion of the FBI, just about everything she knew in connection with the crime. Agent Beane had insisted that Ruth's statement be prepared in both Spanish and English. Ruth had carefully gone through the typed statement in both languages, modifying it repeatedly, penciling in changes and clarifications. She had done this twice.

In the end Attorney Harrod instructed his client not to sign it. In all probability, that would have made no difference. Harrod recognized clearly that the statement would be admissible at any trial. The FBI had been extremely careful in explaining to Ruth her rights, often and repeatedly, and she had signed waivers.

As it turned out, this statement was never released. In preparation for this book, Robert Mackle inquired of J. Edgar Hoover of its availability. Hoover replied courteously that policy prohibited the FBI from making it available until the case was finally adjudicated.

On that March 16, though, Attorney Harrod wanted his client to tell more about the mitigating circumstances of the crime in the hope that any difference between the confessions could be magnified in a courtroom. He also hoped to attack the translation.

The FBI, perfectly willing to let Ruth confess again in the presence of her attorney, consented. Consisting of thirty-one double-spaced typewritten pages, it eventually came to light publicly in Atlanta, Georgia. Attorney Harrod had mailed it to Ruth's new defense counsel there.

She made the statement in Spanish. An interpreter for the FBI translated it into English, using the standard police practice of capitalizing proper names.

As a confession of a principal in a major crime, it was an absorbing document. It was also a highly self-serving one:

I, RUTH EISEMANN-SCHIER, make the following statement voluntarily to JOHN W. BURNS and JIMMY D. CLOOS, both of whom have identified themselves to me as Special Agents of the Federal Bureau of Investigation and have exhibited their credentials to me. . . .

On September 23, 1968, while a student at the University of Miami Marine Institute, Miami, Florida, I participated with other students and researchers in a scientific cruise aboard the ship *Pillsbury*. . . . I fell in love with DEACON and we became inseparable companions. DEACON and I discussed our life's dreams which included, on his part, an intense desire to be wealthy. . . .

Upon return on October 7, 1968 . . . I saw his wife and one child right after leaving the ship. I wanted to observe his wife in order to see for myself the status of their marital relation . . . because I wanted to be certain I wouldn't create any unhappiness for this couple. . . . He had talked with his wife about a possible separation, inasmuch as they were incompatible. . . . Approximately two or three weeks after the cruise we considered running away together. I had decided to do this and to live with him without marrying him, since I could still tell my mother that I was single. He did not want to run away without sufficient financial resources, therefore we did not do it. . . .

He astutely outlined to me a plan which he thought would be successful in raising a considerable amount of money for both of us. This plan included the design and construction of a capsule-type box in which a prospective kidnap victim could be buried beneath the ground . . . I did not assist DEACON in the design or construction of this capsule, nor did I contribute financially . . . I specifically recall that on my 26th birthday, November 8, 1968, DEACON informed me that he had selected the person. At this time he did not furnish me with the person's name . . .

Sometime in early December, 1968, DEACON drove me by the residence of Mr. ROBERT F. MACKLE in Coral Gables, Florida. He pointed out the house to me as that of his prospective abduction person and identified her by name as BARBARA MACKLE. At this time I observed a man whom DEACON identified to me as Mr. ROBERT MACKLE in the yard speaking with a workman. . . .

On this occasion, I observed what appeared to me to be a light gray Lincoln automobile, which DEACON informed me was MACKLE's car. No other prospective persons were ever discussed between myself and DEACON.

Also, in early December, 1968, I first entered the trailer parked at the Marine Science Institute where DEACON was constructing the capsule. Because I was concerned for BARBARA, I climbed into the capsule and asked DEACON to close the lid, in order that I might know the type of feeling a person would experience while imprisoned in such a capsule. I asked GEORGE if he would let me sleep a whole night inside the box to convince myself the girl would be all right. GEORGE would not permit me to spend the night in the box; however, I did lie in the box with the lid closed for about an hour. It was a frightening experience, but in spite of everything, knowing she was an intelligent person, I convinced myself she would probably be all right . . .

After this experience I became very worried and decided that it might be best for me to withdraw from any participation in this abduction plot. . . . He would not let me do this, and told me that I knew too much, and besides which, he could not live without me. This discussion lasted about four hours, and with his intelligence and astuteness he made me understand that I could not escape from him. . . . DEACON told me that the principal reason he needed me was to take care of BARBARA MACKLE after she was abducted and en route to the burial location, because he could not watch BARBARA and drive the car at the same time.

I wish to explain at this time that I was very much in love with DEACON and I was prepared to do anything he asked of me . . . He told me that the best manner of proving my love for him was to stay with him and to help him with the project; because in spite of everything he was determined to carry it out. Since I was so worried about BARBARA, I understood that it would be best to resign myself and try to help BARBARA in every possible way that I could.

On an unrecalled date in early December, a few days before we left for Atlanta, I accompanied DEACON to downtown Miami where he purchased a Polaroid camera and two handie-talkie radios for use in the abduction plot. . . .

On the evening of December 11, 1968 . . . DEACON again drove me by the MACKLE residence and I observed him leave the car and place a small article beneath a palm adjacent to the MACKLE residence. He informed me that he hid the ransom note . . .

Upon arrival in the Atlanta, Georgia, area, I was very tired, restless and worried, and I urged DEACON to stop at the first opportunity so that we might get some sleep. He also was tired and it was agreed that we would stop. At approximately 12:15 A.M., December 14, 1968, we stopped at the Rodeway Inn Motel and immediately went to our room and retired. We parked the Volvo, with the box protruding from the rear, outside of our motel room. . . . Sometime during the day [December 14] DEACON and I stopped on the campus of Emory University. DEACON made two or three telephone calls to various offices on the campus inquiring as to the exact whereabouts of BARBARA MACKLE. Through these telephone calls he was successful in ascertaining that BARBARA MACKLE was temporarily residing at the Rodeway Inn Motel. This surprised and somewhat amazed us both since we had checked out of the Rodeway Inn earlier that morning.

Subsequent to the visit to the university we continued looking for a prospective burial location and eventually we arrived in a remote area in the vicinity of a small lake. We drove around the lake and got lost on one occasion. Ultimately DEACON selected a site to bury the box in a highly remote wooded area. He specifically selected the area in which the box was to be buried because he could drive the car into the wooded area immediately adjacent to the spot where he would dig the hole. This eliminated the necessity for carrying the heavy box for a long distance. Upon arrival at the burial site, DEACON slid the box out of the Volvo onto the ground. I assisted him in camouflaging the box with leaves and sticks. We did not dig a hole nor bury the box at this time. To the best of my memory, we dropped the box in this area late in the afternoon of

December 14, 1968. . . . We returned to the Atlanta area and checked into the Clermont Motor Inn Hotel. . . . DEACON made a telephone call to Mrs. ROBERT MACKLE at the Rodeway Inn. He did not identify himself but stated to her that he had a certified letter he would deliver to her. He explained to me that the purpose of this call was to verify the fact that Mrs. MACKLE and BARBARA were present at the Rodeway Inn.

On Sunday morning, December 15, 1968, DEACON and I returned to the remote area where we had placed the capsule the day before. DEACON began to dig the hole in which he was going to place the capsule. The digging was difficult for him and he complained that I wasn't helping him, so I attempted at one time to help him, but it was much too difficult for me and he had to dig the entire hole himself. No one was present at the time besides DEACON and myself. . . . DEACON completed digging the hole and placed the capsule therein. He was physically exhausted at this time. . . .

On Monday, DEACON . . . drove me to the dormitory where BARBARA MACKLE usually lived. He instructed me to go into the dormitory and make an inquiry at the room ordinarily occupied by BARBARA MACKLE. I was to go to BARBARA's room and determine if anyone was present. If either BARBARA or her roommate was present, I was to ask for the one not present, thereby covering my entry to the room. I located the room and found neither BARBARA nor her roommate, RAMSEY OWENS, present and I then returned to the car. He made me enter the dormitory to see if I could find some pretext to enter the room of BARBARA in the motel.

Sometime after leaving the university campus DEACON and I stopped at the Pancake House Restaurant at the Rodeway Inn for something to eat. While there he observed a uniformed policeman's cap and DEACON, for reasons known but to himself, decided to steal the officer's cap, which he did. Upon returning to our room at the Clermont, DEACON decided he would use the policeman's cap and by impersonating a police officer he could easily entice Mrs. MACKLE to open her motel room door at an early morning hour. He liked this idea but decided that policemen ordinarily do not wear beards and he, therefore, shaved off his beard.

At approximately 4:00 A.M. on December 17, 1968, DEACON

drove me to the Rodeway Inn, at which time DEACON was wearing a yellow sweater and the policeman's cap . . . He was successful in enticing Mrs. MACKLE to open the door and he immediately lunged in and I followed. . . . DEACON had instructed me while en route to the burial site to apply a chloroformed cloth to BARBARA MACKLE's face but in my excitement and due to my nervousness, I hastily got into the car and sat on the chloroform-soaked cloth. The chloroform penetrated the seat of my clothing and inflicted a considerable burning sensation to my buttocks. This caused me to squirm in the seat . . . and I was so frightened at the time . . . I was badly burned in the buttocks area and my skin is still marked from this burn.

When we arrived at the burial . . . I was so concerned for the well-being of BARBARA that I desired to enter the capsule with BARBARA and actually remain with her until DEACON could effect the ransom procedure and return with the ransom money. I realized the box was not large enough for both of us because I entered the capsule when I forgot the siphon tube she would use to drink water while inside the capsule; so I pleaded with DEACON to let me remain at the burial location with BARBARA until DEACON obtained the ransom money and returned to pick me up. . . . DEACON would not permit me to follow this course of action and instructed me to accompany him. . . .

To my knowledge, no provision of any kind was made which would permit the victim to escape from the capsule in the event DEACON and myself had been killed in an automobile accident or some similar tragedy. Therefore, I pleaded with GEORGE to let me stay with BARBARA and he could buy milk and some apples for me and I could stay in the woods.

The only concern DEACON had displayed about the welfare of BARBARA after placing her in the capsule had been in making several telephone calls prior to digging the hole so he could get detailed weather information to be sure that no heavy rains were imminent which might result in the flooding of the capsule at the burial location. I would like to point out that during this entire ordeal, BARBARA MACKLE was very well behaved, quiet and cooperative. She at no time cried out and appeared to remain calm throughout the ordeal.

The lid to the capsule was then closed and I held a light while DEACON placed the screws through the lid and screwed them into the body of the capsule, securing the lid. At this point DEACON and I began covering the capsule with soil approximately twelve inches in depth. When the capsule was completely covered we again camouflaged it with leaves and sticks. After camouflaging the capsule, we returned to the Volvo station wagon, at which time DEACON told me he did not want me to be seen in the car so I lay down on the floor of the car between the front and rear seats and he covered me with a canvas tarpaulin. . . . I remained there crying intermittently until arrival at Jacksonville. . . . It was I who requested DEACON to return to Miami by way of Jacksonville since I wanted to mail some post cards from there to various friends in Miami for the purpose of confirming to them that I did, in fact, arrive.

. . . On December 18 . . . GEORGE was very angry with me, saying that I was a "poor sport" and that I was not cooperating with him. From that moment he was very abrupt with me and did not explain anything that he was doing. I was feeling very bad, like a robot, and I was trying to be as silent as possible, just doing what he told me to do. . . .

I do not know when the Polaroid photograph of BARBARA MACKLE was mailed to the MACKLE residence as I did not mail the envelope. I have a vague recollection that DEACON used one of the stamps I had purchased in Jacksonville for the post cards . . .

At about 3:00 or 4:00 P.M. DEACON was complaining of a bad skin rash in his groin area. He decided to visit a dermatologist for medication and did so in Coral Gables . . .

. . . After selling the [U-Haul] trailer, DEACON and I proceeded to an Italian restaurant near the shop where the trailer was sold. He ate a good dinner but due to my nervous condition, I was unable to eat at all.

During the evening of December 18, 1968, I accompanied DEACON to the Miami International Airport where he purchased two airline tickets to Chicago in the name of SCHULTZ. I recall that these tickets were paid for with two one hundred dollar bills which I provided to him. . . .

After having left the Miami International Airport, DEACON drove to the area of Virginia Key where the Marine Science Institute maintains some boats and other facilities. I walked along the beach to some bathhouses which I entered and changed my clothing. I then returned to the car and pretended to be straightening out the luggage therein while DEACON was preparing a small outboard motorboat . . . I was really watching for the guard as instructed by DEACON to make sure that DEACON was not interrupted . . . DEACON returned to the car and wanted me to drive it back to the area of the Fair Island Bridge and when I told him I couldn't do it, he tried to give me a quick driving lesson which was unsuccessful. He thereafter took me to the Fair Island Bridge . . . I waited for him in the middle of the Fair Island Bridge and observed the boat come down under the bridge and where he beached it on Fair Island just south of the bridge. I went to join him and he had a bag containing some articles and a box which he wished to carry back toward the center of the Fair Island Bridge. The time was about 1:00 A.M. The box we carried to the center of the bridge was one of the boxes used by the Marine Science Institute to carry gear on their cruises. It was constructed of wood with a top and had rope handles on each end. DEACON had installed a light of some type on top of the box to which he had attached a long coil of wire permitting him to flash this light from a considerable distance away. On the south side of the bridge in about the center he held the box over the railing and a rope was attached thereto which he put around my neck and asked me to hold the box while he attached it to the bridge with a delicate wire. He cautioned me to be careful since if I dropped the box, I would probably go with it into the water. He explained that the box would be attached in such a way that when the additional weight of the ransom money was placed therein, it would automatically fall from the bridge to the water where DEACON would recover it in some manner. Once he had the box attached to the bridge he asked me to return to the Miami side of the bridge and watch while he tested the light. Once again he tried to make me feel that I was in his hands and I didn't have any will power. . . . He was threatening me with ugly words.

I observed as the light flashed several times and returned to the center of the bridge. DEACON instructed me to walk now to my vantage point behind a Chinese pagoda which he had shown to me earlier in the day. I had with me my binoculars and handie-talkie radio. This was the last time I have seen GEORGE DEACON to this day. My assignment was to act as a lookout and to inform DEACON by radio when Mr. MACKLE appeared in the area in his Lincoln automobile. I was also instructed to inform him of any impending dangers, such as a police vehicle or helicopter in the area. He was very conscious and fearful of helicopters.

I remained at this position until I saw the car of Mr. MACKLE leave the area. I made only one radio transmission to DEACON, and that was to inform him that I had observed Mr. MACKLE's Lincoln approaching the area of the Fair Island Bridge. . . .

I had been at this vantage point for several hours and I had become frightened for fear that I might have been observed . . . While proceeding to the Florida Bible College, I found myself in a dense thicket, as a result of which my blue jeans and shoes became very dirty and torn. I decided while in this thicket to abandon the handie-talkie and the binoculars, which I did. As I approached the Bible College, I crawled underneath of an abandoned car . . . I used a protruding piece of steel to cut off the legs of my blue jeans and the sleeves of my shirt so I would not look so dirty. I crawled out from under the car and went to the Bible College where I abandoned my shoes, shirt sleeves and pant legs in the trash barrels . . . At this point I did not know whether or not DEACON was successful in collecting the ransom money and I considered the possibility that he had run out on me since we had argued earlier. . . .

After waiting more than a reasonable amount of time, I took it upon myself to depart . . . and I walked towards the Coconut Grove section of Miami. En route I looked around the residential areas in hope of finding some clothes which I could use on a clothesline, but was unable to do so. I did, however, find an open garage door. I entered the garage and located a brown flowered curtain which I took and wrapped around myself and continued my walk to Coconut Grove.

I had $80 in cash on my person and went to a Five and Ten Cent store in Coconut Grove where I purchased some clothing, including shoes and a small purse. I thereafter went to a nearby gas station, changed clothes, and cleaned myself up a bit. I took a taxi to the Greyhound Bus Terminal in downtown Miami. I . . . decided to take a bus to Houston, Texas, since a bus was leaving in a few hours and I could afford the fare and I knew there were many Spanish speaking people in Houston among whom I might not be noticed so easily. While waiting for the bus I walked a few blocks to a nearby library. . . .

I specifically remember this trip since a fellow passenger on the bus suffered a heart attack . . .

I would like to repeat that I left Miami in the afternoon of December 19, 1968. DEACON had no knowledge of my means of departure or my whereabouts at any time since that date. . . .

I certify that the content of these pages is true and correct to the best of my knowledge.

/s/ RUTH EISEMANN-SCHIER

DATE March 16, 69

TIME 10:37 P.M.

To a highly bizarre crime, Ruth's account added a few more peculiar touches, some of them almost laughable.

Where had she hidden during the first ransom drop? A Chinese pagoda, of all places. Actually, Ruth had hidden in the Japanese-styled garden of Gunther Steen, a German-born plastics executive who had built a bridge, pond, and hung potted orchids from a sea grape tree in front of the oriental doors of his home at 1734 South Bayshore Lane—a block from Fair Isle Street. One might wonder if she had had to stand and wait because her buttocks were so sore she couldn't sit down.

And what had the kidnaper done upon return to Miami? He had seen a family doctor about jock itch.

The incongruity extended to Krist's meticulous planning. He had devised an incredibly complex scuba-diving method of retrieving the ransom money, supposedly submerged in Biscayne Bay in a lidded box attached to Fair Isle Causeway—after rigging up a flashing light and apparently lining the interior of the box with metal to foil electronic surveillance. And what had he done just prior to his expected performance of this feat? He had tried to give his partner in crime a quickie driving lesson.

Her inability to drive from the marine lab, where Krist stole the boat, to her lookout post in the Chinese pagoda, may have contributed to the late 3:47 A.M. call to the Mackle residence. Krist had to drive her to the pagoda, park the Volvo near the entrance to Rickenbacker Causeway, then return to the lab to get the boat. From the Volvo to the marine lab it was three and a half miles.

How did he get there? Quite probably, he walked. He may have had to. The last bus on the B-2 run had made its final 7:30 P.M. trip hours before. Conceivably, Krist could have hitched a ride. Key Biscayne residents often picked up marine lab students at the tollgate after the buses stopped. Krist might have caught a taxi. Scrutinizing radio dispatches of all companies, the FBI learned a call for a cab had been made late that night from a public phone booth at a nearby Holiday Inn. No cab driver, however, acknowledged picking up the fare. A walk seemed a logical explanation.

Months before Ruth's apprehension, in the days immediately after Krist's capture, the Bureau had pretty much ruled out any third-person involvement in the crime. The two policemen, the FBI believed, saw Krist twice, not two persons. By their own accounts, the officers had glimpsed the figures separately and at different times—not together—by the light of a street lamp from a distance of about 600 feet during a pursuit situation.

Ruth's confession pointed up another oddity. Although Ruth and Krist had missed each other by six hours at their rendezvous at the Florida Bible College, they were directly across the street from each other in downtown Miami on Thursday afternoon, December 19, and didn't know it. Krist was in the office of Northwest Orient Airlines cashing in Ruth's ticket at the same time she sat in the reading room of the Dade County Public Library.

Some portions of Ruth's confession, however, appeared to be pure embroidery upon the truth. She claimed that Krist wouldn't trust her with the rifle and that he made her go get the supplies at the burial site. Barbara was certain that Ruth did not leave her. Ruth asserted that she had secretly promised Barbara that she would stay with her. Barbara said she did not.

Ruth's claim that she wanted to crawl inside the box and remain with Barbara amounted to nonsense. Krist had erupted in anger at the site and ordered Ruth to find the water-siphon hose for Barbara. Ruth had climbed in most reluctantly and scrambled out quickly.

In the conversation with Ruth Eisemann-Schier, one question kept coming back again and again: If Ruth was so concerned about Barbara, Barbara's welfare, Barbara's very survival, why had she not made any attempt to tell anyone where Barbara could be found?

Thirty-six hours had elapsed between the time Ruth and Krist were separated. To be sure, Ruth had used most of that time in flight on a Greyhound bus. Yet she had done nothing.

Asked why, Ruth burst into tears.

There was no answer.

My Only Sin

Two days after Ruth Eisemann-Schier made her last confession in Spanish, she wrote a letter to Robert Mackle from a jail cell in Atlanta, Georgia. She had been transferred there to await trial.

She wrote in a stilted English, her fourth and most difficult language, and her writing reflected her ineptitude in grammar and punctuation:

"Sir, I am writing to you with tears in my eyes and with all my heart I am pleasing you Mercy and Forgeaveness.

"You can't imagined how I have suffered through all this Tragedy and how much I have fight to avoided it!

"Believe me Sir I tryed with all my power to protect your daughter and I did all what I could to help her. I was never interested and your money and I did not conspired against you. My only Sin, if you Could described as a Sin is to love with all my being to a Man, who I did not know had a terrible trauma. . . .

"I don't know if He has realy love me or if as the FBI agents told me, had only used me and have take adventage of my love and my person, I am not God to judge him, and after all what I have suffered I still love him, that's why I am asking you Mercy, not only for me but also for him, He is so young and intelligent and I don't think he knew exactly what he was doing, He was posses by rebelion feelings He developed in being in a Prison before . . ."

By the time Ruth contacted the Mackle family—not to inform them of Barbara's whereabouts but to beg forgiveness for herself and her lover—the state of Georgia and the United States Department of Justice had reached accord on prosecution.

Initially, even before the capture of Krist, William A. Meadows, Jr., United States Attorney for the Southern District of Florida, had authorized the filing of charges. On December 19, 1968, he charged George Deacon and Ruth Eisemann-Schier with con-

spiracy to violate the federal kidnaping statute, the Lindbergh
Law.

Congress enacted the law in 1932, the year of the most famous
kidnaping in America. Charles A. Lindberg, renowned for his
flight across the Atlantic in the flimsy Spirit of St. Louis, paid
$50,000 in ransom through an intermediary after the abduction of
his twenty-month-old son from his crib in Hopewell, New Jersey,
on March 1, 1932. His child's battered body was found May 12,
1932. Bruno Richard Hauptmann, an immigrant German carpen-
ter, was arrested for the crime September 19, 1934. Police recovered
some of the money from a hidden compartment in Hauptmann's
garage. He was charged with murder, convicted, and executed on
April 3, 1936.

The Mackle kidnaping, however, lacked one essential factor for
prosecution of the federal statute. Barbara had not been taken
across a state line.

The Department of Justice in Washington felt that the facts
warranted an initial prosecution for kidnaping, not for anything
else, and that only Georgia could properly try Krist and Ruth for
kidnaping; the federal government could not.

The federal government could—and did—file other charges
against Krist and Ruth. As United States Attorney, Meadows asked
that United States Commissioner Swan dismiss the original charge
on December 23, 1968. He filed new charges that they had violated
the federal extortion statute as well as a law against interstate
transportation in aid of racketeering.

The telephone call from Atlanta to Miami in connection with the
kidnaping comprises one count; Barbara's photograph mailed
in extortion another count, and the travel to Georgia and back to
Florida constituted two more counts. In all, conviction could mean
sixty years imprisonment. These charges were held in abeyance,
depending upon what happened in Georgia.

On January 13, 1969, a grand jury in DeKalb County, Georgia,
the scene of the abduction, indicted both Krist and Ruth for kidnaping for ransom. Conviction there meant either life imprisonment
or death in the electric chair. There was no other choice. Superior
Court Judge H. O. Hubert, Jr., issued a writ requiring the U. S.
Attorney in Miami to produce Krist for trial. Meadows honored
the request, ordering U.S. marshals to deliver Krist to the Fulton
County Jail in Atlanta.

Krist learned of his impending departure late Friday night, January 24, 1969, only a few hours before he was to leave. He became agitated. He began pacing his cell. The federal government was relinquishing control. Soon he would be in the hands of the Georgia authorities and the prospect did not appeal to him. He knew full well he could be electrocuted in Georgia. He also knew that life in a federal penitentiary probably would be far more tolerable than life in a Georgia prison. One of the FBI agents who saw him that night thought Krist came within a fraction of making a full confession in the hope that the federal government would retain jurisdiction. Krist, agonizing, decided finally to take his chances on a death sentence rather than confess. U.S. marshals arrived for him shortly before midnight. In his best wild-West bravado, Krist said, "I never thought I'd see the FBI pull the riders-in-the-night bit."

In Decatur, Georgia, the county seat for DeKalb County, Judge Hubert appointed two experienced criminal lawyers to represent Krist, James R. Venable and Mobley Childs, and on March 7, two days after Ruth's capture in Oklahoma, Krist stood for the first time in a courtroom. He had grown back his black bushy beard. Krist said nothing. His lawyers pleaded him not guilty, claiming he was mentally deranged and unable to assist in his defense. They petitioned Judge Hubert for a sanity hearing and they also asked that he be tried separately from Ruth. Judge Hubert granted both motions. He ordered Krist examined psychiatrically and set April 21 for a sanity hearing. Should he be found competent at the time, said the judge, trial would start May 19. Things were moving right along.

Judge Hubert appointed Dr. Merton B. Berger, a Peachtree Street psychiatrist considered one of Atlanta's finest. Dr. Berger found his subject fascinating and his report to the court reflected this:

"In accordance with Court Order ⌗10425 dated March 10, 1969, I performed a psychiatric examination on the above-named on March 11, 1969, March 12, 1969, and March 14, 1969. I spent approximately two hours each day performing this examination.

"Mr. Krist's mood and attitude varied in each of the three examining sessions. At times he cooperated readily and answered the questions directly, but at other times made it quite clear that he had no wish to cooperate and withheld data. During the time of the first examination he stated, 'I don't know why I should give anyone any more ammunition against me than they already have. I don't see why I should confide in a psychiatrist who is going to testify against me. I don't wish to participate in this farce. I wish to terminate this session.' At another time during the first interview he stated, 'You can't establish my competency or incompetency without my cooperation so why should I cooperate? You are not going to do it so you just might as well give up.' In the second two sessions I found Mr. Krist more willing to answer questions directly and he cooperated reasonably well with the mental statute examination.

"Throughout the entire three interviews he delivered lengthy discourses regarding his opinion of the law and the judicial process as it exists. 'The law is unjust in its conception and its application. It doesn't work. It's mechanically unsound. It is bound to disintegrate and fall apart. It's very poorly conceived. It declares some people able to take life and for others it's a crime. It sets up a social caste system and a moral system founded in power forces working for their own good. The system has basic hypocrisies. Superiority by itself doesn't permit you to cope with the Phillistines and overcome them with the jaw-bone of an ass like Samson did, so what it boils down to is that they've got the rule book and the enforcement capability.' During the second session he stated, 'I began to observe a number of years ago that power and money are the only things that count.' He then went on to describe an episode when he was 13 or 14 years old when he was at home all alone while his parents were out in a fishing boat and he suffered an attack of appendicitis. He described ten days when he was unable to eat or care for himself and had to lie in his own excrement. When he regained some of his strength he stated that he went to the general store in the community to get something to eat. The store was owned by a Mr. Freeman who informed Mr. Krist that his parents had overdrawn their account by $300 and, therefore, he could extend Mr. Krist no further credit, 'so later I went back to Freeman's store and splashed it with gasoline and burned it down to the ground.' He states that this experience convinced him that if he was ever to be secure and safe it would require money because he feels that money and power are the most important forces in life today.

"During the second interview I tried to establish whether Mr.

Krist was aware of the charges against him and he stated, 'I won't dignify this interview by even mentioning what I'm being charged with. It's beneath my dignity.' He then went on to state that he has absolutely no confidence in his legal counsel, stating that he would prefer to have a lawyer who is 'not a member of the establishment.' At another point during the second interview Mr. Krist discussed morality and stated, 'The current system of morality doesn't hinder me. It's as farcical as this examination. I have no misapprehensions about our system of morality. There is no one or no thing that exists that can determine whether my activities were justified.' At other times during the interview Mr. Krist stated, 'I've been charged with violating the integrity of the system.' At another time he stated, 'I have offended the cartel that runs this country in case you don't know it.' At other points he stated, 'I'm in jail now simply because I was overpowered. I wasn't as ruthless as I should have been. I should have fought fire with fire.' Another statement he made was, 'My only mistake was a minor miscalculation of the concentration of forces.' At still another point he stated, 'The crime I am accused of is seeking to have what other people have, but losing out in the completion. It's a question of power. You can't ever be wrong if you are rich or have power.' At still another point he stated, 'I'm going to be in court because I'm intrinsically a threat to their security.'

"I found that Mr. Krist did have a keen understanding and comprehension of the court proceedings, including the principles involved, possible verdicts, the penalties, and certainly his legal rights. He did not hesitate to remind me that he has an option as to whether or not he would answer any question I asked and reminded me that he did not have to comment in any way regarding the crime for which he is being charged. . . .

"He showed no signs of being out of touch with reality. He was oriented to time, place, and person with no difficulty in his sensorial state. His thinking was clear and his productions were coherent. He denied ever having had hallucinations. He was able to comprehend without difficulty whatever questions I asked him and seemed to enjoy engaging in philosophical debate with me rather than answering some questions directly. I found this man to have a very keen and retentive mind, and based on the areas he was willing to discuss with me, I would gauge his I.Q. to be, if not at the genius level, then certainly in the near genius category. Mr. Krist seems quite well aware of his mental capabilities, stating, 'I am a superior human being. I've never found anyone who could match me in my field or at my level. It's due to genetics. It's an offshoot of biologic sports.' I found Mr. Krist to be conversant and expert in such areas as physics, crystal growth, X-ray diffraction, thermodynamics, electronics, some aspects of biochemistry, and history. For instance, he could speak authoritatively on such physical concepts as absolute temperature, and when I asked him to define absolute temperature, he gave the figure as 273.1642 degrees below zero centigrade. I was not able to check the correctness of this figure beyond the second decimal point, but the World Book Encyclopedia gives this figure as 273.15 degrees centigrade below zero. Mr. Krist was also able to talk about desoxyribosenucleic acid. He was also able to tell me who discovered penicillin and how Roentgen discovered X ray and the contribution of the Curies regarding radiation. He also talked about quantum theory and was able to give Einstein's formula concerning the relationship between energy and mass. When asked to give the speed of light he stated that it was 186,242 miles per second. According to the World Book Encyclopedia the figure given there is 186,282 miles per second. When asked to give the speed of sound he stated that it was 1130 feet per second and, according to the World Book Encyclopedia, it is 1100 feet per second. He was able to comment on Dante's *Inferno*. He knew the author of *Paradise Lost* and the author of *Don Quixote*. When asked who wrote the *Odyssey*, he stated Homer, and he also went on to state that Homer was the author of the *Iliad*. When I asked Mr. Krist to define hieroglyphic he stated, 'It was something found on the Rosetta Stone. This stone was found in the ruins of Alexandria and had writing on it in Roman, Sanskrit, and Egyptian.' I then asked Mr. Krist to discuss mythology with me, and he mentioned that his favorite god was Thor whom he described as a Norse god. 'He was cool. When he felt things weren't going right, he picked up his hammer and blew the shit out of it.' He then was able to discuss the Valkyries, stating that these were 'female Brunhilde types who took people off to Valhalla.' He was able to discuss with me the composer Wagner, and then took delight in discussing his liking for chess and the strategy of playing chess, stating, 'It's like personal combat on a board. When you kill off all the knights and pawns there's no blood on the floor.' He was able to discuss logic in terms of Aristotle's concepts and then went on to define both deductive and inductive reasoning. He also had an understanding of Socrates, stating, 'His basic contribution was to teach us how to die with dignity. They gave him a choice of dying, either being beaten to death versus drinking a poisonous substance derived from the bark of the hemlock. This was a sulphurous substance.' He went on to talk about the Sophists, describing them as 'priests who wandered around for a certain amount of money and would prove or disprove things. They were connected with Hellenic civilization.' He then talked about ancient Roman history and he was quite conversant in this area as well. I asked him who Caligula was and he described him as a Roman Emperor in about 45 A.D. and stated, 'His biggest contribution was killing off a bunch of people who professed to be pacifists. He preceded Tiberius. He fed Christians to the lions.' When I asked him how he became so conversant with ancient Roman history, he stated that he had read *The Rise and Fall of the Roman Empire* by Gibbons, stating that he had read all twenty-six volumes.

"His affect was labile and appropriate. He had an excellent capacity to abstract proverbs and in general I would say that the examination, including the mental status, showed no evidence of psychosis or any other severe or disabling mental illness.

"In my opinion this man has sufficient capacity to comprehend the nature and object of the legal proceedings in which he will be involved, and he is very well aware of his own position in relation to these proceedings. Further, he is able to advise his counsel rationally in the preparation and implementation of his own defense.

"Diagnostically he can be classified as having a sociopathic character disorder with no evidence of psychosis.

"Thank you for allowing me to evaluate this very interesting patient."

Dr. Berger submitted his report to Judge Hubert on March 22. In those days of March, Krist talked freely about his past, and Ray Moore, Atlanta's best-known television newscaster, took full advantage of it. Moore knew Krist's lawyer, Jimmy Venable.

"Your client," Moore told Venable, "has been depicted as a black impersonal beast. Why don't you let me interview him on film?

Let's see if we can't flesh him out. Show people he talks, he breathes, he thinks."

Venable figured he didn't have much to lose.

The newscaster found Krist articulate and willing to make six two-minute film presentations for use on WAGA-TV Channel 5. They could make them all at one time for use later over six nights. Moore had his cameraman roll in a color camera, and Krist, the bearded kidnaper, seemingly at ease, commenced his recitation in the best manner of the TV talk shows.

He chatted amiably of his childhood, relating how he hit his baby sitter in the solar plexus with a kitchen pot and fired a shotgun at his big brother. "I missed, you know. It was a big shotgun and it sort of overbalanced. It threw me right on my *gluteus maximus,* which is a kind word for your posterior."

Speaking extemporaneously, he timed his speeches to the second, one reel after the other, explaining how he dynamited a school-yard as a boy, led a posse into a train tunnel, and bluffed his way into the Massachusetts Institute of Technology.

"I served quite a bit of time for justifiable reasons. My total amount of time in prison is about four and one half years. However there was one time when I served—or almost served a five-year stretch for something I didn't do. In California I was committed to the Deuel Vocational Institution for stealing a car—I really didn't feel that five years in prison was justified by a lousy car.

"So I contrived to cut the bars out of my cell in the middle of the night and go over a fence. The man who was in the room with me also went over the fence, not at my bidding, however. And he was killed in the process. I have often wondered about the mentality of a society which allows some people to kill and be paid for it. In California, for instance, a guard that shoots an inmate going over the wall gets a one week leave and fifty dollars for the effort that he went through. Well, it is hard for me to understand that. Earl died that night and I remember the bullet hitting his side. It sounded as if someone had slapped a watermelon."

And then, dramatically, Krist added, "I still hear that sound an awful lot sometimes. Especially when I sleep. I can almost feel it hitting me."

He paused, believing newscaster Moore had ceased to film the sequence.

"Now, boy, if that isn't a tear-jerker, I don't know what the hell is," he said.

Krist's televised commercials for himself might not have been construed everywhere as helpful to his cause. He certainly did not look like a crazy man, unable to help in his own defense.

The date for the sanity hearing was approaching. Krist was aware that the psychiatrists would deem him fit to stand trial.

On March 21, presumably to prove something, Krist stopped eating. "I asked him why," said DeKalb County Sheriff J. Lamar Martin, "and he told me, 'You're not going to poison me.'"

"He sits there naked most of the time, writing on a pad with a pencil," said the sheriff. "He never lets us see what he has written. He doesn't talk much."

Krist's fast was not complete. For a while he drank two gallons of water daily, and after two weeks one of the guards, Thomas Blaylock, described Krist as "still flabby."

"Every morning we offer him fresh biscuits, fried bacon and toast and jelly. We put it right under his nose," said Sheriff Martin during the second week of the fast. "I think it is really getting to him."

If it did, Krist did not show it. The sheriff, increasingly concerned, offered to bring in canned food himself, take a can opener inside Krist's cell, and "let him have it right there. So he could see it wasn't poisoned." Krist declined.

"I think his hunger strike is just a way to get us to take him to a hospital—or a more escapable place," said the sheriff during the third week. "We'll turn the jail into a hospital first." The sheriff offered Krist "the finest steak in town" if he would end his hunger strike.

"If you let me go get it," Krist countered.

Idly almost, Krist one day threatened to stick one foot in a commode and his finger in a recessed electrical socket. "It would save the state the expense of electrocution," he said.

Workmen soon invaded his cell to fasten a metal plate over the electrical outlet. They also installed a metal plate over an exposed rod in the ceiling. There was no way. Or so they thought. The guards watched him around the clock.

The only place Krist could not be seen in his cell was a shower stall and he would take three or four showers a day.

On one occasion he walked out of the shower stall with a pair of wet socks knotted tightly around his neck.

The guard yelled for help, a jailer hurriedly unlocked the cell door, and they charged in.

"It is impossible to choke yourself to death," Krist proclaimed.

During the fourth week of his fast, Krist stopped drinking water, and on April 22 he collapsed. By court order a doctor administered glucose intravenously.

Semiconscious, Krist consented—until the doctor told him that he also intended to feed him by inserting a tube into his nose. The doctor had taken the precaution to have him strapped to his bed. Prior to the forced feeding, the doctor administered an injection to calm him.

Krist asked if he couldn't please go to the bathroom first. He was allowed up. He promptly dropped to the floor and frantically began doing push-ups. The doctor and jailers watched in awe.

"Now it [the drug] won't take effect," Krist announced gleefully. He was right. It didn't.

To avoid a forced feeding, Krist agreed to start eating. His first meal consisted of a bite of chicken, two beans, a few forkfuls of potatoes, and a pinch of bread. He said he had fulfilled his promise. His fast had brought his weight down to a reasonable 170 pounds.

On the day prior to the scheduled sanity hearing, Krist's lawyers withdrew their plea. They decided they could raise the issue of insanity in the course of the trial if they wanted to. They asked the court to appoint another psychiatrist and a psychologist of the defense's choice to examine Krist. Judge Hubert granted the motion. Krist's trial would go ahead as scheduled, May 19.

For all practical purposes, lawyers Venable and Mobley represented Krist as a charity case. For the defense of a capital crime, the state of Georgia would pay them the sum of $500. They could divide it.

When his bond had been set at $500,000 months before, Krist had acknowledged his financial plight. He turned to Inspector Shroder and said, "I had that much twice the past few days—and dropped it."

Now he had only a partial pay check from the University of Miami, which had terminated his services the day it learned of his role in the kidnaping, and in California his wife Carmen wanted that.

The university had sent him the wrong amount of money, Carmen declared. "Gary told his lawyer to send it back with a snotty letter telling him they owed him $600—not $400—and he wanted to be paid in full."

It appeared, however, that Krist had miscalculated. The university treasurer, Eugene E. Cohen, in consultation with the university's law firm of Mershon Sawyer Johnston Dunwody & Cole, reworked their calculations and informed Krist that the university was right the first time. He was due $468.70, check enclosed, which was minus his withholding tax and FICA. It was the last honest dollar he earned.

From the senior scientist at MIT's magnet lab in Cambridge, Massachusetts, a University of Miami professor also received a communication about Krist.

"I am writing to see if you want me to recommend any more technicians," wrote Dr. Henry Kolm to Dr. Mahlon M. Ball. "I see you lost the last one for a while. What in the world do you do to corrupt people like that? In just three months you drove him to a life of crime. This couldn't be a scheme to raise research money, could it?"

The F.B. and I.

In Decatur, Georgia, on the gray and sunless Monday of May 19, 1969, Gary Steven Krist went on trial for his life.

Unusually pale, his weight down from 235 to 174 pounds, his beard trimmed neatly, Krist walked that morning through a tunnel from a jail across the street to the modernistic slab-and-marble courthouse of DeKalb County. He wore a dark colorless tie, a dark brown suit, size 39 long coat borrowed from the younger of his two lawyers, a restraining belt for his handcuffs, which were removed a moment before he entered the third-floor courtroom, and a pair of black shoes so new the soles were unscuffed. They squeaked. Six sheriff's deputies, their seven-point-star badges pinned prominently on their coats, positioned themselves around the courtroom, and the elected sheriff, J. Lamar Martin, joined them and greeted pleasantly his constituents he recognized in the summoned assemblage of 250 veniremen. The body heat soon taxed the air conditioning.

In a ritualistic daylong selection of a jury, Krist sat between his two lawyers, alert, intense, taking copious notes on a legal yellow pad, nodding and whispering his approval or rejection of prospective jurors. His lawyers complied.

They were James R. Venable and Mobley Childs. Venable, paunchy with thinning gray hair at sixty-four, pink-faced, blue-eyed, and apple-cheeked, was something of a legend in rural Georgia. Folksy, unpolished and countrified, quite deliberately so upon occasion, Venable survived as a courtroom relic of the old school of bombastic oratory. He could rant and cry tearfully of his inadequacies in a closing argument, "I wish I was a William Jennings Bryan, I wish I was a Clarence Darrow, I wish I was a Billy Sunday," all the while conjuring up the inevitable comparisons. Much of Venable's fame rested on his position as an imperial wizard of the National Ku Klux Klan, Inc. Once he had candidly told the House Un-American Activities Committee he had been a card-carrying member since 1924 and that he had bankrolled a movement to "expose the kosher-food racket." Not only had he served as "Imperial Klonsel" for his brother Klansmen in trouble, he had once defended a group of white-hating Black Muslims charged with insurrection in Louisiana. (They, too, were strict segregationists.) As a criminal lawyer for thirty-nine years, he had practiced in thirty-seven states and knew his way around a jury box as well as any attorney in Georgia. Among his diverse clientele he numbered a Communist, a Temple bomber, and a rare 1932 marijuana smoker, as well as uncounted rapists and murderers, two of whom confessed prior to his representation and paid for their statements with their lives. His cocounsel, Mobley Childs, was a swarthy and urbane former insurance adjustor of thirty-five who had worked several years as an appellate attorney in the office of the Georgia Attorney General. He was quick and he tried hard and he considered the Krist trial his most important case. "You don't get too many millionaires' daughters buried whose friend is the President," he said.

Richard Bell, the straightforward, methodical and austere district attorney of the Stone Mountain Judicial Circuit, had given Krist's lawyers a list of 330 prospective witnesses prior to trial, and Bell and his assistant, Dennis Jones, a bookish, erudite, quiet man big in Little League Baseball, were quite prepared to call everyone if necessary, including Ruth Eisemann-Schier, a listed witness for the prosecution. She was to be tried separately from Krist. Her trial was scheduled the following month, June 16, 1969.

About one in five persons questioned that first day was excused because he disbelieved in capital punishment. Most were not. Again and again, Prosecutor Bell arose to ask a single direct question: "Do you know the punishment for kidnaping for ransom in this state is death in the electric chair, or upon recommendation of mercy, life imprisonment?"

And one after the other, the prospective jurors replied, "Yes."

"No further questions," Bell said, promptly seating himself.

Attorneys Venable and Childs alternately probed the backgrounds of the veniremen, and if the panel was representative of the 360,000 populace of DeKalb County, the community was almost totally Protestant (mostly Baptist) and white, the personification of mature suburban Atlanta middle- and upper-middle-class respectability. Everyone wore a suit and tie. There was no long hair. No one could be considered a laborer. And no one belonged to the Klan.

"Are you a member of any secret or fraternal organizations?" Venable asked repeatedly. He asked the question so often an audible buzz swept the courtroom.

The one man with a beard in the courtroom other than Krist was an associate professor of philosophy at nearby Spelman College and neither he, nor the only two women on the panel, a heavy-set divorced mother of four, and a librarian at Emory University, were selected. Prosecutor Bell rejected the two women in using nine of his sixteen pre-emptory challenges.

Krist's lawyers used twelve challenges, knocking out, among others, a deputy sheriff who said he wasn't prejudiced. At the end of a tedious day, as distant Stone Mountain glittered in the breaking sunlight, the twelve men and two alternates grouped themselves in three clusters in the jury box and stacked their hands on three Bibles.

Declared Prosecutor Bell: "You shall well and truly try the

issue formed upon this bill of indictment against Gary Steven Krist, who is charged with kidnaping for ransom, and a true verdict give according to the evidence, so help you God."

It wasn't a question. It was a command.

They responded in a unisoned, "I will."

The peers of Gary Steven Krist, as sworn and sequestered, were Cleason L. Pool, a chemistry lab technician; James David Lemming, an executive of the Atlanta Transit System; G. R. McClure, a pharmaceutical salesman who remembered that he had played high school football against Prosecutor Bell "a century ago"; Hubert T. Jenkins, chief of the camera section of the National Medical Audio-Visual Center; Julian G. Fluker, an engineer for the Georgia Highway Department; C. P. Mathews, Sr., a television station engineer; E. D. Foskey, Sr., a retired manager for a Western Electric outlet and the oldest juror at sixty-five; John M. Haney, an accountant and the only bachelor; Edwin E. Webster, a salesman whose uncle was a sheriff; Parker Little, a General Motors executive; David M. Searcy, a computer program analyst and the youngest juror at thirty-two, and Herbert I. Rainwater, a friendly white-haired gentleman of fifty-four who smiled a lot. Rainwater, a salesman for an optical equipment company, would become the foreman.

The trial of Gary Steven Krist moved swiftly. Judge H. O. Hubert, Jr., a plump and round small man of sixty-two years, wise in the ways of the law, determined to avoid the pitfalls of reversible error, willing, nay eager, to give the defendant every possible legal advantage, ran his courtroom for six days without raising his voice unduly or touching his gavel. He knew the law, the lawyers knew he knew the law, and they afforded him the respect of the good judge that he was. Judge Hubert suffered one noticeable and distracting ailment: emphysema; and because of an addiction to tobacco, he permitted cigarette smoking in the courtroom. In breathing, he would open his mouth frequently, as if chewing gum. With his head tilted and his face blemished by warts, he looked not unlike a kindly bullfrog.

In a terse twelve-minute opening statement, District Attorney Bell declared:

"The State will expect you to find a verdict of guilty without a recommendation of mercy." For the defense, Venable, adopting a wait-and-see strategy, said nothing, preferring to make the first and last closing speeches to the jury in the event his client did not take the witness stand.

"Call your first witness, Mr. Bell," Judge Hubert said.

Assistant Professor Marshall Casse took the witness stand and gave his account of how Krist, reminding him of Al Hirt, and Ruth Schier, whose name sounded almost identical to his own secretary, Ruth Scherer, tried to find Barbara at Emory University the Saturday before the crime. He said he overheard Krist telephoning.

David Slier, a freshman working at the Emory student information center, testified he received three unidentified telephone inquiries that afternoon about Barbara, but Judge Hubert cut him off quickly. "The court doesn't feel that the fact somebody was interested in Miss Mackle is evidence in this case."

Aldin F. Miller, an FBI agent, set up the proof yet to come. He removed three telephone books from the wall where Professor Casse had overheard the conversation and forwarded them to the FBI laboratory in Washington for fingerprint examination.

Had Ruth been on trial, District Attorney Bell probably would have called three Emory coeds, Diane Crews, Ellen Seay and Pam Pickens, all of whom saw Ruth at McTyeire Hall that Saturday.

Next came three gas-station attendants who saw Krist and Ruth the Saturday afternoon prior to the kidnaping. Horace King said he saw a man drive into his Shell station at Buford Highway and Clairmont Road in a station wagon with "a long box, kind of like a casket sticking out under the deck lid. The one I seen was a tall, bearded fellow, had on a police cap, come into the station and asked for an Atlanta map, and I told the fellow I didn't have one, and he thanked me and turned around and walked out again."

"Do you see the man in the courtroom today?" asked Bell.

"Right there," said King, pointing to Krist.

Charles Taylor, an attendant at a Standard Station, testified next and identified Krist. "That's him, sitting at the table." Taylor said he had seen a "mattress or something flat" on the "Volkswagen or something" with a "blue and white license plate."

"Whose gas station was that?" Bell asked.

"Jake's Standard Station."

"Jake," J. C. Mann, forty-seven, was not in the courtroom. He underwent surgery for a hernia that morning. He could have testified that Krist introduced himself as a "doctor so and so," and told him he was looking for a "small town, a town with a small population." Mann suggested Norcross or Duluth or Highway 23, and Krist drove off in that direction.

Stitched in red across the left pocket of Mann's uniform was his nickname, "Jake."

Was he then the fictional "Jake" of "Jake and the boys?" It was as good a guess as any.

At a Texaco station on the same route, Walter Schobel, a forty-four-year-old Rumanian immigrant, noticed the Volvo that same afternoon. "I am a mechanic, as a mechanic I work for thirty-two years on foreign cars, that is why it was unusual to see a Volvo come in," he said in a heavy accent. He saw Ruth in the front seat, bouncing up and peeking out the window "like some kids like to do and so I thought it was a boy.

"I saw the box, see, so I said, 'What you got in the box?' So he turned around very excited, you know, 'bout fell over the step and he said, 'That is dynamite, man,' and so this aroused me, and I made the remark to my wife that maybe he got somebody in the box like to bury, you know." Krist, he said, asked him for directions to a "remote area" where he could conduct a scientific experiment "and I was very excited about the whole matter, and so I was about to call the police and my family told me, you know, be quiet, that is foolish talk."

Schobel's daughter, Jana, a haunting beauty of twenty-three and a senior at Georgia State College, followed her father to the witness stand. She was doing the bookkeeping when Krist drove into the Texaco station, and she noticed the "trunk or crate" that "stuck out over the tail gate three or four feet under a greenish canvas."

"He wanted a map, a road map and we didn't have any, and he apologized because he didn't have a topographic map," she testified.

"He said he was going to carry on scientific experiments, was going to bury a box which contained scientific instruments and he needed a remote area. He said he was going to set off dynamite charges and measure the refractions of the charges.

"I asked him if he was studying for his Ph.D. and he said,

'No, I have one.'" She identified Krist, "The beard and the eyes
and the face, it is a striking face; he looks a little like Al Hirt."

She also directed him toward a "remote area"—Norcross—where
Barbara would be buried. Jana Schobel had notified the FBI
of her suspicions on Thursday, December 19, a full day prior
to Barbara's recovery.

Just north of Norcross "on the 23 highway, Buford Highway,"
that Saturday of December 14, Frank Roper noticed a "foreign
station wagon" stop under the narrow canopy of his two-pump
combination gas station-grocery store." "Nobody local ever comes
under there," he testified, identifying Krist and Ruth as his patrons.
"They bought three Pepsi-Colas, three packs of crackers and
three honey buns, as I remember," he said.

"Isn't it just the beard that makes you think he is the man?"
Attorney Childs asked on cross-examination.

"I'm pretty positive," Roper replied. "I noticed his eyes. His
eyes sit eager."

For the repeated identifications of Ruth, a deputy would
bring her to a side door of the courtroom and she would pose
in the doorway, nodding and smiling slightly, removing her hair-
band, turning for a profile view at the request of Assistant
District Attorney Jones.

Krist, writing furiously on his yellow pad, would pause and
look up. It was the first time they had seen each other since
he left her at the "Chinese pagoda" before the aborted first ransom
drop.

Late Sunday afternoon, December 15, Hoke Cooley was driving
toward the Buford Highway on McGee Road from his new and
as yet unoccupied home in the City of Berkeley Lake.

Suddenly and unexpectedly, he saw a "European car, one of
those squarebacks, but not a Volkswagen bus, coming right out
the woods to the left." He didn't know there was even a road
there. He saw two forms in the car, no box. Krist stopped taking
notes. He stared in silence at the table top. The testimony had
put him almost precisely at the burial site.

Glenn S. Loudermilk, Jr., a gaunt and intense young desk
clerk for the Clermont Hotel at 789 Ponce de Leon in Atlanta,
next identified Krist as the man who registered as "George S.
Price" at 8 P.M. Saturday, December 14. "He was wearing a beard

and I thought he was an entertainer and I put him in room 14A on a terrace over the lounge."

Later Loudermilk noticed the initials MIT on the registration card under "company representative." Loudermilk said he waited an hour for "Mr. Price" and his "female companion" so that he could change their room. He didn't want them demanding a refund after paying a week's rent in advance, $46.35. "I don't trust anyone wearing a beard," Loudermilk testified. "You get stuck with a few going out the back door on you." He never saw his guests again.

On Sunday morning, December 15, Susie Mae Clark, a Negro maid, made the bed in room 14A and emptied the trash and beer cans. She noticed a Polaroid camera and two photographs on a dresser. She looked closely at the photographs. They were of Krist, fully bearded, and Ruth. Later these same photographs would be found in the Volvo in Miami at the aborted first ransom drop. The maid identified them. "I never did see any human people there at all," she testified.

On Tuesday morning, about nine o'clock, five hours after the kidnaping, the maid received a checkout notice for room 14A. The guests had checked out in a hurry. "In the kitchenette in the refrigerator there was a lot of beer and eggs and canned goods, and there was a pot of hot chicken soup on the stove, real hot as if it had just been turned out." On the bathroom floor she found a towel covered with black hair. It was the hair from Krist's freshly shaved beard. It clogged up her vacuum cleaner.

"Your Honor, I really don't know how this can be material," interposed Childs.

"That would be immaterial, let's go ahead," said Judge Hubert.

Moving ahead, FBI agent Carl Clairborne testified that three days later he lifted fifteen latent fingerprints from room 14A. He found the venetian-blind cord had been cut and most of the cord missing. He took the remaining cord for laboratory analysis. The evidence was rushed to Washington by special FBI carrier.

"Could it be because the President of the United States was directing the operation?" Attorney Childs asked.

"I don't know about that, sir," replied agent Clairborne.

Agent James Riordan testified he took the evidence to the crime lab on a Delta flight.

"Are you what they call a runner?" asked Venable.

"No, sir, I am a special agent," Riordan replied.

Barbara's mother took the stand as the fourteenth witness and in subdued preciseness in a barely audible voice she told of the abduction of her daughter and how she screamed and screamed and screamed for help. "I wasn't frightened. I was more angry with myself for opening the door." She was asked if she could identify the kidnaper. Looking at Krist, she said, "He resembles him, but I cannot positively identify him . . . The man was clean shaven, didn't have a beard."

Krist stared sullenly at the table top, his head bowed.

Walter Perkins, the Rodeway Inn's resident poet and night clerk, followed her to the stand and he identified Krist and Ruth, she again standing in the courtroom doorway, as "Dr. and Mrs. Johnsen Rarik" who checked into Rodeway Inn at 12:13 A.M. on the fourteenth. For identical rooms, Perkins had charged Krist $14.42 and the Mackles $16.48.

The two DeKalb County detectives, Mac E. Dover and Harvey Hopkins, testified how they took five pieces of sash-type white cord, a two-inch reel of Johnson and Johnson Red Cross tape from room 137 and mailed it to the FBI lab in Washington.

Only hours after the crime, Krist and Ruth checked out of the other hotel room in Atlanta, 14A at the Clermont Hotel. It was eight o'clock, "give or take a few minutes," on Tuesday morning, said Michael S. McGovern, a desk clerk. He could not identify Krist. He remembered that Krist wanted a refund. He didn't give it to him.

Theodore King, the Georgia security manager for Southern Bell Telephone and Telegraph and a former FBI agent, testified that someone telephoned the Mackle residence from Atlanta at 9:10 A.M. Tuesday morning. The caller deposited a dollar and thirty cents and talked one minute and thirty-four seconds, according to the long-distance operator's toll card. King said the caller gave his pay booth number of 874–9244, which may or may not have been accurate. That booth was on the west side of the football stadium of Georgia Institute of Technology.

William O'Dowd, the Deltona treasurer, testified that he received a call from the kidnaper at the Mackle home at that time, and agent Joseph H. R. St. Pierre told how he and the gardner dug up the ransom note under the clump of palms. Agent

James H. Downing testified of his flight to the Washington lab with the ransom note.

"Is this a normal procedure in FBI work to run a piece of paper to Washington?" Venable wanted to know.

"Depends upon the type of case, sir," said Downing.

Assistant State's Attorney Jones, peering through his thick gold-rimmed round glasses, read the note into evidence, State's Exhibit 32A, B, and C: "Robert Mackle: Sir, your daughter has been kidnapped . . ." and a silence gripped the two hundred and twenty spectators in the packed courtroom.

In the newspapers the next morning Jane Mackle would read the ransom note for the first time—six months after the crime.

One of the more unusual arrivals in the courtroom was Buddy Ayers. An admirer of Venable, known for his Ku Klux Klan activities, Ayers' local fame rested on his alleged role as an undetected usher at the funeral of Martin Luther King.

A highly knowledgeable FBI agent, Joseph A. Ciminera, sat at the state table with prosecutors Bell and Jones. He helped keep the sequence and chronology of the crime unfolding smoothly.

Agent John P. Brady told how the First National Bank of Miami prepared the $500,000, and William W. Hillhouse, the microfilm operator, identified the print-outs from two rolls of film he initialed when he put the bills through the Recordak machine.

To his lawyers, Krist muttered that it was against the law to photograph money. The FBI had taken the trouble to request permission of the Treasury Department.

The head teller, James Sumpasis, (pronounced "some passes, more than one pass,") detailed the bank's counting procedure, and a vice-president and an assistant vice-president C. Ellis Clark and Thomas Pendray, identified specifically page 101 of the serial numbers they had copied and double-checked. The bills were those found on Krist.

Agent Edward F. Brandes, keeping intact the chain of evidence, told how he accompanied Billy Vessels and agent Frank Smith to the bank the next morning to get the money for Robert Mackle.

Agent Ben Cantey, Jr., told about picking up the letter at the Coral Gables branch post office which contained Barbara's ring and the Polaroid photograph with the "kidNAPPED" sign under her chin.

And Attorney Venable, beginning to grope for a diversion, cross-examined Cantey on Bill Vessels' reputation.

"Don't know if he was a strong-arm man, bodyguard?"

"I don't know that," Agent Cantey responded flatly.

Robert Mackle took the stand next, and in a direct, low-key, unemotional manner, he recited his role, the trip to Atlanta, the telephone call from the kidnaper, the drop at Fair Isle. From the witness stand he smiled frequently, disregarding several awkward interruptions because of rules of hearsay. He made no attempt to convey the torment and anguish and agony he suffered. The questioning of District Attorney Bell extracted nothing of this.

On cross-examination, Venable took an inordinate interest in Billy Vessels. He was looking for a scapegoat.

"Could you run with the suitcase, could Vessels run with it?"

"I didn't attempt it, sir," replied Robert Mackle.

FBI agent John R. Ackerly read to the jury the kidnaper's instructions he had recorded on a Magnetcorder in the basement of the MOhawk exchange building. Ackerly had had two conversations with Krist at the Dade County Jail and he identified positively Krist's voice as the voice of the kidnaper.

Krist balanced a pen upright on his legal pad, seemingly disinterested. "I'll probably be convicted," he said during a late afternoon recess the third day of trial. A newsman had asked him what he thought of the trial.

"It's a disaster," he said.

Several reporters began to crowd around him, and Krist warmed to the occasion. "The trial is an interesting farce," he declared. "Predestined, you might say, but interesting. But you can't ever tell what a jury will do. It is like prodding a bull.

"I had an ant colony once," he continued.

"Are you comparing the trial to the ants?" someone asked.

"The ants were a little more industrious," he said, grinning.

"Humans are supposed to have greater capabilities than chimpanzees, but I haven't seen it here."

It was then he pretended to notice his audience. "My God," he said in mock chagrin. "What have I done?" He appeared highly amused at himself.

By Thursday, the fourth day of the trial, Krist had brought into the courtroom a scientific textbook, *The Origins of Pre-*

Biological Systems and Their Molecular Matrices, and flipped the pages, seemingly oblivious to the trial.

Frank Mackle testified of the second call from the kidnaper after Robert had left the house for the first run. Attorney Childs seemed more interested in Billy Vessels. "Do you know anything about his background?"

"I know he played football, for the University of Oklahoma, and he played for the Baltimore Colts, and he came, I believe, from the Colts to us in public relations."

"Is he a sort of bodyguard?"

"He is in public relations with our company and he is also a good personal friend of ours."

Deputy Paul Self, followed by Miami officer William J. Sweeney, testified at length on finding the Volvo, the chase, the gunfire, and the discovery of the green suitcase filled with $20 bills. FBI agent Andrew A. Armstrong, Jr., again keeping intact the chain of evidence, told how he picked up the $500,000 at the Miami Police Station and returned it to agent Homer A. Newman, Jr., head of the accounting section at FBI headquarters. Agent Newman said he and four agents rechecked every serial number to make sure the bills were the same. He also identified the 109 bills Krist spent in West Palm Beach as the ransom money.

Agent Edward J. Sharp testified he took the $500,000 in the green suitcase to the Mackle home and helped repack it in the blue Samsonite. For a moment, Sharp could not identify the blue one positively. He had forgotten he had written his initials and the date under the lining. Prosecutor Jones refreshed his memory on redirect examination, and Attorney Childs made the most of it, "You forgot the one thing that you did do, is that correct?"

It was an insignificant point. The defense had only insignificant points.

Albert Bischoff identified the Volvo as Krist's, pointing to the defendant he knew as George Deacon at the Al-Ril Trailer Court, telling the jury how the wire under the hood opened the hood. It couldn't be anyone else's Volvo.

Attorney Venable tried futilely to keep the jury from hearing about the contents of the Volvo, claiming the FBI had "trespassed illegally."

"I don't think the defendant can object unless he claims to be the owner," needled Jones.

Lyndall L. Shaneyfelt, a photographer and FBI lab expert from Washington, methodically recited the inventory of the Volvo —the ski masks, the airline tickets, the Rodeway Inn key, the xylocaine and syringe and needles, the Polaroid swinger camera. He had prepared huge photographic blowups of the torn edge of the number-three photograph found in the Volvo and the "kidNAPPED" picture mailed to the residence.

The torn edges fit perfectly. "The picture had to have been made with this Polaroid camera. It could not have come from any other source," Shaneyfelt testified.

He identified item after item, photograph after photograph, and he pointed to the long and faint diagonal scratches he had made with a sharp instrument on the metal trim of both suitcases before the drops. "They couldn't be seen unless held to the light just right," he said.

"I notice all of you call yourselves special agents," Venable countered lamely. "You got any regular agents of the FBI?"

Dr. Robert J. Hurley, the Vandyke-bearded oceanographer, identified Krist as his employee, George Deacon, and photographs of Krist's laboratory trailer at the marine institute. He also identified by photograph the Boston Whaler stolen from the marine lab. He knew it was his. "I drilled holes in the gunwale to install a bimini top," he said. In a rambling cross-examination, Childs questioned the scientist about his beard. "Isn't it an old fable that you can't trust men with beards?"

"It depends on whether you wear one or not. I won't belabor the point," Dr. Hurley responded, glancing at the bushier Krist.

Agent Frank J. Smith, the office Santa Claus, testified that he found in Krist's trailer a piece of fiberglass cloth, screws and nails, and a bit for a drill, and a flap-lid plywood box with the name International. He identified photographs of the rectangular epoxy outline on the floor—Krist's "capsule."

Harold Shofner, the Yellow Cab Company driver, put Krist at Miami International Airport at 4:25 P.M. December 19 before the second drop. He had driven him to Budget Rent-A-Car and Merlin Rent-A-Car on $2.30 and $.70 fares, and heard Krist tell him he had been injured. "Said he was thrown out of the car, the automobile had struck a construction sign and he was thrown out of it and fell on top of a hurricane fence."

Ray Hoadley testified he rented "George Deacon" the two-door lime-green '69 Fairlane, tag number 1E-24848, about 4:45 P.M. that day, and a few days after it had been found in West Palm Beach, he gave permission to the FBI to examine the car.

"Do you remember the name of the agent?" Venable wanted to know.

"No, sir, I don't. There were so many of them I lost track of the names, must have been six or eight."

Hoadley identified Krist and Venable ranted, "You come up here and identify this man and can't tell the court and jury whether his pants was red or green or blue, can you?" Hoadley said he remembered the face.

Father John C. Mulcahy, the assistant pastor at the Church of the Little Flower, told of his two conversations with the kidnaper. On cross-examination, Childs asked him if he was Catholic.

Billy Vessels then took the stand, and if he suspected that Attorney Venable would attack him by contrived innuendo and grossly unfair insinuation, he betrayed no emotion. In a straightforward manner, Vessels recounted his role in a restrained manner. He said nothing of the frantic trip to Fair Isle to help Robert Mackle. He was not asked.

Vessels made one misstatement of fact. He thought that agent Lee Kusch had lain on the back seat with a shotgun during the second drop. Kusch had a revolver. The FBI had substituted agents. Agent Larry Coutre had the shotgun. He didn't go.

Attorney Venable, attempting to conjure every conceivable diversion from his client's guilt, asked Vessels if he had ever been out in the company of Barbara Mackle.

"No, sir," said Vessels.

Venable questioned Vessels about the hotels he had frequented in Atlanta and the size and weight of the suitcase.

"And you couldn't run with it, it was so heavy?"

"Probably if I had to, I would have tried," Vessels replied.

"Did you know that this girl called Ruth Eisemann-Schier was captured in Oklahoma—Norman, Oklahoma?"

"Yes, sir."

"And are you telling this court that the only hotels that you have ever been in in Atlanta are the Marriott and the Air Host?"

"Well, sir, I have stayed in the Dinkler, I believe."

"And in the Clermont?"

"No."

"Isn't it true, Mr. Witness, that you have stayed at the Hotel Clermont and they made preparations there for you, isn't that true."

"No, sir, it is not," Vessels said, his anger controlled.

"Did you know what type of car you was to meet out there and what type of person you was to meet out there, didn't you say you was to go to this spot and put the money there in this spot?" Venable asked, almost incoherently.

"I put the money out in the middle of the road."

"Isn't it true, Mr. Witness, that the stock of this company you work for has gone up greatly."

Jones objected. "I will sustain the objection," said Judge Hubert. In all, it was a wild and baseless attack, typical of some criminal attorneys in desperate straits.

In the courtroom Vessels retained his composure. But when newspapers published what happened in the courtroom he was hurt deeply.

Agent Leroy L. Kusch followed Vessels to the stand and testified that he was in the back seat during the foggy delivery on Tamiami Trail. And Attorney Venable, again using his imagination, asked, "Were you aware of the fact that Mr. Vessels was disappointed that you were going with him?"

"No," said Kusch.

"Was he?"

"I did not get that impression, no sir."

"He did not want to go by himself?"

"I never received that impression," the FBI agent said harshly.

In an easy and gregarious recitation, Norman Oliphant then told about the "Arthur Horowitz" purchase of the Orlando Clipper with $20 bills from a brown paper bag. He quoted Krist, "'You might as well have the bag to put the money in, when you put money in a paper bag, nobody knows you have it.' And then he waved and bid me adieu."

Agents Robert Schachner and Patrick A. Philbin traced the ransom money to the purchases in West Palm Beach and told of the impounding and fingerprinting of the rental car found at an Allright parking lot at the intersection of Narcissus and Clematis streets.

Gerald J. Doyle, the telephone security manager, testified about the call from West Palm Beach, and Trisha Poindexter, the FBI switchboard operator, started to tell of receiving it in Atlanta.

"I will object to testimony about the telephone call unless she identifies the caller," Venable interposed. It was one of those unthinking automatic objections. In the advocacy system of American courts, lawyers sometimes oppose by reflex. Here was one act of the kidnaper which might go a long way toward mitigation.

The jury never heard the girl. She could not identify Krist's voice. Judge Hubert sustained the objection.

Prosecutor Jones, taking over the direct examination, began to pound at the defense, as if to nail shut the State's own coffin-tight case. Agents Edward James Tully, William A. Sullivan, Irwin Frank Davis and Joseph Santoiana reconstructed the chase and capture of Krist. Santoiana identified aerial photographs from the helicopter, a man running to the shoreline.

"Isn't it a fact, Mr. Agent, that the reason why you identified this man was because he was brought into El Jobean and they said, 'Here he is'? and he had on the same or similar clothes to the man that you saw on the beach?" Attorney Childs suggested.

It wasn't.

"Mac" and "Butch," Richard N. McLeod and Milton Buffington, retold the capture and Attorney Childs tried again. He wanted to know if Krist was armed with a "fingernail clipper, too."

"You said that you advised this man of his rights when he, like a Hollywood production, said, 'I have rights'? Is this correct?"

"I don't believe I put it that way," said McLeod.

Sheriff John P. Bent, of Charlotte County, and his chief deputy, John Shannon, told how they took custody of the $18,000 found in the satchel. They left no loopholes. Agent Santoiana identified the seven moist and sandy bills taken from Krist's billfold— G81315805A, C55341014A . . . They matched the ransom serial numbers prepared at the First National Bank in Miami, page 101 of the list.

On a bier borrowed from the A. S. Turner & Son Funeral Home during the fifth day of trial, deputies wheeled into the courtroom the long gray plywood crypt, State's Exhibit 161. A gasp of awe sounded through the courtroom. Jurors stood.

"Was there anything to your knowledge to keep rats, snakes, tarantulas from getting into that box?" District Attorney Bell asked agent Declan J. Hughes.

"Not to my knowledge," said Hughes, who was the wrong man to ask.

Krist, rapidly chewing Doublemint gum, whispered fiercely to his lawyers.

"What do you see over those holes?" Venable asked.

"Screen wire."

It was one of the few times the defendant smiled. He seemed pleased.

Agent Declan Hughes, following to the stand the agents who found Barbara, Robert S. Kennemur and Vincent J. Capazella, said he took a few measurements. The burial site was 130 yards from the road on the downward sloping side of a hill twenty feet below the surface of the road. The pit measured nine feet long, two feet nine inches wide, and three feet three inches deep, he testified. It took seven men to lift the box from the hole.

Agent William J. Watry said he drove the box to the FBI lab in Washington on the next day in a rental truck. It took him twelve hours and ten minutes.

Agent Morris Samuel Clark, an expert in hairs and fabrics and a botanist with a master's degree in forestry from Harvard University, testified that the white braided cord found inside the box was the same in diameter, color, construction and composition of cord taken from Krist's room in the Clermont Hotel. The cord, sixteenth of an inch thick and with a sleeve braid formed from six piles, four white cotton and two rayon, was also the same as the cord the kidnapers bound Jane Mackle with and "could have" come from the same source.

A roll of fiberglass cloth found in Krist's trailer at the marine lab, he testified further, was the same in color, weave and construction as a specimen removed from the box.

Agent Clark inventoried the box: a green-and-white striped foam pad with a Sears, Roebuck and Company label; a yellow blanket; a green bedspread and a yellow bedspread, both cotton; a foot square three-inch thick sofa pillow with a button in the middle; a three-gallon milk jug-styled plastic container with a molded handle and a screw cap used for water; a white plastic pail and blue lid with a compartment for a deodorant used for refuse; a white muslin bag; Xeroxed copies of three pages of instructions, torn and smudged; a box of Kotex; a blue plastic drinking glass; a piece of black plastic tubing for the water; two rolls of toilet paper; roll of waxed paper; white facial tissues; a package of Nabisco saltine crackers; a sixteen-ounce jar of Sue Bee honey; three packs of gum, Beechnut Spearmint, Wrigley's Spearmint and Wrigley's Doublemint; a nine-ounce bag of candy "Bonomo" peanuts; a box of Post's Sugar Crisp cereal; an unopened loaf of bread; a bag of caramels; six red apples and the brown paper bag containing the apples.

"Did you test these apples to see whether there was any poison of any type in them?" Venable asked on cross-examination.

"No, sir. I did not," agent Clark replied. The State submitted photographs of everything, the apples included.

A young black clerk from the fingerprint department of the Atlanta Police Department, Bernard Wayne Crockett, testified that he took prints from Krist on January 28, 1969 and Ruth on March 17, 1969, for comparison purposes. Attorney Venable didn't like it. He argued that no comparisons could be made because Crockett was an "inexperienced and unqualified Nigra."

"The objection is overruled," droned Judge Hubert.

John Walker, an FBI fingerprint examiner of twenty-five years experience, dwelt upon the intricacies of ridge characteristics, much as a dull college lecturer, and then got to business.

He found Krist's right thumb on the rear mirror of the Volvo. He found seven of Krist's latent prints in the loose-leaf unruled notebook paper in the Volvo; he found eight of Krist's prints on the Delta Air Lines ticket, and he found five of Krist's prints on the lime-green rental Ford. There were others. He didn't bother with them all. They were not necessary.

Walker also testified where he found Ruth's prints, her purse in the Volvo, her marine lab premise pass. There was one print that linked her inextricably to Krist. She left her right thumbprint on the back of the Polaroid photograph of Krist in the nude. Agent Walker found Krist's print on an unused six-cent stamp found in the Volvo.

This wasn't quite all.

Arley P. Crotts, another fingerprint expert, examined three

Metropolitan Atlanta telephone books removed from the basement of the Rich Building at Emory—where Professor Casse testified he overheard Krist telephoning.

The FBI dismantled the books, using a silver nitrate processing for every page.

On page 613 of one book, the Mc's, where someone might logically look for Barbara's dormitory, McTyeire Hall, agent Crotts found four of Krist's latent prints—his left index, left middle, left ring, and left little finger.

Crotts said he also found two of Krist's prints on the registration card at the Clermont Hotel. He found a latent print of Ruth's on a doorframe inside room 14A.

In a feeble cross-examination, the defense brought out that the FBI had failed to lift any latents from the suitcases and the Boston Whaler. The failure wasn't significant. There were no latents to be lifted from Krist's "capsule" either—not even Barbara's.

At a recess, Krist buttoned up all three buttons of his coat, sipped an iced Coke, and acknowledged that the State had an impressive case.

"I'm waiting for them to bring on the dancing elephants," he mused.

He admired the construction of the box. "It's very well constructed," he said. "Maybe after I'm electrocuted, they can bury me in it. I understand the state has to pay $97 for a coffin."

Krist informed reporters he did not think he belonged in the courtroom. "They wouldn't bring a chimpanzee into court for assaulting a human being. Why should you bring a superior being to court and expect to obtain justice?"

And was he a superior human being?

"I think I am a different species. I don't think scientists have genetically classified me."

He declined for "ethical reasons" to discuss the performance of his lawyers. "You wouldn't ask a mechanic to assess his work on a motor half-torn down."

Would he take the stand? Georgia, alone of all states, possessed a unique "unsworn statement" law. A defendant, should he so desire, could take the witness stand, forego the usual oath to tell the truth, and testify as he pleased without any cross-examination whatsoever.

The jury could attach whatever significance it deemed appropriate. The defendant could also choose to take the stand in the usual manner.

Did Krist wish to deny he was the designer, manufacturer, transporter and gravedigger for his coffin-styled "capsule"?

"It is irrelevant if I do," he said. "I don't expect to obtain justice from a court of human beings."

Robert Frazier, an FBI firearms and tool identification expert, next took the stand. He shifted his body so he would face the jury, and he spoke clearly and distinctly.

By microscope, he had examined the one-quarter-inch Douglas-fir plywood of the box, three layers glued together, scrutinizing the grain structure, the width of the growth rings.

Then he had made a comparison. He compared the edge of the partition in the "capsule," as he too called it once, to a piece of Douglas-fir plywood found in Krist's lab-trailer at the Marine Institute more than six hundred miles away.

"They were originally one piece of wood," Frazier testified. "They were sawed apart irregularly, possibly by a handsaw."

From Krist's trailer at the lab the FBI had also discovered a bit for a Black & Decker power screw driver, number 31041.

Frazier tested the screw driver bit on a soft lead screw in his lab in Washington, noting that when he applied pressure, the bit twisted out of the slot and made distinctive scratch marks.

He made another comparison. Under a microscope, he compared his marks to the marks left by the person who originally put the four screws into the foot end of the box for a handle.

They were identical. The bit found in Krist's trailer—and only that bit—could have been used to put a handle on the 231-pound, two-foot square, eight-foot-long box removed from the Georgia hillside.

Frazier illustrated his conclusions with huge microscopic photographs taken at the same time. "Gather round, gentlemen, you will have to get close," he said to the jurors.

George W. Finger, an agent in the FBI's radio engineering section, examined the twelve-volt automobile-type wet cell battery in the smaller 25-inch chamber of the box.

"I would estimate that if it burned continuously for the fan only, it would have lasted another thirty-five or forty hours," Finger testified.

"If the pump had run continuously off this source, could you tell us how long the battery would have lasted?" Prosecutor Jones asked.

"The pump probably would have depleted the battery in about two hours, maybe three," Finger replied.

He noticed a curious defect in the designed use of the pump. It didn't have any place to pump. Had water actually accumulated in the box, the pump, which had a short piece of garden hose attached, would have merely squirted the water back into the main 71-inch chamber of the box.

"It wouldn't keep it from filling up then?" Jones asked.

"I don't believe so," Finger replied.

"In fact, if the box is waterproof on the outside, the box would fill up, wouldn't it?"

"I think before the box filled up, the pump would be shorted out."

"There is no way for the pump to pump water out of the box?"

"I don't see any place to pump it out of the box."

Finger testified that the filament had burned out in a bulb requiring two amperes at twelve volts, roughly twenty-four watts. He couldn't tell when it had burned out.

"How long you been with the F.B. and I." Venable began. Finger had begun in 1940.

Venable later made his points.

"Assuming this light bulb was turned on and the fan, how long in your opinion would they run, not the pump, just those two items?"

"Probably a hundred thirty or forty hours," Finger replied.

If Barbara had left on the pump, she would not have survived. She would have suffocated. The battery would have gone dead, Finger estimated, in a "little over fifty hours."

Joseph Gormley, an agent with master's degrees in both chemistry and law, analyzed the pale amber liquid in the container left for Barbara to drink. It contained chlorpromazine, a potent tranquilizer and anti-emetic to prevent nausea and vomiting.

Here, then, were the tranquilizers Barbara had looked for and could not find.

Chemist Gormley found approximately seventy-five milligrams per hundred milliliters of water—or just about the quantity of a hundred middle-strength tablets dissolved in water. A yellow dye on the tablets probably made the water turn amber.

Dr. James H. Christy, an internist at the Emory University

Clinic who examined Barbara at the FBI agent's house, testified on the same matter. He found her suffering from dehydration.

"Could a part of her inability to walk be from having stayed in a lying position?" Attorney Childs wanted to know.

"There is a possibility this could have contributed to it."

"How about the chlorpromazine, could that also be a part of the cause of her weakened condition?"

"If enough had been ingested, it could."

"Then if enough chlorpromazine had been ingested over the three-day period to cause that, then she would not normally have been dehydrated?"

"That is not necessarily so at all. She could have taken only three hundred milliliters of fluid, a little over a glass and a half, and would have been thoroughly tranquilized," he said.

Palmer Tunstall, an FBI examiner of questioned documents, next attached to a wall two enlargements—a page from the ransom note, and a page from instructions left in the box.

Tunstall, using a pointer, directed the jury's attention to slight blobs on both notes. Both had been Xeroxed. Both had been Xeroxed on the same machine. The blobs were from dirt on the glass or faint defects of the machine.

He put up a third enlargement, a seemingly blank piece of loose-leaf notebook paper taken from Krist's Volvo.

Faint typewriter indentations were clearly visible when light was projected from the back. "They were used as backing sheets when the original ransom note was typed," Tunstall testified.

The FBI was not able to identify positively the typewriter used. Turnstall said the kidnaper had probably used an upright standard or portable Underwood machine. The Xeroxing had obscured a definite determination. The FBI did not find the specific typewriter used.

Prosecutor Richard Bell called his seventy-fourth and last witness, Barbara Jane Mackle, and Barbara, wearing a blue knit dress with a white front, a trace of make-up, her black hair flouncing to her shoulders, walked quickly through the stilled courtroom.

Composed, speaking rapidly, smiling frequently, she testified for thirty-eight minutes.

Weeks later she would receive a letter from George P. Hardin, Emory University, class of 1937, a genealogist and close friend of Attorney James Venable. He would have to be considered a biased observer.

"Miss Mackle, your presence upon the stand was a fresh breeze blowing across a sick scene, because of your most forthright and unadorned narrative, and, pardon me, your natural charm.

"The defense thought you a wonderful witness so far as Krist-the-sick was concerned, since you conveyed no attitude of vengeance, nor did you dilate upon your most singular experience. I was delighted myself to see you unscarred, and even Krist hissed at me across the defense table just as you were nearly finished, 'She's got more guts than everybody in this room, you understand that, George?' 'More than I have, surely,' I hissed back.

"Also the equanimity of your family upon the stand, as well as that of Mr. Vessels, was remarkable, and was remarked upon by many of the audience, with admiration.

"When you stood up to identify Krist, I was the man with the mustache sitting at the end of the defense table."

Prosecutor Bell had asked his last witness to stand and look around the courtroom. "See if you see the man who kidnaped you that early morning."

"Yes, I do."

"Where is he?"

"Between those two gentlemen," Barbara had replied. A moment later she identified Ruth Eisemann-Schier, grinning foolishly in the doorway.

"Miss Mackle," said Attorney Childs on cross-examination, "I am six feet tall, I weigh a hundred and eighty-five, I have dark hair, I don't have a beard. Could I have been the person who put you in this box?"

"No, sir," said Barbara. "Honestly I will never forget the face; really, I am quite positive."

There was no defense. There was no attempt to argue the insanity. The psychiatrist and psychologist appointed by the court at the request of the defense, Sheldon B. Cohen and Herbert W. Eber, both had deemed Krist sane and able to tell the difference between right and wrong.

Krist elected not to take the stand. As Hardin, Venable's friend, later explained, "We would have run the hazard that the defendant, once upon the stand, might have become intoxicated by his own voice and eloquence and so might have aroused some new slumbering hostility in the jury. Thus it was prevailed upon the accused with the wisdom of his sitting mute."

It took Assistant District Attorney Jones two hours and thirty minutes to submit formally the State's evidence. In all, he listed 207 exhibits, many of them multiple, and they ranged from the 231-pound coffin to a six-cent postage stamp with Krist's fingerprint on it.

Preserving his appellate rights, Venable objected to each exhibit. He objected to the admission of key 153 of the Rodeway Inn, where Krist and Ruth had stayed. "There is no evidence presented that the key fits the lock," he protested.

"Overruled," said the judge.

As was the custom, the court stenographer, Mrs. Ruth Harris, ceased to record as the closing arguments began.

"I wish I was a William Jennings Bryan," Venable began, and in a two-hour impassioned discourse, he wrung his hands in the personified agony of the old South, called even upon the granite images of Confederate generals on nearby Stone Mountain to bear witness, and delivered such an orgy of summation observers feared he would collapse. Literally, he frothed at the corners of his mouth. He wept. He damned the "brave hawk-eyed characters from the F.B. and I.," and said they conducted "a shameful case." "God help you and God pity people charged with crimes if you are gullible enough to believe this kind of evidence from the Boy Scouts," he cried. He said the FBI was bankrupting the nation. He assailed the "albatross—I call him a buzzard"—who identified Krist from the helicopter. He ranted against the two "niggers"— "that's what I call 'em," and castigated a Marine Institute Scientist of "foreign extraction" and "proud of whiskers all over his face." "Billy Vessels," he said, "knows more about this case than anyone on trial."

He preached to the jury an old Southern adage of the courtroom: "You sit in there until the roaches bring you out the keyhole."

In a terse argument, Prosecutor Bell said he had proved his case "almost to a mathematical certainty."

He neglected perhaps to say he had everything but the instant replay. The FBI would have given him that, too, possibly, if it could have installed the infrared camera in the Lincoln.

Dramatically, Bell stalked across the courtroom, flipped open the lid of the coffin and turned on the noisy pump.

"Stick your head in there and listen," he exhorted the jurors. "The normal person, the usual person, would have gone crazy.

"Mercy? The state says no. He deserves none. Punishment? There is but one.

"Barbara Mackle could have died in there except for the grace of God. She is not alive because of Gary Steven Krist, but because of the FBI. God bless the FBI—except for them, she might still be buried in the cold red mud of Georgia with the honeysuckle over her grave."

Bell defended vigorously the character of Billy Vessels. "If ever a fellow was maligned, it was he. He was the right hand of Robert Mackle."

Bell, though, was sandwiched between the two defense attorneys, and Mobley Childs also assailed Vessels. Then, hardly pausing for breath, Childs set up an equally improbable target, Stewart Woodward. "They had witnesses crawling out of the woodwork and where was he? Does he drive a dark blue Volvo? Could he have Massachusetts plates on it?"

He made one salient point. "How much easier it would have been to bury a dead body? I ask you that."

The shouting ceased finally, Judge Hubert charged the jurors, and the twelve men tried and true retired to deliberate.

In the emptied courtroom some hours later, waiting for a verdict, Gary Steven Krist held court.

"No kidnaper who returned his victim alive has ever been executed," he announced. He said he had looked it up in the World Almanac.

"If this jury returns a verdict of death, it would only persuade all other kidnapers never to return the person alive."

Kidnaping? "The only kidnaping I know anything about is Robert Louis Stevenson's."

The proper punishment for the kidnaper of Barbara Mackle, he suggested, "would be to bury the guy in a box for three months and see how he likes it. That's an interesting proposition, isn't it? An eye for an eye."

"It would be logical to assume that the kidnaper had on his person a map with detailed instructions to the burial site of the capsule," Krist said at another point. "And in the event of his death," he continued, speaking in the third person, "the map would have been found on the corpse."

He described Attorney Venable as a "priceless character." "Of course, Jimmy was incoherent and not right 90 per cent of the time."

And not unlike his lawyer, Krist denounced the FBI. "The Canadian Royal Mounties always get their man," said Krist. "The FBI always gets a man.

"The kidnaper had to be certain the infallible FBI would find the girl, and despite specific instructions, the dumdums didn't know where to look. They dug her up with tin cans because they forgot shovels.

"You don't play parlor games with human lives."

When taken to the hospital after his capture, "suffering from dehydration, exposure and exhaustion, they stripped me stark nude," Krist complained.

"And they never gave me a property receipt."

Then he paused. "I have the greatest respect for the FBI's technical ability—but they are built-in witnesses for the prosecution."

What of his marriage to Carmen? "I'll leave it to her. I'm not the injured party. A marriage is a binding contractual arrangement."

And what of Ruth? "The kindest thing I can say about her is to say nothing."

Did he expect a guilty verdict without mercy? "Yes. I'll probably get the chair—or whatever these barbaric humans use these days."

At 9:50 P.M. Monday, May 26, 1969, after four hours and five minutes of deliberation, the jury trooped single file into the courtroom. The foreman, Herbert I. Rainwater, remained standing. The eleven others took their seats. The verdict was written on a piece of paper. He handed the paper to the district attorney. Bell read it silently.

Krist, standing, looked straight ahead. He put his right fingers to his left wrist to take his own pulse. It raced upward to 120, he would calculate.

Then, reading still, the prosecutor's words rang loud and clear. "We, the jury, find the defendant guilty with a recommendation of mercy and life imprisonment."

Gary Steven Krist would live.

Jimmy Venable, beside himself with joyous relief, wiped tears from his eyes.

"Does the defendant wish to make a statement?" It was Judge Hubert.

Krist whispered into the ear of his lawyer. "The defendant wishes to thank you," Venable replied.

The next day Krist would regret that he had not spoken himself. "I should have thanked them for wasting their time." "Cracker-barrel justice," he called it.

The jurors had begun their deliberations with a prayer. They had talked nearly two hours and sifted through the exhibits before taking a first vote by secret ballot.

Ten voted guilty. One abstained momentarily. One man voted for acquittal.

Without any sort of direct confrontation, they talked some more. No one would argue innocence. "There was no use going on until we found the party and could discuss the problem," said Rainwater. "When the gentleman admitted he was the one, it came out that his religious beliefs prevented him from voting to kill anyone. He wasn't a fanatic; he was quite religious and very sincere. He had tried to make himself think there wasn't enough evidence, but that certainly was proven otherwise," said Rainwater. The vote then changed to 12 to 0.

The issue of mercy arose. "We all knew that no one had been electrocuted in Georgia for years and they weren't about to start now," said Rainwater. "But there was strong feeling that the sentence should be imposed. We would have like to have given him ninety-nine years."

In the end, Gary Steven Krist owed his life to the family he wronged so terribly.

The courtroom demeanor of the Mackle family—a father, mother, and daughter—influenced immensely the jurors' decision.

The poise, calm, and sheer vivacity of the victim, a stable and resilient young woman weighed heavily.

"There was no hatred, no animosity," Rainwater said. "Neither the father, his wife, nor the young lady demanded retaliation.

"And, of course, there was the swaying factor of no bodily harm. It seemed as if Krist did everything he could to keep from hurting her—except putting her in the box."

The jurors viewed Attorney Venable with some embarrassment. "The mercy was despite Mr. Venable, not because of him," said Rainwater.

The vote was close: Six for mercy; five for execution; one abstaining.

In his jail cell the next day, an exuberant Krist, sitting in his jockey shorts, announced that "life imprisonment is absolutely not the right way to reform my character."

He said he did not expect to be released for a long time.

"In the vague and distant future, when I have rheumatism and gout, I will step out of prison doors onto a moving sidewalk, dodge the jet-propelled hovercraft, stumble around and wonder how I got into the twenty-first century," he said.

"I am convicted of taking a rich man's money and using inordinate means and that's the highest crime in the book. That may be a twisted morality, but Robin Hood did it and he became rather famous for it, didn't he?"

Some moments before Gary Steven Krist was transferred that day from the DeKalb County Jail to the Georgia State Prison in Jackson—where he would get a shave—a deputy had him fill out a personal history form.

The last line asked for the names of his relatives and closest friends.

Krist answered in a single word: "None."

In the same courtroom three days later, Ruth Eisemann-Schier pleaded guilty.

Judge Hubert sentenced her to seven years' imprisonment. She left the courtroom smiling.

Ruth's two court-appointed lawyers, LeRoy C. Hobbs and Thomas W. Elliott, had informed District Attorney Bell that Ruth would plead guilty if the State of Georgia reduced the charge from kidnaping for ransom to the lesser charge of kidnaping.

Bell pondered and accepted. The Krist verdict had disappointed him. He had hoped for a verdict of death. He did not look forward to a second trial and he realized that the U. S. Immigration and Naturalization Service would deport Ruth to Honduras upon her release—regardless of how long she served.

He knew that the two defense lawyers would argue that Ruth had abandoned Krist prior to the collection of the ransom, and that she had co-operated fully when captured.

Technically, the lesser charge would make her eligible for parole in two years and four months from the time of her first incarceration in Georgia—or as early as July 1971. Depending upon the judgment of a parole board, she could remain imprisoned until March 1976.

Wearing a two-piece yellow knit suit, Ruth stood between her two lawyers that day of May 29 as Prosecutor Bell questioned her.

"Do you understand you are pleading guilty?" he asked. She nodded.

"Do you wish to enter a plea at this time?" he asked.

"Yes," she replied in a low voice.

"What is that plea?"

"Guilty," she said.

Judge Hubert sentenced her to the maximum time under the lesser charge and said, "The court has always had the feeling that Miss Schier was not the principal culprit, that Krist was."

As she left the courtroom, soon to be sent to the Colony Farm Women's Prison at Milledgeville, Georgia, she paused long enough to reiterate a familiar restrain.

"I wish to explain that I was very much in love with George Deacon. I was prepared to do anything he asked of me.

"I was so worried about Barbara. I decided it would be best to resign myself and try to help Barbara every way I could."

How Is She *Really?*

I always feel a little awkward when people come up and ask, "Are you Barbara Mackle?" Most of the time they don't know quite what to say. And neither do I. They say things like, "I prayed." And I thank them. I always want to get it over with as quickly as possible. I guess I respond both ways. It is awkward and at the same time it is very touching.

Even after this long, more than a year later, most of my friends don't know quite what to say. They want me to bring it up and if I don't, they think I'm afraid to talk about it. I'm not really. I just don't like to.

Since the kidnaping it has been a little hard to make new friends.

I'm afraid I've had to rely pretty heavily on those I already had. Very much so. And even with them, when the subject of crime comes up, everyone suddenly realizes I'm there. They stop. They don't know whether to go ahead or back off. I just smile. I try to tell them to go right ahead. And then, I guess, they wonder if I really mean it or not.

It hasn't been easy for my friends either. But sometimes it is almost funny. My roommate at Emory, the first semester after the kidnaping, was Berri Davis, and it got so that when someone would ask her who her roommate was, she would say "Barbara mumble-mumble-mumble."

The one question everyone always asks is, "How is she *really?*"

Mother kids me about it. She says, "Now, Barbara. If you ever do anything odd or peculiar during the rest of your life, everyone is going to say, 'I knew it. I knew it all along.'" I guess Mother is right. Some people just don't want to believe I'm all right. Some people want to think I'm in shambles. And no matter what I say will not convince them, I guess.

But I'm fine. I really am.

I came out of it all right and I am certain that a lot of other persons could survive a lot easier than they think they could.

I haven't seen a psychiatrist. I don't think I need one. Right after I got home, Dr. Lauth and I talked about it. He asked me if I thought I should, and I said no, but that I would if he wanted me to. He said not unless I wanted to.

Dr. Lauth was so helpful; I trusted him completely. He knew the family so well and he told me that if I ever needed to talk about anything, any kind of problem, he would be there. Probably the nicest thing anyone ever said about me was Dr. Lauth. It was right after it was all over and we had talked and he said, "Barbara, you are one hell of a woman."

His death shocked me terribly. He died of a heart attack about a month after the kidnaping. Anyone that close, you just can't accept it. I went to the funeral and I've driven out to his grave at St. Mary's Cemetery four times by myself. I remember the funeral. It was the only funeral I've ever been to. When they put the dirt on the casket I had this strange crazy feeling. It all came back to me, and it was like I was talking to him.

I really don't think about the kidnaping very much. It is there all the time, of course, something that happened, something that

I will never forget, but I am not conscious of it. I didn't really try hard to concentrate on it until this book when Gene Miller interviewed me and we tape-recorded our conversations. That was about the worst time. I woke up suddenly at nights and I was afraid—and I didn't know why. I just felt fear. Then, when I realized where I was, I smiled and relaxed and went back to sleep. I left the night light on in the bathroom all week. I felt a little, well, a little silly. But it helped. I still wake up occasionally, startled and afraid, not knowing where I am for a few seconds. But it goes away very quickly and it doesn't happen so often any more.

I kept pretty busy in the days and weeks right after the kidnaping. Daddy and I went down to the bank together to thank Mr. Bruce. He told me he had put himself in Daddy's position. I think he has a daughter my age, exactly. When he heard about the kidnaping, he called his own daughter just to be reassured; no real reason; it wasn't rational. He just did. Daddy also bought Mrs. Bruns a new suitcase to replace the one she loaned us. The FBI kept that one and it was introduced as an exhibit in Krist's trial. Krist's boat sort of belonged to us, too, I guess. So when the FBI told us they wouldn't need it for the trial, Daddy gave it to the Charlotte County Sheriff's office over at Punta Gorda near Hog Island. The sheriff didn't have a police boat and he was glad to get it.

On the day before Christmas, just four days after I came home, Bobby and I had an appointment with the eye doctor to have our eyes tested. We'd had the appointment for a long time, and we kept it. While we were there in the waiting room around noon, we got a telephone call. Bobby took it. They wanted us to come home right away. Mr. Nixon was coming over to our house. Bobby and I were laughing and kidding all the way home.

I'd seen Mr. Nixon once after the convention the summer before. I was with Daddy over at the Villas when he and Bebe Rebozo were staying there. We ran into them in the parking lot and Mr. Nixon said, "Well, I'm finally home." This was before he bought a home on Key Biscayne.

This was the day the FBI fingerprint men also came to our house. They wanted our prints, mine, Mother's and Daddy's, Bobby's, just everyone's, for comparison and elimination purposes. They were taking them on cards in the kitchen and it seemed as if the whole

house was full of FBI agents and Secret Service men for Mr.
Nixon.

I didn't know what to call Mr. Nixon exactly. He hadn't been
inaugurated yet, and I didn't want to call him Mr. President-elect.
So I decided not to call him anything.

He came to the front door and we hugged each other. He
said, "You've lost weight. You've got to put on some pounds." He was
telling me how concerned he had been, and how he wanted to
come over to see the celebrity, something like that. We all laughed.
He was very casual, golf shirt, tennis shoes. And, of course, I was
all dressed up. He stayed for forty-five minutes to an hour and he
met everyone. Agnes and Walter came out of the kitchen. He shook
hands with all the Miami FBI agents, and he would ask them
where they were from and they would say Indiana or somewhere
and he would start talking Indiana. A superb politician; that was
my thought exactly, and I don't mean to be unkind. Mr. Vessels
brought up the kidnaping. He said there were no bad effects. So I
explained briefly what had happened and what it was like being
buried alive and how the FBI found me. Mr. Nixon is an extremely
good listener. When I finished he said it was one of the most unusual and exciting crimes that had ever happened. I kind of
laughed and he said I ought to tell everyone how well I came out
of it and how efficient the FBI was. He said, "I want you to think
about writing a book." I laughed again and he said he was serious.
"This is a story that should be told," he said. "This is a book that
should be written." It was the first time I had really thought about
it.

That same afternoon we went to the Villas to visit Mr. Hoover.
Everybody calls him the Director. Although he often comes
down at Christmastime, I had never met him before, and I guess I
expected someone gruff. He wasn't at all. He had on this Hawaiian
flowered shirt and he was grinning and he was absolutely fascinating
to listen to. He started talking the moment we walked in and
hardly anyone else said a word. He speaks very fast and he knows
so much history. He was telling us all about the other kidnaping
cases. He really opened up and talked. He went into great detail
about the Lindbergh case. He mentioned the Sinatra case and how
difficult it had been to work with Frank Sinatra. That was a real
kidnaping, he said. He said Daddy was an asset in our case. He
knew all about it. Everything; he really did. He said he thought

I was very brave and that he couldn't have come out of it like I did. He was adamant on Krist. He said he wanted a quick trial and quick punishment; a quick trial without a lot of legal delays, and a severe and harsh punishment; I forget his exact words. He felt very strongly about it. He was very much for capital punishment.

I'm not sure how I stand on capital punishment. I know I have great qualms about the entire principle.

I know that I did not want Krist to be executed. For one reason, it was he who called.

I guess I have more feeling for Krist than Ruth. I've been told not to say this, but it is true.

I have no hatred for either. I just don't. Perhaps I would have felt differently if anything would have happened to Mother or Daddy—if Mother or Daddy had had a mental breakdown or anything like that. But we've all come out all right, Mother especially.

I don't feel that I know either Krist or Ruth very well. Except for seeing them at the trial, I saw them only that morning, thirty, forty, fifty minutes. If it was that long. It certainly didn't seem that long. I don't know them well enough to have much insight into their characters.

When I was buried I kept reassuring myself that even if the man did not call, Ruth would. She seemed so concerned. She gave me her sweat shirt. She said, "Oh, we should give her nose drops." She said, "We'll stay with you Barbara. I'll be back, Barbara." For some odd reason, I trusted her. I trusted her completely. I guess I had to. I thought that she would be the one to call and tell someone, Bobby or Daddy, where I was.

Afterward I had just assumed that she had called. It was a real shock when Inspector Shroder told me that she had not called; Krist had.

Why didn't she call? She was separated from him for almost a day and a half. There is just no answer to it. Her behavior was her answer. She did nothing.

Then she said she wanted to crawl into the box and stay with me.

I'm sorry. I just don't accept that. I felt betrayed. I think she is quite a little actress.

And I think she was lucky. Very lucky.

I think about them often. I often wonder if Krist would have called if he had gotten the ransom money on the first attempt without a hitch. Daddy doesn't believe he would have. I wonder if the box was just sort of an insurance policy against the possibility of failure? What would they have done if no one would have found out immediately who they were? I don't know. I honestly don't. But this could be one explanation why Ruth didn't call when she was separated from Krist.

Every once in a while I think I could still be there. And I thank God. We all take life so much for granted.

The trial didn't bother me too much. The only really bad thing was the distortion on Billy Vessels. From what everyone tells me, he was the real iron man during the kidnaping. He lived some of the finest and most unselfish hours of his life; then they had to make those insinuations. I've thought a lot about it and maybe I shouldn't say this, but if it had to be anyone, I'm glad it was Billy Vessels. A lot of other persons simply couldn't have taken it. He could and he did. Outwardly, he was very calm and cool. I know it must have torn him up inside pretty badly.

Krist looked at me the whole time I testified. I had a crazy kind of feeling because he was just sitting there smiling. I thought he might put his head down but he didn't. He had that strange sort of smirk, grinning, as if he was enjoying it. I have sort of a neutral feeling about him. I don't like to think about it.

I was scared of the cross-examination. Actually, it was very perfunctory. The lawyer said, "You don't mind if I cross-examine you, do you?" and I said no and I smiled, but I felt like saying, don't you dare. Bobby had told me, "If they get to you, Barbara, you start crying. Make yourself cry. And they'll stop."

I think the whole thing was harder on Bobby than anyone. He was convinced I was dead. Stewart told me about Mother at the Rodeway Inn that first morning. "If anything has happened to Barbara, my life is over," she said. This is what she said to Stewart. She said, "Bob and I just can't go on." I put myself into Bobby's position. If something happened to Bobby, I just don't know how I could handle Mother and Dad. He had to be the hardest hit. He had the hardest job.

I knew I was safe. I knew I was there. And I knew that Daddy would do everything possible, everything. My faith in him was absolute. If anything conceivably could be done, he would do it. I knew that.

When I think about the kidnaping now, it is usually my family.

Coming home. More than what happened. Meeting Dad; seeing Mother at the hospital, and especially Bobby. Their faces. I could see the mental agony in their faces, and for a long time afterward, Bobby just couldn't stand to be around if the subject came up. He would get up and walk out of the game room. He is better now. He doesn't do that any more.

But sometimes I see them sitting quietly with a certain look on their faces and I know. I know that they are remembering.

Most of the time, though, we're able to talk about it freely when it ever comes up. I went back to Emory and one weekend last autumn, Mother and Dad and I drove from Atlanta over to Hendersonville, North Carolina. It was my twenty-first birthday and my parents wanted to buy me another opal ring. We found a beautiful little ring in a small jewelry store in Asheville. Anyway, I was driving on the way back to Emory and we approached Atlanta and I noticed a highway sign that said, "Gwinnett County." This wasn't too far from Norcross, Georgia, and I cried, squealed almost, "Oh, Daddy. Let's stop and see where I was buried."

I was putting him on. But he didn't know it right away. And he said, "No way, Barbara, no way." He was really upset. "How can you even think of such a thing?" And then I was laughing at him and he began to laugh too.

I skipped a quarter at Emory right after the kidnaping, and I had to work pretty hard to make it up. Not really, I guess, but everyone knew who Barbara Mackle was, and I worked harder than I ever had before for good grades. I made straight A's during summer session and I graduated with my class in June 1970. I'm not real sure of the future. I may apply for graduate school after a year or so but I think I want to work in Atlanta for an airline in an economic-business capacity for a while. I'm not sure.

The kidnaping, I know, has changed my life in some ways forever. I never truly understood how profoundly other people could care about someone they didn't know. We had so many letters to answer. I answered all the personal ones to me, and Mother and Daddy and Bobby and my uncles answered all theirs. I even have a Czechoslovakian Fan Club of all things. We had to have a Kelly Girl to help with some of the others and she was so overcome by emotion she couldn't type. Daddy had to get her a box of Kleenex.

You hear so much about the insensitive nature of man today,

and I was amazed to see that so many thousands of persons identified themselves with our family. People who cared. I am convinced that compassion is the basic nature of man.

This is one of the reasons I decided—and the family decided—to write the book. I was very reluctant at first. We realized, of course, that someone else probably would write about it. By doing it ourselves, we could do it as honestly as possible. It is about as factual as we know how to make it.

The FBI is another reason. The law enforcement people take an awesome amount of criticism these days. Some people just don't realize what a magnificent organization the FBI is. There is no crime, I believe, that quite affects the FBI like a kidnaping. Again and again I heard the agents say that they felt as if I was their own daughter. I believe them. If this book deters even one crime, it will serve a useful purpose.

And the final reason for writing all this is personal.

I wanted to tell it once—completely and as honestly as I could—so that it will be behind me.

I want to end it. I want to put it behind me. Once and for all, I want it to be over. For ever and ever.